dedicated to the memory of
Jimmy DeSana
and
Felix Gonzalez-Torres

Between Artists

Between Artists

Twelve contemporary American artists interview
twelve contemporary American artists

with an introduction by
Dave Hickey

Edited by
Lucinda Barnes
Miyoshi Barosh
William S. Bartman
Rodney Sappington

A·R·T· Press, Los Angeles

Between Artists is dedicated to Marion Bolton Stroud.

Project editor: Rodney Sappington
Editors: Lucinda Barnes, Miyoshi Barosh,
William S. Bartman, and Rodney Sappington
Copyeditor: Patricia Draher, Seattle
Proofreader: Laura Iwasaki, Seattle
Designer: Lausten/Cossutta Design, Los Angeles
Film output: PrePress Studio, Los Angeles
Printer: Publishers Press, Salt Lake City

Distributed by:
Distributed Art Publishers
636 Broadway, Room 1208
New York, N.Y. 10012
800 338-2665

ISBN 0-923183-20-5

This publication was made possible in part by the generous support of The LLWW Foundation, our Library Fellows, which include The Lannan Foundation, Ruth and Jake Bloom, and The Ganz Foundation. We would also like to thank many individual contributors whose support has made our publishing efforts a continued success.

Art Resources Transfer, Inc., founded in 1987, is committed to documenting and supporting artists' voices and work, and making these voices accessible beyond conventional art spaces and outlets by establishing innovative methods of distribution and access. A.R.T. Press books are based on an in-depth collaboration between artist, designer, and editor.

Contents

Preface

When I began this project in 1987, I had no idea what form it would finally take. All I knew was that the most stimulating and important parts of my life had all been connected to art and artists, both visual and performing. Since I had been diagnosed with AIDS and was given a maximum of two years to live, my dream was to create an organization that would permit the world to know art and artists the way I had been allowed to over the years. I had no idea then that I would survive and be able to witness A.R.T. Press take on a life of its own. I also did not have any idea how hard it would be through the writing of these few words to express the complexity of feelings that are surrounding me. The art community has been consumed by the AIDS pandemic. My own personal grief and sense of loss have been compounded by the death from AIDS of, first, Jimmy DeSana and, just last week, Felix Gonzalez-Torres, both of whom became intimate companions on a journey that you share only with someone who has become part of your personal creativity. I have been searching for a way to bring some kind of meaning to the hopelessness, loss, anger, and just plain emptiness that I feel. Finally, I am able to hold on to their voices—the same voices that they openly shared with all of us and that will remain, along with their art, as a permanent record that they were here. All of us who knew and loved them have this small piece of their spirits to hold on to as a gift from them.

I set up several restrictions for the production of our books. First, they would each contain an interview with the artist conducted by an artist of his or her choice. Second, the artist was to edit the interview so it truly expressed his or her own voice, and, finally, the book was to be conceived and designed with the artist and the designer working closely together through the final press check. I really had no idea how this would eventually work, but as you will see in this collection of conversations, many of which read like one-act plays, both the personality of the artist and that of the interviewer are integral and clear.

Most of my friends are artists who are anything but the elitist aesthetes they are pictured as in the popular press and art magazines. If anything, they are just plain people going to work every day, except the result is a work of art rather than an automobile or a toaster. There have been far too many reviews, interpretation, and unreadable drivel written about contemporary art, and I felt this project had a chance to make the artists' voices clearly their own, without interpretation and without unreadable artspeak. Little did I know that the books would be distributed all over the world. In this collection we are attempting to emphasize the voices of the artists involved by concentrating on their words and only putting in a few images. In a small way, it is a history of a certain period of art.

To the artists, editors, and designers who gave of their time and energy, I am forever grateful for making my dream come true. I hope the reader can see the ideas that are repeated in each interview, and for the first time in many years, if ever, think of the artist as a person first, a worker second, and ultimately as the artist who has created a harvest waiting to be shared. They're just like you and me.

William S. Bartman
Publisher
January 26, 1996

Notes on Distribution

Over the years, our books have gained wider distribution and have found their way into international bookstores. But what if an entire network of public libraries could no longer afford to purchase these books or any art books? What if the very people these books were designed to reach never had the opportunity to read them? In fact, this is exactly what we discovered in 1990, and as a result, we developed a distribution program that places books on art and culture into rural and inner-city public libraries. It is a frightening reality that public libraries must struggle daily to provide books and materials that reflect our changing culture. Libraries are a primary resource for millions of readers, who can gain access to information by simply requesting cards at their community libraries. The Distribution to Underserved Communities program (D.U.C.) reaches readers in eight states, in six hundred public libraries, and to date has placed 16,000 books out in the world.

Through discussing the needs of librarians, library patrons, and publishers nationwide, we have assembled an alternative distribution system that not only places A.R.T. Press books into the hands of library patrons but also distributes to them, free of charge, books on art, cultural studies, and multicultural education, as well as children's books and international fiction. Bay Press, City Lights Books, The New Press, Lannan Foundation Literary Videos, and the Museum of Modern Art are among the award-winning presses that are part of this remarkable program.

Between Artists will be available in bookstores, but it also gives me great hope for the future of art publishing to know that readers of all ages and backgrounds will have access to the lives of these wonderful artists with the simple use of a library card. The fact that these books are provided free of charge to thousands of people who could not afford them, and that school curricula are being based on these materials, represents a remarkable step toward new ways of disseminating culture. It is our hope that this book and the books we distribute will dramatically increase a real understanding of how artists continue to shape the culture in which we live.

Rodney Sappington
Editor and Executive Director

Rosencrantz and Guildenstern Redux
The Artist's Voice after the Death of the Author

Dave Hickey

The provinces of his body revolted,
The squares of his mind were empty,
Silence invaded the suburbs,
The current of his feeling failed; he became his admirers.
—W. H. Auden, "In Memory of W. B. Yeats"

In a recent *New York Times* story about the death of artist Ray Johnson, the reporter quoted one of Johnson's friends as saying that the artist's suicide was probably a "smart career move." In black type, on an inside page of the *Times,* the remark sounded pretty cold—and the reporter doubtless intended it to sound this way—but there are good reasons for believing that the artist's unnamed friend was speaking more wistfully than cynically. First, the remark is exactly the sort of thing that Johnson himself might have said were the situation reversed, and second, the statement was true. Dying *is* a good career move. Dead artists, in this culture, are presumed to have paid for their transgressions by dying; no longer in a position to profit from our respect and attention, they thus become worthy of it—and vulnerable to our characterization of their life and work, since they are unavailable for comment.

This cultural proclivity for loving dead artists and hating live ones, of course, is a strident cliché of modernist culture—so much so that the tantalizing prospect of an artist taking advantage of this hypocrisy by *appearing* to die is a staple plot device in popular narratives about the art world, which usually purport to be parables of "art" and "commerce." With only a moment's reflection, I can think of two movies, a novel, a television miniseries, and an episode of *Perry Mason* in which a charismatic male artist, having achieved a "critical reputation," attempts to cash in on his paper fame by feigning his own death, thus setting off a feeding frenzy of demand for his now-valuable work.

For the greater part of this century, such narratives have presented a plausible scenario and a reasonable explanation for our affection for dead artists, since this sort of postmortem affection is, indeed, a function of the market. When an artist dies, his or her production becomes, for the first time, an absolute, finite commodity, subject to the astronomical price escalations that characterize any market situation in which proliferating demand is focused on an absolutely limited supply. Market economics, however, cannot tell the whole story. Not anymore. Most critically, they cannot explain why the cultural inclination for nurturing dead artists should hold true at the symbolic level of cultural discourse as well, beyond the material discourse of actual objects and real mortality, and continue to hold true long after the practice of visual art in this country has ceased to be a market-driven enterprise.

The fact remains, however, that American culture in the twentieth century began dispensing governmental and academic patronage upon the people who make visual art at the exact moment that the "artist" died—at the precise moment in the late sixties when the idea of the artist as an originative, independent, litigious voice in the forum of cultural politics became intellectually discredited, when the artist became a mere cultural producer whose work constituted a "collaboration" with the culture at large. At this point, the work of art, which high modernists chose to regard as a symptomatic objectification of the artist's individual consciousness, became an object that postmodernists regarded as symptomatic of *cultural* consciousness, variously construed as societal neurosis or class bias—or, at best, as embodying the consciousness of a marginal subculture within which the artist situated his or her identity.

In this way the work of art, which had been rendered mute and symptomatic by modernist theory, remained mute under the new regime, a voiceless symptom, while the artist, who had previously been allowed the occasional *cri de coeur,* was rendered mute as well. He or she became a mere collaborator, dead as an author, robbed of authority by the social, cultural, and critical co-option of his or her performative expression (and thus eligible for patronage and available, if needed, for comment on matters of technique and theory, rather in the manner of a shop foreman). At this point, I would suggest, *all* living artists in the United States and Europe achieved that peculiar condition of "living deadness" hitherto restricted to those fictional artists on television dramas who faked their own demise. They became widely respected, academically accredited, nonspeaking cultural instrumentalities. Officially dead.

✶

There are those, of course, who would suggest that contemporary artists did this to themselves out of a failure of nerve, that they "committed suicide as a career move," selling their voices and their right to be wrong for the privilege of institutional and academic patronage. I disagree with this interpretation. In fact, I would suggest that this disenfranchisement of the artist's voice is the consequence of a failed project by pop, minimalist, and postminimal artists in the late sixties to suppress the artist's presence in their work, so the work itself might speak to its beholder—so the work itself might comment on the cultural context we all inhabit, rather than reflexively referencing the artist. Because, as Willem de Kooning remarked at about this time (and I am repeating this remark as it was paraphrased to me by Elaine de Kooning), "One can hardly expect a work of art to do *anything* in the world when it is trivialized as a scrap of evidence pertaining to its maker's eccentricity. You make a painting about a crazy world, they say it was made by a crazy artist. That's a loser's game."

So the artists of the sixties, having learned from the public trivialization of postwar American painting, strove to cleanse their works of the allegory of self, sought to present their works as public *declarations,* as transitive, rhetorical instruments of advocacy in the forum of cultural politics. These works, however, were almost immediately reconstituted as symptomatic objectifications of "societal consciousness" (rather as the British government was initially predisposed to regard the Declaration of Independence as an interesting symptom of "societal consciousness"—in this case, of colonial agrarian truculence). In the case of late sixties art, however, the powers that be were never disabused of this notion. So the efforts of these artists in the late sixties to cleanse their works of self-reference, so the work might speak, only resulted in these works being silenced again, wrested once again from the political consciousness of the beholder and reallegorized by Freudian, Marxist, and deconstructionist theories as objectified symptoms of cultural eccentricity, historical specificity, or the artist's "identity group."

As a partial explanation of this allegorical appropriation of American art, I would propose Pierre Bourdieu's maxim that, in the case of intellectual or symbolic property, the issue is rarely what it *means* but who owns it, who speaks it, whose power it enhances. Thus, when the artist dies, "he becomes his admirers," as Auden says, and the artist's works revert to the culture, and redound to its credit. As a consequence, members of that culture are happy to acquire works which are, by rights, their own. And when the "artist" is declared dead by the fiat of intellectual fashion, when the American government is assured by no less an authority than Paul de Man of Yale University that works of art, made in America, are the products of America itself and not of its individual citizens, it should come as no surprise that this government would feel free to endow a practice that produces works which are, by rights, its own.

Nor should it come as any surprise to anyone that this government would ordinarily seek to suppress those works that it deems unrepresentative. The fact that this cultural appropriation of the artist's production by academic and governmental fiat amounts to crediting the disease with its cure, of course, is never considered, since this would amount to characterizing works of art as performative declarations made by free citizens of a republic. And we all know that artists are professionally trained manufacturers—culture workers who produce works symptomatic of their culture, or their particular part of it, at the moment of its making. And we also know that this work is primarily destined to provide the bureaucrats and academics who administer high culture with material evidence that must be analyzed in order to ascertain the degree of "correctness" or "false consciousness" in which any particular segment of the populace languishes at any particular moment and in any particular place.

✶

Which brings us to the collection of interviews that this essay introduces, and hopefully provides a context for the special edge and sense of vertigo that accompany our reading of them, since—as thoughtful and interesting, as urgent and heartfelt, as these texts are—we are never quite certain *to whom* we are listening. On every page, in every question and response, we are confronted with the question of who is speaking, in what role, from what position, upon what authority, and to what end. You might say, "Well, we are listening to *artists!*" But what does that mean? What is an artist in 1995? A courtier? A jester? A civil servant? A pensioner? A critic? A manufacturer? A visionary? A cultural researcher? An exemplary sufferer? No one really knows anymore, least of all artists, and certainly not myself, and I have spent the greater and happier part of my life in conversation with them.

The problem (or the virtue) of this situation is that the word *artist,* having been robbed of its cultural authority by Barthes, de Man, and Foucault, no longer has any stable cultural signification. Thus, we have no context in which to locate the "voice" of the artist, nor any overriding cultural imperative even to listen. What's more, the voices themselves, the ones that speak these interviews, seem equally unsure of their location and their authority. They seem, somehow, to be aware that they are dead. They could hardly have failed to notice. So their remarks are diffident, thoughtful, remote—and we never quite know: Are we listening to the "artist" as traditionally constructed: the possessor of an informing moral vision? Or is this the voice of the artist as cultural producer who manufactures work in collaboration with the culture? Or is this the artist as subcultural ombudsman, embodying the desires of a particular sector of the populace? Or is this the "professional" artist dedicated to maintaining standards and dealing with issues of consequence within the profession? Or, finally, is this simply a citizen of the republic who has, through the complex interplay of chance, choice, and desire, ended up making art?

In these interviews, thankfully, we are dealing for the most part with the latter, with the artist as quotidian citizen. So we learn, in some detail, how one becomes an artist in this nation at this time. Most powerfully, I think, we learn how little the tradition and traditional artifacts of "high art" have had to do with these artists' acquisition of their vocation. Conversely, we learn just how much the intellectual and visual complexities of American popular culture *have* contributed to their endeavors. Again and again we discover that the "threshold experience" of these artists took place on the street, that it has little or nothing to do with the experience of high art within the confines of high culture. Mike Kelley may be beguiled by Jackson Pollock, but he finds his roots in Sun Ra and Iggy Pop. David Reed may be a devotee of baroque painting, but that devotion is grounded in his experience of film and the landscape of the west.

This inclination to ground one's practice in the vernacular is stable throughout these interviews, but we should probably keep in mind that our perception of this proclivity is probably skewed by the fact that most artists become artists because they find the art available to them unsatisfactory. "Artists make things because they want to see them," Terry Allen remarked in an interview, "They make the art that's not there for them to see." Moreover, the disinclination of the artists in the interviews to talk about "real art" is probably reinforced by the fact that their interlocutors are artists themselves, who, almost by definition, may be presumed to have differing tastes and agendas.

The fact that we are listening to artists talking to artists in these interviews, however, marks them as profoundly of this moment. We have no interview by Willem de Kooning with Jackson Pollock, by Lee Krasner with Grace Hartigan, by Andy Warhol with Roy Lichtenstein, or by Eva Hesse with Richard Serra. Nor can we imagine such interviews, because prior to 1970 the idea that all artists belong, somehow, to a "professional community" did not exist. For the previous one hundred years, artists regarded themselves as entrepreneurs in a field of independent competitors, struggling to gain the public eye. To this end, they would form stylistic or ideological alliances, of course, but never communities. This competitive struggle to gain the public eye, however, evaporated when public did; and even though one need only read between the lines of these interviews to discover that competitiveness has not completely evaporated, the struggle today takes place almost completely within The Art World—a garrison of recent construction that bears a distinct resemblance to The Art World created by Louis XIV in seventeenth-century France, a roundelay of courtiers and academicians.

As a consequence, one must necessarily read *all* these conversations between the lines, since there is no longer any articulated "outside" position from which one can attend to the proceedings, no exterior cultural vantage point, beyond The Art World, from which we may view the responses. Nor is there any conventional journalistic relationship that we may assume between interlocutor and respondent. Traditionally, the interviewer is the representative of the reader and, by extension, of the culture at large. In these interviews the interviewer is, first and foremost, a representative of his or her own private artistic practice, so the experience of reading these texts is less like our experience of consulting documented, secondary sources and more like our textual experience of reading postmodern fiction.

The questions and responses are full of mystery and fluid contingency, lost precedents and covert politics, repartee and passive aggression. So we do not so much read them as overhear them, as we overhear the bemused colloquy of those two classic postmoderns in Tom Stoppard's *Rosencrantz and Guildenstern Are Dead.* Stoppard's protagonists, of course, are as cognizant as these artists are of their ghost-like status. So they spend the duration of the play discussing their contingent existence, uncertain—as any artist must be today—of the roles they have played and are expected to play in the tragedy going on around them.

Moreover, the speakers in these interviews are saddled with the tragicomic injunction to talk about that which they cannot: their art—to discuss that practice, which, were it explicable, they should not be pursuing, to explain those objects which, had they known what they were making, they almost certainly should not have made. Thus, Isaiah Berlin's distinction between the hedgehog and the fox is applicable here. "The fox knows many little things," Berlin explains, "the hedgehog knows one big thing," and artists, as artists, are almost always hedgehogs. They know one big thing, the thing that drives the engine, that perpetually eludes articulation. So what we have here, between these covers, is the conversation of hedgehogs playing at being foxes. We do not get that one big thing, nor could we expect it. But we do get the *atmosphere,* the filigree of little things, of accident and incident, of nuance and desire, that surrounds the enormous absence that the work of art must, necessarily, fill in our lived experience.

✶

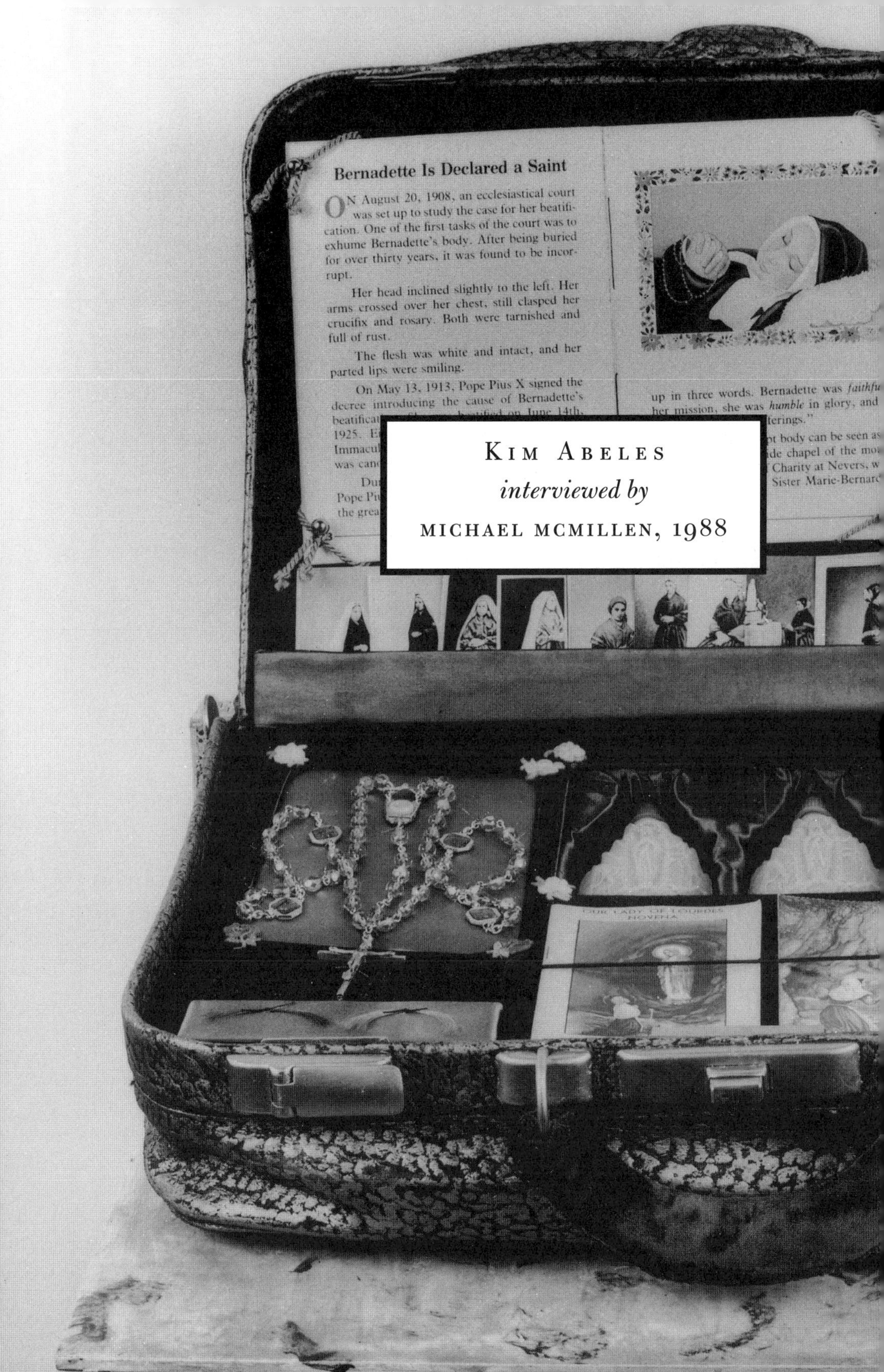

KIM ABELES
interviewed by
MICHAEL MCMILLEN, 1988

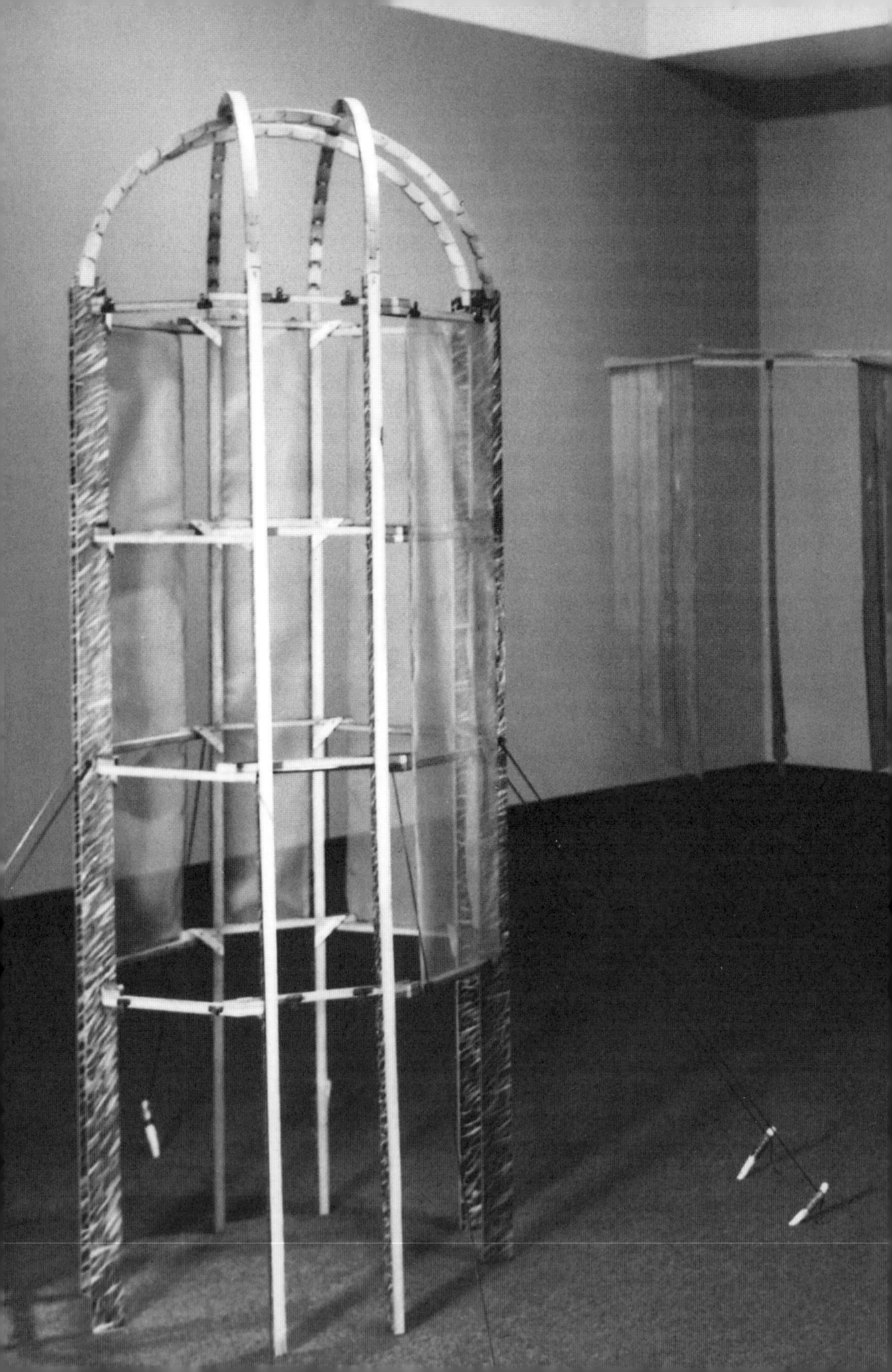

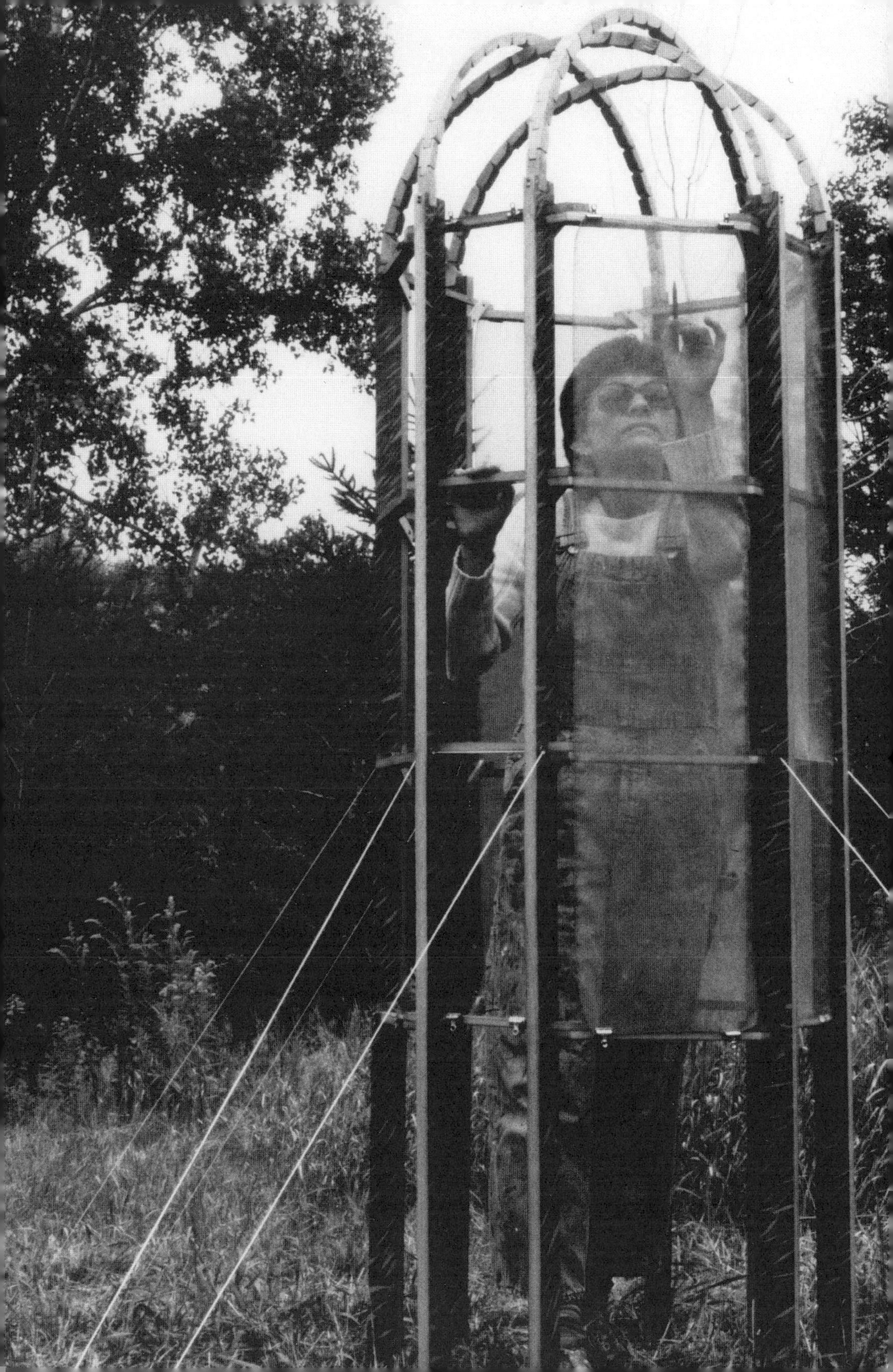

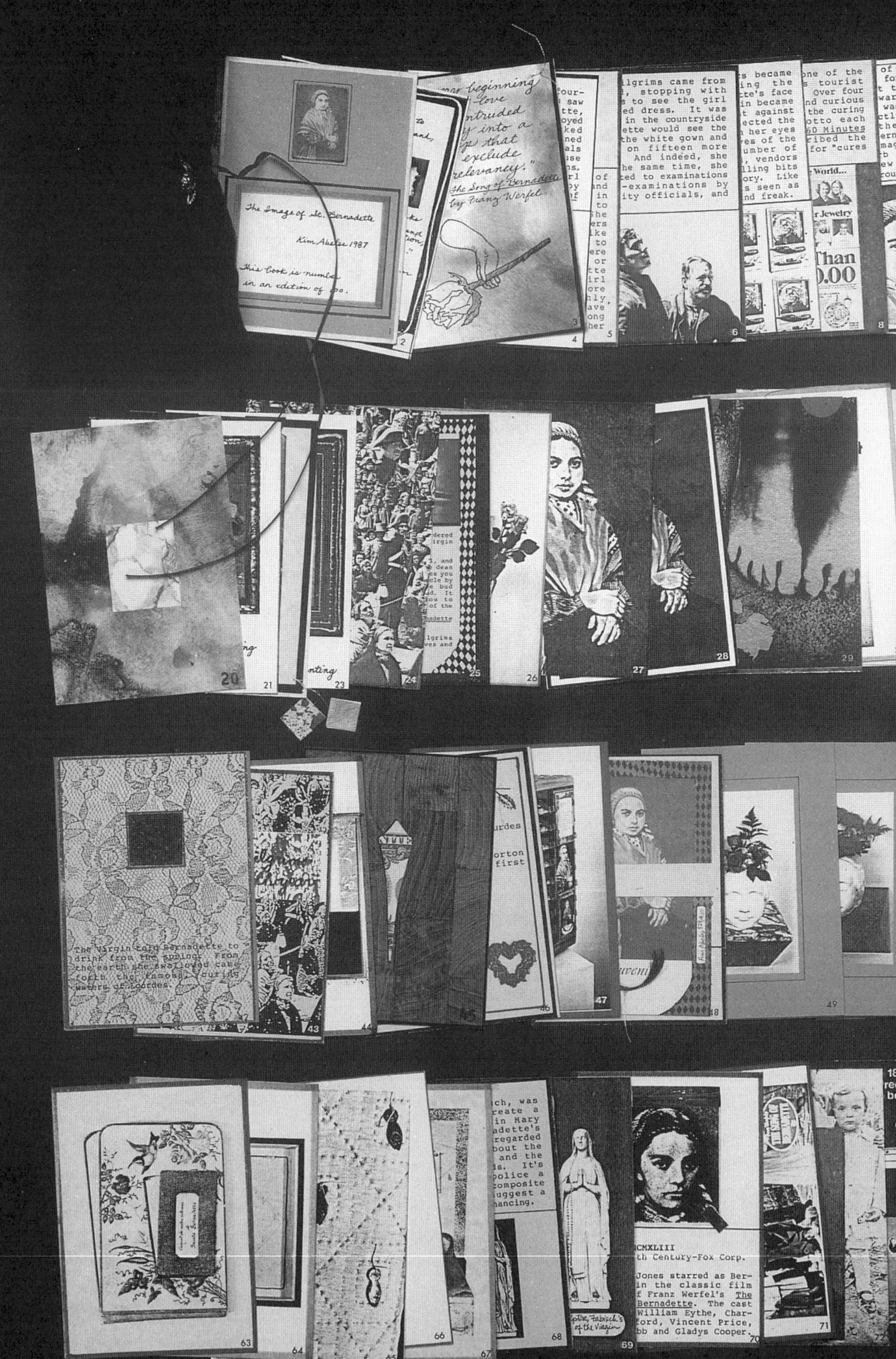

The Image of St. Bernadette
Kim Abeles 1987
The Song of Bernadette by Franz Werfel
The Virgin told Bernadette to drink from the spring. From the earth she swallowed came forth the famous, curing waters of Lourdes.

KIM ABELES

interviewed by

MICHAEL MCMILLEN

Michael McMillen: Have you always wanted to be an artist, or did you make a shift from another area?

Kim Abeles: I always wanted to be an artist. In school I minored in psychology, so in a sense I was thinking about something practical, but you get to a point as an artist where there's only one direction you can really go. Nothing else quite makes sense. My art incorporates other avenues and other disciplines, so I don't feel that it's limited to a dialogue that's just about art.

McMillen: One of the fascinating aspects of your work is that you reach into history and culture and drag out and synthesize things into something that's not quite historical or formalist but more interesting than both.

Abeles: I'm interested in making my art interdisciplinary because usually you see history as a package deal in a museum, especially in the United States. In Europe you can walk the streets, and history surrounds you. Because I grew up in this culture, the only sense of history I ever had was if I went to a museum and paid for my ticket. I would go in, and history was in a little box, neatly labeled. That makes it hard to get a feeling for your position in history.

McMillen: The fact that an object is in a museum represents one person's point of view or a school of thought, whereas that's not really what history is. It's only one of many views.

Abeles: Right, because when people see history like that, or when they read a book, they assume that a fact is absolute. They forget that there's poetic license, that there are editorial changes, so in a sense, it's not real history, even though the packaging looks real.

McMillen: Yes, there's the point that history is written by the victors.

Abeles: Exactly, the history books in America are definitely like that. You don't see blacks in history books, even though they played a critical role in the Civil War and all the wars after that, because white males wrote

page 1:
Traveling Sales, *1987, from the series The Image of St. Bernadette, 28½ x 19 x 19 inches*

page 2:
Observatory/Territory, *1984–85, from the series Observatory/ Territory,* Observatory: *85½ x 29 x 29 inches*

page 3:
Observatory/Territory, *1984, Kim Abeles charting the celestial paths in her construction at the Hand Hollow Foundation, George Rickey Workshop, East Chatham, New York*

page 4:
The Image of St. Bernadette, *1987, book, edition of 100, 5½ x 4 x 1½ inches*

the whole damned thing. Women aren't included in that dialogue either. And when they are included, it's always in an isolated way, making them tokens instead of a part of what went on. They're an addendum to the main part of history.

McMillen: You have a wonderful facility for material things, objects. You use found objects as well as synthesized things that you build. And you do it with such seeming ease. Did you just pick that up as you needed, or were you familiar with manual arts technology before you became an artist?

Abeles: Well, to a certain extent I've always been good with my hands, but I think a lot of it has been just struggling through it. I wasn't trained in wood shop. I suppose girls are now, but when I was growing up and going to school, we just took home economics. So when I started making sculpture, I was very aware that I had to figure out my own process for building something. I didn't have standard forms of building that somebody growing up with that kind of technology would have had. When male sculptors would come into my studio and I would tell them what I was doing, they'd always say, "It'll never work, it'll never work." But if you have a kind of naiveté, and you decide that you're just going to plunge in and start, you can do anything. You know, you can practically defy gravity until somebody tells you it's not possible. I think that's a plus women have sometimes in sculpture. They have to have guts to go into it because they don't have a lot of role models. If you have the courage to say, "I can go into sculpture," then you create your own vocabulary because no one has given you one to follow.

McMillen: Your work seems very much about human beings, either real or imagined, and in that sense they're like portraits without the traditional sensation of a portrait. They seem to depict aspects of a personality through objects and little narrative passages. Obviously, you're a humanist, and your interest is in people as opposed to formal objects.

Abeles: Any person has a story, and all you have to do is tap into what their story is. It's always the details of human lives that are striking to me. That's where their real qualities come out. It's not so much what people's professions are, but how they deal with the intricacies of their lives. It's the details that are most revealing. If you name historical characters, anybody in a room can grab on to the grander description: "President of the United States," "the person who developed the atom bomb," or "the first woman to vote." It's really their intimacies that we want to know. I don't think it's about being voyeuristic, but that the intimacies are most difficult to share with someone.

McMillen: It makes the heroes more human. I just finished reading a biography of Jackson Pollock, and he's a good example of a person who was completely lionized as an innovative person but whose personal life was just a minefield. I don't think we want to gloat over someone's misery but rather to learn of the hardships and personal doubts that have been overcome.

Abeles: It gives us a kind of hope and courage because we suddenly realize that these others were also normal people. That's what interested me in the Saint Bernadette series. She was a very young girl, fourteen years old, and in other circumstances she would have just lived out her life and nobody would have known about her. But she had a vision, and, really, whether you think she saw the Virgin Mary or not doesn't matter at all. Because she said she did, everything changed. Millions of people still go to Lourdes, buying icons, buying cigarette holders with her image, and lighters, and can openers. She was just a little girl who suddenly everybody made into an icon. She became bigger than life, in the same way that you would say Pollock did.

McMillen: Another aspect of your work is the kitschlike memorabilia you use. There's a kind of secondary industry of manufacturing ersatz mementos for an event that people imagined happened, as Saint Bernadette.

Abeles: I went to Lourdes the year following my Saint Bernadette show. The commercialization of Bernadette is just as grand as going to one of the services in the cathedral. People go there buying up stuff as fast as they can because they can take a piece of the story home. In the Saint Bernadette legend there's a rose bush that was made to bloom in the middle of winter as proof of her vision of the Virgin Mary. People started plucking the roses off until finally they just uprooted the whole bush. If they have to buy it or they have to steal it, they still want that part of it.

McMillen: I'm reminded of the medieval practice, and rather lucrative business, the church had of selling relics of saints' bones and hair and little weird detritus from some imagined personality.

Abeles: Still, in Italy, you can go into churches and see the knuckles of a saint or even entire dried-up corpses of saints. We all have a morbid curiosity. I think that's a lot healthier than not discussing death at all. I suppose that in our culture, as close as we get to accepting death is our morbid fascination with it.

McMillen: When you're working on the creation of a new work, do the objects suggest the work, or do you find the objects to suit the idea?

Abeles: Actually, in that sense I work differently from many assemblage artists. I'm very concerned with the concept. I pick the topic, whether it's a person or some social issue I want to discuss. Then I look for the objects. Sometimes I already have them because I collect a lot and people give me things. Sometimes I have to make them. There's a strong seductive quality to old stuff. Once you start making assemblage, it's almost impossible to walk by a trash can if you see something halfway rusty sticking up. Some people follow a strictly formalist approach. I don't want to be seduced by the objects in that way. Yet the color of rust, for instance, is such a beautiful thing that you almost can't duplicate it. The oddly shaped things we've created in postindustrial society interest me. They become organic creatures that we then incorporate in the same way that I suppose primitive cultures incorporated trees and branches and rocks.

McMillen: They're like icons of our age, like detritus from the age of manufacturing.

Abeles: Some of the objects are semi-identifiable. You sort of recognize a function. Some people could pick one of these things up and say, "Yes that's a capacitor for this or that," but most people would pick it up and see that it's very intricate and once had a purpose.

McMillen: You look at an object like that and see all the time, design energy, and manufacturing that went into it, and now it's a piece of junk that's been discarded.

Abeles: And it never had a signature either. Yet somebody sweated over the damned thing. Somebody figured out how to make it and design it in the first place. Then twenty people put it together and there's never a signature, ever, in all the time that it was used, discarded, and then made into art. And then somebody makes two hundred thousand dollars off of it.

McMillen: I am struck by your ideas of transience in life and how things change and always will change.

Abeles: That issue appeals to me because it's something that's hard for me to face. In some ways, change is one of the loveliest things in life, but it's always difficult to cope with change. I think people have an inner desire, a secret desire, for everything to be identical from one day to the next, even though they'd fall asleep. Change makes good subject matter because, as someone making art, you realize that you never can quite get a grip on what you're looking for, which is the reason for continuing. Henry Moore said if he ever made a piece of sculpture that he thought was perfect, he would never make another one.

McMillen: It's like a search. You keep going on, and you're trying to reach a level professionally that no one could ever reach. And yet, you don't want to reach it. Would you talk about the influence your trip to Japan had on you?

Abeles: My mother always has said that I was never the same after I came back from Japan. I was sixteen years old. I hooked up with a Buddhist priest there who knew a lot of the national treasures and the artists. He'd take me to see ceramicists and calligraphy artists. A girl of that age, who loves art anyway, is so impressionable. I was exposed to this in a very casual way. It had an influence on me later in terms of making the kimonos. I wrote a thesis on Shingon Buddhism, which was this priest's sect of Buddhism. So in a way it had a very direct effect, but it also affects the way I question reality. I never quite accept what is given to me. This comes through in my work in terms of my combining fact and fiction a lot. It's different than simply being skeptical. I think that it's realizing there is always a flip side of a coin. No matter how argumentative I am about certain issues, I'm always keenly aware that the other side is there.

And yet, the scary thing is that this can make you think you can almost throw everything away. Nothing is real, so let's not believe anything and not even care to learn anything. I think that if you see the flip side and you add humor, it is a healthier step. There is a tinge of humor in the most serious of events.

McMillen: It casts an ironic shadow over everything. That's a Zen attitude. You realize that life is an illusion. Would you talk a bit more about the kimonos?

Abeles: They really functioned as personas housing various social issues. They were very popular, and people wanted them like crazy. When I stopped making them, everyone was annoyed to death. The art world is designed to make each artist easily identifiable, to keep them producing the same thing. Collectors want it that way, and curators want it that way, because it makes their selections a little easier. Writers want it that way because they don't have to scramble with a new line of thinking every time an artist has a show. Ultimately, all these people would really like you to maintain this one thing. I stopped making the kimonos when I felt they were becoming a form of appropriation. My point was quite genuine at first. I had had a strong connection with Japan. I had learned kimono making there. I made the kimonos in relation to Shingon Buddhism.

I am bitter about the kimonos now because after stopping them, a lot of people were upset and became disloyal. I just wanted to keep experimenting like artists should. It should always be sort of dangerous to do another piece. We should have the option to completely shift gears. Some of the kimonos are really beautiful and really fresh, but you can't retain that freshness by plugging them out over and over again. I saw that happening to them. When I described the story behind one of the final kimonos to someone visiting my studio, she said the story was more interesting than the piece. I looked at it, and she was absolutely right. I was not capturing the beauty of the tale because I was trying to force issues on a form that had nothing to do with the story.

Once my sister made a T-shirt with one of my kimonos on it, and it said "Kimono, Kimono, Kimono, Kimono" over and over again, and then it ended with "Kim." That was it. I had had it. It was as if I had a pure vision in my heart, but suddenly I had to open my eyes to the context. The context for showing my work had changed too much. It was putting me in places where I never intended to go with the work.

I was angry that so many people thought I had nothing more in me. This is why my work never follows the same format anymore. There is a sensibility that's obviously mine, but I am very resistant to mass producing unless my point is to make a statement about what it means to mass produce. The kimonos were really beautiful for me when I worked on them. They were very important. They moved me into more narrative work, into new materials.

McMillen: Do you see yourself as a visionary?

Abeles: How do you describe a visionary?

McMillen: As a social critic or person who looks at the zeitgeist, the whole picture, and reflects on what's happening.

Abeles: Yes and no, especially talking about my historical pieces. I feel that I'm just now working myself up into the twentieth century. I did a series with the Dead Sea Scrolls. Then I got to the 1850s with Bernadette. The most current people I've dealt with are Ethel and Julius Rosenberg, from the 1950s, in a piece I did not so long ago. It's strange—a lot of the issues never change. When I did the series on the Dead Sea Scrolls, the three basic concepts I had in mind were greed, naiveté, and courage. In the series there were three characters with those qualities, but those are things you could say about someone living today. Humanistic themes never seem to alter. Only the façades and personas change a bit, but basically, underneath you have the same characteristics. This is partly why the historical aspect seems good for me and my viewers. It gives a little distance. If you work on Ronald Reagan right now, a lot of people still would get very uptight and close their eyes to the issues. Though I'm often tempted to deal with living characters, because there sure are some lively ones around, you have no distance. So many things can happen as another decade transpires.

I did a piece on the Monroe Doctrine and its influences on American imperialism. A lot of people have trouble with that piece. It's just a little too close. The piece is a play off of H.G. Wells's story "The Island of Dr. Moreau." The correct title is on the flip side of the sculpture: "The Island of Doctrine Monroe." At the gallery some guy really liked the piece. He was just sucked right into it, and when he realized that in the mouth of the creature there was a map of the U.S. and Central America and then related that to what the Monroe Doctrine means, he became furious. Most political work you can identify across the room. You either believe it or you don't. If you don't like it, you just don't approach it. In this case he was actually having a romance with a piece that was completely contrary to his political beliefs. He started yelling at me. Then a friend of mine joined in, and the man rolled up his sleeves and wanted to knock it out with my friend.

McMillen: What was he yelling about?

Abeles: He thought I was a communist and anti-American. Pretty wild, huh?

McMillen: At the University of California, Irvine, were you influenced to a significant degree by any of your instructors?

Abeles: There was one that I must say, yes: Allan Sondheim, who was a visiting artist at the time. He's sort of a hell-raiser type. If you're a painter, he'll give you a long list of reasons why painting is dead. He really caused me to rethink the way I was approaching my work and introduced me to a lot of conceptual work which I wasn't familiar with because of my background. When I was in undergraduate school, Kienholz was very interesting to me, but only because there happened to be a Kienholz color plate in Janson's *History of Art.* I remember I cut it out and kept it in my notebook for years, ten years or more. It was *The State Hospital* (1966). I'd look at it and look at it. None of my teachers ever presented work like that to me. I would just stare at that picture and think, "What is that?" I didn't really care if it was an installation or whatever. I just couldn't get a grip on it. It didn't look like a painting.

McMillen: It didn't look like art?

Abeles: It didn't, but I knew that it was. I knew somewhere in my heart. That's like Duchamp's work for me. It is almost as if you can learn to love Duchamp's work by osmosis. It's not something that you can really read about. You either connect with the work, as if you've breathed it from the first day you took a breath, or you don't get it. I could almost duplicate all his work without ever seeing it—that's the way I feel about that work.

McMillen: How do Observatory Territory *and* The Mountain Wedge *fit into the rest of your work?*

Abeles: I think a lot about that work. My environment is really interesting to me. I don't understand it. It's too big for me. I did *Observatory Territory* because I simply did not comprehend the paths of the moon and the sun and the way they interact with one another. And I didn't want to read about this and take someone else's word for it. I thought that if I built an observatory and got into it, even if I had to do it twenty-four hours a day, which toward the end of the project I had to do, I would see how the paths related. Similarly, in *Mountain Wedge,* though I realized there is smog in L.A. (you'd have to be crazy not to know that), I had to have a way to make it seem more tangible. One day, from my studio fire escape, I saw a clear, gorgeous view of a mountain fifteen miles beyond the city that was wedged visually between the buildings. I wasn't satisfied just to say, "I don't see this normally because there is smog." I wanted to chronicle the whole thing and see how long it would take to get a clear shot of the mountain wedge with a camera. It took over a year.

There are ways of interacting with the environment in which one's presence doesn't matter. This means getting out there and really getting involved in it. It is difficult in the city, and I think that's partly why I do these pieces. When you live in the city, it's not like you can go for country walks picking berries. You have to figure out a way to interact with a city that doesn't want you.

McMillen: It's not user friendly.

Abeles: Exactly, not at all.

McMillen: Would you talk about Calamity Jane*?*

Abeles: This piece is a biographical portrait of Calamity Jane. It also addresses the issue that many things we consider to be factual may not be true at all. Calamity Jane was a notorious liar, and it's really hard to know whether or not the facts about her life are true. Information about her is conflicting, even the spelling of her name. So I started to check every encyclopedia and text to compare the data. For instance, there was the question of whether or not she was married to Wild Bill Hickock. The whiskey bottles suspended from the piece contain conflicting data. In one it says they were married; another says she was too ugly to have been more than his trail companion. The lie detector image on the top of the piece I actually got from the L.A.P.D. I asked to go to the polygraph department and photograph one of their lie detectors. This is another thing I really like about doing this kind of work. It takes me to places I'd never go normally. All I have to do is say I am an artist and they say, "Oh, let her in, she's just an artist." Since we're assumed to be dimwitted, we're not really going to do any harm, so we have carte blanche to go where we want. Calamity Jane contains images that are part of her life, photographs of her as well as a garment that replicates the garment in one of the photographs. She was considered a terrible alcoholic, which is why I used the whiskey bottles. But they also look like medicine bottles, which is perfect because they thought of her as an angel of mercy, too. She once helped in a smallpox epidemic in a town where others were fleeing while she was in there helping people.

McMillen: You have incorporated photography in several pieces. How do you regard your use of photography?

Abeles: My use of the photograph is most influenced by *On Photography* by Susan Sontag. The book talks about the photograph as a very real thing, as an object. It made me see materials in a different light. Instead of just selecting materials because they are beautiful or the texture is right, I suddenly understood that the choice of materials could also be dictated by the idea. As in *Calamity Jane,* I used the photograph to replace something real. For another piece, *She Said I Saw This Sparrow and Thought of You I Said,* I had a dried bird outside my studio window for quite a long while. I was thinking about this piece and what it meant, and I realized that because of perspective the image of the bird was the same scale as the people below on the street. It was important to have a photograph of the view out the window to really complete my view of what the bird implied. That is, it symbolized human beings. Sontag also sees the use of the photograph as an act of power. This became apparent to me in pieces such as *Rickety-Tickety.* I was trying to get a photograph of the knee-down view of the world as somebody stretched out on the sidewalk, like the street people in downtown L.A. When I went to shoot the photographs, everybody to the right and left of me stopped because I had a camera and they didn't want to intrude in my picture taking. Well, it was very ironic to me because the piece was about street people, and they are usually just stumbled over. That kind of courtesy isn't extended to them, and so the very act of taking these pictures had a lot to do with the nature of this piece itself.

Another way I use the photograph is as documentary material, as a collection of data, such as in pieces like *Experiment to Identify Change.* I'll photograph over a period of time in order to prove something. I want to use that kind of documentary material in a way that is captivating to the viewer.

McMillen: How about Bayeux Tapestry?

Abeles: It tells the history of the Bayeux Tapestry on an etched brass plaque in front of a very worn ironing board that's obviously had a long history of its own. When I did the piece, I was interested in the fact that artworks, and objects in general, change so much through time in terms of their worth. At one point, the real Bayeux Tapestry was going to be ripped up to make covered wagon covers. Years later it was considered a national treasure. Its history has been very volatile, which is true of many objects. There are celebrated artists today who won't even be known to the next generations, and many struggling, unknown artists who will be critically acclaimed decades and decades from now.

When I did *Bayeux Tapestry*, I really wanted to go all out with it. To choose the colors for its display case, I took paint chips to the Los Angeles County Museum of Art and matched the colors in the new wing. The guards kept following me. I would go to blank walls in order to avoid artwork—I didn't want them to think in the least that I was hurting anything. I don't know what they thought I was doing. Then I crawled on the floor and photographed one of the temperature control boxes. My version wound up being a sort of collage with a real metal box and photographs of LACMA's temperature control box. It was lovely being belly down at the museum. How many times do you get to belly down in a museum with a camera?

McMillen: Tell me about Leon Trotsky's Eyeglasses Found in East Chatham, New York, Where He Considered Visiting.

Abeles: That's a Fact-Fiction Box. Trotsky had eyeglasses that were similar in shape to the ones I actually used in the piece. I also did a pretty funny one with my IUD in it. It's based on the idea that its shape was once considered a numerical symbol in North America. Recently, archaeologists excavated a camel skeleton implanted with a similar device, proving that there was once an isthmus connecting North America with Africa. There's a little map on the bottom of the piece with an isthmus connecting the two continents in the shape of the Copper Seven. All you have to do is add a map and a brass plaque to an object and everybody believes it.

McMillen: Are issues about the environment the reason behind your horizon drawings?

Abeles: They remind me of primitive technology in a world filled with gadgets that can do everything. Basically, we haven't changed much. We've just created all these items that need to be plugged in. So the horizons are like translating a megalopolis into a primitive form, with just the hand and the pen. I draw different cities. I did one of Berlin that actually makes one friend homesick because he sees the Mercedes sign on top of a building. And there are other distinctive peaks in the landscape that identify the city. It is like a primitive way of writing a diary. Some of them are funny. I did one of Washington, D.C., in which the Capitol building is surrounded by construction cranes that seem to be holding it up. Your image of cities is most often from picture postcard views, and even if you're really there, you still see it the way you remembered it from *National Geographic.* These drawings expose all the junk in the scenes. I did one from L.A. to Del Mar that in a way defied the very possibility of doing it. The piece is called *Mile-a-Minute* because I figured that's how fast I had to draw in order to get everything. I was drawing as I looked out the window of a train. The landscape was just whizzing by. It's not scientific. If I really wanted to be factual, photography or film would have been a lot more logical. But this was more intriguing somehow. It was more like someone's own language.

I've actually been doing research for a drawing from L.A. to New York. The drawing itself, end to end, would stretch a couple of miles. The smartest way to do the drawing is to make a computer program that uses a light pen on a horizontally moving screen. The most beautiful way of doing the drawing, and this would send you to the madhouse, is to make a sort of pump sewing machine that shifts the paper. In a sense you would be walking that distance. Think what that would be like. You'd go through areas of the Midwest and see practically straight lines or maybe just a few telephone poles. A funny thing happened when I did the L.A. to Del Mar piece. There were children on the train. At first they didn't know what I was doing, but obviously I looked like I had a mission. I had a sense of determination about me. The next thing you know, these kids were asking their parents for drawing paper so they could try to do the same thing. I worked on tablets that were then transferred. That's why the sewing machine would be great. It's very in tune with the way I do things. If there's a chance to reinvent the wheel, I'll do it. That's the fun of it.

McMillen: Tell me about the contraption pieces.

Abeles: *Experiment to Identify Change* is a contraption piece. It was done because someone told me that the lines in one hand change during your life, but in your other hand they stay the same. I wanted to do an experiment to confirm whether or not this was accurate. I built a contraption, and every day I went to the studio I would get into it, almost like a little confessional booth, and place my hands on a mold that was on top of a structure with a stationary camera. I would photograph my hands each day to see if they were changing. I did this over a five-and-one-half-month period. The question that people like

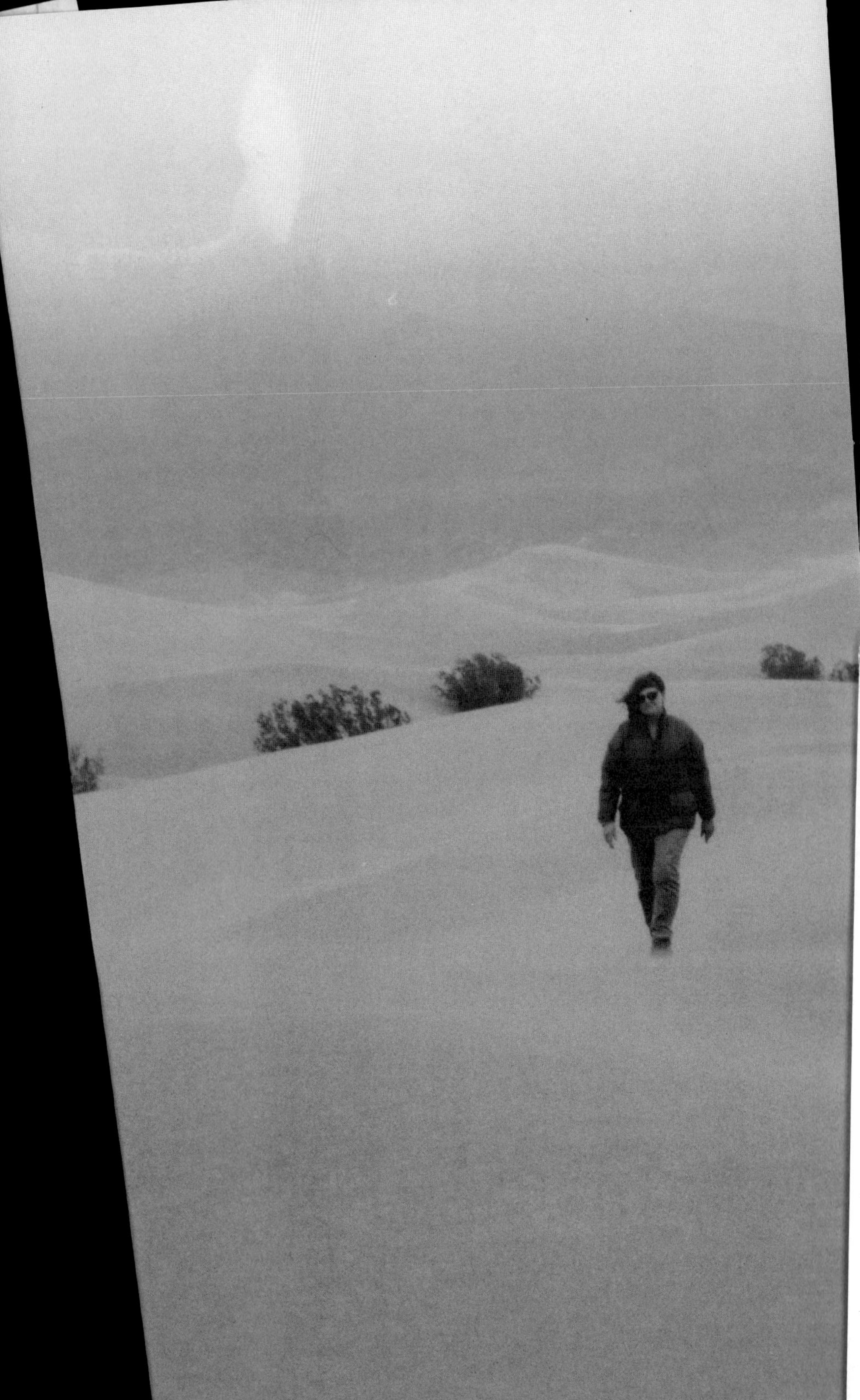

to ask me now is, "Was there any change in my hands?" You know, in the end, I never really compared them because the piece had become such an obsession. I couldn't go to the studio without doing this first, like brushing your teeth in the morning. I couldn't do anything else first. So I had obviously gone through a change, and it was almost as if I didn't want to test my faith in it. I had changed through the piece. It is a good example of my making a structure in order to perform some duty. It becomes sculpture only after this ritual has taken place.

McMillen: It's almost like a shamanistic totem or an object that becomes empowered.

Abeles: The piece feels like that even when finished. A lot of the contraption pieces are certainly like that. They are really performance oriented. In the second phase of the *Mountain Wedge* project I actually walked from my studio to the mountain wedge on a day of a first-stage smog alert to see how close I'd have to be in order to get a clear picture. As it turned out, I had to be at the foot of the mountain. I went as the crow flies. I walked in a completely northerly path, so if I had to cut through lawns and yards and houses, I had to knock on the door and ask. I had to go over barbed wire and down cliffs and under freeways, with dogs barking and grabbing my pants. By the time I finished, it had become a fourteen-hour walk. And I wasn't in good shape. I didn't do this after an athletic fitness program, plus I was a chain smoker at the time. By the time I reached the mountain, I looked like I had been trashed. My glasses were broken, my hair was full of brambles and thistles. I had been bitten up by red ants at one point when I sat on an ant hill. I was literally a mess, pants torn and dirty, blood and everything. Somebody asked, "Did you take a picture of yourself at the end?" because in a way that was a logical thing to do. I said, "Well, no." I guess the point wasn't really me. The point wasn't that I was a martyr in doing this.

My memory of that walk will be one of the most tremendous memories in my whole life. I can barely go anywhere in that vicinity without thinking, "God, I was on this street corner, and this is where the kid said 'You're gonna walk in this neighborhood?'" I took photographs at every intersection of every street, and I never even used those photographs. Maybe one day I will, but they just didn't seem to be the point.

McMillen: It really fills out the piece for me knowing that you did this pilgrimage to complete the whole piece.

Abeles: It needed it. It was a closure. There was a need for me to make that whole installation. It wasn't even that I had visions of these pieces or anything. It's just they all more or less described themselves as I became aware of what the smog was like.

McMillen: Tell me about your interest in books and book format.

Abeles: The books originally started because in the topics I singled out I realized that I couldn't do everything in one piece of sculpture. There would always be additional images that were very interesting to me but never quite fit logically in the sculptural format I was using. In the books I could merge all the information. It was also important that the books could be afforded by anybody, that they could be hand-held. The best way to see my sculpture is to see it directly, not to look at a little slide. Because the books are tactile and I can even incorporate little objects, anyone can experience my work. I really believe strongly that art should be much more egalitarian than it is, that it should be accessible to many more people. In a lot of ways I feel we should be exhibiting work at Woolworth's. People complain about the normal person not comprehending art, but we never give them a chance to see it. The books open up another avenue for me and another audience.

McMillen: Do you have a fantasy piece or installation that you would like to build?

Abeles: Well, I guess my answer is that the piece I'm currently researching is my next fantasy piece. Every time I start a project I have this feeling that maybe I can't do it. As soon as I start work, I jump in the water and I see that it doesn't matter how cold it is as long as I just keep swimming fast. That fantasy piece is the next one because it's still sort of dreamy in my head. I see images clearly, but there is nothing concrete I can show you. And it's frustrating when you have an idea and you're dying to tell somebody what you're going to do. They look at you strangely, and you wonder, "Maybe the idea isn't as brilliant as I kept thinking it was, because they can't see it." You can see it, visualize it in your head, but describing it to someone just doesn't work. This is funny because if you describe to someone a piece you have seen in an exhibition, then it works. Somehow you can transmit that.

✶

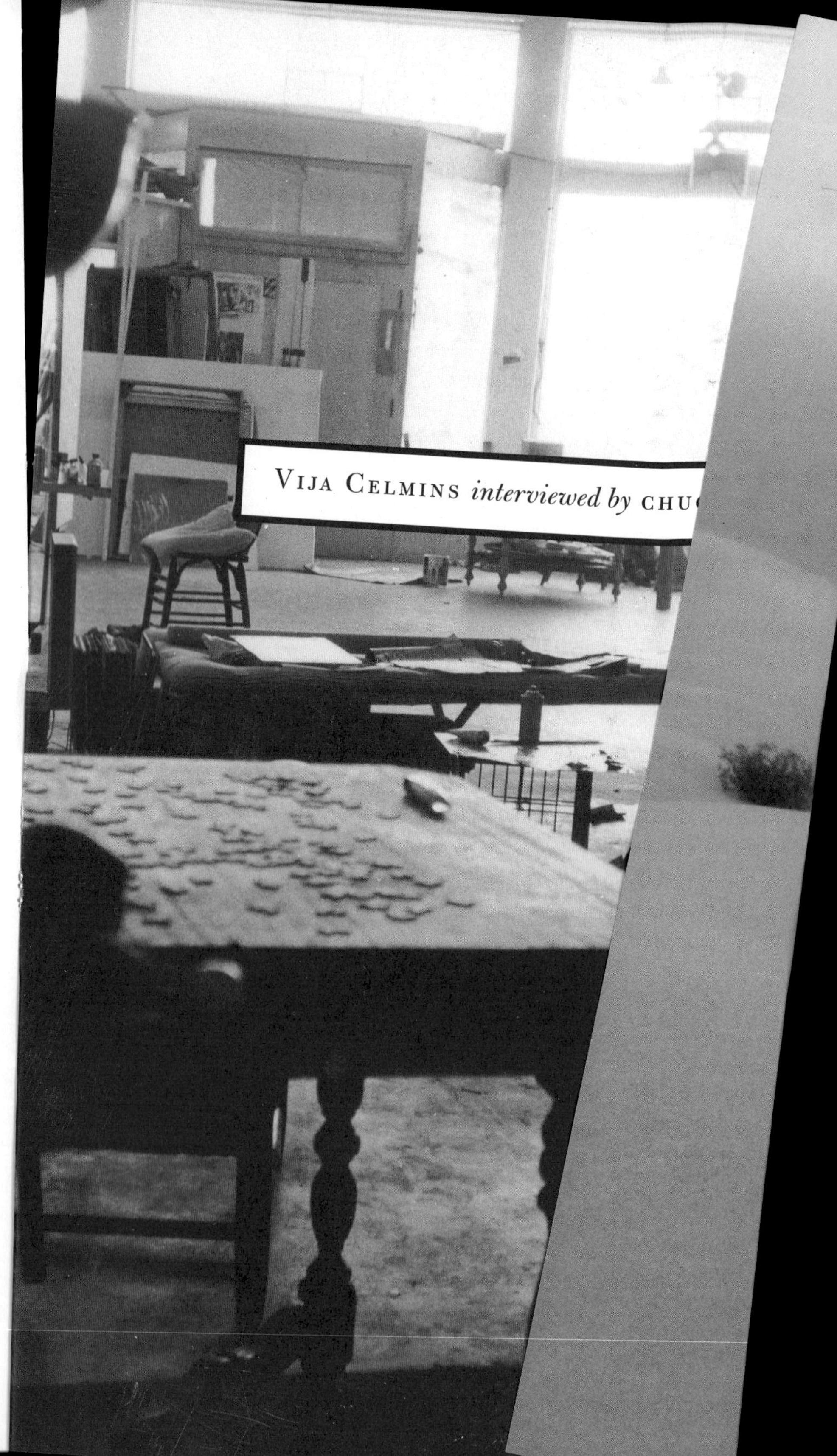

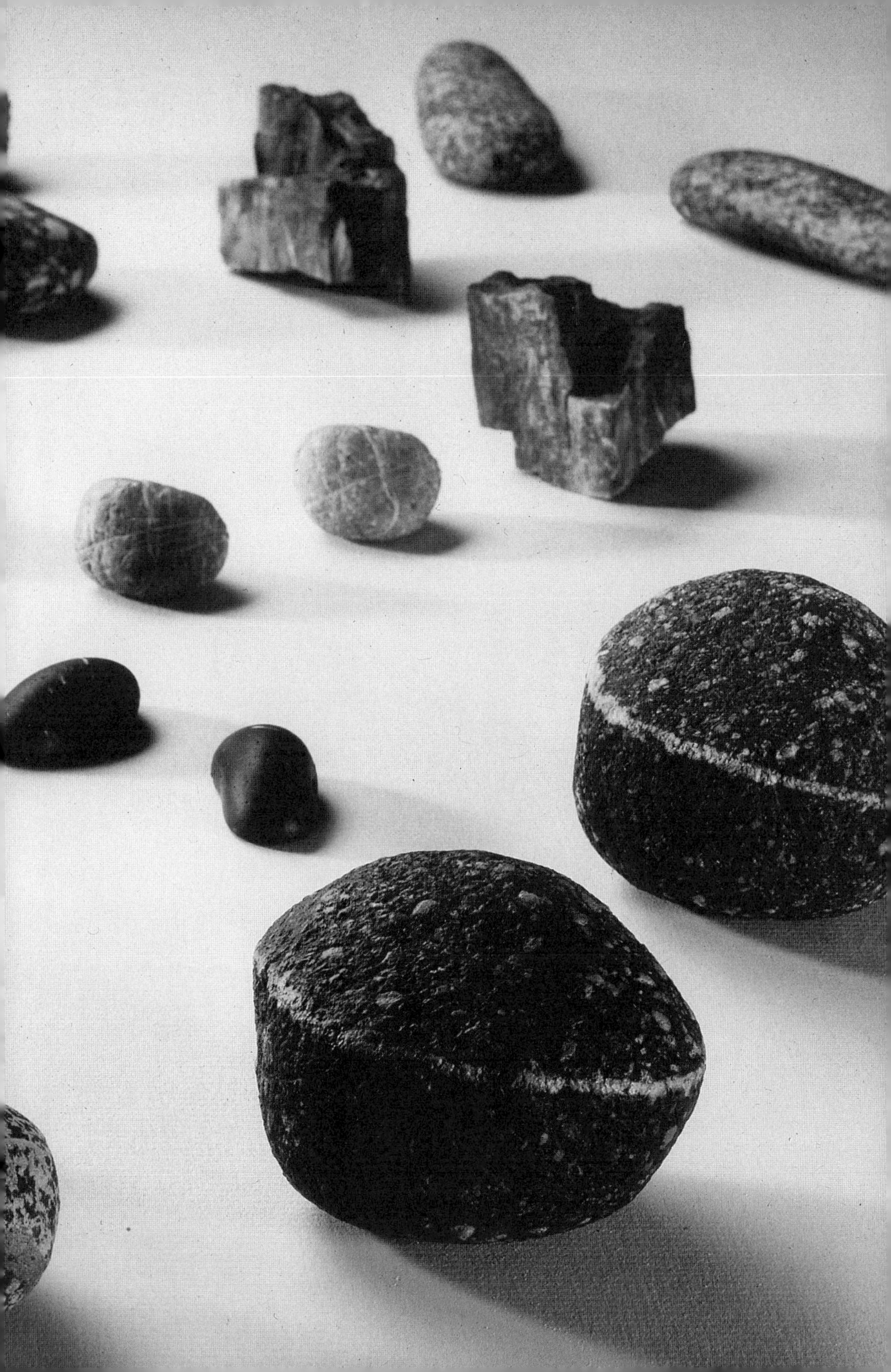

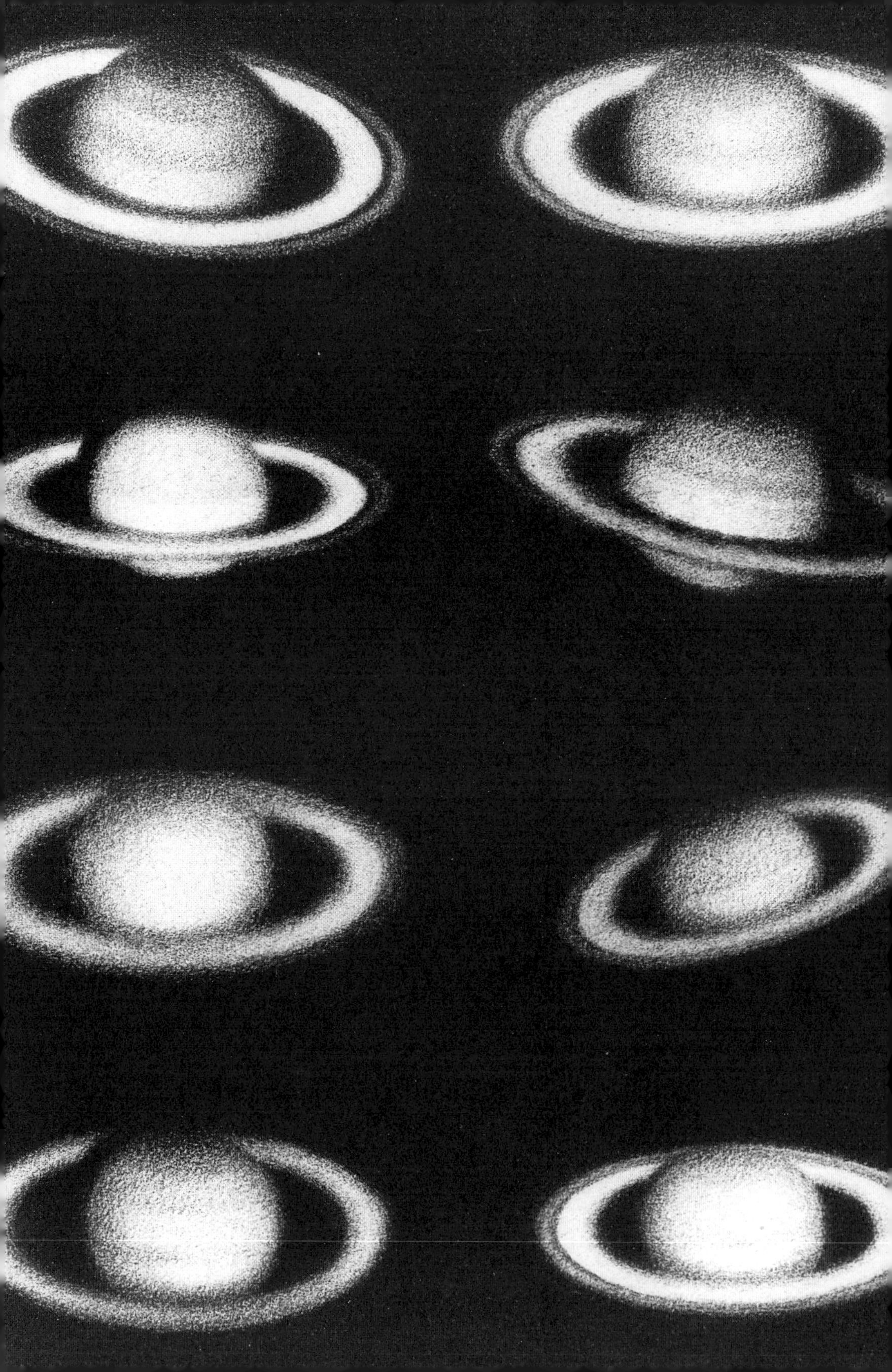

Vija Celmins

interviewed by

Chuck Close

Chuck Close: I was wondering about the various kinds of imagery that you have used over the years. The first kind of imagery you used is very domestic—household items and stuff like that—and we might think archetypically more female. Then there are the planes and violent imagery, which stereotypically we think of as male imagery. And then there is the whole range of images which I consider as an almost overwhelming nature; overwhelming men and women. I was wondering if you had any thoughts about the choice of imagery in light of your being a woman?

Vija Celmins: Well, I don't look at imagery that way; that's all there is to it. I don't look at work from any kind of political standpoint. I look at it from my own making of it. I went through many "styles" in art school, mostly making large, semiabstract paintings. I began to face my own art when I went out to L.A. from Indiana. For one thing, it was the first time I had been away from my parents and I missed them. Also, for the first time I had a giant, empty studio with some secondhand, ordinary household things in it: chairs, tables, lamps, a TV, my hot plate. I started pulling back into myself and painting what I was seeing. I painted the things in my studio; I painted just about everything. Then, as I got more involved with myself and my memories as subject matter, I moved back into my childhood, into the war years, as subject matter. I never considered whether that was masculine or feminine.

Close: I don't either, but I was just wondering if you had any feelings about it. I know how personal the imagery is, and I want to talk about that, too.

Celmins: I don't think of imagery from a symbolic, a political, or even a sociological perspective. I don't think of it as private or personal either. I don't mind other people looking at it that way, but I don't look at it that way. So why did you bring up this question?

Close: I thought the viewer might wonder why you chose this particular imagery. I thought that the choice of imagery was far more personal, that the urgency of the imagery was from your life, rather than some overlay.

page 17:
Vija Celmins's studio, Los Angeles, 1966
page 18:
Vija Celmins in the sand dunes of Death Valley, California
page 19:
To Fix the Image in Memory, *1977–82, acrylic-painted cast bronzes and original stones*
page 20:
Drawing—Saturn *(detail), 1982, graphite on acrylic ground on paper, 14 x 11 inches*

Celmins: I think the use of imagery is so complicated, and there are so many different ways of looking at it, that perhaps it's open for interpretation. I'm telling you, at the time I never once thought of it in those terms. Actually, I don't think of it in terms of coming up with meaningful imagery. I used what was at hand. Maybe you can force me to think of it in those terms.

Close: But I don't want to.

Celmins: But it might be interesting. I do think, in retrospect, I have detached myself from my work somewhat. Now I can see it as if I had nothing to do with it. Which is perhaps one of the most interesting things that has happened as I've gotten older—I am able to look back and say, "What is this?" So when I'm forced to look at imagery this way, the imagery has an intensity, especially the early things. They have an ominous, kind of dangerous strangeness.

Close: I think those are the most violent-looking paintings. What appear to be…

Celmins: Benign.

Close: That's right. It is the most dangerous hot plate, or the most dangerous heater, or whatever, that I have ever seen. And they are scary for some reason.

Celmins: Oh, I don't know, do you think so? They do have that ominous feeling that there is something going on besides just still lifes. I think that it came about because I had been painting in an abstract expressionist manner and I had been trying to make my strokes—the painting space—meaningful. I had tried to do passionate kinds of paintings because I was full of this energy, like I think you were, like we were when we were twenty years old. A couple of years later, I began to feel that there was no meaning in it for me. I lost my way; I rejected it. I couldn't resolve the stroke making with the essential stillness of the painting. So then I went back to some basic thing, like looking at simple objects and painting them straight, trying to rediscover if there was anything there that might be more authentic. But the object paintings came out sort of twisted, with more energy in them than was needed.

Close: Do you think that we rejected abstract expressionism because we were coming to it so late, sort of fourth-generation, junior abstract expressionists? We were imitating the look—it's what we learned art looks like.

Celmins: It was hard not to make it at that time.

Close: That's right. Do you feel that you purposely pushed yourself into some corner where you had something more specifically personal to do?

Celmins: The truth is that I have always had a lot of stops and starts in my work. So sometimes it's hard to see a logical development. When I realized that this painting that I was doing was getting so decorative and meaningless, probably for the reasons you said—that I hadn't really originated it and had received most of this information from magazines—I had to leave it. I had to back up and find a place where I felt more comfortable.

Close: In the forties and fifties, art magazines were in black and white. Growing up in Seattle, I went over these magazines with magnifying glasses. As far as I was concerned, all these de Koonings and stuff were black and white. I had never seen any of the originals; I didn't know what color they were. And it wasn't until about 1961, when the magazine It Is *came out, that I saw the first reproductions in color to see what these paintings actually looked like. Both of us have spent a lot of time making black-and-white work.*

Celmins: I think I probably dropped the color for other reasons.

Close: Well, me, too.

Celmins: I was dissatisfied. As I remember, many people moved on from abstract expressionist painting—so did I. I decided to go back to looking at something outside of myself. I was also going back to what I thought was this basic, stupid painting. You know: there's the surface, there's me, there's my hand, there's my eye, I paint. I don't embellish anymore, I don't compose, and I don't jazz up the color.

One of the things that I remember being very struck by was an Ad Reinhardt article. I think it came out in 1957, in *Art News* or something. Remember that article on the twelve things not to do? I believe that I had never seen Reinhardt's work, and I don't think I've ever been influenced by his painting, but I have been influenced by his writing. He wrote twelve technical rules, or how to achieve the twelve things to avoid—I loved that. No texture, no brushwork or calligraphy, no sketching or drawing. Now you see, I drew but I didn't sketch. What I finally did was to leave painting: forms, design, color, and, I thought, invention.

I remember discussing this article in Indiana, of all places, in this very traditional studio where older students had their own little, messy workplaces. I remember being inspired to imagine what is art if you remove all these things. What was left was a kind of poetic reminder of how little a work of art really is art, and how elusive it is to chase the part that excites you and turns one thing into something else. And how tiny that part is, and how hard it is to define. So I was inspired to throw away as much as I could.

Close: Actually, we were on opposite coasts purging our work.

Celmins: Did you do that, too?

Close: Absolutely, severe, self-imposed limitations: I am not going to do this. I can't do that. I am not going to use this material. Get color out of there.

Celmins: Were your first things black and white?

Close: Yes, I didn't work in color for several years.

Celmins: There were a lot of changes going on in the late fifties and early sixties. Johns, Warhol, Rauschenberg, Morley, all those people that started doing dumb objects, dumb painting, commercial-art painting, whatever you call it. I began to look at Morandi, too, because he was showing up in magazines.

When I went to Europe in 1962 to look at some museums, I was turned on by the real presence of works that I'd only seen as reproductions, especially Velázquez at the Prado in Madrid—seeing that removed quality of his later paintings of Isabella and Philip IV. His paintings seemed to have just appeared. They seemed effortless; it was fabulous. And then you go up close to see this brushwork that just seems to have collected there. I remember the somberness of that gray and white. I remember remembering those paintings for a long while.

Close: As much as your work is purged of a lot—trying to get the handwriting out of there, trying to get the brushwork out of there, get the color out of there—it is amazingly physical. There is a tremendous amount of physicality to it. It is not just ethereal. I think that is one of the dichotomies that is really riveting and so engaging in the work. At once they look like they just happened, and yet there's this physicality. The drawings are incredibly physical as well.

Celmins: Sometimes I'm convinced that there is nothing else but the physical act of making the art. Sometimes I refine it too much, which makes it seem ethereal, which of course it's not.

Close: You're talking about how conceptual drawing with graphite is. There isn't so much there, just decisions, just a record of decisions having been made.

Celmins: That's because I see drawing as thinking, as evidence of thinking, evidence of going from one place to another. One draws to define one thing from another. Draws proportions, adjusts scale. It is impossible to paint without drawing. I see the drawing in your painting, too.

Going back to the object paintings I started in 1963–64, I dropped scale and composition altogether and painted the objects one by one, life-sized: hot plate, lamps, refrigerator, radio. I made some of the objects three-dimensional. I think of them as having fallen out of the picture plane. They are not really sculpture.

Close: I don't think of your sculpture as sculpture, but more like painting that comes out of the room and occupies the space with us.

Celmins: That's a nice way to put it. I was grappling with what it meant to work on a two-dimensional plane, and come out of it and go back into it.

Close: I think all this has a lot to do with artifice and the artificial. In a sense, you are decorating a surface with paint, but then there is the desire to actually paint around something. It makes me think of your choice of photographs because you say in your notebook, "My eyes were honed in nature. I practiced seeing the desert." Some people think that you're not looking if you're looking at a photograph.

Celmins: Oh, that's ridiculous.

Close: Why do you put this artificial layer between you and what you're looking at?

Celmins: The photo is an alternate subject, another layer that creates distance. And distance creates an opportunity to view the work more slowly and to explore your relationship to it. I treat the photograph as an object, an object to scan. Actually, the first time I used photographs was really because I had been away from my family and lonely. I had been going through bookstores finding war books and tearing out little clippings of airplanes, bombed-out places—nostalgic images. At first I painted them; later I decided the clippings were this wonderful range of grays for me to explore with graphite. Then I started to do moon drawings from photographs taken by a machine that had recorded the range of grays on the moon and had transmitted them back. Then they had been photographed and printed in a book, and then...

Close: There was a layering in between.

Celmins: I thought of it as putting the images that I found in books and magazines back in the real world—in real time. When you look at the work, you confront the here and now. It's right there.

Close: So you approach these photographs as an object in the same way as the lamp had been an object?

Celmins: Right, I did at first. I think you can see that the whole idea at first was that it might be possible to put something in a two-dimensional plane, or on it, or somehow solve that problem. You can see that the photographs had the same kind of single-object imagery, like the objects that I had been painting earlier. In a way, the photograph helps unite the object with the two-dimensional plane. Although I think that with the airplanes there is this kind of wonderful place where they really float, and then they become dimensional, and they take off as well as staying flat. I did not realize it then, but now I can see that the subject matter has a kind of internal tension that also exists in the work. The paintings tend to have an internal feeling, as if there was something behind what you see.

Close: The paintings are very lush, and, at the same time, they're incredibly restrictive. That is a funny dichotomy.

Celmins: I'm always aware of the limits of painting, and have come to think that the limits are what give it more meaning. Of course, one has to find the limits. I painted so much between 1961 and 1964 that I probably went through five lifetimes of different sorts of painting: Matisse, Hoffmann, Gorky, and de Kooning. I think you can also see quite a bit of a Morandi influence as well.

Close: More in the early color work. It's a world of color but it's really approached monochromatically. Later, when you got color totally out of the picture, the viewer fills in the color in his or her mind. I always thought that black-and-white photographs of war, for instance, were far more scary than color photographs of war because color photographs of war always look wrong—the blood doesn't look like blood, it looks like ketchup or something. But in a black-and-white photograph of war, you fill in the color in your mind and make blood blood-colored. In a way, it's sort of less artificial. By purging the work of color, it actually makes them more naturalistic.

Celmins: Yes, but naturally I didn't think of that either. What I know is that I didn't just wake up one day and say, "I'm not going to use color." I slipped into it through drawing the photographs, which were black and white, because those were the only photographs available at that time. The second thing is that I do believe I wanted a more somber note, and I thought that color was an extra, as if I were decorating something.

Close: I understand that. I got rid of color because I felt I depended too much on it. I'd been told that I had a good sense of color and all that. It just occurred to me that the color I was using was learned *color, was* art *color. It had something to do with other people's paintings. I could see wanting to get it out because it was reminiscent of a certain kind of art.*

Celmins: That's right, though I often think that my removing things was going too fast. It was a series of decisions, arrived at intuitively, to remove stuff. Then I think it may just be my nature to throw stuff away.

Close: Let's talk about your nature. At one time, you described yourself as lazy. To look at your work, the last word to describe you is lazy. When we started talking about compulsion, you said that everyone would assume you're a very compulsive person. I don't think you're a very compulsive person; nor do I think I am. A compulsive person is driven to do things whether they want to do them or not. They have almost no control over themselves.

Celmins: Oh no, I'm not like that.

Close: I don't see you that way at all. I see that you force yourself to behave in a compulsive manner, that is, to sit there and keep doing it. But it doesn't come from some kind of compulsive drive.

Celmins: No, I don't think it's *mindless* compulsion.

Close: Do you think that people like your work for the wrong reasons?

Celmins: Who knows why people like work? At a certain point, you're very happy that people look at it at all; in that way it's good. My feeling is, however, that often people only look at the image. I feel that the image is just a sort of armature on which I hang my marks and make my art. The early imagery, especially the war things, had a more specific emotional tension, but most of my later imagery developed without choosing any specific kind of symbolic meaning. I don't use the ocean in any kind of symbolic way. These first broken-surface images were a way to articulate the surface of the drawing in a cubist way: with individual marks that break up the surface and then build up into a whole.

Close: In your notebook you talk about building a painting: "I build the work like a house, like construction. Hah, all the materials put together—when I was young I had mechanical ability." You could build whatever you wanted.

Celmins: Which is pretty funny. My father was a builder, so I must have identified with building.

Close: I like to think the way I work is almost like knitting a painting, or something like that. I don't think of it as painting it in layers, the way you talk about finding a way to get down to an armature for the individual marks to build upon. That's something that interests me a great deal.

Celmins: I have long been interested in building a form in the painting. It's hard to define the word *form,* but I wanted to make a work that was multidimensional and that went back and forth in space yet remained what it was: a small, concentrated area that was essentially flat. Who knows why you want to do this? So, in a way, I thought of painting as building a dense and multileveled structure. Now I tend to think of it only in physical terms, but you could say that it alludes to a denser experience of life. You have to reimagine it in other terms, which is lead, paper, paint, and canvas. My feeling is that we all do essentially the same thing. I like to talk about it in terms of structuring because when I'm working, my instinct is to try to build and to fill—to fill something until it is really full.

Close: Does it help to make decisions easier to break it down into bite-sized increments?

Celmins: It doesn't make it easier, but I have found it a way of building the space, letting in light, keeping the image close to the surface, moving the eye along. Small strokes keep their integrity.

Close: Were you interested in having a way to make judgments based on things that were outside of art? For example: Did it in fact look like a lamp? Did it in fact look like a photograph? Did it look like a postcard on the wall? Ultimately, it seems to me, when you had the original rock next to the manufactured or built rock, that that was taking verisimilitude to the absolute extreme. I always liked the fact, when I was working from photographs, that instead of inventing an interesting shape I had to accept the shape that was in the photograph. There was a right and a wrong shape, and it wasn't dependent on whether it was an interesting "art shape." It was being determined by things that are outside of taste.

There's something else about the rocks which interests me. Sometimes the one you made looks more real than the real one. So you've conjured up an illusion. It's like a magician who does everything necessary to make a successful illusion.

Celmins: A magician's not bad, but if you look very close, it's immediately clear which rock is painted and which one isn't.

Close: But that's what's interesting to me.

Celmins: So, in a way, it's impossible to ever completely mimic nature.

Close: But again, to use the magician metaphor, you always know when you're seeing an illusion created by a magician. It's not real and that's the pleasure in it.

Celmins: What is the name of this piece? *To Fix the Image in Memory*—can you imagine such a pretentious name that I picked for this piece? It is sort of an exercise in looking, a superlooking, as if the meaning of art was only in looking. I got the idea for this piece while walking in northern New Mexico picking up rocks, as people do. I'd bring them home and I kept the good ones. I noticed that I kept a lot that had galaxies on them. I carried them around in the trunk of my car. I put them on windowsills. I lined them up. And, finally, they formed a set, a kind of constellation. I developed this desire to try and put them into an art context, mocking art in a way, but also to affirm the act of making—the act of looking and making as a primal act of art.

Close: I was really blown away when I saw them.

Celmins: Well, the best part is that they do have a little bit of a magic quality to them. I think that the impulse to make these was so complicated that I can't say much about them without sounding silly. They're really something to experience, I think.

Close: Were they cast directly from the stones?

Celmins: Yes, I decided to put them into a traditional art material, the way that Johns did when he cast his ale cans in bronze. It was the most conceptual piece that I had ever done. Part of the experience of exhibiting them together with the real stones was to create a challenge for your eyes. I wanted your eyes to open wider.

Close: You do need something to measure them against. You don't know how far they've come without the comparison to the original objects.

Celmins: I liked the fact that they were something outside of myself. And I did *love* the fact that I didn't have to make up anything, because I was trying to find something that could still be art after removing obvious composition and obvious invention.

Close: Don't you think extremism is really interesting? Your work is very extreme.

Celmins: Pardon?

Close: Your work is very extreme.

Celmins: I don't think of it that way. Do you think so?

Close: Yes, and that piece is the extreme of the extreme.

Celmins: I must admit, the most extreme works were the bronzes. I thought of it as an invented piece, but most people would say that this was just a work about copying. But it's not just a copy.

Close: I think that it's invention, too. It's what I call an "invention of means," rather than an invention in the way it's normally thought of. You're not inventing the shape. You're not inventing the color. You're not inventing the texture. All that is inherent in the original. What you're doing is inventing the means to reconstruct that, in its own terms. It all has to work as a painting.

Celmins: That's right. It has to work and be redefined in this other context.

Close: It's not a rock. It's not a photograph. It's not a car. It's not a house. It's not a lamp.

Celmins: In the case of the bronze stones, I wanted to see how much I could see—not to project any view, but to test my seeing and making, as if there were some secret to be discovered only there. I left the original for the viewer to relive that process of seeing. Of course, on close inspection, one sees that the "made" piece is invented, an interpretation. At that time, this interested me. In the case of the paintings, I have to admit that I am fascinated, intrigued, with that two-dimensional plane which is the here and now. I have come down to very formal issues. Do you think this is sort of formal? From my little book you must be able to see—it's beyond the word *formal.*

Close: I think the work is reacting to the wretched excess of the last several decades. Ultimately, the choice—just like a writer's choice of words—can make a story very interesting or compelling, and that is the formal level of decision making that is absolutely essential to making anything. People have stopped talking about art this way because the focus has been on the story told rather than on the way it's communicated. It does not mean going back to some kind of Greenbergian formalism. It is what we do in the studio every day. It is what occupies our time. It is the evidence, that residue of the act, that is what engages us. That's why we make art. It seems to me to be the pleasure and the fascination of putting these pieces together that is ultimately what separates one artist from another.

Celmins: I think that sometimes I get too involved in formal concerns.

Close: The work is also profoundly psychological. I don't think one negates the other.

Celmins: I don't like to look at them psychologically, but it is a popular way of looking at art today. When I look back at some of the images from 1964–66, the objects that used images from World War II, especially works like the little house on fire (which is one of my favorite pieces from that time), I am moved even now, and I have to admit that there is a psychological component to the work.

Close: Let's go back and figure out who this person is who made all this stuff, because I've known you since 1961.

(Celmins laughs.)

Close: I've known you since 1961, when we met at the Yale summer school. I've followed your work with tremendous interest over all these years, and I've tried to put it together with what I know to be aspects of your personality. One of the things that is a constant in all the work, psychologically, is that I find you immensely charming, very funny, and, at the same time, there's a melancholy. You operate back and forth—you sort of bump into one aspect of yourself; then you go back the other way. When you're having too much fun, you'll think about something that brings you back down. I was trying to understand the work in light of what I know to be true of your history, which is certainly amazing, about what happened in your life.

Celmins: Well, it's not so amazing. So many people have been refugees from various parts of the world. And, of course, in the United States I would say almost everyone is a refugee from some disaster or another in Europe, Asia, South America. I guess I have more firsthand experience than most of the people you know. Of course, I know a lot of people who went through the same experience.

Close: Do you want to talk a little bit about your childhood?

Celmins: I generally think of my childhood as being full of excitement and magic, and terror, too—bombs, fires, fear, escape—very eventful. It wasn't till I was ten years old and living in the United States that I realized living in fear wasn't normal.

I went back to Riga about three years ago. It was exciting, and, at the same time, shocking. You know, they have so many problems. It was very difficult to really comprehend the whole situation, so I embraced it the best that I could. It was moving to see my relatives and to go back to where I was born.

Close: Are some of these people still living in the house where you were...

Celmins: Yes.

Close: You once told me about how the communists kept filling your house with Russians.

Celmins: There was no place for them to live, as they didn't build houses. The communists have a lot of trouble doing the simple things. They just moved into our house while my family continued to live there, too, but I don't really want to talk about it. What can I say about it? It was an emotional experience. I do regret not having a homeland. I wonder what it would feel like to live your whole life in the same general area where you were born. I imagine that would have been very comforting to me and would have given me a different kind of strength. This is one of my biggest regrets.

Close: What do you feel about what's going on in Latvia now?

Celmins: I would like to go there and help them out in whatever way I can. But I also feel that it is just too complicated to get involved in without changing everything about my life. I have a feeling that they are going to get back some of their self-respect as they gain independence. That's really what's missing because they've been occupied for so long. They've been very brutalized and humiliated. When you go there, you have a strong feeling that someone is sitting on them.

Close: How do you feel about the word displaced?

Celmins: People usually do leave one place to go to somewhere better, to escape some situation. I've always felt that there is a sense of loss. I missed my childhood. Actually, I think I had a very eventful childhood with a lot of adventures. It was not like sitting at home with a TV the first ten years of your life. When I finally left my family and moved to Los Angeles to go to graduate school, I spent years working out my longing for that lost childhood. Because the first ten years of my life had been so dominated by the war in Europe, I found myself reaching back to it. I re-created the toys and puzzles and other things remembered from my school days, like the pencil, eraser, and comb. Some of that work has a childlike quality which seems now to have an edge of humor to it. Maybe I feel somewhat displaced. First we moved to Germany and then to the United States—to Indiana, then to California, and now to New York. I mean, I've done a lot of moving. I do feel a little bit exiled.

Close: Is home where you hang your hat, or is there a home which you've left?

Celmins: Sometimes I think home is Latvia; it will always be my first home. In another way, the studio is a home because that's where everything happens for me. I heard a program on the radio discussing Czeslaw Milosz, and I picked up on an eloquent phrase he had used: "Imagination can fashion a homeland." I liked that. That statement is more than true for me. Where my dog is, that's where home is—that's not bad. That's about as good as anything.

Close: How about translation? Was there a point when you stopped thinking in Latvian?

Celmins: I can't remember exactly when I stopped thinking in Latvian. Somewhere in my late teens, I think. Many words for things still seem best in Latvian. Words that don't have a proper translation into English, like *ăcgārni,* which means you're doing things the most awkward way. It's more than a word; it's a cultural concept that is inside of me. Or words like *pļava,* which means "field" or "meadow." It has totally different images connected for me than the English word *field.* Or a word like *mĕzonīg//s,* which means "fierce" or "from the forest," "beastlike." I think, in some essential way, Latvian words shaped how I saw images.

Close: It seems to me a great deal of what you've always been involved in was translating from one situation into another, from one medium into another—from a photograph to a painting, for example. I've always thought of it as an interesting metaphor for what I do, and that is that one has to completely understand the language—all the subtlety and nuances—before putting it into another language.

Celmins: But I don't think of the seeing part. You mean, you wouldn't be able to see without a language? That is an interesting thought. You mean, you have to really *see* what's in a photograph before you translate it? Well, I think you see what your imagination allows you to see.

Close: I guess what I'm talking about is people think, "Oh, you're just copying photographs." As if there were only one way to make a painting or drawing based on a photograph, that it's just automatic. Whereas to make an effective translation, you have to understand both worlds extremely well. You have to really understand what you're looking at: decode it, break it down, and understand it. Plus, you have to have, I think, tremendous sophistication with the new language that you're translating into—which is the painting language or the drawing language—to really function in that space between the two.

Celmins: I think the way that I put the painting together talks about the modern issues that we ended up with since Cézanne. I think you do this, too.

Close: Do you feel that you knew your subject from looking at it, and then you used the camera to jot it down, or do you feel that you learned from looking at the photographs?

Celmins: I would say both. I can't say that I took the photos in order to make the paintings because what I really liked was looking through the camera lens. I had a job at the University of California, Irvine, and used to drive to it back and forth on the freeway taking photographs by balancing my camera on the steering wheel. I guess I thought of my camera as something to see through. I think later I was inspired by the silvery grays of the moon photos that were sent back from Luna 9, and others from American missions.

Close: But you haven't been to the moon, so you have to depend on the photographic evidence. It never existed as a firsthand experience. There is always this artificial layer between you and the experience.

Celmins: So there's an experience of only being inspired by the surface in the photograph. And the ocean drawings...you see, I lived by the ocean in Venice, and I used to walk my big dog by the ocean every evening. I think I started to treat the camera as something to use, to peek through, and to take pictures with without thinking that I would use these photographs in my work, because I was still doing the war series. Finally, I had so many piles of pictures of the ocean, and I became so enamored with that image that I began drawing them.

Close: It's almost something between you and the experience. It's the difference between going to Europe with a camera and shooting everything that you're looking at, and just going to Europe and looking around. One is almost as if you're making something to be experienced back at home, and the other is just looking.

Celmins: Yes, mine was more like looking. One thing led to another. When I started looking, I began to look more at my own work, and I think I made the work more about looking. Essentially, it's very conceptual work—it's about looking.

Close: I certainly believe that the same kind of looking and scrutiny can be applied to something that is already two-dimensional.

Celmins: Yes.

Close: I have real trouble with faces, in recognizing them. In a photograph, they don't move, and they don't change, and they don't go away. I can come back and refer to them later. It allows me to really scan them, and scrutinize them, and get much closer.

Celmins: You see, you do the more amazing thing; I simply scrutinize surfaces that are much more abstract, while you scrutinize a face.

Close: I'm scrutinizing a photograph.

Celmins: You do scrutinize a photograph, but you just said that you get to remember the face, or you explore the face in another way. I have only been on the ocean a few times—I never think of that ocean experience when I'm making the art. I don't imagine the ocean and try to re-create a memory of it when I'm doing the art. I explore a surface through drawing it. The image gets controlled, compressed, and transformed.

Close: But you're trying to control something as big as the entire cosmos. At the same time, you're trying to control a little eight-by-ten-inch piece of paper.

Celmins: The drawings have allusions to other kinds of spaces, just like your portraits have many allusions to all kinds of portraiture. But I am only interested in controlling the space in front of me.

Close: I'm just now becoming comfortable with thinking about some of those allusions after all these years. Thinking of myself in terms of the history of portraiture is something that I've only done in the last few years. I've always kept very much in my own arena.

Celmins: You may be more open than I am. I am in total chaos now. I feel as if I've closed up this thing that I have worked on: combining the dimensional with the real, with the flat, with the here and now—making the relationship so incredibly tight that you can't even take them apart anymore. It's just paint now. It's just material. I feel that I want to open up my painting a little. I'm struggling with the idea of punching holes in my paintings, which is what I want to do to open them up. I think that I want to make them a little more accessible. I have a tendency to focus down on a thing too much.

Close: At the same time that you might see that as a problem, our problems are always our strengths, our strengths gone crazy. You know what I mean.

Celmins: I have noticed that. The part that you most hate is often also the part that is the most interesting. But I have to walk this line myself, and I have various instincts and various wants, and I have a certain amount of time left to do the work in.

Close: But at the same time, the work is insular and hermetic, and you pull into it. It's your world and your decision making. It's also—I can tell you as another artist and somebody that looks at it—it's also very generous in spirit. You lay it out there for everyone to see. I think you lay out a great deal about who you are, which you constantly deny. You gave me this very personal notebook, then you said something self-mocking and self-deprecating about it not revealing anything, when, of course, it reveals everything.

Celmins: I also said that I trusted you with it.

Close: It seems to me that you appear to not be showing us anything personal, and then, ultimately, it is profoundly personal.

Celmins: Well, I'm speechless. I don't know what I can say to that.

Close: The more limitations, the more things close down, the more they open back up.

Celmins: That's a hopeful thing to say. I could also say the more it closes down, the more it closes down. And the more closed it gets, and the more impossible it gets, the less it communicates. You could also say that.

Close: That's a risk, I suppose.

Celmins: That's a risk, right.

Close: Is there not enough there? Do you feel that you're replowing the same field? Pick your metaphor.

Celmins: I think one of the things I've noticed in doing the drawings is that I tend to take very small increments and steps in changing. An example was that I had been working with the pencil and I began to see that the graphite itself had a certain life to it. So I did a series of images of oceans and deserts using different grades of graphite and pushing each to its limit. I learned a lot about the possibilities of expressiveness in graphite by doing this. Then I moved into the galaxy drawings. Even though you may think they came from lying under the stars, for me, they came out of loving the blackness of the pencil. It's almost as if I was exploring the blackness of the pencil along with the image that went with it.

Close: I think this is how most decisions are made.

Celmins: So I started doing the same image with different hardnesses of pencil. And then the next thing that came out, which wasn't a really big jump actually, was that I would have the photograph beside the drawing. Then I started to do double images.

Close: Were the photographs usually the same size as the drawings?

Celmins: No, in fact, the photographs are very tiny and dog-eared. I tend to make small decisions that evolve one out of another. I guess that makes sense. But sometimes I wish for a bigger leap that would really work.

Which reminds me, I just saw a Dutch film called *The Vanishing*. In one scene, this guy talks about how he is scared to leap off a balcony, and then he finally leaps. Well, I have this feeling (which I've had now since I've been in New York, where it's more competitive) that I ought to be making more of a leap, but I don't know if I ever will. I think, though, my history shows that I develop out of working. So now I want to make bigger paintings, which I have. I did several six-feet-by-six-feet paintings that were not quite square. You can roam over the surface even though the surface is very closed off. It's damn hard to close off this big a surface. It has been very difficult to find a way of doing those paintings so they just don't look totally dumb or corny to me. That's what I'm trying to do now.

Close: I think those pieces will be a different experience. Yet, in reproductions they will be exactly the same.

Celmins: People will think, "She's doing the same thing."

Close: They'll say that there's no change, nothing's happened. Yet you will have orchestrated an incredibly different experience. I think you just have to be driven by your own urgency.

I absolutely understand when you say that you made the sky black because you were driven by making dark pencil marks. That's exactly the curious route we end up taking. But sitting here—looking at the water, the sky, the desert, and the moon—there is something that I'd never really thought about in your work before, which is that they all seem to me to be describing dangerous places. I've been swept out to sea twice.

Celmins: You have?

Close: And almost drowned. I know the force of water and just how dangerous it is. The desert seems to me to be a very dangerous place, as does outer space. They all contain a power greater than that of individuals. It seems a greater power than we're capable of dealing with. I know suicide is pretty high when people live in the mountains because they feel insignificant, overwhelmed by nature, these forces that are so much greater than you. Maybe you don't think this is an issue at all, but to me there is a foreboding and a danger. At the same time, they are lush and incredibly beautiful and seductive, and I want to go right up and look at them. I want to have my eye an inch away from the surface to see how beautifully built the image is. Now, sitting back this many feet away from them, it's the first time I ever saw that as an aspect of the work.

Celmins: Well, I don't know how I can deal with it. I can imagine somebody seeing that. I have found that, aside from art, nature is one of the most amazing and comforting things to me. I usually don't think of nature as a source of danger; I think of it as a place of discovery. I am inspired by it; I depend on it—it's raw material for me. One of the worst things about living in New York is that the nature is all so covered up.

Close: I love nature, too. And I don't feel scared when I'm in the desert or when I'm on the water.

Celmins: I also don't have that kind of romantic thing, that Caspar Friedrich tendency to project loneliness and romance onto nature; to contrast nature's grandness with tiny, insignificant watchers. I like looking and describing, using the images to explore the process of making.

Close: I know that the position you've taken is very flat-footed and neutral. I like that.

Celmins: I've never heard that phrase, "flat-footed."

Close: It's not like dancing around the stuff. You know what I mean. You're just standing there.

Celmins: See, you're doing what everybody does, they read the image only!

Close: I don't normally do that with your work.

Celmins: Making art, for me, is much more abstract, which is what I always want to bring it back to. But I think you could look at it as a way of controlling images that are from nature. In a way, you are controlling it when you work on a two-dimensional plane—I'll go that far. Over the years, the thing that I have felt about working is that it's just another chance to adjust the image to the flat page. I tend to do images over and over again because each one has a different tone, slant, a different relationship to the plane, and so a different meaning. The meaning for other people tends to be a projection of their own romance. For example, with the ocean image.

Close: I don't find your involvement with it is romantic at all.

Celmins: Or kind of corny, or whatever.

Close: I don't find anything about them corny. As a matter of fact, it's wonderful the way it has been purged of all that. You and van Gogh are the only people that have ever been able to handle stars.

Celmins: Me and who?

Close: Van Gogh. Remember him?

Celmins: I love van Gogh.

Close: The last time we were together, we were talking about how important the abstract expressionists had been for us—how we thought we learned from de Kooning, what we thought we learned from them. Now, most people looking at your work would not assume these people had played any seminal role in your deciding to make the kind of work that you make. Yet I see it as absolutely integral to what you do.

Celmins: Good, because I do, too.

Close: Whether it's the all-overness of the American painting: doing away with foreground, middle distance, background, and making the whole surface...

Celmins: Right, although I don't think that started with the abstract expressionists. Another artist I have looked at carefully is Cézanne. Cézanne recognized and gave value to the space that is in front of you, here and now. It is not just an illustration of absent events, he did it self-consciously. The mark was a mark on the mountain, and that mark also indicated the atmosphere in which the mountain existed, and, finally, it is also a mark on the canvas. At a certain point I realized that this work, which can allude to so much outside of itself, nevertheless remains comprehensible only through the organization of that flat arena. This is no limitation, but an essential expressive element of painting. I think that the abstract expressionists, certainly de Kooning, knew that and used it. They added another subject, however, which was the unconscious—but, of course, that's the subject you like to keep bringing up.

Close: I'm sorry. I'm the last person in the world to keep bringing this stuff up. I feel like I've really failed you. I hate it when people ask who my subjects are looking at, and what are they thinking, and who are these people. The whole is greater than the sum of its parts. There is a transcendent quality to your work and to all great art.

Celmins: What do you mean by transcendent?

Close: It's the magic of art that makes graphite more than just graphite. Look at her face—she's going to ask for another interviewer! I don't see anything corny in that.

Celmins: Look at your work. Maybe that's the nature of art. You do one thing and then something else always comes through.

Close: You stack up the bricks, and you build something that is more than just a pile of bricks. That's what you're doing—the approach is bricklaying. It is something that I respond to in your work.

Celmins: I would say that the work, beginning with the ocean drawings, is more like that. It really went into a rigorous building, and letting the material be the material, letting the image be more and more like an armature. In some of these, the image is almost nothing. It just holds you, and it articulates the picture all over. I'm really interested in that. For some reason, I'm able to do that over and over again without getting bored.

Close: Maybe because I know what it's like to build a picture, I see the delight in what seems laborious and the pleasure that one takes in small things having occurred. I find it very life affirming, finally.

Celmins: I guess it's life affirming.

Close: Is there a rocks-in-your-shoes aspect of difficulty, purposely making it into an activity that slows you down? Are there things that you do to make things more difficult, like laying the strings across the drawing?

Celmins: Not the strings. You mean the cross that went through the whole drawing—you can hardly see the cross. I can tell you about that piece. I had so many people that wanted the oceans and they missed the point. They just rushed past them. So I decided I was going to give them one with a big cross through it. It was a really childlike answer to that demand for ocean drawings.

Close: You're going to give it to them, but you're going to hold back on some aspect.

Celmins: I don't know. That's a perverse thing to do, and it was difficult. The cross flattened the surface more and destroyed the pictorial quality of the ocean. I liked it because it slowed the viewer down. It also slowed me down because it was so hard to do. Even harder is making a drawing of a field of stars where the white is just the paper, without using an eraser. This probably took a year and was drawn maybe four or five times so that the image filled up as much as it could. It got real fat with graphite. But there were all these mines in there to go around.

Close: You had to draw those white shapes by not drawing them.

Celmins: They were drawn by not drawing them. They were left so that the paper became an integral part of the piece. I don't know, do you think when somebody looks at the drawings, do you think that they see all of that?

Close: To quote your notebook, you said, "My work does not exist in a world of its own. It is for the spectator. That is, you find your relationship to it physically, not just mentally or by imagination. It asks participation to come alive. I mean spatial, visual participation. The body, the eyes complete the work." Which reminds me of Duchamp's famous quotation in which he says that the artist has only fifty percent of the responsibility, and that's to get the work out there, but that the piece is not completed until it's returned to the artist by the viewer.

Celmins: How clever.

Close: It's essentially what you're saying as well. So all you can do is to stack up the evidence for the viewer, and that's what you do.

Celmins: So this is our bricklaying—stacking up the evidence.

Close: For me, part of the joy of your work is the vicarious reexperience of your having made them. I really love them physically, love their matter. I love standing there and going over the surface with you and reliving what you did.

Celmins: Much of the early work I did while I was in graduate school at U.C.L.A. I destroyed.

Close: Not the food paintings?

Celmins: I don't have a lot of food ones left. I have a soup-bowl painting. I did a puzzle with a stew on it. I did a lot of fish heads. For the most part, those are buried beneath what is now Mountain Gate, one of the fanciest developments in Los Angeles. I would go through my studio every six months, sweep through it, and take another load to the dump.

Close: Me, too.

Celmins: You didn't take them to the L.A. dump. You took them to some other dump. Well, here we are in this studio looking at photographs of paintings.

Close: But they jog my memory of having seen the paintings.

Celmins: The physical confrontation makes a different experience of it even though the paint isn't very manipulated. I wonder if I could ever pile up paint again?

Close: Are you talking about punching holes again?

Celmins: You seem to have more breadth in your work now, which I like. There's a more physical kind of presence. There's much more air in them. In my last things, there's no air in them at all. No air, just all material and image barely hanging on to each other.

Close: I love that.

Celmins: Ah, you see, because you didn't have to do them.

Close: You imply that there is something painful about having to deal with it.

Celmins: It's painful only because it's hard for me to do it. It means I have to consider everything a million times to try to get that little balance just right. My favorite thing would be to have a show, then take it down and paint it again. Then show it again, then take it down and paint it again just to readjust it a tiny bit. My wish would be to work on one painting the rest of my life. It's neurotic, no? I think part of it has to do with not wanting to reveal—I've been quite revealing with *you.*

Close: Earlier we were talking about the pauses and breaks in your work. We were talking about trying to sustain a certain level of involvement and what might happen when at a certain point you can no longer maintain that intensity, and then going into a period of not working.

Celmins: I usually pull back after I show work. Do you do that?

Close: I'm so worried that I will never be able to start working again that I usually have the next piece going before the show is over.

Celmins: In my mind, this is ideal.

Close: I think it's because I'm scared to death that if I ever stopped... There was a time after graduate school and after living in Europe that I stopped working, and it scared the hell out of me. I was drunk all the time, using a lot of drugs and stuff. I kept thinking that if I ever stopped, I would sink back into that. I don't think it's any accident that I've found work that requires that I go to work everyday. I think it's what I need to keep sane. Do you think there's an aspect of that in you?

Celmins: I'm not sure that it exactly keeps me sane. There is some way of living through the work, isn't there? You live in the work even though it's not the same thing as living in life. It's some way of keeping a certain kind of other life going, I don't know. I think my stopping often...I'll tell you, I'm not so happy with it. I think I often stop because I can't stand the trauma of having to look at my own work in a show. The worst part of it is that I think if I keep on working, I might break through to some other plane that's past the mind. Sometimes I think that I think too much about the work I've completed.

Close: You were talking about being engaged and then disengaged; I think I tend not to disengage and question what I've done. Recently I was telling my wife, Leslie, that I had a real crisis of conscience in that I was feeling very self-critical and beating myself up. And she said, "Did it ever occur to you that maybe there is a reason to criticize yourself?" It's as if it's wrong to criticize yourself. She said, "Maybe there's something wrong. Maybe that's why you're critical of yourself." And I realized that I keep working so that I never have to step back and take a break, look at the work, and be critical of it. I think I just keep chugging along in hopes that I will grind it out, that I will just keep moving.

Celmins: We should switch. You can beat yourself up, like I do, and I can just keep going in there, like you do, and maintaining. Look, I like that idea! Of course, it might not be so easy to do, but I like that. I admire you for being able to ask that of yourself.

Close: I think it's driven by my fear. That's not so positive.

Celmins: You think so? But then it doesn't matter what drives you.

Close: We're the flip side of the same issue, in a way.

Celmins: What does it matter what you're driven by? I remember reading this biography of Cézanne about what a terrible life he had. But then you look at the work—it's sublime.

Close: It doesn't guarantee anything.

Celmins: I'll show you some of the clippings that were the inspiration for my work.

Close: These photographs are just about the crummiest little—what do you call these? They're like little souvenirs.

Celmins: What I want to tell you is it wasn't a system. My working from photographs was really an affection for certain little areas in the photographs that I carried around with me and that I reexamined all the time.

Close: That's why I think they can be described as souvenirs. They're not working photographs in the normal sense of the word.

Celmins: Then it didn't occur to me that I could score them either, put them in a grid, which I did later on.

Close: How long did it take before you used a grid?

Celmins: It took me a long time. I think I didn't begin to grid them until I began the ocean drawings because I kept losing my place all the time. They were too complicated, so I thought I would try it. It was sort of an amateur operation.

Close: It is, but it's like going out into the landscape instead of looking out of the corner of your eye. Getting something that you could really see.

Celmins: But I had to really *look* at these "souvenirs."

Close: Of course, but it was a different kind of looking.

Celmins: I would scrutinize these little images in great detail. Their small size allowed for an intimacy with the subject. It allowed me to enter that gray world in a personal way, and I would draw my way out of it. I think of it as taking out the grays and rearranging them.

Close: It reminds me of diving: there's execution and then there's also degree of difficulty. In a way, it almost looks like you purposely increased the degree of difficulty, which is what I meant when I say that there's a rocks-in-your-shoes mentality, or hair-shirt mentality. It's something that you approach in a very different kind of way, with just the barest evidence.

Celmins: You see, I didn't realize that it was so difficult because I approached these in an emotional way. I approached these from a kind of intuitive sifting of my thoughts. I mean, sifting through images and then becoming attached to one. Later, I realized that you could use the opaque projector to draw some of that stuff.

Close: Did you ever do that?

Celmins: Yes. I also used the grid. But my subjects became more difficult to realize as my way of dealing with them became easier. Of course, I also did things from life, like the house and the gun.

Close: No kidding, the guns were done from life?

Celmins: Somebody gave me the gun, and I remember that I took a picture of it in Terry Conway's hand. I bet I have that photograph somewhere.

Close: But he didn't really shoot it, right? There wasn't any real smoke.

Celmins: No, it was imaginary, but he held the gun for me. I wonder what brought me to this point? The Vietnam War was going on, which I was totally crazed about, as many of us were—the world seemed so violent.

Close: I was thinking about that time in the sixties when we were doing this stuff. I think of what a year 1968 was. We were doing our most breakaway work. It happened to be a time when a lot of people emerged, and a lot of people found their mature voices.

Celmins: Yes, people our age.

Close: It was such an exciting and scary time. I remember walking down Greene Street to a friend's house the day that Martin Luther King was killed, and thinking about the meaninglessness of having spent the day making art when all this was going down. And yet, it was a very fertile time. The world was in absolute chaos; there was the need to make some kind of order. Since I've been sick, I think more about stuff like that, that things are more than just what I always thought they were. Certain activities are incredibly important, more important than making work, the way we like to talk about it. We like to talk about it as if we were laying bricks. And yet, I don't know.

Celmins: I get very defensive when you say something that's too close to home. I tend to deflect it, which is one of the things that I usually do.

Close: But I did to you what I hate people doing to me, which is to put some overlay on the work which wasn't the artist's intention. I find myself talking about things which are not the way that I experienced them. When I stand in front of your paintings, I just love them to death. I just love looking at the marks.

Celmins: But I don't know if I want them that accessible. In a certain way, I like them colder.

Close: You know, an artist looks at things because an artist has pushed the material around himself or herself. The viewer is going to look at what you did in a very different way.

Celmins: You look at it like another artist. But when I look at the work, it has a very somber and solitary feeling. I think you have tried to get me to admit that there are touches of melancholy in the work. I don't know whether I would think of my paintings as melancholy, but they do have a kind of solitary look.

Close: I said you *were melancholy, not the work.*

Celmins: Oh, I see. But I have another part of me that fights that. There's another part of me that's the opposite of those peasant qualities—very refined and exacting. I was telling you about the last two little ocean paintings that I had at David McKee; they were so refined that they seemed to be totally cerebral. Physically they were very pinned down, but they also seemed like ghosts. I was quite shocked that I had done that. I had been talking about opening up, showing more basic emotion, and instinctively I had done the opposite. I closed up the painting and kept it more distant.

Close: Let's talk about the difference between drawing with a pencil and painting. Even the smallest brush is a klutzier, clumsier tool; then you use this very sharp thing.

Celmins: You can pin the drawing to the paper on the point. Each point is like a point of consciousness. So it is like a record of having been there, which is probably what you like because we're both artists. You get to be very intimate with the process of putting down the point of the pencil. I like that at that moment. I like the fact that I didn't have to smudge or erase, or push and pull.

Close: So what happened when you came back to painting? I would like to continue talking about the difference between pencil and paint.

Celmins: When I started painting again in the mid-eighties, I couldn't finish anything. I painted on this one painting for about six months, scraping off the paint and putting it back on. The paint looked like an old rubber tire. I layered the paint on dozens of times, trying to reach some place in the painting that I could accept, one layer on top of the other. I feel that painting permits a more complicated spatial experience. I like that experience, but I felt like a baby crawling on my hands and knees. I should have called this first painting *Start Over*, but I called it *The Barrier* because it was an obstacle to overcome, and the overworked surface became a barrier to the image.

Close: Do you work all over?

Celmins: Yes, I work all over. But in layers, one on top of the other.

Close: Which is really the old, abstract expressionist way of working. Slowly bring the whole surface up at once.

Celmins: I went back to painting because I wanted the work to carry more weight. I have this feeling the work has more meaning when it is fuller and richer and has what I call more form. I think I'd taken that pencil lead as far as it could go. I think all the last drawings were really my wish to paint, and I just hadn't switched to the brush yet. They were as heavy as they could be with lead. They were really about mass and weight, but they couldn't carry any more form. I had a longing for more dimension.

Close: Another way that I think the painting is different is that every square inch of one of these paintings has paint on it. So white areas are painted as well as dark areas. White is reflecting off the outside skin no matter how much is underneath it.

Celmins: There are more possibilities with paint. I like to show the support, yet it is harder to do with paint. I've been leaving the canvas showing on the edges, but that's such a common solution.

Close: Somehow, the way the light bounces off the paintings is a lot different than the way the light bounces off the drawings.

Celmins: These paintings that I've just done are matte, so that they don't have light bouncing off them. In fact, the graphite has more light bouncing off it because it's shiny. The white is not painted on the black; both the white and the black develop together. I layer them until they become what I call "fat," so they're like marble. There are more possibilities with painting because I have a feeling that somehow the form is bigger just because there's more layering. There are more shifts in the work. It just is a more complicated spatial experience.

Close: A great deal of the difference between drawings and paintings is that when you're humped over a drawing board it's insular and personal. There's a rapport between you and the object, and you're very close to it, as if you're guarding it.

Celmins: For the most part, my drawings don't call upon the viewer to have those kinds of personal, intimate experiences, even though the process of putting them down on paper was like that.

Close: You don't use pencil like anybody else. You use pencil as a medium, not as a tool. In fact, I don't consider your work in pencil to be drawing.

Celmins: It's not *just* drawing.

Close: That's what I mean by saying that it is a medium, not a tool. They're paintings in which the medium is pencil lead.

Celmins: Museums sometimes give drawings second- or third-rate status; they are put in dark little rooms. Often, in houses, people arrange drawings in little groups—it's just totally inappropriate. I like to have my drawings out in the open because they need space and careful looking.

Close: I just recently came to the conclusion—and I think it's something that I wrote about for the Modern catalogue—I began to think about the activity in the studio as a kind of ritualized dance. I go through these motions. I do these things. These are my habits. These are the things that I do. And then I do them in front of a rectangle. In a sense, I'm sort of a performing artist, but there's no audience. The canvas, however, ends up being a kind of record of that ritualized dance. Then it goes out in the world and stands for that as evidence so that the viewer can become reengaged in…

Celmins: That ritual dance. Especially in your work, because I have found myself running around your work, seeing where it jells in a certain way and where it doesn't in another way.

Close: But that's the pleasure that I'm talking about—which I think you'd like to deny—the pleasure that someone can have in front of your work. You seem to think if you have pleasure making it, it's not rigorous enough.

Celmins: No, no, no. But I evidently like the pleasure.

Close: But that's where I am engaged with and dancing along with you, enjoying the quality of the decisions you have made and the notation system which you have found to record these decisions. There's something very engaging and something very connecting in your work. Let me just say one thing—often my questions are longer than your answers.

Celmins: But I like that.

Close: I'm interested in questions that push you to a place other than where you wanted to go.

Celmins: Your questions managed to get me to talk about a lot more things than I wanted to.

✶

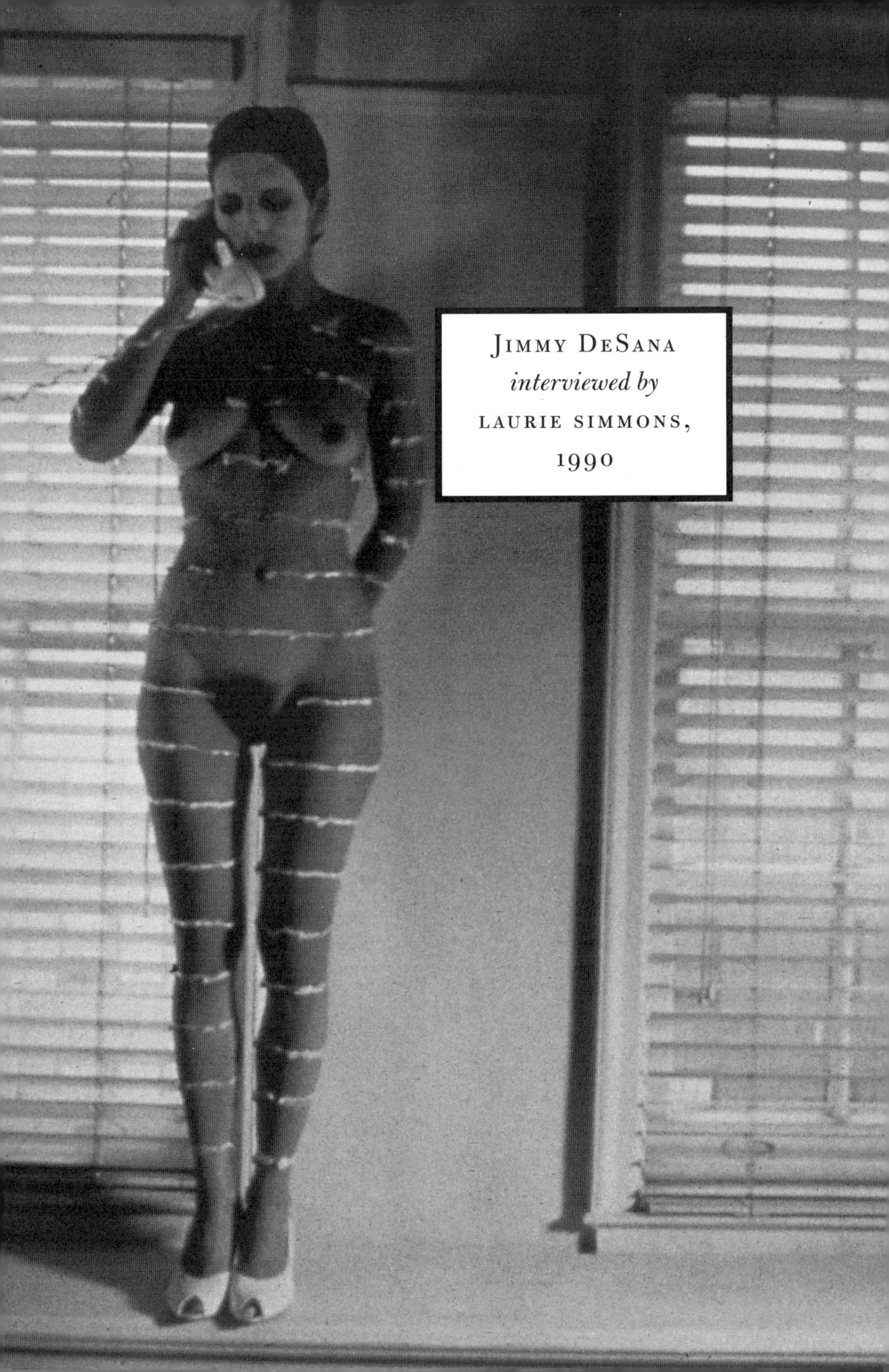

Jimmy DeSana *interviewed by* Laurie Simmons, 1990

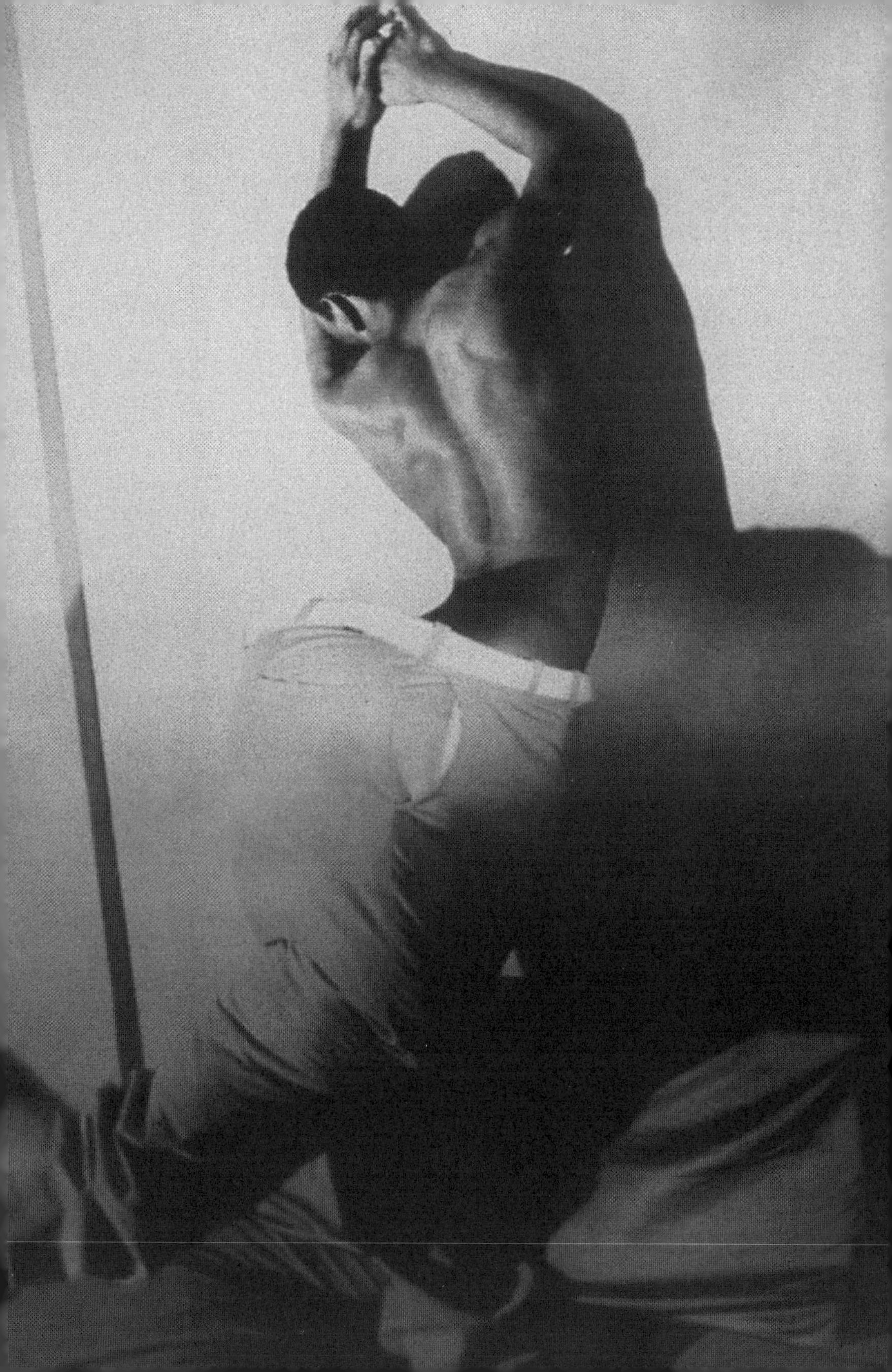

mons: But it does have a relationship to the abstract work that you're g now. How do you account for the fact that your vision has remained -course, so directed towards one kind of thing?

I think of my work as very eclectic, but I guess in a sense it does all e of lighting, technique. A lot of things have happened because I prints myself. The *101 Nudes* was very grainy, but it was grainy of the printing process. It was done on a little printing press. There her way to do it, so the technique was something that I didn't have rol over. It became part of something that I really liked. I'm still using iness.

ons: Certainly there's a real visual thread through everything you've but more interesting to me is the fact that pornography became your t when you were in your late teens, and still is.

Well, I read a lot of William Burroughs in the late sixties, and it was lly oriented. I realized that this stimulated me so much more than lse. I had to explore it to see what I could do with it, make a state- it, and those feelings stayed with me for over a decade.

ons: Do you feel that you grew up in an environment of real sexual sion?

wouldn't say real sexual repression. I did feel it in the South, but not y particularly. I don't remember a lot of sexual experiences when I as some people do. I can remember false starts and that sort of thing.

ns: The basic suburban sexual starts and stops.

didn't ever quite click, and I know that it did with others in their ys.

ns: That's interesting, because sex/suburbs becomes a theme in your the late seventies and early eighties. I'm referring to the kind of where you combine artifacts from the five-and-dime with people in postures. You seem to have an interest in a sort of banal suburban ment with people doing clumsy yet erotic things to each other.

on't really think of that work as erotic. I think of the body almost , which is what I am doing now in photographing objects. I use the body but without the eroticism that some photographers y. I think I de-eroticized a lot of it, particularly in that period, but y the suburbs are, in a sense. They're not about sexuality, to me city is much more about sexuality. The suburbs are people in cars tely to their houses. There's not a lot of contact between people s.

: You're talking about isolation.

hat period, for that work particularly. I think of it as not very ted even though they were nudes. The body was treated almost used with objects, then set in a suburban situation.

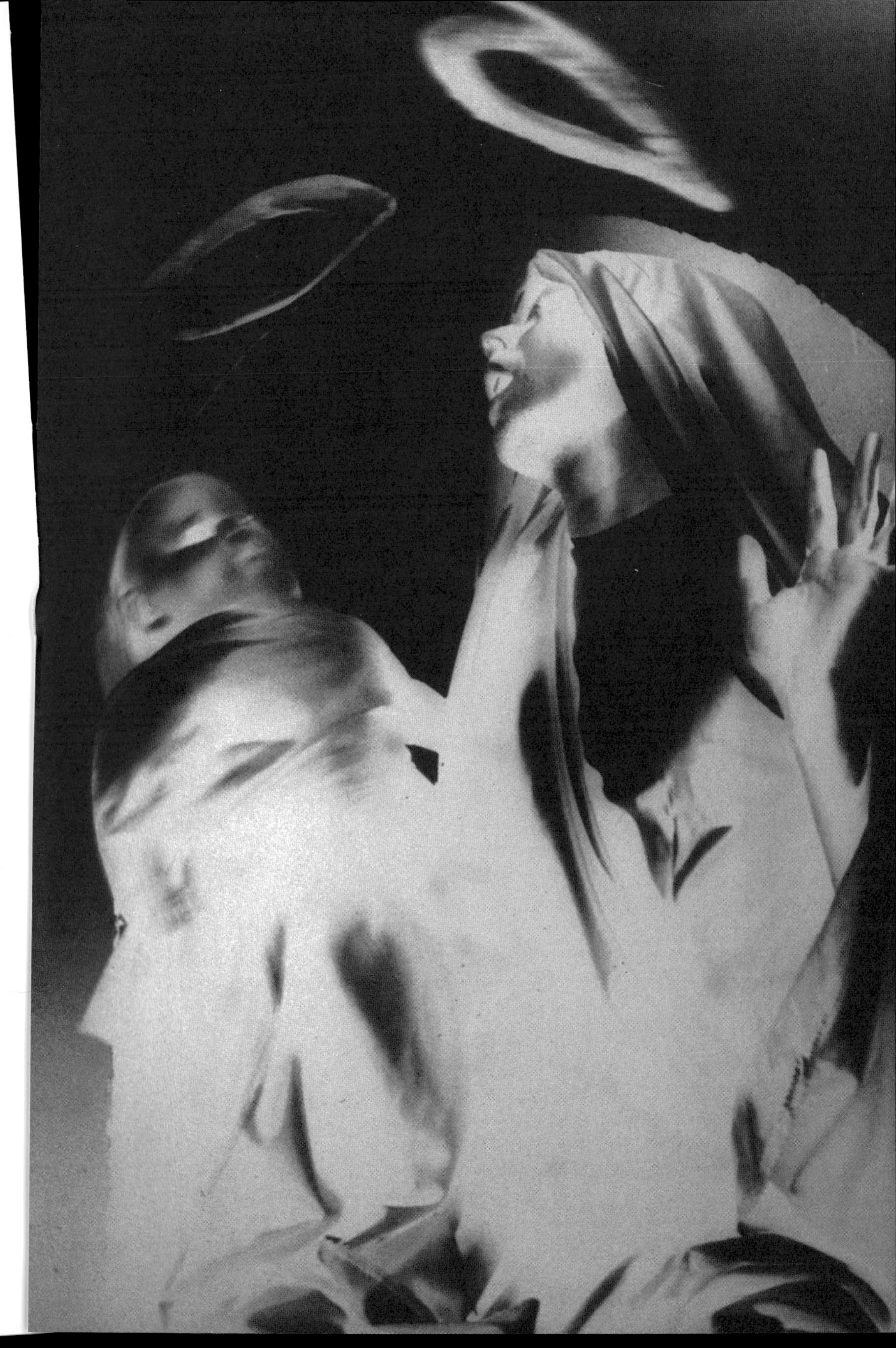

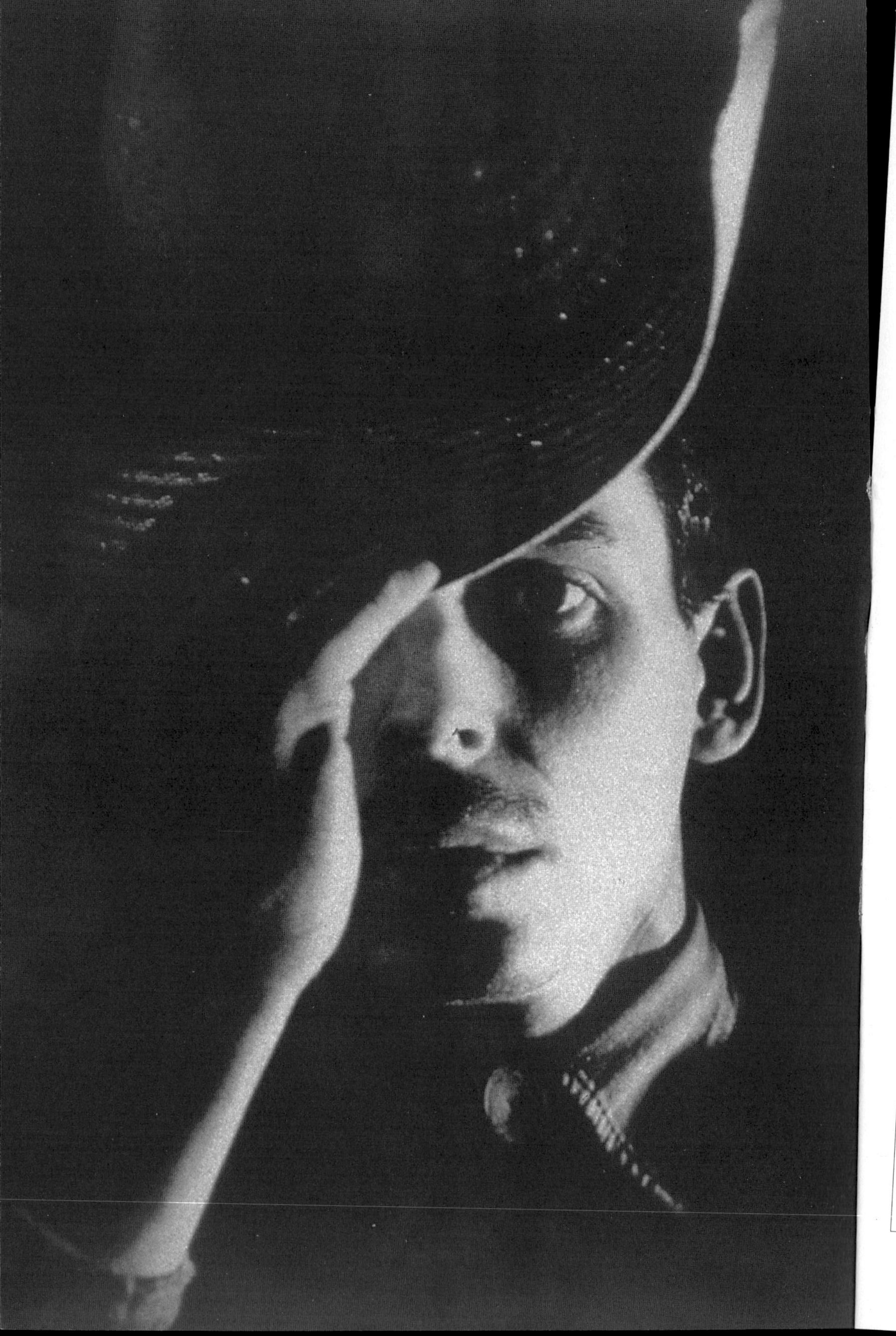

J I M M Y D E S A N A

interviewed by

L A U R I E S I M M O N S

Laurie Simmons: I remember the first tim
the fall of 1973. A group of us were takin
can't remember why. A mutual friend w
studios in Manhattan introduced us. (T
thousand-square-foot loft in Soho toge
Panama hat and a Yashica around you
white. I'd heard you were Southern and
101 Nudes. *Can you talk a little bit abo*

Jimmy DeSana: It was really a portfolio. It
and basically the imagery was very porno
from traditional pornography—photogra
rake-off on them. I used a lot of friends as
up, I saw little bits and pieces of pornog
were often shot with a flash camera and g
my *101 Nudes* and went beyond pornogr
that I was going for. We had people stan

Simmons: You refer to pornography
found secretly in your parents' hous
growing up in the South—how did y

DeSana: My friends had it. I don't kno
had it under their mattresses.

Simmons: Kind of contraband mat

page 45:
Toothpaste *(detail), 1980, photograph*
page 46:
Pants *(detail), 1983, photograph*
page 47:
Pizza Crusts *(detail), 1985, photograph*
page 48:
Smoke Cowboy *(detail), 1985, photograph*

DeSana: Yes, yo
look at pornogr
rabbit tobacco.
which we used
at all.

Simmons: 101
did it when yo

DeSana: I did

Sim
doi
so o
DeSana:
relate: u
made th
because
was no o
total con
that grai
Simr
done,
subje
DeSana: V
very sexu
anything e
ment with
Simm
repres
DeSana: I
in my fami
was young,
Simm
DeSana: It
younger da
Simmo
work i
imager
strange
environ
DeSana: I d
as an objec
attempted t
use frequent
that is the w
at least. The
driving priva
in the suburb
Simmons
DeSana: In t
sexually orien
as a prop and

Simmons: Would you say that those pictures were antisex?

DeSana: For me, in a sense, they were. I didn't even use models that were sexually interesting to me. Well, I used myself.

Simmons: You mentioned William Burroughs and that he was an influence on you. Didn't you actually meet him?

DeSana: I had a suicide self-portrait that got published, *Rope.* It was a nude with an erection. William Burroughs's associate tracked me down and said that Burroughs would like to meet me. He was curious to know if I was actually sexually interested in hanging myself and getting an orgasm from it. He had a lot of case histories on file which he pulled out and talked about. So that's how I got to know him. I'm not into that sexual kind of thing, but I did it for a photograph. That's how I met him. Later he wrote the introduction for my book *Submission.* We've been in and out of touch over the years, and I've done his portrait many times. In 1981 I did a portrait for a record cover with him and John Giorno and Laurie Anderson.

Simmons: Was that the image where the three of them were holding canes, kind of like vaudeville actors?

DeSana: Yes, that's the one. The title was this long thing that was something about money.

Simmons: In the early seventies you shot some photographs that set the tone visually for the punk era. I'm thinking particularly of pictures of the Talking Heads you did for their album.

DeSana: I did the photo for their first single, when there were only three members of the band. Then I helped them with the Polaroid cover for their second album. Then I photographed them for *The New York Rocker* newspaper, the cover with Brian Eno, and some other magazines, too.

Simmons: And wasn't there a Debbie Harry photo, a cover shot for File?

DeSana: For *File,* yes.

Simmons: And various others?

DeSana: Patti Astor for *Artforum,* that's all part of that same period.

Simmons: You used a very particular kind of lighting and a particular kind of style. I think your work may have influenced a lot of the photography done at the time, portrait photography, album covers, etc., for the punk period. Where does that fit into your own idea of your work? Do you see it as something separate and commercial, or do you see it as some integral part of your own development?

DeSana: I see it as part of my life, really, because these people were my friends. I didn't pursue them on a truly commercial basis, and I usually didn't make much money from it. It felt very natural to shoot them. It seemed like an extension of my own personal work. In fact, I used some of these portraits in a show in 1980 on 57th Street. So the portraits became part of my art.

Simmons: It seemed at that time there was a real crossover, that your own work and that kind of portrait work were really compatible. It was also the way that you made your living. One week you might sell an art photo and the next week you might have a commission to do some portraits, and they sort of blended together.

DeSana: Right.

Simmons: You made your work your life and the way you made your living.

DeSana: It was like a lifestyle.

Simmons: Let's talk about the book Submission *(1980). It seems like your dark side.* Submission *seems like your secret work, while the work you were exhibiting at the time was your public work. Perhaps you could explain how two such disparate bodies of work could be in progress at the same time.*

DeSana: *Submission* was a special project. It was almost a black-and-white documentary of a certain aspect of my life. A friend of mine gave me a leather mask and it fascinated me. I realized that I wanted to do a photo series that involved S & M. The activities were always staged for the photographs. Since I and my close friends were the models for the photos, it became very close to me in a way. From looking at the first photos, I realized that I wanted to make a book. Then, a year later, I started shooting more open, suburban things. It took over a year for *Submission* to be published, so by the time the book was released, I had already completed a large body of color work that was completely different. Its subject matter was more suburban in nature, without the heavy S & M look. I wanted to be more humorous and lyrical, and *Submission* didn't really feel that suburban or humorous or lyrical. This play on suburban life was shot in color with a kind of brilliant color saturation.

Simmons: Why the combinations of strange sex and objects?

DeSana: I think that in *Submission* I was trying to push sexuality to the limit. As long as I could come up with an idea that related to bizarre sexuality and still make an interesting statement about a product, the photo was successful for me. There was always a product involved in those photos. In fact, straight through my career there has always been some sort of object.

Simmons: I thought the suburban works were shot simultaneously with Submission.

DeSana: No, *Submission* was really shot in 1977–78 and came out as a book in 1980, but by 1979 I had started shooting in color and had dropped all the leather and sexual gadgets totally. I was looking more in terms of treating everyday products the same way, but with a different look.

Simmons: The explicit depiction of sexual acts in Submission *made a lot of people very uncomfortable, which leads me to my next question. I always felt the subject matter in* Submission *was very, very risky to be dealing with. It involved danger, pain, and death. I had a sense that you were acting as voyeur, not a participant. Maybe that was something that I needed to believe as a friend, but I never sensed a direct involvement. I felt that you were approaching the information as an intermediary, a liaison between that world and the straight world. That was a subterranean world, and you were saying, "I have access to this. I can show it to you. I can bring it to you."*

DeSana: I have to say that there was some participation. I would set up the whole thing. I was even a model in some of the photos; my penis is in that book pissing on someone. The ideas were really mine, or maybe a friend might suggest something that I might want to work with. So it's not that I documented real sex acts in progress, even though in the introduction to the book Burroughs made it sound like that's what I had done.

Simmons: Well, if it's set up and documented, and you're the photographer, again, there's the sense of voyeurism and of you being somewhat distant and removed.

DeSana: But there's also the fact of being the actor in it. In certain images, I was so intimate with the other person that we were actually responding to each other. The purpose of all of this, however, was the photograph, not the sexual relationship of the actors.

Simmons: Do you think that the color photographs of the late seventies were some sort of announcement to yourself that you were moving away from all that? Or just "Okay, on to the next project"?

DeSana: I think I just wanted a change. I think it is very important for an artist to change. I wanted a new look. I never felt like putting the *Submission* photos in frames and exhibiting them. They've never actually been exhibited. It was a project and a package for a book, whereas the color work was intended to be presented on the wall. I think that there is a lot of humor in *Submission,* but there's a lot more humor in the color work that followed. I mean, I found *Submission* to be humorous, but a lot of people did not. They couldn't see the humor at all. There are certain images that I still find very funny.

Simmons: Can you describe one?

DeSana: The egg coming out of the ass. To me, it's just funny. There's nothing heavy about that at all.

Simmons: It's a very particular kind of humor.

DeSana: Yes, if you're into eggs in asses. There are also definitely some heavy images there.

Simmons: We've been talking about the move to color in the late seventies and the decision to move on. It was at a time when photography was really coming into its own, photography that didn't come out of a photographic tradition. Photography was coming from the art world, and it was starting to shake things up, starting to be regarded in a completely different way, particularly color work.

DeSana: There was a small group of art photographers at that time, including you. There are many more now, and I think that people forget how few of us there were in the beginning.

Simmons: Now a large-scale color photograph doesn't have the shock value it had in 1979. Your color prints were not exactly vibrant and happy. They weren't like Dorothy arriving in Munchkin land.

DeSana: I used an exaggerated kind of color for the portraiture as well as the sexual images. For a while it seemed like my style. It came from trying to produce a new look. It was different from *Submission,* which had a gloomy black-and-white feeling to it. It made things just a little bit more upbeat. Also, it was a way of making a color print that looked different from anything that I had seen. Maybe that's what I was aiming at. So that anyone who saw one of my photos would know that it was mine. It had this signature colorization. And I think it worked fairly well.

Simmons: It is very interesting that you use the word colorization, *because it looks a lot like what is being done to old black-and-white movies. The photos do have this feeling that you went back in and worked on them and decided that red would be here, blue would be here, and yellow would be here. And oftentimes it was a dissociative kind of color. It didn't work where it was meant to work, but in the end the whole thing looked right.*

DeSana: I've had bad reception on my TV since I've lived in midtown (ten years). It would turn a face green. I think that was partly an influence.

Simmons: You'd think from your photos that you were a nocturnal being, but knowing you, I have to say that isn't true. You're up at the crack of dawn, out for your walk. Breakfast at seven. Lunch at noon. Why this attraction to nocturnal feelings and emotions when you don't really participate? You're a day person.

DeSana: I think a lot of friends sort of pulled me out, and I actually became a night person. Particularly that period in the late seventies—it was an exciting moment with the club scene. I realized that I really could get to know a lot of people. It was like going to a party every night. But it's true that I would sleep very little and be up the next day trying to lead a normal life. It didn't really work for very long, but it was a great period.

Simmons: You must have seen things then that really affected you.

DeSana: It was just a way to see people. It would basically be the same people every night or every couple of nights you'd go out. But maybe I felt there was something lacking in that night life. Those photos were sort of wishing that there was more sexuality in it. Because there really wasn't that much sexuality in it at that time. The use of the sexuality in photography was a little more shocking then. Even with my very weird friends and the punk scene. It felt very desexualized. And maybe, actually thinking back on it, my upbringing really did feel very desexualized also.

Simmons: And where does religion fit into this? You're Southern Baptist?

DeSana: Methodist with a little bit of Catholic in the family.

Simmons: Do you feel like there are any religious influences in your photographs?

DeSana: Only recently. The very newest work has a little bit. In the old work I think it just wasn't much of an issue.

Simmons: What about the South itself or growing up there? That's pretty powerful.

DeSana: I lived in the Bible Belt. I always tried to ignore it, thinking that I would move away, which I did. But I'm sure it had quite an effect on me. I used to get headaches regularly on Sundays.

Simmons: In New York?

DeSana: No, in Atlanta. The big change in my life in terms of religion came with an operation. That was in 1984. I had my spleen removed. To some extent it may have brought on a questioning of religion and how to really look at life in a different way. Before that, I looked at life as a big party, a big joke. I still look at it as a big joke, but in a different way. It's a big bad joke. I think that I attempted to bring religion into my life after that operation and basically failed. I found very little there that I could relate to. But I think I brought in some bit of religion to my work. There was the use of African death figures and a kind of Zen aspect with the language. Little bits of references to religion, maybe making a little fun of religion in the way that I made fun of the suburbs in the earlier work.

Simmons: It sounds as if you're talking about an attraction to religion, but as you moved closer…

DeSana: A disappointment with it. It didn't offer me what I wanted. So I turned that into art. And I think the artworks were what I wanted out of it. So in a sense I did get something from it, but I didn't get a feeling of satisfaction.

Simmons: More than any other artist I know, you have a desire to turn every experience in your daily life into art. There's very little separation, and you want to use everything as material.

DeSana: My house is jammed with objects. At this point it's totally out of hand because I can't part with things. I'm always thinking I might use them. Or even if I've already used an object, that I might use it again. I still have the leather mask from *Submission.* I still have a lot of the props I used in the early color sexual work. Now I go to flea markets and look for odd kinds of objects to photograph. I used to go to Woolworth's and places like that to shop for products, which I really don't do much anymore.

Simmons: You're talking about props, but wouldn't you say it's really true of emotions, too?

DeSana: That I get attached?

Simmons: Not only attachment, but that you use everything you find. You see everything in your life as a potential prop, even your emotions: days when you don't feel well, days when you feel great. You don't let yourself take any vacations or have any distance. Your emotional and physical selves become material for your work. What's it like to translate all of that stuff?

DeSana: I guess it's that art is habit forming, and I've arrived at this obsession with art, and it's very hard to pull away from it. I think that's the way it's always been for me, even going back to *101 Nudes.* I used friends and I used houses that I was living in.

I would like to say something about anger. There are issues in life that I have been unable to satisfy through my art, and I find that really disappointing, but I'm still trying. A book like *Submission* was seen as shocking by a lot of people, and I liked that aspect of it. I also like that it was what I considered quality photography and a new sort of statement that people were not seeing. And it was dealing with a lot of anger, but on a different level. There are issues that I don't seem to be able to photograph or that I'm not satisfied with my attempts at, so I may discard them.

Simmons: I think you're beginning to talk about the thing that I'm trying to get you to talk about, which is the, for lack of a better word, feverish quality with which you approach your work—this almost, well, "hysterical" is a little strong, but this urgent way you've always worked, as though you'll run out of steam or can't keep up with your own ideas.

DeSana: Some days it's not that way. I'm trying to incorporate my art and my life and make a statement that I'm happy with, and that I feel is worthwhile for other people to see and think about. Along the way I've done self-portraits. I often don't call them self-portraits. It's all part of my life.

Simmons: I get the sense that you used yourself for lack of a model who could do exactly what you wanted him to do.

DeSana: It's me looking at myself as a prop, as an object, but it is me.

Simmons: Then it's not about self-transformation as much as it is about you turning yourself into that thing which you want to photograph?

DeSana: Exactly.

Simmons: In 1983 you started making yourself fat in photographs. Why?

DeSana: I was making fun of myself at the time. That's what I wanted to do. Also, so many friends were dieting, particularly lady friends. I realized that America had this obsession with food and dieting, and I just wanted to make some sort of crazy statement about that aspect of American life. So that was my statement.

Simmons: How many of them did you do?

DeSana: Successfully, about three or four images. I had an idea of becoming a fat woman. I started to have a suit made that would actually look like flesh, that I could actually be zipped into, but I never followed through. I just went on to another project.

Simmons: Did you become a woman in any of your photos?

DeSana: Yes, I did actually. I used the Andy Warhol Marilyn Monroe painting as a reference and used myself with an aluminum-foil hairdo.

Simmons: Looking back over your work, the move to abstraction seems like a pretty big jump. What did the change feel like to you?

DeSana: I actually did do abstract work much earlier. I touched on that thing way back in school. Then I dropped it. The period when my spleen was removed changed my life and my way of looking at things. I wanted to deal with nonsexual imagery. So I started looking at objects and pulling them apart, collaging. The abstract photos are always real objects, even though they're called abstract.

Simmons: There's always something that you can find in them, a pair of legs or a piece of fruit. Some of them look like Tantric art and some of them look like the June Taylor dancers on the Jackie Gleason show. Is the idea of repetition and lack of resolution in them hard to talk about?

DeSana: I do want to say something about that. I was thinking about the kind of nothingness of life and how to make a photograph of nothing. That's sort of what I was looking for. But you can't really make a photo of nothing. That ambiguity interested me—that there was that ambiguity, and how far could I go. Could people actually figure out what it was? How far could I take the object, collage it, destroy it, and rephotograph it? I think my life changed a lot, and that changed my way of looking at things. I didn't want to joke about sexuality. I wanted to talk about death and nothingness, the way that I perceived death.

Simmons: Are you talking about a process of emptying your photographs of the kind of content that they had before, of removing possibilities for a meaning, for an interpretation?

DeSana: I think it's like jumping from hot to cold, in a sense. It's going from one extreme to another. From extremely hot, sexually charged images to extremely vague, ambiguous images.

Simmons: You bring up death now. Death always has been a subject of yours, going back to the suicide photo in 1973. But do you think there is a point where the subject of death really gripped your work in a stronger way, or do you think it's been pervasive throughout?

DeSana: I think it has been pervasive throughout, but I started looking at life and death in a new way after the operation. It was a very major change for me. I think that prior to that I was looking at death as a joke. After the operation I think it became more real. I had always fantasized about it. I had committed suicide repeatedly in photographs. After that operation it took on a more serious tone. I was trying to look through Zen and refer back to my past love of dada, and trying to figure out how death and dada worked together—still trying to bring humor into death, however. I have some new pieces that are dealing with suicide that are quite different.

Simmons: What are they like?

DeSana: There's going to be a list of artists who committed suicide. It's going to be kind of a name game called Connect the Artists. It will be a list of first and last names. The idea is that you connect the first name to the last name and get a list of artists who committed suicide. So I'm still dealing with death but in a different way. It's hard for me to talk about the new work because it's new and it's coming out of my life again.

Simmons: By the mid-eighties you had deemphasized portraiture.

DeSana: I had been photographing friends, and I started to realize that it was becoming an obsession to photograph famous people. Why did I feel that I must photograph Debbie Harry again? So I began to think, "Well, I just won't do any more portraits." Because it's all part of the celebrity thing. It's become the same way in the art world over the last decade. It's turned into a real celebrity kind of scene. It's about money and celebrity.

Simmons: Did you feel that by photographing somebody you were bestowing a kind of celebrity on them?

DeSana: In a sense.

Simmons: And you just didn't want to do that anymore.

DeSana: It would make me sick. It became like a kind of sickness. It was obviously something that I did very well with.

Simmons: You'd built part of your career around it.

DeSana: But it turned very sour in the eighties, and I realized that I wanted to focus on being an artist.

Simmons: You were good at it. You had a style, a way with people. It's something you could have done a lot if you had chosen to.

DeSana: Definitely, and I may turn back to it. I don't know. I often think that I would like to do it again. It would be a way of meeting new people, a sort of opening up. I think I really closed down over the last half of the decade. I started working on a very, very personal level with collage, not even dealing with models. Maybe I'm heading into another change. I hope so.

Simmons: Do you think of yourself as any kind of technician, or do you think that you just have the basic rudimentary skills to do your work?

DeSana: No, I think that I've actually done some things in the darkroom that as far as I know were not done before, pretty minor things, little tricks that I've figured out in the darkroom, but they've given my photos the look that they have.

Simmons: A lot of art photographers today tend to emphasize their lack of technical skills. That's clearly not the case with you. I know from my own experience. I've learned a great deal from you technically.

DeSana: It's been an asset for me. It hasn't bogged me down. Some photographers are obsessed with equipment, but I'm not at all. There are just quirky little things that led me into creating certain photographs that might not have been made if I hadn't been in the darkroom.

Simmons: I also think of you as a creature of habit. You seem to derive a lot of comfort from repetition, from having your life be very orderly. Do you think that comes out in your work?

DeSana: I wouldn't say it has to do with repetition. I don't use repetition the way I see it in Warhol's work, for instance. My work is very eclectic. It pulls together whatever comes my way, even though my lifestyle is pretty organized. If I had printing to do, I'd get up and do it in the morning. I just generally could not do it in the afternoon because it was not the way I wanted to live my life. I wanted the afternoons free.

Simmons: What's your relationship to gay politics?

DeSana: More and more I am involved with the politics of living in a heterosexual world. There is a realization as a gay person in the art world that there is a little distancing from the mainstream. This is something that I never even considered ten years ago. I never even thought about it until the AIDS epidemic appeared. It has pulled the art world together, but in a way it's separated gays from the regular heterosexual crowd, which I think is pretty dominant in the art world now. I don't think of the art world as very gay particularly.

Simmons: Did you used to?

DeSana: I used to think about it that way. People have died or disappeared. The power structure is primarily heterosexual. That's made me pull away from the art world a little bit socially because I just don't feel a part of it. It's like living on an island. Actually, I don't even need to be in New York. I feel that I could be living anywhere and still be a New York artist. It's kind of scary. The emphasis is so much on celebrity and money. Art as money, fame as art. It's hard to watch people dying at the same time that the art market is booming. This has been a decade of death glossed over with media hype.

Simmons: Do you think the turn to abstraction in your recent work is directly related to the climate of New York, the AIDS climate?

DeSana: For me, it's an escape. AIDS is such a sexually oriented disease, for my group at least. I think I had to get away from sexuality for a while. I was running in fear of AIDS and sex, and so naturally that affected my art. The abstract work is a statement about attempting to deal with nothing, a nothingness that is the way I see death, and I see all art through the eyes of death. If the photo looks like nothingness, then it's a good statement for the moment. Because that's the way I'm feeling. I almost want to do nothing. I want to make art about nothing.

Simmons: Do you feel you've turned away from political activism and support systems in favor of a more solitary existence?

DeSana: I took part in a little activism, but it made me too angry. I thought, "No, this is not going to be productive for my own way of life." I support the politics of AIDS and will do what I can. I feel I'm better at making statements about the times, but hopefully my own statements, through exhibitions.

Simmons: So in order to understand that your current work has to do with AIDS, one would have to know your previous work and that, in fact, you have turned away from sexual imagery. Is that what you're saying, or is that a misrepresentation?

DeSana: I don't think that it's necessarily important to know the earlier work in viewing the new work. I actually hope it isn't.

Simmons: You speak about the recent abstract work as though it's obviously about AIDS. People have responded very positively to this work but don't immediately see the connection with AIDS.

DeSana: It's not my style to inform people. I like the idea of putting a work of art on the wall and waiting for a response. The voyeur comes out again. I want to watch and see how people relate to it.

Simmons: So you're counting on the melancholia and moodiness of these pictures to suggest these feelings?

DeSana: I'm already moving into an angrier period, and I don't know if that melancholia is going to continue. That was a moment; that was a statement. The show of large-scale abstract work at Pat Hearn Gallery in 1987 was basically a statement of my own death, in a sense. So I've died now, and the next step is to be angry or in heaven and to produce imagery that will relate to that. I'm really glad that I made that sort of quiet statement about death and what's happening now in terms of AIDS. For myself, I feel really good about it. But I'm on to other things now. I really would like to be able to upset people now that that's the feeling I have—I'm so upset. Life is a mistake. Life is a bad joke and everything is upside down. So that's the way I'm thinking, and I'm working on various things.

Simmons: What do you think about when you think about death? What sort of image do you have in mind?

DeSana: A nothingness, an emptiness, but maybe a very warm emptiness. Just a security, nothing—no product. No time. No art.

Simmons: No afterlife, no...

DeSana: Yes, but very simple: like you're stuck with one kind of very simple feeling that has some emotion, but it's not an emotion that we ever have when we're alive. It's something different.

Simmons: Do you think it's better?

DeSana: Oh yes, I think so. We all die, so there must be something to it. It must be good in some way that we can't imagine. You couldn't really make art about it, but I'm trying.

Simmons: It's odd, but somehow to me, to someone who doesn't really know, your description feels very right.

DeSana: Does it?

Simmons: You've talked about being a voyeur and wanting to watch people's reactions to your work. Have there been any extreme responses that you can recall?

DeSana: There have been letters written to magazines in which portfolios have been published suggesting that I should be sent back to the other side of the moon. The story was about photos from the dark side of the moon. It really outraged middle Americans.

Simmons: This was before the recent Jesse Helms extravaganza.

DeSana: I was delighted when it became part of my press book. I can't imagine anyone responding quite like that to the work I'm doing now. The work is really going in a different direction, but I would love to make a statement that would get that kind of response. That's what I'm really working on, desperately working on.

Simmons: To try to outrage again.

DeSana: Yes, in a totally different way. Obviously, sexuality just wouldn't do it. Use of language with images might work.

Simmons: Use of cold hard facts. This is who I am, this is the way I feel, this is what's going on in my body.

DeSana: In terms of a lot of the politics of AIDS, the cold hard facts have been presented through the press and through art already. If I could do a show that people would walk into and at one moment be laughing and at the next moment they would be nauseous and have to run out of the gallery, that would satisfy me because that is the way my life feels now. There are moments of happiness, but there is nausea behind it. If I could do a show that confused people so much, that was so ambiguous that they didn't know what to think, but they felt sort of sickened by it and also entertained, then for me that would capture the moment that we're going through right now.

Simmons: It sounds as if you want the viewer to feel your feelings along with you.

DeSana: Exactly.

Simmons: As if to exorcise your own feelings. If they could experience your feelings through your pictures, you would be neutralized, or at least purged.

DeSana: Left to the challenge of just getting through the day.

Simmons: Do you have a strong relationship to magic and fate: "If I do this ,then that will happen"?

DeSana: For me, money falls out of the sky. I never know why. It just comes or doesn't come, but I know it will come again. Yes, I think about superstition and all. It doesn't control my life, but I think about it.

Simmons: You feel that in some way you can control everything.

DeSana: Yes, control is a big thing. I think the older I get, the more I want to control and the more I realize I can't control a lot.

Simmons: That seems to be your greatest frustration—feeling that things are out of your control.

DeSana: Exactly, which would be medical things. They're totally out of my hands. But they're not really, because I can always say no. And I do like to say no.

Simmons: The greatest power that a person has is the power to say no.

DeSana: And I've applied that now to every aspect of my life.

✦

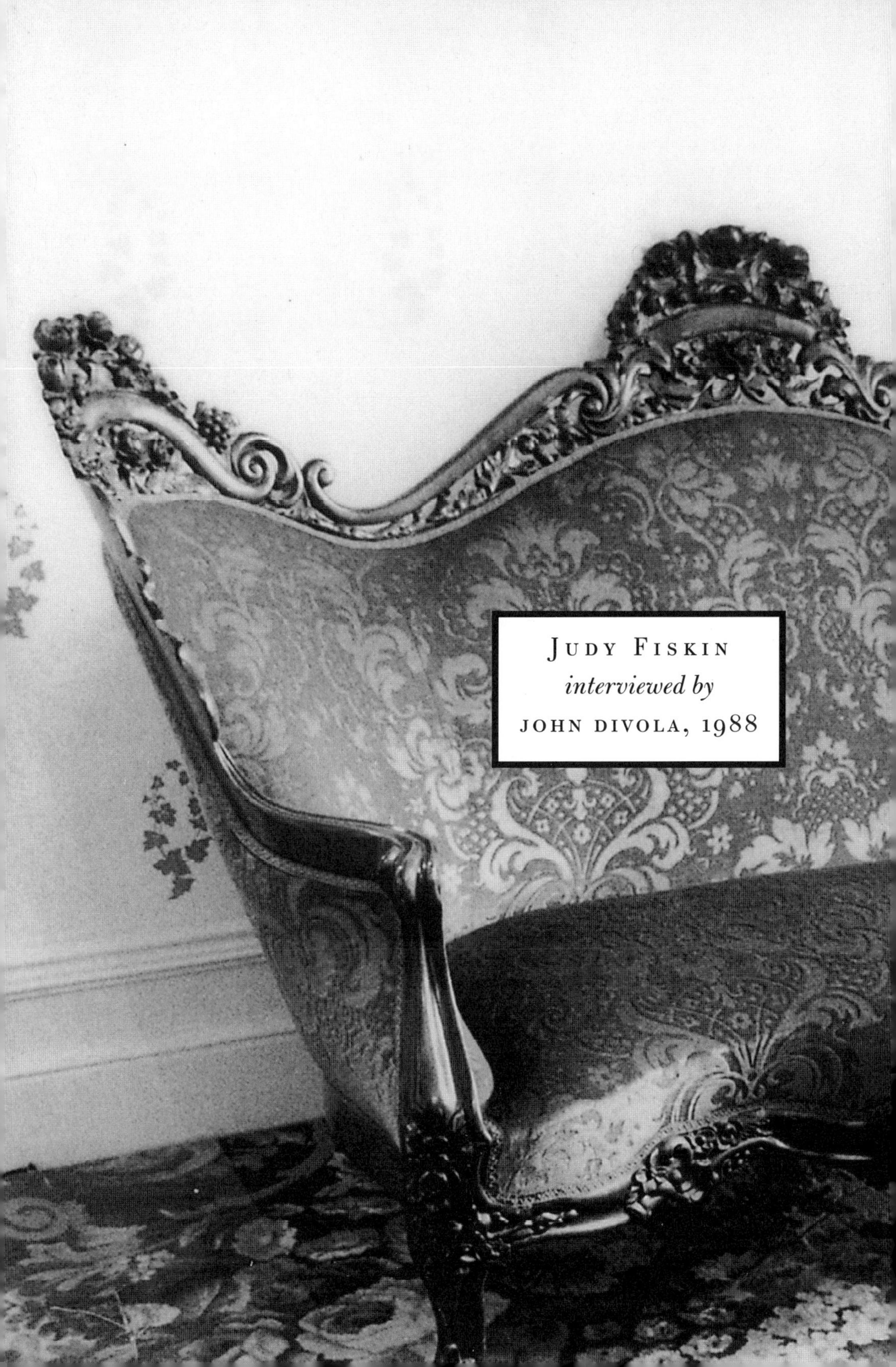
JUDY FISKIN
interviewed by
JOHN DIVOLA, 1988

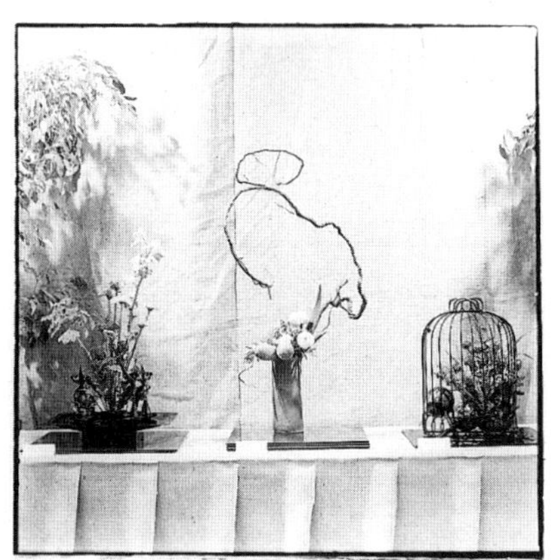

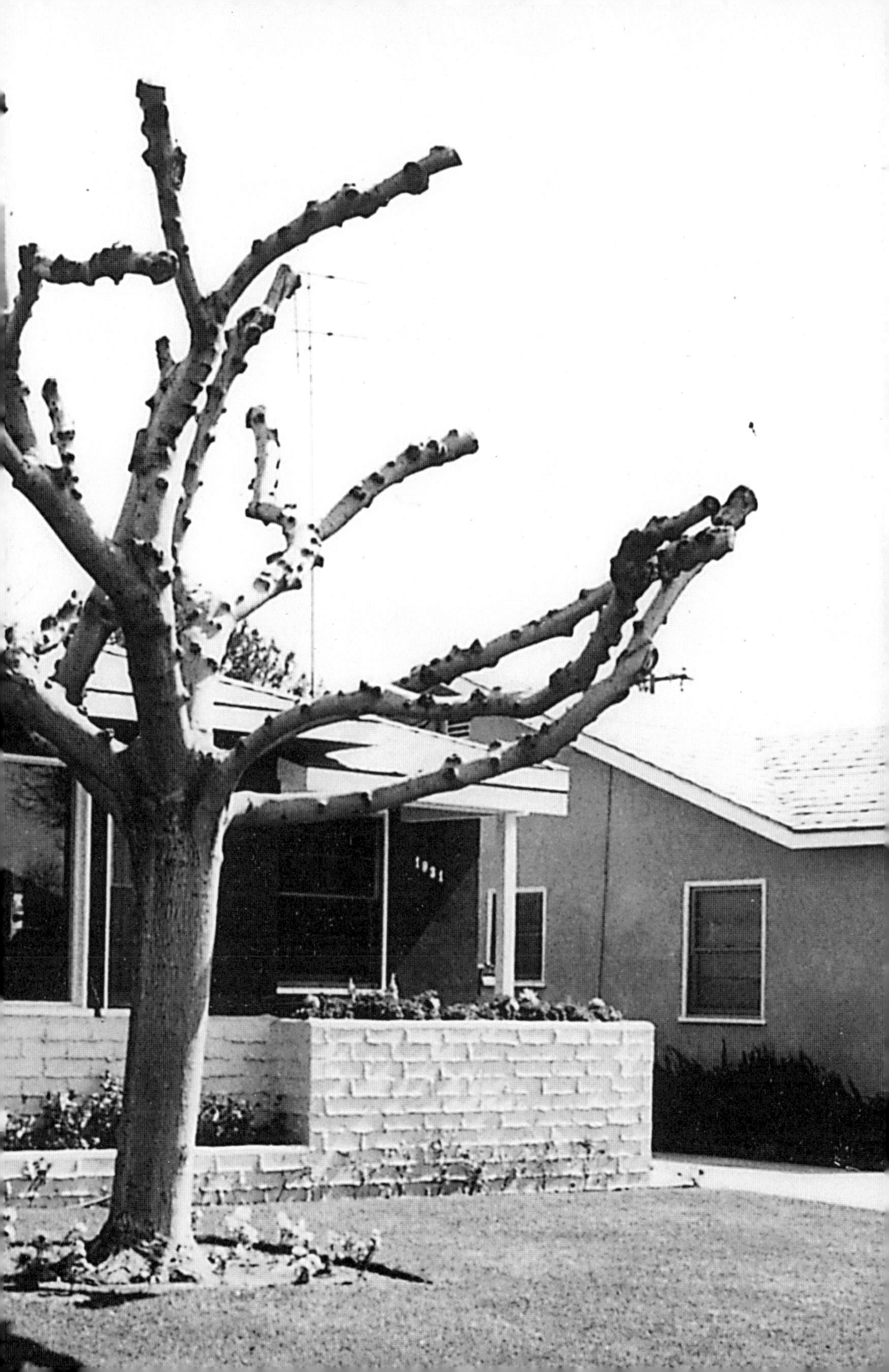

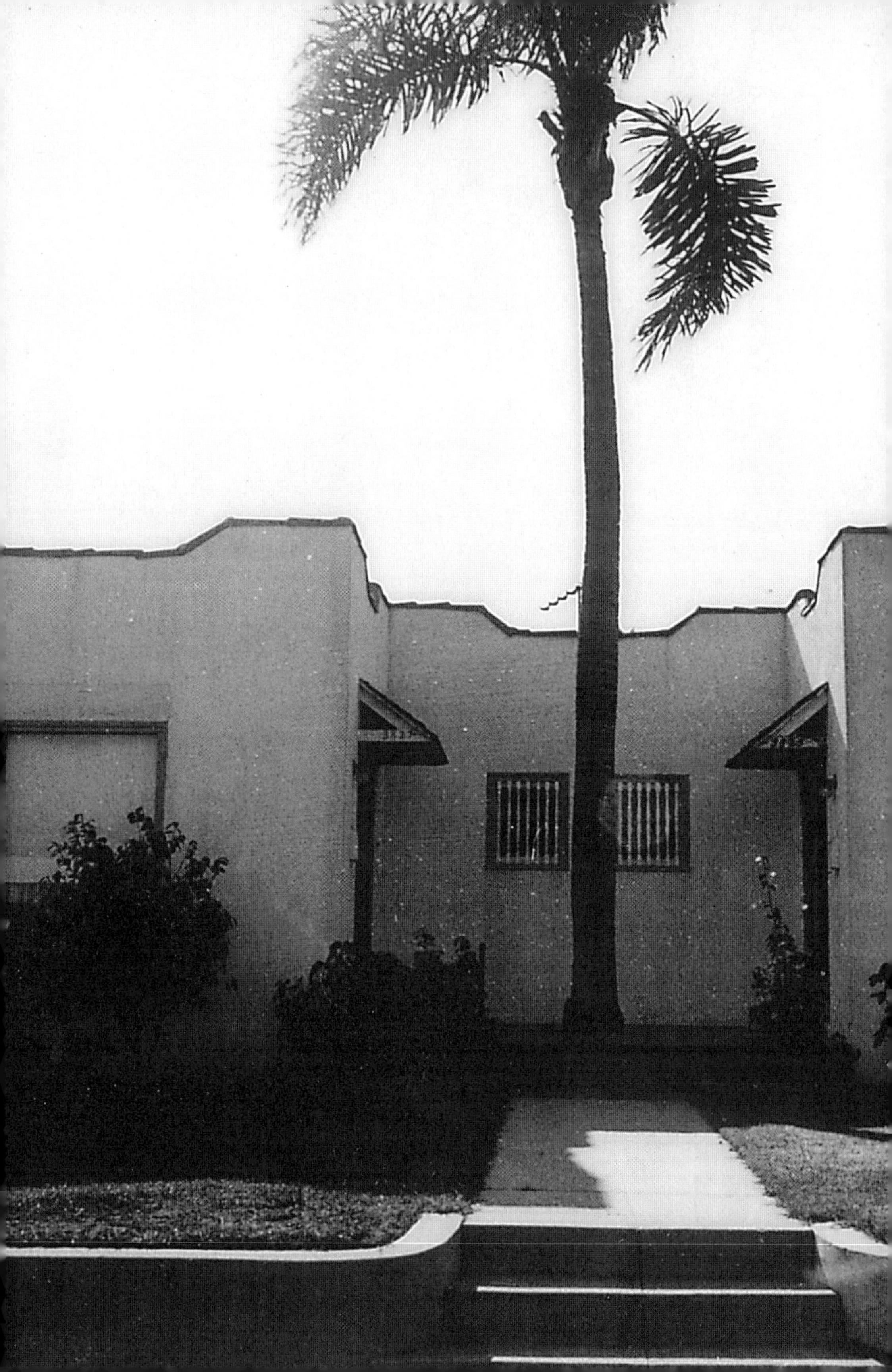

Judy Fiskin
interviewed by
John Divola

John Divola: Your background was in art history. How did you decide to become a photographer?

Judy Fiskin: After the first week of graduate school at Berkeley, I realized they had changed the game on me, and I quit school. I went over to the university employment center and found out that the only thing I qualified for with my B.A. in art history was clerk typist. So I reenrolled and decided to stay in graduate school until I figured out something else to do. After a year, I came down to L.A. to finish at U.C.L.A. I was taking seminars on modern art with a really wild guy; his name was Kurt von Meier. This was the late sixties, and he was having us do Happenings. We would all get together and go to the airport and watch the planes come in, or he bought a small TV and we all threw it off the pier. For one seminar, he told us to get hold of a camera and document some image of popular culture. I was given the heart. This was after seven years of art history, looking at lots and lots of images. I don't remember using a camera before this. I looked through the lens and right away I thought, "This is what I want to do." I learned the basic mechanics from my then brother-in-law who had a darkroom in his garage and was teaching himself. It was enough to get me going, and it accounts for my rather peculiar take on technical things, because he taught me wrong. I mean, he didn't know that much. Then I just taught myself after that.

Divola: What do you mean when you said they changed the game?

Fiskin: In college you're just having a great time discovering all this stuff. I was in it for the appreciation and not for the information. In graduate school you were supposed to be thinking about dates—dating every work, putting everything in the proper slot. And even though now in art history there's more of an idea of work in its broad historical context, I wouldn't be interested in that either. When I had to get serious about it in an academic way, I didn't want to.

page 63:
From the series Portraits of Furniture (detail), 1988, photograph, 2½ x 2½ inches
page 64:
From the series Some Aesthetic Decisions, 1984, photograph, 2½ x 2½ inches
page 65:
From the series Thirty-Five Views of San Bernardino (detail), 1982, photograph, 2 x 2¾ inches
page 66:
From the series Stucco (detail), 1973, photograph, 2 x 2¾ inches

Divola: Did studying art history influence your work as a photographer?

Fiskin: What I think directly translated into my work was the idea of looking at art in tiny reproductions. A lot of my experience of looking at art was in reproductions that weren't that much larger than the size that I make my work now. In Los Angeles at that time, there weren't too many examples of real art to look at. Also, after spending hundreds of hours in dark rooms looking at thousands of slides, I had quite an image bank stored up in my subconscious.

Divola: For the last eight to ten years, I've never seen a photograph of yours any larger than a couple of inches square. Has that been the case from the first, or is that something that you evolved into slowly?

Fiskin: It took me about a year to get down to that size. I did take one class in photography, a summer school class at U.C.L.A. Everybody was doing 8 by 10s. By the end of the class, everybody was trying to make 11 by 14s or 16 by 20s, and I had already started trying to make them smaller. They just looked too gross to me. I worked in 5 by 7 for a while. Then I got down to 4 by 5, and within one or two years I got down to the size now: 2¾ inches square. I arrived at that size because it was the farthest that my enlarger would go down. I didn't realize that if I had put a book on the enlarger table, I could have made the prints even smaller, and I'm grateful now that I didn't because I don't know how small I would have made them.

Divola: How do you think the small size affects the reading of the image?

Fiskin: For me, looking at small images somehow re-creates the experience of looking through a viewfinder. When you are looking through a viewfinder of a thirty-five-millimeter camera, the scale disappears; you don't know the size of the object you are looking at. It's like receiving an image directly into your brain. And when you have to get up to the photograph and peer into it, you lose the sense of separation between yourself as a body and that picture as a separate entity.

At this size the images are edible. You don't just scan them. You take them in all at once. The small scale organizes the image visually in a really graphic way. It gives it an immediate impact. Then if you want to look for detail, you can.

Divola: You employ other strategies that further undermine an attempt to read detail: your exaggerated tonal scale, the highlights being blasted out. Is that a conscious device for reducing that kind of information?

Fiskin: I never started out with the idea that I wanted to reduce the information in the image. I wanted the photographs to act on me in a certain way and to look a certain way. At the time that I got interested in photography, I also discovered Atget. The first two years I tried to make photographs that looked as much like Atget photographs as I could because I thought his prints were so beautiful. But he was using albumen paper and a big view camera, and I was using silver paper and thirty-five millimeter. Reducing the print size and printing high contrast was my version of reproducing the look of albumen paper, which has bleached-out whites and very strong blacks. On silver paper you couldn't make such an extreme print large, so detail had to go.

But suppressing detail also did something I was very interested in. I was trying to match my mental image of the world, rather than the world itself, and mental images of objects aren't full of detail. If you think "house," you're going to get something very general, and if you want detail, you're going to have to make an effort to add it. Dropping detail made the photographs more general, like mental images.

Divola: Does that particular kind of print have anything to do with creating atmosphere?

Fiskin: When I first started, I was really interested in atmosphere. I've developed away from that, but that's true of the first stucco bungalows I did and then the stuff I did in San Bernardino—and even the military bases to some extent. I was interested in a sort of Raymond Chandler atmosphere—too much sunlight, making you squint, everything really menacing. That's how I picked San Bernardino. I grew up in Southern California, and on my childhood map, after San Bernardino there was a big void that you would fall into if you went any farther. And then one day I was driving through there, and the smog was so thick it was palpable. It made the place look filthy and disgusting, and that was very appealing to me. In my mind, it was a very creepy place. That's why I wanted to photograph there.

Divola: To photograph is often compared to an act of redemption—to select from an infinite number of choices that which is to be remembered. In some of your early work there was a sense of redeeming from popular culture certain gestures which otherwise might be dismissed. However, in your new work dealing with furniture in museums, the objects which you photograph already populate a catalogue of redemption. Their context, the museum, is an assertion of their significance.

Fiskin: In a way, you can't avoid that act of redemption as a photographer, especially if you're doing anything that looks at all documentary; the work is going to be read that way anyway. I didn't try to avoid or undermine that reading, but I was more interested in something else: a feeling of the arbitrariness of the world. A metaphor that I've always used for that is aesthetic choice. I've always dealt so much with kitsch material because arbitrariness of choice in popular architecture and popular art is quite obvious since the choices are, from our point of view, so often wrong.

That's why I photographed flower shows. Flower arranging has such a frozen aesthetic. The judges at those shows would take me around and say, "See, that rose is half an inch off." I would nod my head. I couldn't see anything wrong, but this was an aesthetic that had very, very strict rules. It was an aesthetic, but it was completely awkward. What appealed to me was the idea of so much meticulous care being put into something that turned out so wrong.

Furniture in museums has already been designated and canonized as high art, but a lot of it fits into the same category as flower arrangements. I didn't go photograph Shaker objects in museums. I photographed wild Victorian furniture. I photographed rococo French furniture from the eighteenth century. Because it's canonized in the museum, people look at it and tick off all these examples of "good taste." But in fact a lot of them are quite bizarre, which puts them in the right territory for me. It gets back to the idea of the photograph as redemption when you say, "Let's look closely at these things and see what's really there." The furniture is being redeemed from conventional notions of beauty. In the photographs the objects are freed to take on a different kind of beauty.

Divola: When you photograph a piece of furniture from the eighteenth century, the context it operates within is the present. To some degree it undermines the notion of history.

Fiskin: By making objects appear slightly off, the way that I do in the photographs, by making them appear different from the way they're presented, you have to deal with them as objects of the present. Once you do that, you have to ask, "What are they now?" We're used to understanding them as direct links to the past—if you have contact with this, you have contact with Louis XIV. In fact, it's not true, and once you throw that notion out, then it becomes very unclear what they are or what your attitude toward them should be. That is always the feeling that I'm trying to get at in whatever I do.

Divola: Yet all of your work seems to be anchored in a representation of particular historical eras.

Fiskin: The eras that I've dealt with up until this furniture series have been close to the present, starting from the bungalows of the twenties and thirties, and that does bring up the question of the nostalgia. I want to deal with that a little bit. For instance, the desert landscapes—it wasn't just that I wanted to go out and photograph the desert. I was going out and photographing an idea of the desert. That idea of the desert was set in the forties, and I'm sure it came from forties movies. But I was also working from my own memories of having a lot of childhood vacations in Las Vegas and Palm Springs. But I still don't think of the way that I dealt with it as nostalgic. A friend recently looked at the furniture work and said he thought I was casting a cold eye on my own nostalgia. I think it's nostalgia with a distance, a step back from nostalgia and an acknowledgment that what you're longing for is just another image.

Divola: Your work often addresses aesthetics as subject. In more recent work, it was the aesthetics of high culture, the objects which literally populate the museum. Your work is a kind of catalogue of the stylistic codes which characterize an era.

Fiskin: I'm looking at the idea of how those definitions are put in place. One way to define each era is through this kind of visual shorthand that gets constructed. Once you've got some distance in years from that, it looks more and more arbitrary. In Some Aesthetic Decisions, the flower show images, I was dealing with an aesthetic that had been frozen in the fifties. This was already 1984, and here was this whole group of people who were doing something very consciously aesthetic, but the aesthetic was thirty years old, and they didn't have any idea that that was so. I found that an interesting thing to be dealing with.

Divola: The idea of arbitrariness sounds metaphysically bleak.

Fiskin: It is. What I am dealing with over and over is having your ease in the world pulled out from under you, because I don't feel easy in the world. The flip side of that, the positive side of that, is that it makes a clearing where you can see the world with fresh eyes, see the world with a sense of wonder. Once the comfortable meaning of things slides away, it makes you aware of your own contingency in the world, but it opens objects up for you to really see them and have a strong experience of them. That's a positive thing, and it can be applied to everything—even sixties apartment buildings.

Divola: Weren't the emotions you wanted to inject often emotions of detachment?

Fiskin: They were about being detached when you didn't want to be detached.

Divola: There's an emphatic reticence about them.

Fiskin: Yes. During my career as a depressed person that was part of my personality. In fact, at that time of my life, I didn't talk much. I hung around with people who would talk for me. But I also think that the reticence in the work is an attempt to allow a thing to speak for itself. If I leave an object seeming like it doesn't have enough meaning, I think it just allows it more room to be there, to have presence.

Divola: That notion of presence is interesting because your work has often seemed impenetrable. All that's allowed to come through is this stylistic code or idea of a type of an object.

Fiskin: Impenetrable, opaque, obdurate: these are good terms to apply to the work. They all express something about what the world feels like to me.

Divola: To call all aesthetic decisions arbitrary undermines the whole pretense of the arts as humanizing the world, or inflecting objects with a sense of individual character and value.

Fiskin: But that is just what makes it arbitrary. For every era of art making there is some new agreed-upon code. If you don't agree on it then it doesn't mean anything. That's one of the things that conceptual artists explored: that is, looking at art is an activity that depends on consensus. If the consensus dies, then the object is up for redefinition. The game changes all the time; for me, if you look at that too closely, you're getting into real queasy territory. How do you say anything means anything if that's the case? I'm not making art in which everything that I'm doing is meant to lead you to that conclusion. Instead I'm trying to make that into a visual experience that leaves you somewhat uneasy. I do appreciate these objects that I'm looking at. But I have to make up my own terms of appreciation, redo the objects; then I can appreciate them. In that sense, I am doing a kind of photographic rescue mission, but I know its limits.

Divola: I'd like you to talk about the cataloguing approach that exists in your work. You often work with the methodology of the catalogue, exploring variations within a group of similar objects.

Fiskin: I think there's something basically appealing about variations on a theme. A lot of people in photography have done that. I think photography is a great medium for cataloguing because you can gather information endlessly. In the Dingbat series, I did a lot of photographs of apartment building façades that were decorated with geometric motifs. You could drive through Los Angeles and say, "Boy, there's all these apartment buildings, and some of them have circles on them, and some of them have triangles, and some of them have squares," but you couldn't have the experience of seeing them all together except in a series of photographs. That kind of serial structure is a benign way of working out greed. It's a kind of stand-in for owning things. It satisfies your acquisitiveness.

Divola: Photography often has been described pejoratively as a form of shopping.

Fiskin: Yes, and I'm a great shopper, too. But if that's all it was, it wouldn't be enough. The catalogue structure does lots of other things. It lets me put things together in a way that feeds into the idea of the arbitrary. That showed most clearly in the Dingbat series. I had so many photographs that I was able to divide them into several different subseries. On the surface it looked like an encyclopedia of sixties architecture, but underneath, if you looked at all the different categories, they didn't make sense as categories. One category was buildings with side stairways, another was geometric motifs, another Japanese roof lines. Those categories don't really add up to anything when you put them together. I had one category of peaked roofs and another category of Japanese roof lines, but Japanese roof lines also have peaked roofs. They could have all gone in the peaked-roofs category. It started to fall apart on you if you were paying attention. It was about dissolving order, but I did it in a playful way. I put together three buildings that had decorative screens on their façades with a building that had a tiny diamond-patterned window, because that looked like a screen to me.

Divola: You generally emphasize the concrete, discrete objects as opposed to photographs of broad yields of information. It seems very consistent, even in the desert work.

Fiskin: I think that's a question of sensibility. One of the reasons I chose a desert landscape as opposed to a mountain landscape is that the desert is where you can see things discretely. I got images of a cactus or a bush just sitting out there by themselves. I was able to silhouette them, so they really stand out. I also had a verbal idea, which was *rock, mountain, sagebrush.* I was going to try to come up with some primal image of those three things together. I got one photograph that I think finally did that. That goes back to the idea of working from idealized images in my mind.

Divola: One of the fascinating things about photography, as opposed to many of the other media, is that it pulls you out into the world. It pulls you into what's outside the house. Is that any sort of motivation in relation to the work?

Fiskin: When I come up with something I want to look at, some part of the world opens up. When I was looking at little stucco buildings, since L.A. is so full of those, L.A. became a whole playground for me, because I was not just looking at them and appreciating them, but I could really focus on them. I was looking at them with a purpose. The interesting and unfortunate thing is that when I'm through with the series, I couldn't care less about those buildings. The world keeps opening up and closing down through this process.

Making something that you really like is like getting a shot of morphine. It's pleasure. Unfortunately for artists, you can't keep getting that hit from the same thing over and over again. That's why your work has to keep changing to some extent. You get bored within the work. That's what keeps me going, to have that pleasure and not be bored.

Divola: All of your work is shot either in the Los Angeles area or the New York area. Why is that?

Fiskin: First of all, shooting in L.A. was a matter of circumstances. It's where I grew up; it's where I mostly went to school; it's where I discovered architecture; and it's full of different kinds of interesting architecture. There was fertile ground for me here. When I started, I was interested in the atmosphere of this semi-arid place with lots of light. I think, again, I wanted to re-create something about my memories of childhood that way. For many years I felt like I couldn't live anywhere else, couldn't have an identity anywhere else. That's no longer true.

I went to shoot in New York because of what I would see when I took trips there, driving in from the airport, going through Queens. At one point in Jamaica the expressway is elevated, and you see all these little houses with all kinds of different siding—weird, at least to West Coast eyes. I was fascinated by that. At a certain point I realized I could go there and photograph those houses. There was a whole different kind of vernacular architecture there.

I would like to shoot in all different kinds of places. I'm interested in domestic architecture in Germany, pictures I've seen of vernacular architecture in

Africa, especially Mali. This stuff is on my mind. In fact, I don't enjoy travel that much, but I have this terrible feeling that I might actually get myself to some of these places to do this. On the one hand, I would really like to do the work. On the other hand, I think I would hate the trip. So we'll see. In the meantime, I'm about to go to New York for six months to shoot stick-style Victorian architecture on the Jersey shore.

Divola: Is there any difference in working in New York or Los Angeles?

Fiskin: Yes. People reacted differently to what I was doing in each place. People get upset when they see you outside photographing their houses. I learned to tell the story that seemed to satisfy the most people the most quickly. When I first started in L.A., I used to tell the truth. I would say, "I'm a photographer" or "I'm an artist and I'm doing this series on small houses." Nobody believed that. I learned to say something else when I was in L.A.: "I'm a location scout and there's going to be a movie made and your house might be in it." There's nobody in L.A. who didn't go for that. Really, it's just a question of what people are used to and know about.

Then I went to New York, and I was photographing in Brooklyn. The first person that came out to question me, I said, "Well, I'm an artist." Total relaxation. They got that right away. They said, "Oh, you're an artist. We have some artists moving in around the corner. If you think this house is interesting, there's an even more interesting house around the block." This happened over and over again. In New York the concept of being an artist has reached everyone. No matter what people say about L.A. as an art center, it does not get you anywhere to tell people in L.A. that you're an artist.

Divola: What was it like to shoot in the desert?

Fiskin: I always went out there alone. Before I went, I was really interested in reading survival books. I was pretending to myself that I was going to go out there and get lost. So I learned all this stuff like how to burn the tires on your car to signal for help. I sent away for a huge orange plastic tarp that spelled out HELP, to throw over the top of your car if you got lost. I put together a whole survival kit. I had a little snake-bite kit. I carried boards in case the car got stuck in the sand, even though when I did get stuck in the sand I had no idea how to use them. I had to go find someone who was parked in a trailer nearby to get my car out of the sand. The truth is, when I went out there, I never went more than a five-minute walk away from the highway.

Actually, I've had lots of fantasies about being in danger when I'm shooting, and I've heard other photographers talk about that, too. When you're walking around behind a camera, you lose track of what's going on around you, and I think that makes you feel vulnerable. There was the danger of hostile people coming out of their houses at me. How was I going to handle them?

Divola: What was it like photographing military architecture?

Fiskin: I thought it was going to be incredibly difficult to get permission to photograph. In every case except for one, all I had to do was to call up the public information office at that base and say that I was interested and sound like my interest was positive, and they rolled out the red carpet for me. Someone there would take me all over the base. Nobody ever questioned what I was doing. Nobody ever checked my references. Nobody ever called me to see if I was at the right telephone number. At some bases they let me go around by myself.

The best place for my purposes was a Seabee base in Ventura. The Seabees are the construction battalion, and in peacetime they go all over the world to help rebuild in places that have had natural disasters. There were these big fields of what my guide called "materiel," which changed from week to week. There were things like giant rubber water bags that they would drop on places where there had been earthquakes. But most of what was there was unrecognizable, and there were acres of it. For me, it was like finding miles of functional minimal sculpture to photograph.

The other thing they did on this Seabee base was to train soldiers in construction. They had a miniature block of houses that they would have the trainees build. Then, when new people came in, they would tear down the houses, trim the wood, and rebuild them. So the houses kept getting smaller and smaller until they used up the lumber. They also had two-foot-high telephone poles so the guys could learn to string telephone wire without worrying about falling off the pole.

Divola: Is the perspective of a woman evident within your work in any way?

Fiskin: I think so. It's subtle. It can only be seen in a certain context. When I first started showing my work, some of the ideas I was working with were generally in the air. There was a bunch of photographers who were grouped together at that time after a show called *New Topography*. New Topography was work that dealt with the landscape and the urban landscape in a very neutral-looking way, coming out of the documentary tradition of Walker Evans. It wasn't totally documentary because a lot of emphasis was given to a certain kind of beautiful print, but an air of absolute neutrality toward the subject matter was essential. All the work of the New Topographers was men's work. My work came out at the same time, and there were ways in which it was related to theirs. I wanted the work to look objective in a certain way, too. On the other hand, arbitrariness and depression and bleakness are not so present in the work of the men who did New Topography. I wanted to inject certain kinds of emotional states into this neutral-looking work. That, I would say, is more female and less male.

When I photographed the flower arrangements, part of what drew me to that was the milieu. It was such a paradigm of the options traditionally open to women. I got to know some of the women, and when they felt comfortable with me, they would say, "We're not doing flower arranging; we're doing sculpture." But they're not doing sculpture in a creative way, and they're not doing sculpture in a professional way, although the competitions they go through have all the trappings of something highly serious. It's a picture of an activity in which women were doing this thing that was parallel to what men did, except the stakes and the rewards were very low. Women get to pretend to do what men do. These women were all middle class and upper middle class, and very conventional, something I feel that I narrowly escaped in my life.

I remember sitting in an auditorium when one of the clubs was giving a demonstration of flower arranging, and I had the fantasy that the doors were going to swing shut. We were all going to be locked in there forever. I was going to be the only one who wasn't really a part of this world, but I was going to have to live in there, the flower-arranging world, for the rest of my life. I think that's in the work.

Divola: Could you talk a bit about the influences that surround your work?

Fiskin: The specific influences started back when I was studying medieval architecture. I liked Romanesque architecture, which is heavy and squat, with powerful, generalized spaces. I was drawing on this taste for heavy and somewhat awkward architecture when I decided to look at vernacular architecture. Then there was Atget. And after Atget, Walker Evans was a strong influence because of the way he centered objects, the way he was interested in looking at objects, in vernacular architecture, and the way he made vernacular architecture look monumental. My earliest work on architecture was trying to make the stuff look monumental. It doesn't any more, but it did at the beginning. After that there was an influence that I didn't see at the time, even though it was all around: minimal sculpture. When I look at my photographs of simple buildings centered in the middle of a square frame, I have to think that somehow something about the minimalist aesthetic filtered into me.

Then there are things that look like influences, like the Bechers, that I just don't think were influences at the time this work was developing. As for the work of the New Topographers, I had pretty much gotten to all the essential elements of what I was doing before I became aware of them. I was dismayed to find out that this bunch of other people were doing such similar work.

Divola: Often based in the aesthetics of minimal sculpture.

Fiskin: I think it also comes from looking at a lot of nineteenth-century landscape photography and really loving it, but having to deal with the fact that it had already been photographed. How do you make those photographs again in a contemporary way? I think that was a problem that they were solving and that I was solving, too. That was another very heavy influence: nineteenth-century American landscape photography.

Divola: How do you know when you're finished with a body of work?

Fiskin: Usually these days I just make work for a show. When I have the show, that's it for the series. For instance, I think when I had the show of the Desert series, I didn't feel like I was finished. I still wanted to go out to the desert. I was still interested in it. But once I had the show, it was dead. I couldn't do it anymore.

Other times, you see things on the proof sheet that you know would make good photographs for that series, and you just don't want to do them anymore. It just gets boring. You've tapped it out in some way. You just know—it's as simple as that.

Divola: The process of art history is to take a category of objects and reduce it into propositions about what it means. It seems to me that you have great skepticism about that reduction.

Fiskin: Yes, it's because I'm more interested in creating an experience than in summarizing experience. My work a lot of times gets talked about as if it were documentary work. My definition of documentary work is photography in which the information is the most important part of the work. In my work the information is the least important part. It's there, and the work wouldn't mean the same thing without it—I don't deny it—but it isn't structured around the information. The most interesting part to me is the visual play: how many different kinds of one thing I can put together, how these things look when I make them into prints. The most interesting part is looking at this little universe of representation that I can make out of the world.

✦

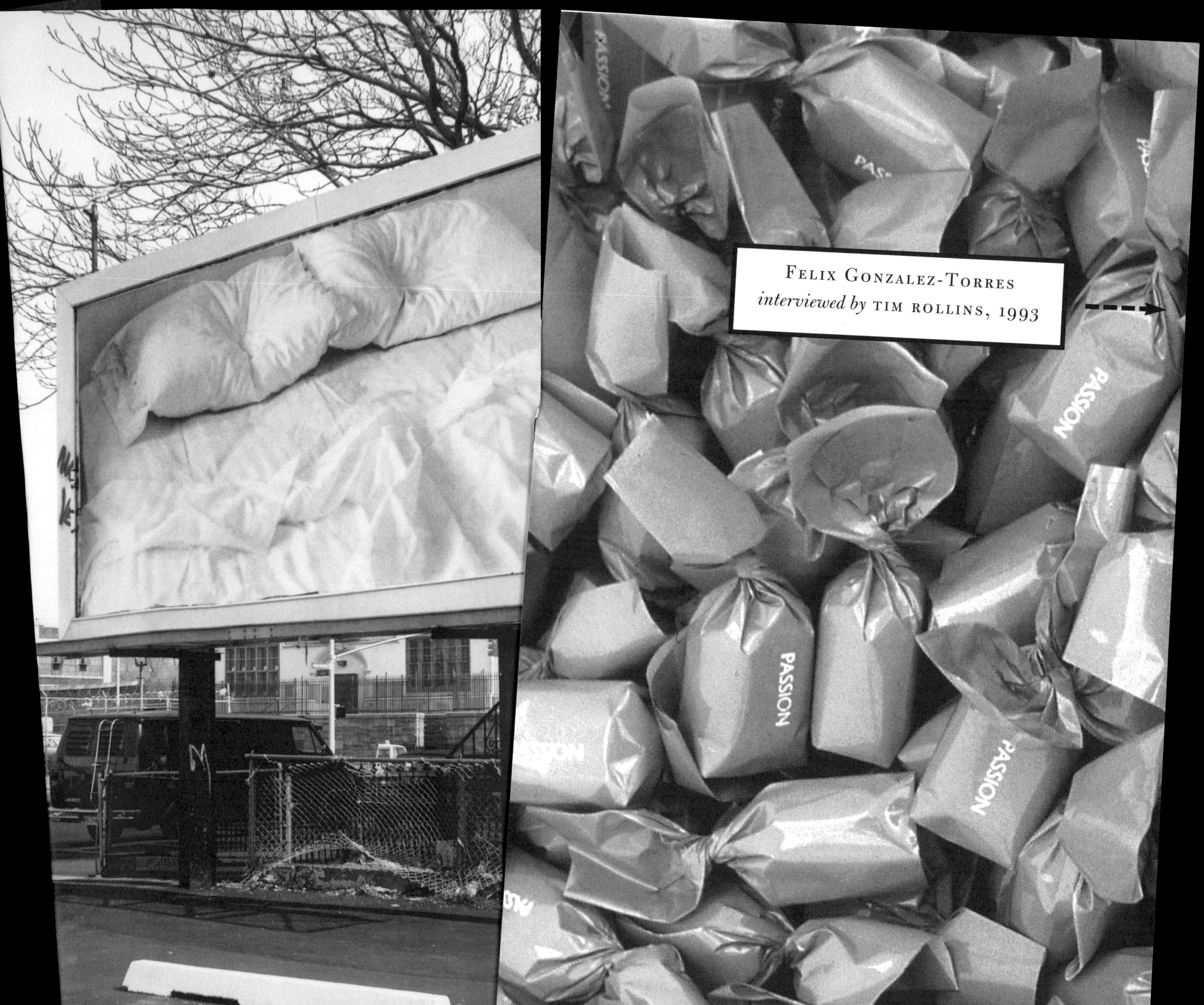

Felix Gonzalez-Torres
interviewed by Tim Rollins, 1993

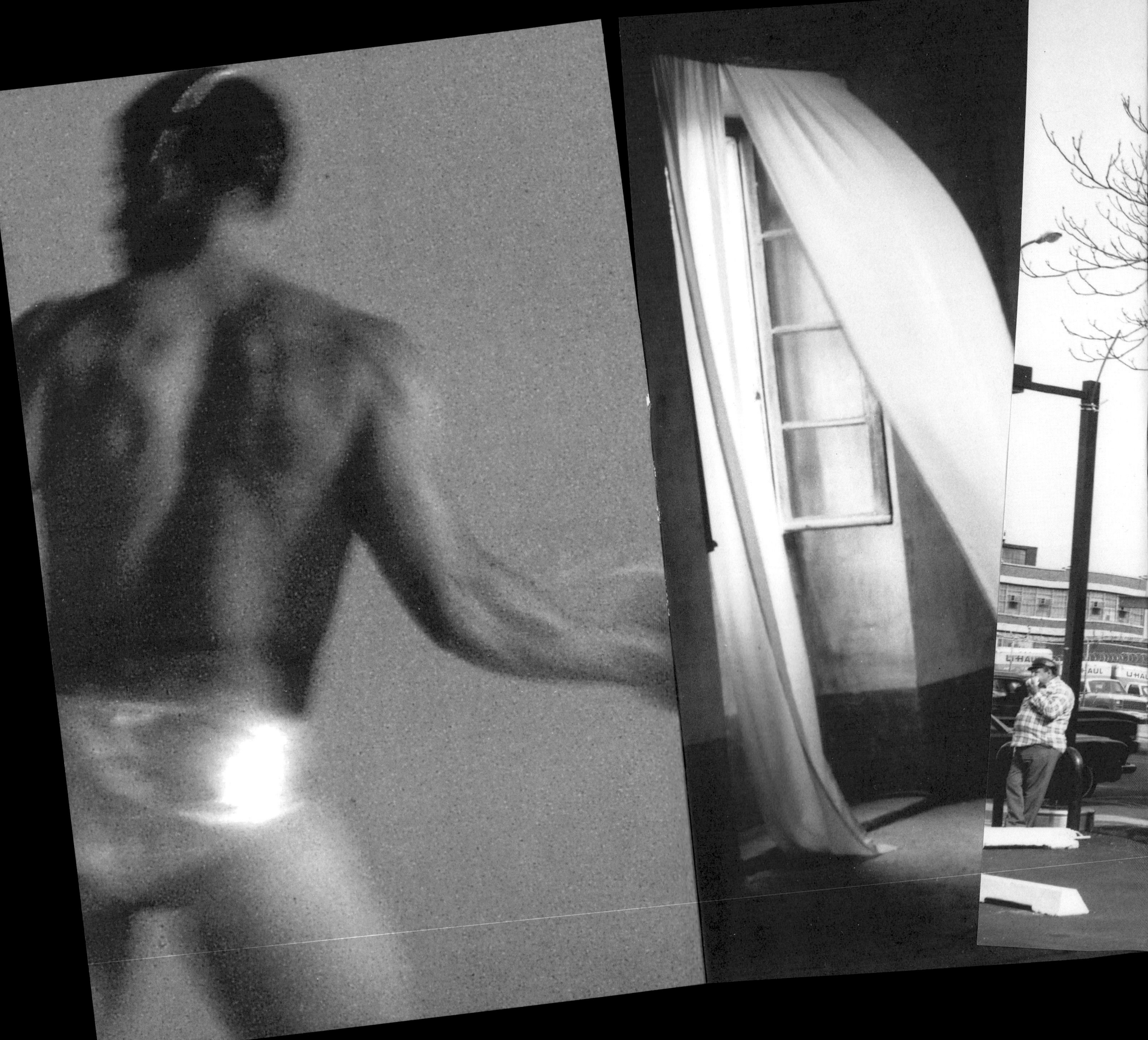

Felix Gonzalez-Torres

interviewed by

TIM ROLLINS

Tim Rollins: How long has it been since you've been to the movies?

Felix Gonzalez-Torres: Two and a half years. I used to go to movies with Ross, mostly. Nowadays it's so much easier to rent a video; I got used to being able to replay the important parts. At the movie houses you can't say to the projectionist, "Hey Joe, can you replay that part?"

Rollins: So much of your work seems cinematic—drawn from films, the movies. The date works remind me of credits, really great movie credits, and your stacks remind me of an accumulation of frames from a film. You also often integrate photography in the work. The new work with the curtains. All these ghosts of cinema and screen are living in your work.

Gonzalez-Torres: I think a movie house is a place of loneliness—one of the few places where I feel comfortable being alone. It's dark. You can just sit there and watch movies. When I first moved to New York, I used to go to movies a lot because I had no friends. It was a nice way to spend two hours alone. Also, at that time there were some great old movie houses—art movie houses—you could see three films one right after the other for very little money. I used to do that a lot. It really was about loneliness and empty frames. It was not about any particular movie; it was just about a place. The movie was an excuse to be somewhere in the dark. Once I met Ross, the movie house had different connotations. It was a place where the movie suddenly became important: the movies became part of our dialogue, part of our exchange of ideas.

Rollins: Most artists today deal with two powerful traditions inherited from the eighteenth century. There is the realist tradition where the artist simply reflects what's going on in society— the "vision thing." Then there are other artists like Courbet who transgress that, who create social statements, project something. Which tradition are you from?

Gonzalez-Torres: It depends on the day of the week. I choose from many different positions. I think I woke up on Monday in a political mood and on Tuesday in a

page 79:
Untitled *(Portrait of Marcel Brient) (detail), 1992, dimensions variable*
page 80:
Untitled *(Go-Go Dancing Platform), 1991, wood, lightbulbs, paint, wire, 21½ x 72 x 72 inches*
page 81:
Untitled *(Blue Curtains), 1989–91, blue fabric and metal rod, dimensions variable*
page 82:
Untitled, *1991, from the series Projects: Felix Gonzalez-Torres*

very nostalgic mood and Wednesday in a realist mood. I don't think I'll limit myself to one choice. I'm shameless when it comes to that, I just take any position that will help me best express the way I think or feel about a particular issue. Formal strategies are there for your use.

When I first made the date pieces with the empty screens, I was working as a waiter. I used to come home very late at night and watch TV to forget the daily specials before I'd work on any art. I'd scan the channels. There's really not much to see. Everything boiled down to the same low level of meaninglessness. Everything was a fragment of a total spectacle: the most horrific news next to the most glamorous gold ring next to the most glamorous celebrity next to cooking oil. News, events, fiction, data, scandals, starving children are all collapsed into a level of historical inaction—a dark landscape, sterile, meaningless. I feel so anemic tonight; it must be the rain.

Rollins: This is something that I've always wanted to ask you: why have you deliberately, obstinately decided for some reason not to have a studio?

Gonzalez-Torres: Do you really want to ask me that?

Rollins: Yes, because it's very curious to me. It's almost like making art on the dining-room table as a hobby. This is an amazing limitation. You don't have the trappings of a studio: assistants, visitors, and all that. Issues of space and light are gone since your work is so sensitive to place and context.

How do you determine the pieces? You say you don't do drawings, but I know you must do drawings. You must have some idea of what the piece is going to look like, so how do you begin?

Gonzalez-Torres: I really don't plan pieces using drawings. First of all, I usually dislike drawings by sculptors, they're just so academic and expected. I don't follow that prescribed mode. I do make drawings and photographs, but they have their own specific function. They are not sketches of the sculptures; these are drawings that represent a parallel set of ideas.

The reason why I don't have a studio—I think that I'm very neurotic. Actually, I guess I am neurotic. So having a studio would paralyze me completely. Just the idea that I would have a place where I had to go to work and make "something" scares the shit out of me. The studio is a scary stage set.

Rollins: Stage fright?

Gonzalez-Torres: Maybe. The only time I had a studio, I didn't make a single thing for six months. I guess that's good; I saved the world from more unnecessary artworks. I've always wanted a studio, a studio that looked like an "artist's studio" with all that stuff: all the lights and the stereo music and the assistants like in *House and Garden.* I never had a penny, so by the time I got around to having some money, I realized I didn't really need a studio. It was a revenge, a sweet one. Now I'm very happy I made that decision because I don't produce objects all the time.

Rollins: So let's get down to it, how do you determine a work? For example, Lover Boy: *How did you decide how big it was going to be? The dimensions of each sheet of paper? What kind of paper to use and how tall the stack would be? How did you decide on which blue to use? How did you know it would go against the wall in that certain way?*

Gonzalez-Torres: Well, it goes against the wall because the blue reflects on the wall. The paper is a light blue and is a standard commercial brand trimmed to twenty-four by twenty-four inches.

Rollins: But how did you know that that would work?

Gonzalez-Torres: I didn't. Not until I did the installation. When you don't have a studio, you take risks. You change your underwear in public. I'm not afraid of making mistakes; I'm afraid of keeping them. I have destroyed a lot of pieces—I like the excitement of fucking up royally. Some artists can "rehearse" in their studios before they go into the gallery; I find that too easy. I don't know, I never had anything to lose so I've always done it my own way.

Rollins: But how do you know it will work? You must keep a notebook.

Gonzalez-Torres: Well, no.

Rollins: Don't lie to me! You have a notebook. You must know how...

Gonzalez-Torres: I have a notebook! Sometimes.

Rollins: All right! There must be some kind of—it might not be a sketch, but you must have the measurements written down. You must have taken some piece of paper and cut it the right size and said, "This is the right size." I know your work isn't completely arbitrary or intuitive.

Gonzalez-Torres: I do like certain uncanny numbers. Things happen to me around certain numbers: five, twenty-four, twelve. Those are the numbers that sometimes determine the height of the stacks and the size of certain papers.

Rollins: A mystical minimalism?

Gonzalez-Torres: Yes and no. Some of the stacks are made thirty-two by twenty-nine inches because that's also the size of the paper. If the piece is about something that is very distant to me, then numbers like seventeen, thirty-five, and twenty-one sound perfect because they are numbers that I would never use for anything except for a piece that is very uncomfortable. In terms of the height, it's really determined by how it looks installed in the actual space.

Sometimes I think, well, eight or nine inches is going to work all right. But once it's in the gallery, nine inches really doesn't work. It just doesn't look right. Then I have to increase or decrease the amount of paper sheets in the stack. With the new work, the light strings, I leave those decisions for others to perform. I don't decide how the strings of lights are installed; I only specify that the piece must have forty-two twenty-watt lightbulbs.

Rollins: Don't you have to give yourself a lot of installation time?

Gonzalez-Torres: I usually do it in just one day. Some shows just take two hours to install—that's it. I'm out of there. I think about the work and the installations for a very, very long time. I lose sleep over these things. I just came back from Vienna with photographs from Peter's [Pakesch] gallery, and I've been getting up in the middle of the night to write something about how it will be installed in the show so that when I go up there...

Rollins: So you do draw?

Gonzalez-Torres: Sometimes. Stuff that goes into the trash can once the show is over. These aren't saved—not signed, numbered, or dated. They're just things to help me through the final piece—which is what I want the public to really be engaged with. The voyeuristic idea that whatever the artist sketches or does is interesting is not interesting to me. That's stuff for *People.*

Rollins: So you don't think these sketches might be interesting or useful to others?

Gonzalez-Torres: No, because I don't want people to be involved with the insecurity that comes with making these things. There's a lot of fear that goes into these things. I honestly think that when I made those stack pieces I was still trying to understand Walter Benjamin. I read Benjamin for the first time while I was in the Whitney program, and I didn't understand it then because I was so green. I had just come out of Pratt Institute, where I had just wasted four years.

Pratt Institute is the kind of place where a teacher can look you straight in the eyes and easily tell you to be "honest and truthful to the space," as if that had some kind of meaning. Pratt is a place where people preserve their jobs by fucking up and confusing young people's minds. They have wasteful courses such as "Space, Form, and Shapes"—Bauhaus theories without the social commitments or interest. From radical forms to empty styles in four easy steps.

Rollins: I would like to talk about theory. I think we both come from backgrounds where books were considered with suspicion.

Gonzalez-Torres: It's a queer thing, I mean, at least from my background.

Rollins: I think it's about wanting a larger world. I think it's about wanting to be involved with the world of ideas, and it takes a certain amount of courage to really go into that other land. That's the danger of being too involved in theory: you get to a certain level in your education where you equate theory with practice.

Gonzalez-Torres: Tim, I must say that without reading Walter Benjamin, Fanon, Althusser, Barthes, Foucault, Borges, Mattelart, and others, perhaps I wouldn't have been able to make certain pieces, to arrive at certain positions. Some of their writings and ideas gave me a certain freedom to see. These ideas moved me to a place of pleasure through knowledge and some understanding of the way reality is constructed, of the way the self is formed in culture, of the way language sets traps, and of the cracks in the "master narrative"—those cracks where power can be exercised. It is also about influences and role models.

Films as texts, such as movies by Godard, have been very influential to me. There is also, of course, Yvonne Rainer's *Journeys from Berlin,* and a movie by Sarah Gomez called *One Way or Another,* which is a feminist view of the Cuban revolution, Santeria, and other issues. This movie is very interesting because it's also about the meaning of love during a particular historical period. I saw that movie the same week that I saw *Hiroshima, Mon Amour.*

Rollins: That's a great movie about love.

Gonzalez-Torres: No, it's about meaning and how meaning is dependent on the context. Last but not least, Brecht is an influence. I think if I started this list of influences again, I would start with Brecht. I think this is really important because, as Hispanic artists, we're supposed to be very crazy, colorful—extremely colorful. We are supposed to "feel," not think. Brecht says to keep a distance to allow the viewer, the public, time to reflect and think. When you get out of the theater, you should not have had a catharsis; you should have had a thinking experience. More than anything, break the pleasure of representation, the pleasure of the flawless narrative. This is not life; this is just a theater piece. I like that a lot: this is not life; this is just an artwork. I want you, the viewer, to be intellectually challenged, moved, and informed.

Rollins: Some people don't like that.

Gonzalez-Torres: Of course not, because they have an investment in the narrative. The artist is expected to be someone who "feels," the idiot savant. I admire artists that break the rules, that break with the expected functions of an artist, that push the limits of artistic practice; artists that can recite economic facts at the drop of a hat; artists that can tell you how much money has been eliminated from programs for pregnant woman and infants over the last twelve years by the Republican "pro-family" administration; artists that can tell you that even though Exxon was fined a few million dollars for the Valdez oil spill, we, the famous taxpayers, will end up paying billions on behalf of Exxon's real crimes.

Rollins: But you're definitely not Brecht, and you're not Althusser, and you're not Celia Cruz either. Would you have a heart attack if I asked you if Dan Flavin was a mentor?

Gonzalez-Torres: I would not have an attack at all. It's very heroic and poetic to take a fluorescent light and make it into something more than a fluorescent light without adding paint to it! But that is as far as I can go in my admiration of Flavin.

Rollins: And to personalize it. What's quite obvious is that you've taken formal strategies from Russian constructivism to minimalism and collapsed all that into artworks that are as industrial as Donald Judd while being as personal as Emily Dickinson.

Gonzalez-Torres: That's true. They're very industrial; you can say that.

Rollins: It's obvious that you aren't as interested in the battle between form and content as you are in method: how the work is made, distributed, and shared. Where did the stack pieces come from?

Gonzalez-Torres: It's really difficult to say. I don't really remember, seriously. The first stacks I made were some of the date pieces. Around 1989 everyone was fighting for wall space. So the floor space was free, the floor space was marginal. I was also interested in giving back to the viewer, to the public, something that was never really mine to start with—this explosion of information, which in reality is an implosion of meaning. Secondly, when I got into making stacks—which was the show with Andrea Rosen—I wanted to do a show that would disappear completely. It had a lot to do with disappearance and learning. It was also about trying to be a threat to the art-marketing system, and also, to be really honest, it was about being generous to a certain extent. I wanted people to have my work. The fact that someone could just come and take my work and carry it with them was very exciting. Freud said that we rehearse our fears in order to lessen them. In a way this "letting go" of the work—this refusal to make a static form, a monolithic sculpture, in favor of a disappearing, changing, unstable, and fragile form—was an attempt on my part to rehearse my fears of having Ross disappear day by day right in front of my eyes. It's really a weird thing when you see the public come into the gallery and walk away with a piece of paper that is "yours."

It's a riot when I show these pieces in a museum because people aren't supposed to touch the art, much less take it with them. At the 1991 Whitney Biennial people would ask the museum guard if it was true that they could really take a piece from the stack of paper. The guards got into it. But I had a show once here in a New York gallery and this East Village artist got upset with the work. She just couldn't take it. I saw her take twenty, twenty-five sheets from the stack and dump them in the corner trash can. That was really upsetting to me.

Rollins: Because it was rude?

Gonzalez-Torres: Very upsetting because I had never seen so much bitterness with respect to my work. It was very strange. I was really upset. I thought she was taking them because she needed paper to do work on. So at first I was very, very pleased, but then she just acted maliciously.

Rollins: I think you're experiencing the underside of democracy.

Gonzalez-Torres: I guess there's a lot of trash on the underside of democracy, unfortunately. Still, I prefer democracy, as faulty as it is.

Rollins: Love and fear seem to be the two great themes of your work.

Gonzalez-Torres: It's funny you say that. Earlier I mentioned *Hiroshima, Mon Amour*—it took me a long time to understand the opening sequence. The female character says, "You are good for me because you destroy me." I finally understand what that means. You can be destroyed because of love and as a result of fear. Love is very peculiar because it gives a reason to live, but it's also a great reason to be afraid, to be extremely afraid, to be terrified of losing that love.

It's not as if I have different bodies of work; I think I just have many fronts. It's almost like being in drag. I'm in a different drag persona as needed. Sometimes I make the stacks, sometimes I do the curtains, sometimes I do text pieces, sometimes I do canvases, sometimes the light strings, sometimes billboards or photos. There are pieces that grow and change all the time. There's a piece where I mail the owner something every so often and it goes into this big box. This piece should never be shown. I don't know if you know about this piece.

Rollins: Explain it some more. Who gets these things?

Gonzalez-Torres: The person who buys this empty box gets these things in the mail.

Rollins: How does this person get the box?

Gonzalez-Torres: They buy it from Andrea. This piece is not meant to be shown. There are other pieces that are not only meant to be shown but are meant to be taken all over the place. I like working with contradictions: making completely private, almost secretive work on the one hand, and on the other, making work that is truly public and accessible. As we know, some so-called public art is really "outdoor art." Just because it's out on the street doesn't make it public.

Rollins: Getting back to how you make decisions. I wanted to ask you how you chose the blue that you use. What's the difference between your blue, Felix Gonzalez-Torres blue, and Yves Klein blue?

Gonzalez-Torres: First of all, my blue is not an international blue, as Yves Klein's was. Mine is just a light blue that you can get anywhere, in any hardware store.

Rollins: It's more specific. It's not just light blue.

Gonzalez-Torres: Actually, I change it all the time. It's a light blue that I change all the time.

Rollins: It's close to the blue the Italian architect Aldo Rossi uses; that's why I know.

Gonzalez-Torres: Really? It just has to be light blue.

Rollins: Okay. Why is it light blue? Is this a baby blue for boys? A robin's egg blue?

Gonzalez-Torres: It's more like a Giotto blue in the Caribbean—saturated with bright sunlight.

Rollins: It's lighter than Giotto's blue.

Gonzalez-Torres: But when you go out in the Caribbean sun, the colors get very washed out. It's almost like what Giotto's blue would look like in *Last Year at Marienbad*—a memory of a light blue. For me, if a beautiful memory could have a color, that color would be light blue. There's a lot of positive dialectic, you know, in blues.

Rollins: It's very baby blue, you know, the blue of your first flannel blanket—if you're a boy. You don't use a royal, rich, velvety blue; you use this innocent blue.

Gonzalez-Torres: That's a good word for it—an innocent blue.

Rollins: Is it a gay blue?

Gonzalez-Torres: No. You know, I really didn't have much of an investment in light blue as a kid because we didn't have that kind of luxury of choice. You just got whatever you got: either blue or pink or whatever. If you got a blanket at all, you were lucky—forget about what color it is.

Rollins: You paint whole walls with it.

Gonzalez-Torres: Yes.

Rollins: So it's a big deal.

Gonzalez-Torres: I love blue skies. I love blue oceans. Ross and I would spend summers next to a blue body of water or under clear, Canadian blue skies.

Rollins: I've heard a lot of grumbling, Felix, about the lack of an overt political or Latino content in your work.

Gonzalez-Torres: (laughing) Well, I just want to start by saying that the "maracas" sculptures are next! I'm not a good token. I don't wear the right colors. I have my own agenda. Some people want to promote multiculturalism as long as they are the promoters, the circus directors. We have an assigned role that's very specific, very limited. As in a glass vitrine, "we"—the Other—have to accomplish ritual, exotic performances to satisfy the needs of the majority. This parody is becoming boring very quickly. Who is going to define my culture? It is not just Borges and García Márquez, but also Gertrude Stein and Freud and Guy Debord—they are all part of my formation.

The best thing for me to do with those people is to ignore them, because I question someone who tells me what I'm supposed to do or be. I always feel like asking them why don't they do it? I think the same thing happened with you and K.O.S. It's very elegant for some Calvinist critic to judge your project. Anyway, people criticize some of the contradictions—as if there are things in life that don't come with contradictions. Everything is part of a contradiction; there are just different levels of contradictions. You decided to do something, something other than just teach art to young kids. You decided to push the limits. It is very exciting to take something that is there in everyday life and create from it something out of the ordinary, to give that ordinary object or situation a new meaning with a great economy of means.

I had a problem just recently in Copenhagen, where I went to give a lecture. A man in the audience immediately started talking about winning the battle for multiculturalism. I said: "Look, okay, first I have trouble with that kind of language about winning battles. That's too male-oriented for me. That's too macho; that's too much about war." Then he said something about numbers—a certain amount of women, a certain amount of Hispanics, etc. No, multiculturalism is not about numbers, it's about inclusion. It's about opening up the terms of the argument, opening up the terms of the discourse so that everybody can participate on an equal footing. It's not about naming two females, three Hispanics, four whites, five blacks. It's not about quotas. Sometimes quotas are necessary when it comes to concrete things like businesses, but in culture it's more complex. It's about opening up the terms of the argument, and it's about readdressing the issue of quality and who dictates and defines "quality."

It's funny what you said earlier about books, about trying to escape the world. That's very true. Where I come from, there were no books. My father only went up through the fifth grade and my mother was a housewife—there were never books. The first book that came to my house was a Bible. That was the first book I came in contact with.

Rollins: The "Text of Texts."

Gonzalez-Torres: That's right. It was an illustrated Bible. And I have to say, the illustrations were really beautifully perverse: images of Christians being fried in hot oil and things like that. I mean, people being fried alive in oil! Imagine what that can do to the mind of a six-year-old kid. "Pro-family" values are so perverse; their negation of sex is all about an obsession with it. In other words, it's all about sex. Raw. The sexual thing, the guilt, the fear—it's very Latino. Which then makes sexuality even more exciting by means of repression.

Rollins: It's New England Baptist, too. It's universal.

Gonzalez-Torres: It's universal. But I never really grew up surrounded by those things, as some people have assumed. So I don't know what they look like. I don't know the ghetto. I have never lived in the jungle, and I despise altars. I grew up in San Juan, which is like a small New York City without subways. So when people say, "Oh, you should be doing this. You should be looking like that," I really think that that expectation comes from guilt. It comes from expecting us to wear grass skirts. They don't really know what we're about. They don't know about our experiences, how hybrid we all are. They are stuck with images from *National Geographic* circa 1950. These assumptions are rooted in ignorance and in a condescending attitude.

Rollins: It wasn't like you were standing in line at Roseland or Casa Galicia.

Gonzalez-Torres: No. Once I started becoming aware of feminist issues I became very suspicious of salsa music. Some of the lyrics are too heterosexual, too pro-family, and too sexist. I never liked salsa much except for Celia Cruz and some other Cuban musicians. I like black music, deep-house music, and rock more than anything else. Salsa never really hit me in the right spot. But I do love La Lupe—my idol!

Rollins: Some artists regress with success. When do you get to the point that you make what you want to make as opposed to making what you think you need to make, or what society needs to have out there? This is the dialectic or contradiction that Brecht suffered as well. All artists who are interested in social change labor under the tyranny of necessity.

Gonzalez-Torres: How do I define the need? It could be a personal need and/or a political need. I'm a person who lives in this society, and I'm a product of this society and this culture. I'm not only a reflection; I'm that culture itself, and therefore whatever I make... I hope that everything that I make is needed by my culture. I always think that when culture foregrounds something, it is because it is needed. It could be an idea, an object, whatever. It could have been there for a long, long time, but it is only when culture feels that it is ready that this object or idea becomes important.

I always tell my students that as cultural producers we should be very aware of what the culture is doing. We must read the newspaper; we should watch the news; we should be finding out what is new, because even if we don't take them on as issues, that stuff will affect us one way or another. For example, what is happening right now in Yugoslavia with men in uniform killing innocent people, I think that should also be part of the studio. I think that should also be a part of your "inspiration" the way that the horror of being the homeless person down on the street should also be part of your life. Artists should be well informed.

Rollins: Your work reminds me so much of arte povera*—using industrial materials and making arrangements on the floor. On one hand, there's something free and casual about it. On the other hand, it's clean, it's printed, it was farmed out to industrial shops. The workers who made this stuff have no real connection to what you are doing. You buy, let's say, a hundred dollars worth of paper, print something simple on it, and sell it for eight thousand dollars as fine art. So you're involved in that nexus of profit yourself.*

And even though everyone is invited to take a sheet of paper from the stack, there will be a collector who will buy the entire stack and have it in their house where dinner guests are privileged to take sheets. The mechanisms of the market can turn works of art into novelty items. I was curious to know what you thought about that contradiction.

Gonzalez-Torres: For me, it makes a lot of sense to be part of the market. It would be very expected, very logical and normal and "natural" for me to be in alternative spaces, but it's more threatening that people like me are operating as part of the market—selling the work, especially when you consider that, yes, this is just a stack of paper that I didn't even touch. Those contradictions have a lot of meaning, as we know.

Rollins: I think your knowledge of manual labor comes from something.

Gonzalez-Torres: It comes from serving too many plates of spaghetti as a waiter, I guess! The contradictory use of hiring manual labor comes from the need to keep a healthy distance from the work. I'm for pushing the limits. I love it when people say: "But it is just paper. It is just two clocks next to each other. It is just lightbulbs hanging." I love the idea of being an infiltrator. I always said that I wanted to be a spy. I want my artwork to look like something else, nonartistic yet beautifully simple. I don't want to be the opposition because the opposition always serves a purpose: "Improve your arms against me." But if you're the spy—always "straight acting," always within the system—you are the person that they fear the most because you're one of them, and you become impossible to define.

Rollins: By giving an interview like this are you being a "good spy"?

Gonzalez-Torres: I think so. I'm always shifting. There is also a lot of power and threat in that. This type of work, the stacks, has this image of authority, especially after so many years of conceptual art and minimal art. They look so powerful, they look so clean, they look so historical already. But in my case, when you get close to them, you realize that they have been "contaminated" with something social.

Rollins: You are a political person, yet you're very concerned with form, and you're not apologetic about it.

Gonzalez-Torres: I love formal issues. Actually, they have a very specific meaning. Forms gather meaning from their historical moment. The minimalist exercise of the object being very pure and very clean is only one way to deal with form. Carl Andre said, "My sculptures are masses and their subject is matter." But after twenty years of feminist discourse and feminist theory, we have come to realize that "just looking" is not just looking, but that looking is invested with identity: gender, socioeconomic status, race, sexual orientation. Looking is invested with lots of other texts.

Minimalist sculptures were never really primary structures; they were structures that were embedded with a multiplicity of meanings. Every time a viewer comes into the room, these objects became something else. For me, they were a coffee table, a laundry bag, a laundry box, whatever. So I think that saying that these objects are only about masses is like saying that aesthetics are not about politics. Ask a few simple questions to define aesthetics: whose aesthetics? at what historical time? under what circumstances? for what purposes? and who is deciding quality? Then you realize suddenly that aesthetic choices are politics. Believe it or not, I am a big sucker for formal issues, and, yes, someone like me—the Other—can indeed deal with formal issues. This is not a white-men-only terrain. Sorry, boys.

Rollins: How do you go about making the "portraits"?

Gonzalez-Torres: As you know, in our culture we read photographs in two ways: by what's denoted and by what's connoted. The denoted is pretty obvious: color or black and white, a photo of a person or of a building, a portrait or a landscape. The connoted are all the other characteristics that we bring to the reading of an image according to our particular historical formation and position. So when you look at a portrait photograph of someone you don't know, you pretty much bring your own connotations to a denoted set of characteristics. In other words, from an image you switch to language, which is the only way we humans can "read" an image. In these portrait pieces, I try to reverse the process. I start with language and then I ask the viewer to provide an image.

I start a portrait by asking the person to give me a list of important events in his or her life—intensively personal moments which outsiders have very little knowledge of or insight into. Then I add some relevant historical events that, in more ways than one, have probably altered the course of and the possibility for those supposedly private or personal events. These portraits are always changing, and whoever owns them can alter, add, or take out information. They usually get painted directly on the wall, way up close to the ceiling, all around the room like a frieze.

Rollins: What is the function of duplication and repetition in your work? The stacks of paper or piles of candies that, through accumulation, comprise a work are internal forms—each individual piece of paper or piece of candy exists as a piece on its own. But they also exist as external forms when you place identical pieces in different sites and contexts.

Gonzalez-Torres: All these pieces are indestructible because they can be endlessly duplicated. They will always exist because they don't really exist, or because they don't have to exist all the time. They are usually fabricated for exhibition purposes and sometimes they are fabricated in different places at the same time. After all, there is no original, only one original certificate of authenticity. If I am trying to alter the system of distribution of an idea through an art practice, it seems imperative to me to go all the way with a piece and investigate new notions of placement, production, and originality.

In terms of different contexts, that's a very complex issue that needs to be nailed down to a more specific example. As we know, context gives meaning. The language of these pieces depends, to a large degree, on the fact that they get seen and read in art contexts: museums, galleries, art magazines.

Rollins: Are the works a metaphor for the relation between the individual and the crowd?

Gonzalez-Torres: Perhaps between public and private, between personal and social, between the fear of loss and the joy of loving, of growing, of changing, of always becoming more, of losing oneself slowly and then being replenished all over again from scratch. I need the viewer; I need the public interaction. Without a public these works are nothing, nothing. I need the public to complete the work. I ask the public to help me, to take responsibility, to become part of my work, to join in. I tend to think of myself as a theater director who is trying to convey some ideas by reinterpreting the notion of the division of roles: author, public, and director. Your question is more puzzling to me than I had previously thought because, yes, an individual piece of paper from one of the stacks does not constitute the "piece" itself, but in fact it is a piece. At the same time, the sum of many pieces of the identical paper is the "piece," but not really, because there is no piece—only an ideal height of endless copies. As you know, these stacks are made up of endless copies or mass-produced prints. Yet each piece of paper gathers new meaning, to a certain extent, from its final destination, which depends on the person who takes it.

Rollins: Do you attach sentiment to your mass-produced materials? For example, your works are often untitled, but then you go ahead and make some evocative reference that becomes part of the piece's "titlelessness."

Gonzalez-Torres: No, I don't attach sentiment to mass-produced materials or objects; they already have it. I just make them obvious. Sometimes I feel very democratic about the stacks—things you can take—but sometimes I feel very stingy. Sometimes I want the thing to hang on the wall and I don't want anyone to touch it. I want this pristine, beautiful object that is just there. Sometimes I do have the desire to be democratic, of affecting people, of moving people to a different place with knowledge, pleasure, love, inspiration.

Rollins: Do you think that has a lot to do with distribution?

Gonzalez-Torres: Absolutely. It's very beautiful when the work changes by being placed in different contexts. A page or stack in a gallery reads differently from one you see in an artist's studio or one you see in a home or museum. I once went to the employees' toilet in a museum in Germany and found one of my pieces, *Death by Gun*, pinned to the door of the toilet stall. The employees told me that they loved reading about all those people's violent deaths while they were sitting. It helped them "go."

Rollins: A laxative.

Gonzalez-Torres: That's another function of my work that I hadn't really ever envisioned, you know!

Rollins: You've had your revenge on Benjamin, in a way, because those individual works do have an aura. Benjamin claimed that a reproduction of a work of art could not have the aura of the original, one-of-a-kind piece, but you made a work of art that is an original reproduction.

Gonzalez-Torres: I never agreed with that. The reproductions or facsimiles of the original always point toward the source of emission—the "real" thing. And as signposts to the original, they become desirable.

Rollins: Isn't the stack the original in a way? It's the book instead of the page?

Gonzalez-Torres: It's always the original because in my case there is no original—the stacks are endlessly reproducible editions.

Rollins: You know, celebrities deal in aura. The pop star, the person, becomes the original object. They don't call them stars for nothing. It's about this light that they generate. People rush to a concert even though they've heard the record a million times. They go not so much to hear the music but to see the words coming out of the mouth of the human "star." The stack is a star in a funny way.

Gonzalez-Torres: I never saw it like that. That's interesting.

Rollins: Engels thought it was a law that any increase in quantity necessitates a decrease in quality. The great challenge to our generation is to find a work that's popular and democratic but doesn't kiss butt, doesn't pander. It's a supremely difficult task.

Gonzalez-Torres: It's a very tight rope, and I think one way of going about it is by being flexible and by saying, "Okay, sometimes I'm going to be democratic. Sometimes I'm going to do a billboard that is just text about health care, and the next time I just want to do a billboard that is about something perhaps more obscure that I need to see in public." I do have a political and personal agenda with this work, and in a way they are very interrelated, but I haven't been able to find a perfect union for both. So in the meantime I do both things. It feels very satisfying, in a perverse way, to be working on different fronts: not to have a style, not to be easily defined, not to be easily named.

Rollins: What about the situation where you have somebody like Sigmar Polke whose stylelessness, like Picasso's, becomes a style. How do we deal with that?

Gonzalez-Torres: That's a good point. I was just thinking about the fact that I don't like to be photographed and how suddenly that becomes a persona. You know, the artist that doesn't like to be photographed.

Rollins: Works like a charm.

Gonzalez-Torres: Right, I know. Still, there are contradictions within everything, but I think that I would rather live with that particular contradiction: the not-photographed persona. To have a nonstyle is risky, but at the same time, it's more liberating for me. I just can't get up in the morning and do the same goddamn work.

Rollins: Do you see a correlation between minimalism and Vietnam?

Gonzalez-Torres: Oh, absolutely. That work could only have been made because of the extreme positions that Vietnam created. Cultural or, in this specific case, artistic production is not only related to cycles of fashion but to larger social situations. The horror of the Vietnam War was being brought to American homes nightly via television. There is no way one can evoke that inferno through any other means of representation. Perhaps film can come slightly closer. The minimalists' answer to the social, political, sexual, and cultural upheaval of the time was to produce rather shocking objects of art that even today don't look like art at all.

In another example of social movements affecting artistic production, during the eighties, parallel to the vital and progressive cultural critiques of artists like Louise Lawler, Barbara Kruger, Jenny Holzer, Cindy Sherman, and Sherrie Levine, we had a very scary return of the bohemian painter, as if twenty years of an intellectual and conceptually based artistic practice had never existed. This was a very dangerous, anti-historical, anti-intellectual movement that served, very clearly, the needs of an artificially wealthy new clientele who wanted some art to decorate their new lobbies, apartments, and (now empty) offices.

It doesn't take a rocket scientist to figure out that a Holzer or a Kruger will not improve business. You don't want to remind stock traders about moral issues; you want to give them some color, to make them feel good so they can commit crimes with a happy face. And so they did. Unfortunately, we will end up paying for all that. Cultural production and socioeconomics are intertwined; either you do work for it or against it. There is never such a thing as an apolitical or inert artwork. Art always serves a function—it either furthers and helps the master narrative or it tries to disrupt it. And it should also be underlined that the reactionary forces that ruled us for the last twelve years are still very active, just waiting to strike back and impose once more their agenda of homophobia, sexism, racism, and divisiveness. Their exclusionary practices are being perfected as we speak. We should never underestimate their vicious power and violence. By the way, Tim, I always say that Group Material is the best-kept secret in the art world.

Rollins: I think the problem with Group Material is that they operated outside of the art market. A lot of people claim that they hate the commercialism of the art galleries, but if you're not visible in those mainstream venues, you're invisible.

Gonzalez-Torres: That's why I make objects. Otherwise, I would be doing performances. But aside from the objects, I love the process more than that final product. That's what I love the most. But I understand the rules of the game: you have to circulate an object in the market in order to have a more direct access to power. I've been waiting for the revolution for a long time and it hasn't come. The ones that have come have done very little to change our ways. Therefore, I don't want a revolution anymore; it's too much energy for too little. So I want to work within the system. I want to work within the contradictions of the system and try to create a better place. I think revolutions were a really nice idea in the nineteenth century and in the early part of this century, but we must take into consideration the technological advances that are being made right now. These technological shifts are happening in a world that has become very fragile and also very small.

Rollins: I know you consider teaching to be an important element of your work. What would you like to see come out of your students?

Gonzalez-Torres: I'd like them to be generous. I don't know what I'd like them to be. I know exactly what I don't want them to be—I don't want them to be self-indulgent. I would like to see them involved with the process of working in addition to being involved in the final product. More than anything, I would just like them to be happy.

Rollins: That is the philosophy of a good parent.

Gonzalez-Torres: I think happiness comes from knowing what you want to do. I don't want to discuss the objects that much. I think the issues, the processes, the needs, and the pleasures around the works are more important.

Rollins: You've taught at several colleges, right? Doesn't it disturb you that there are so few Spanish-speaking students?

Gonzalez-Torres: When I went to art school at New York University, there weren't any Hispanics around except for the elevator man. When I started to teach at N.Y.U. in 1987, I used to joke that the elevator man's name got onto the teacher's list by accident. On the list of fifty-five teachers, I had the only Hispanic-sounding name.

Rollins: So obviously that bothers you.

Gonzalez-Torres: Of course it bothers me. As a young man I didn't think that being an artist was a viable thing to do because there were not many role models. Now that has changed, and it is great to see the variety of voices. I see the practice of teaching as an integral part of my work. Teaching for me is a form of cultural activism, a form of creative change at a very basic level, and it is a way of redeeming the profession of art teaching. As a student you always got these teachers telling you what is right and what is wrong without any doubt or questioning. I want my students to learn the tools of critical thought and to always doubt, to learn how to doubt themselves and to be self-critical. Only through acts of self-criticism are we able to discern which work is better or worse, hopefully. It's based on the Brechtian model. It is not about good or bad. You try to give them the ability, the tools, to see for themselves what is important, what is needed, what is moving, and what is not. I also make very clear to them that they should not trust me—I'm not the voice of authority. I make mistakes, I might be wrong. I do have a very clear agenda, and that is a desire to make this place a better place, and I'm an artist; that is the position where I speak from. But I'm an artist who tries to redefine the role of the artist. I see myself as an instigator, someone who questions not only the function of the art object and the practice but also the act of teaching art. Is it valid to teach art in the late twentieth century? I constantly question my voice, my opinions, my suggestions. What do I know? I don't give my students the comfort of expecting me to be the voice of knowledge, the father, the master narrative. Even if I wanted to, I couldn't.

I had some Hispanic students at CalArts [California Institute of the Arts] and at N.Y.U. Some were great and some were not. I expect more from them than from other students. Coming from that background, you know, there is a lot of struggle, a lot of fights. Things are not easy, but you shouldn't let those temporary things stop you. You should work harder. It's very easy to say, "Poor little me." It's just too easy to feel sorry for yourself—that's what some folks want us to do. They want us to roll over. The only thing they want to hear from us, through our art, is how difficult life is for us, the Others. Hawaiians had to wear grass skirts in *Hawaii Five-O* to make white folks happy. Never mind that our lives are more complex than altars, palm trees, colorful landscapes, and gangs. Never mind that we already had universities when some of your ancestors were sitting at a table thanking God for pumpkins and turkeys.

I also want to make sure I'm not romanticizing the American Dream, especially now after twelve years of trickle-down economics in which one percent of the American population owned as much as the bottom ninety percent. All I want to say is that I always expect much more from my minority students. I always tell them we have to work against two negatives: First, we have to prove we're not bad, but that's not enough; after that, we must prove we are good. When we come into a room, we are automatically bad. When someone like you, white, comes into a room, you are given the benefit of the doubt. We don't get that benefit; we are already suspicious—bad.

Rollins: I keep thinking that if we were doing this dialogue ten years from now, I honestly think we would be doing it in Spanish. That would be real progress because everybody would be able to read it.

Gonzalez-Torres: I had a problem with the idea of making this book bilingual. Why does my book have to be bilingual? Why not the other books in this series?

Rollins: I think we're more interested in making America bilingual. Making art is obviously some sort of offering to somebody somewhere. Would you agree with that? Would you agree that to make a work of art is to assert a belief in meaning? Maybe even to assume the presence, existence, of God?

Gonzalez-Torres: Let's get out of the area of God quickly! I have a major problem with the cultural traps and constructions of God. I think that it is a good excuse for us to accept any kind of situation as natural, inevitable. Once we believe that there is no God, that there is no afterlife, then life becomes a very positive statement. It becomes a very political position because, then, we have no choice but to work harder to make this place the best place ever. There is only one chance, and this is it. If you fuck it up this time, you've fucked up forever and ever. Therefore, God becomes a kind of lollipop you give people: "Look, you are suffering now in this life. I'm making you feel and live miserably. I'm making things really horrible for you, but in the next life things will be better—believe me, and believe in God."

Once you agree that there is not any other life, that there's nothing except here—this thing, this table, you, me—that's it. That becomes a very radical idea because you have to take responsibility to make it the best. By the way, just recently—350 years after Galileo found that the earth moves around the sun—the Vatican accepted their "small mistake" and admitted that the earth really does move around the sun. Galileo, after all, was right. It only took them 350 years to get rid of this dogma! Pity, it could be so funny except that they have so much power, hate, and dogma.

Rollins: So what role does art play in that?

Gonzalez-Torres: It leaves a mark. It leaves a statement that you were here, that perhaps it is possible to have a different view of life.

Rollins: Why bother?

Gonzalez-Torres: I think one of the reasons I made artwork was for Ross.

Rollins: And for your audience? The public? The people that come to see your shows?

Gonzalez-Torres: I also make art to describe how I feel about other issues that are outside the so-called private sphere.

Rollins: I've rarely seen an artist that loves his audience as much as you do.

Gonzalez-Torres: You have to start by loving what you have at home. You don't go out and preach if your house is not in order—you cannot preach a new social order. And going back to the question of why make an art object, I must also add, it is a way of working out my position within this patriarchal culture. I recently saw a very traumatic photograph of a Yugoslavian soldier beating and kicking the bodies of two dead Muslim women. This soldier is a man who probably has a god, a man who performs his duty, a family man, a hero. And of course, these are all my connotations of this photo based on the preconceptions of our own Western, Judeo-Christian culture. How do I process that picture?

Another reason why I make works of art is to try to get that out of my system in a healthy way. Here is a family man who has the kind of respect that I, as a gay man, will never have. How do I deal with a culture that will give him a medal of honor? How? In a way, I'm trying to negotiate my position within this culture by making this artwork. What am I supposed to do? How am I supposed to feel? Who am I supposed to identify with? And finally, above all else, it is about leaving a mark that I existed: I was here. I was hungry. I was defeated. I was happy. I was sad. I was in love. I was afraid. I was hopeful. I had an idea, and I had a good purpose, and that's why I made works of art. Maybe, given enough time, I'll think, "Yes, well, maybe it has to do with the denial of God—that I tried to negotiate the fact that there is no God." Right now, I don't think I'm consciously involved in any notion of God. I hope.

Rollins: It's a big problem, you know.

Gonzalez-Torres: Really?

✦

Mike Kelley
interviewed by JOHN MILLER, 1991

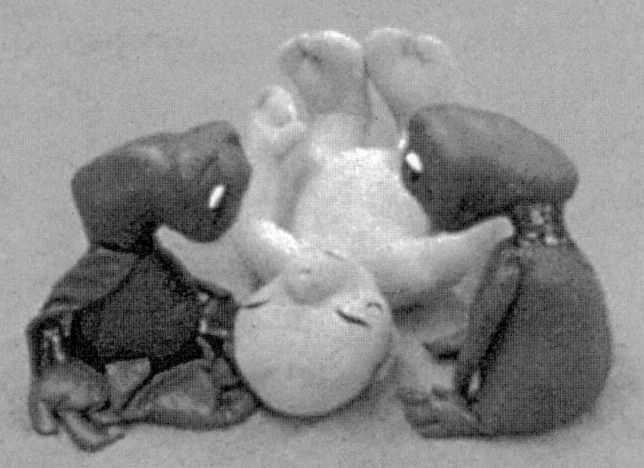

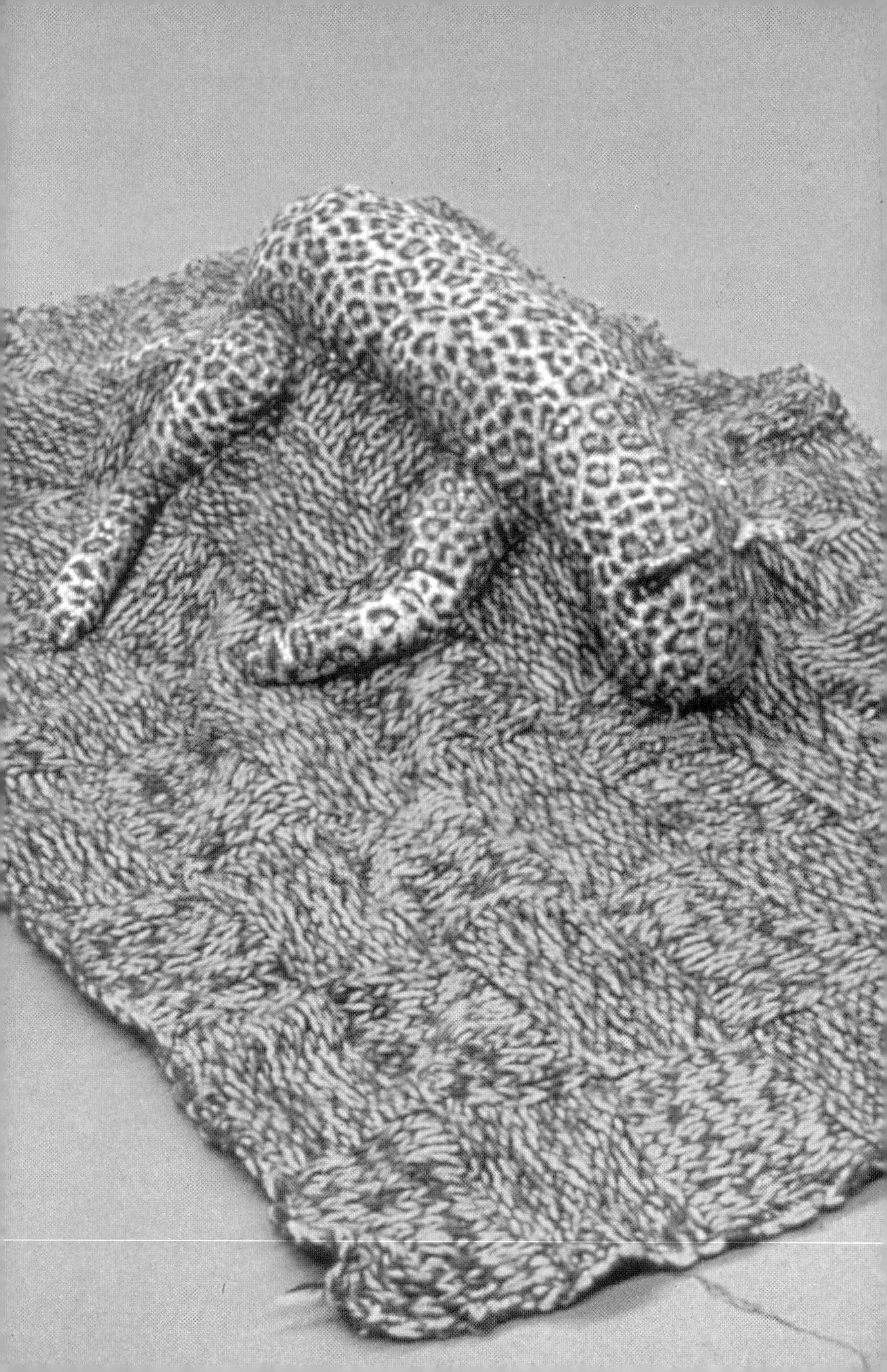

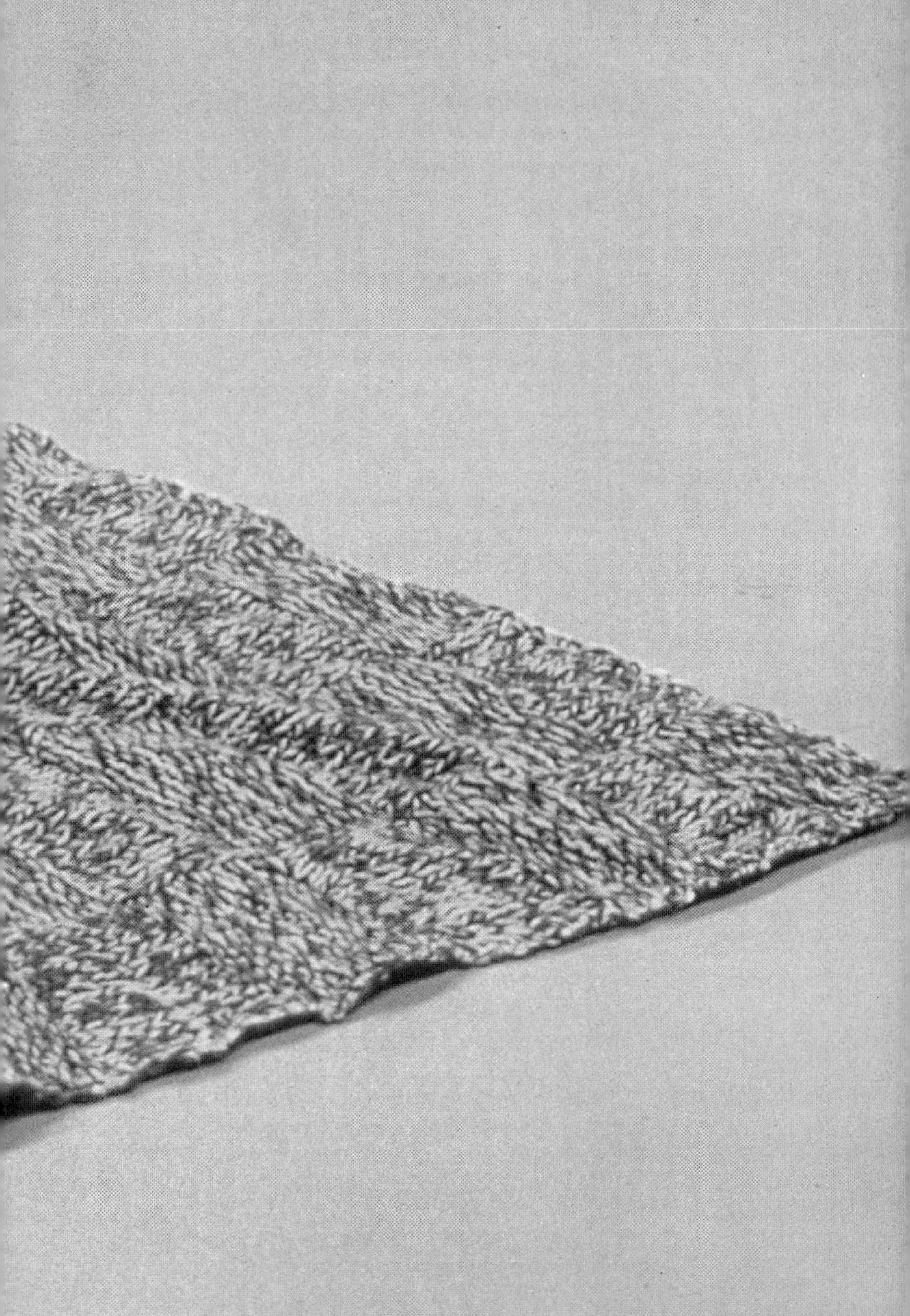

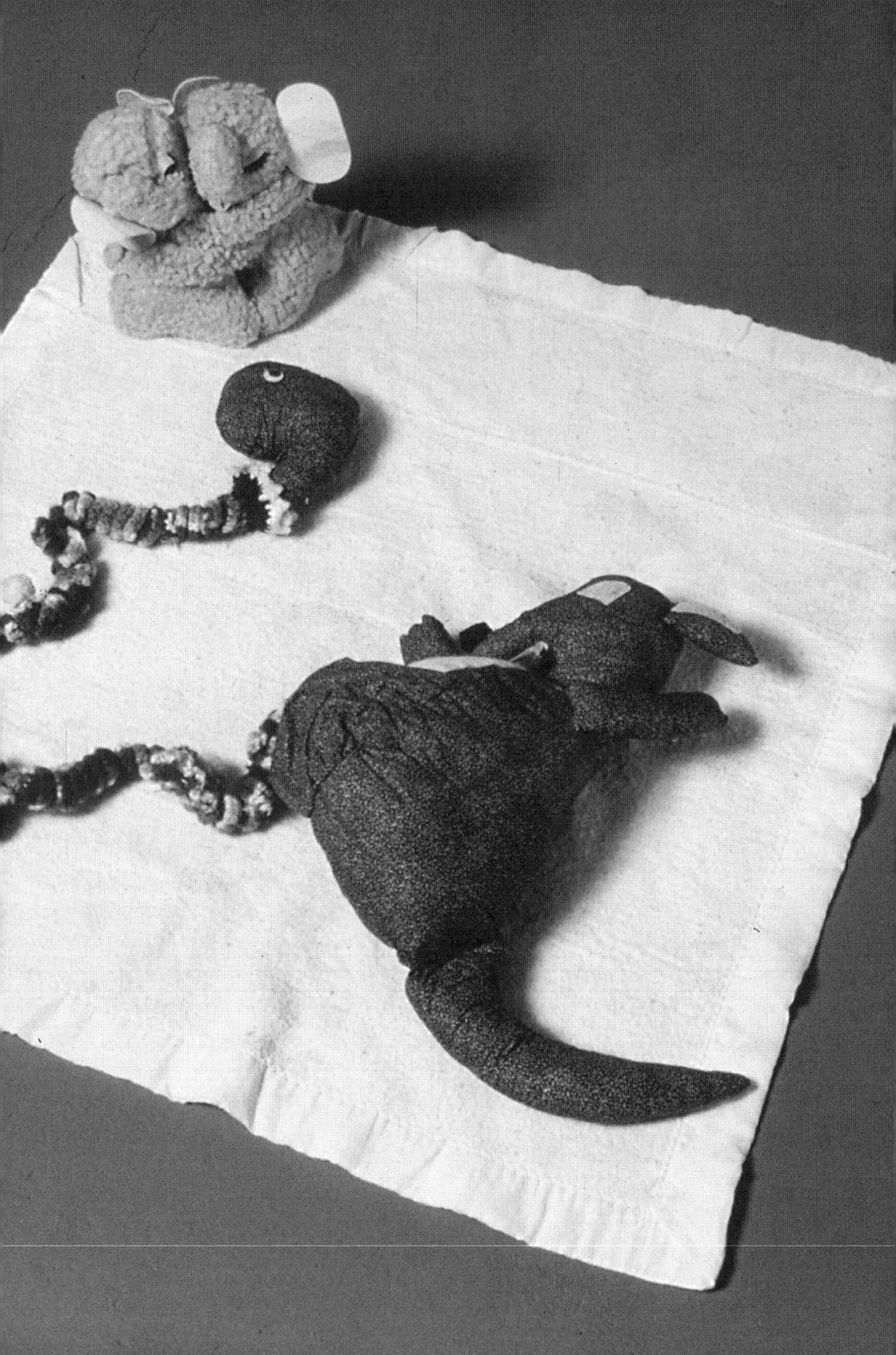

Mike Kelley
interviewed by
John Miller

John Miller: Why don't we start by going back to the birdhouse sculptures you made for your graduate show at CalArts [California Institute of the Arts, 1978]. As a theme for a sculpture series, a birdhouse is almost ridiculously unprepossessing. It's a miniature house and it's for a bird. The anthropomorphizing of the bird is so silly that it undercuts ordinary architectural expectations, monumentalism especially.

Mike Kelley: Those birdhouses were very popular—Richard Armstrong, who was then the curator at the La Jolla Museum, saw the show and that resulted in my having a show there soon after graduation. I think even though the birdhouses were ridiculous, they were acceptable within the terminology of the time because they were reductive, they were primary structures of a sort, whereas the paintings I had been doing up until that time were totally unacceptable in any *art* kind of way.

Miller: But they played on a kind of reductivism other than reducing to an essence; their reductivism was a diminishment of some other form.

Kelley: They reduced to a cliché. The reason that I started doing them was that I wanted to get away from my drawing methodology. I was originally trained as a formalist in the Hans Hoffmann tradition at the University of Michigan: sort of half-push-pull theory and half-automatist. So my work was a strange hybrid of styles, sort of like Sigmar Polke, who I was unfamiliar with then: a style later termed "postmodern." I was confused as to whether I was engaged in a strictly formalist practice of bouncing different styles together—popular imagery and gestural painting—or whether there was some sort of allegorical impulse at work, or whether I was interested in the meanings of these styles at all.

page 103:
Arena #5 *(detail), 1990, found stuffed animals, blanket, 97 x 87 inches*
pages 104–105:
Arena #8 *(detail), 1990, found stuffed animal, blanket, 69 x 47 inches*
page 106:
Arena #2 *(detail), 1990, mixed media, blanket, 40 x 44 inches*

The reason that I first started doing the birdhouses was to do something that I thought at the time was blank, to clear my mind. A lot of that had to do with the expectations of CalArts: that kind of reductivist conceptualist aesthetic led to the making of blank things.

Yet the only things that I could think of as "blank" were crafts. In my suburban working-class background, the most invisible things were crafts. So I decided to do some work that I thought was totally outside of myself, or anti-allegorical, and that was to just build something out of a how-to manual that would require lots of time. So the first couple of birdhouses that I made were from how-to manuals. As far as I could see, they didn't have anything to do with me at all. Of course, as soon as I started to make them, I realized they did have something to do with me.

Miller: So you ended up not only having a reductive object, but the normally "heroic" process of making art was reduced to craft. Even though there may not necessarily be much material difference between art and craft, I think the distinction turns on what an audience is led to invest in a certain set of objects or a certain set of practices, and those become adequate sublimatory vehicles. In a way, you were confounding those expectations, parodying them.

Kelley: Yes, I definitely was. But at the time, everybody talked about them as some sort of flip of minimalism. As if minimalism was being inscribed onto some everyday object.

Miller: A use value.

Kelley: They talked about some of the oddball conceptualists, like William Wegman or Robert Cumming, the same way. It's only in the last couple of years that you hear any discussion about those works in the terms that we're using now: that the impulse to raise the status of things is the main sublimatory tactic of art. At the time, people would generally talk about the bird-houses as formal jokes. It was really frustrating to be stuck within the confines of formalism. Of course, I wasn't totally freed from that myself; I was schooled in that manner and to try to separate myself from it was difficult. I think it was only after I went through a long period of doing work that was dealing with the confusion of logic systems—like all the performances and the drawings—that I could go back to this craft material that I had not worked with for many years, and start to see it as both having a certain social edge, talking about certain social subjects, as well as being about failure or sublimation.

Before, people wouldn't consider sublimation as an aspect of art production except in some heady, Freudian way, like, "Oh, these bad impulses are being nicely put into this object," instead of saying maybe it's not so nice that these impulses are put into these objects. Maybe it's pitiful that all these energies are pumped into a birdhouse. That's what I realized I was going for, not some one-line joke like, "Here's a birdhouse that's minimalism." Rather, "Here's a structure that's loaded with pathos," and you still don't like it. You don't feel sorry for it; you want to kick it. That's what I wanted out of the thing—an artwork that you couldn't raise; there was no way that you could make it better than it was. Its function as *art* actually makes it more uncomfortable. A birdhouse is something that's normally "nice," but if it's *art,* then it becomes a problem, and it's not just simply about transposition. It's acceptable to see a Duchampian found object as an artwork, like the bottle rack, because there is something heroic about the art world that makes his bottle rack better than another bottle rack. That was never my intention. My intention was always to keep things on the same level, or reduce them to a lower level than the one they began with.

Miller: It implies a kind of dysfunction.

Kelley: Where art is some sort of interesting area where dysfunction is allowed.

Miller: Yvonne Rainer once said that one definition of art filmmaking was simply bad filmmaking; art writing is bad writing—right on down the line.

Kelley: Right, but it's *allowed* bad filmmaking; it's *allowed* bad writing. That's the interesting part of it. My early sculptures were an oddity, and I pretty quickly went back to doing two-dimensional works.

Miller: But they foreshadowed your later concerns. Also, I don't think you broke with craft completely because much of your early sculpture doubled as props in your performances. There was still this idea of making something that implied some kind of use, another life.

Kelley: They were useful objects.

Miller: The performance objects became more didactic, and they alluded to things like science demonstrations or lecture props.

Kelley: That was the purpose of them. I mean, interestingly, it was sculpture that led me to writing. I had never been able to write before, and when I think back about it now, it was perhaps that painting is more analogous to writing. So if you're painting all the time, maybe you lose the ability to verbalize. I don't know if it makes that much sense, but it's something that I think about. When I started making objects, I was suddenly able to verbalize in a way that I hadn't been able to before, simply by making something to talk about. So they were really props for verbalization.

Miller: They had a strong rhetorical component.

Kelley: The birdhouses developed quickly from ones that were built out of how-to manuals to ones that did become allegories. I realized, at that point, that my interest was more in that direction—how meaning is inscribed. I started building birdhouses that weren't birdhouses anymore but things that had double meanings or things whose functions needed explaining. Then I started building things that were demonstrational sculptures, and that's how the performances developed. The earliest performances were just groups of demonstrations of objects; by talking about them, their meanings changed. If you talked about them this way they meant this, and if you talked about them that way they meant that. It totally denied the whole notion of a primary structure. Then they started becoming subsumed by the language, and that's how the long performances developed where the language became the controlling factor and meanings changed by virtue of the change in language over time.

Miller: Unfortunately, none of your performances ever really got written about in any substantial way. They didn't fit into the shift from performance-as-ritual to performance-as-entertainment.

Kelley: I'm sort of lost in the midzone.

Miller: Well, your performances were entertaining, but they never aspired to be stand-up comedy, or to be theatrical in the usual sense.

Kelley: That's why I think I got written out of performance-art history. The people on the one end, who are in favor of a kind of agitprop or ritual-based performance, didn't like them, and people on the other side, the kind of East Village stand-up aesthetic, didn't like them either. So I got stuck in this weird middle group—the kind of late-structuralist performance people. They're just gone; they're written out of the history.

I was really influenced by Michael Smith's early performances and somewhat by Stewart Sherman. I also liked Julia Hayward's work, Guy de Cointet, Vito Acconci, and Matt Mullican's performances. Earlier, I'd also seen a lot of—I don't know what to call it—kitsch stuff: early Pat Oleszko and the Cockettes. I was familiar with that really low stuff, and with the traditional tactics of the counterculture: to use the worst and trashiest stuff that the main culture abhors. At the same time, I didn't like the ghettoization of that. Maybe it was my school-bookish side, but I wanted my work to be hard to swallow, even if it was low—that it wouldn't be fun. It probably comes from my Catholic upbringing: everything has to be painful.

Miller: Your performances exuded a kind of black humor, but they were never terribly painful. They were bland and slightly distasteful, but not excruciatingly so.

Kelley: William Burroughs was somebody that I liked, as a student. I always hated the dry tone of surrealist literature. You could tell its associative qualities were programmatic. The great thing about Burroughs was that you could see all these references to stuff that you had grown up with: juvenile literature, pornography, science fiction, and detective novels. It's all scrambled and turned into a quite private thing—really morose and at the same time howlingly funny. It doesn't have those elements of teary-eyed expressionism. That quality is there, but it's intelligent.

Miller: Do you still keep notebooks and make lists of associations?

Kelley: Yes, I do. I still work that way, though I think in the early times, probably because of the CalArts scene, the work was much more fired by language. Now it seems equal parts note taking and language association, with parallel visual associations. I might make something just for the visual kick of it and then the writing comes afterwards.

Miller: The proportion of text to image has definitely diminished. But even without text the work is still enmeshed in word association.

Kelley: It's there, but it operates somewhat differently. I think, early on, it was about this intense running monologue excusing something. If you have a certain flow of language so convoluted that you can't make any sense out of it anymore, the object that it's associated with—that's going to be the thing that explains this morass of weird language. That becomes the excuse.

Miller: The rationale?

Kelley: The rationale, yes. Even if it doesn't make any sense, you assume it does. That's an interesting lead into why I started drawing in this flat, cartoonish manner. In the early days, I got lumped in with the discussion of East Village populism: "Oh, these are *cartoons*." It was never that.

Miller: The irony is that your vernacular was so localized that at first a lot of Europeans didn't get it. They didn't have a way in. Take Meditation on a Can of Vernors.

Kelley: That's a whole other problem about why Europeans didn't get my work. That has to do with cultural differences, too.

Miller: So even though you were drawing off of pop culture, it wasn't in a populist way. The allusions were pretty arcane—a lot of Americans don't know what Vernors is.

Kelley: But they were important allusions, I wasn't trying to produce a deep secret—I'm *telling* you about the image. You don't have to know what a can of Vernors is because I'll tell you what it is and how it transmutes through all these other things. People talked about the drawings as cartoons, but the way I thought of them was that they were just the most boiled-down way of imaging. This is how you picture something clearly, what you see when you look in a dictionary or a training manual. It has this authoritative look, so you could draw the most meaningless thing and it had this look of authority. The populist overtones really bothered me early on; I was afraid of being associated with pop art. I wanted people to think about how these images operated. I was always interested in work that when you first looked at it you said, "I know what that means," because it had this socialized veneer. That's why I don't like dadaist works or punk works: when you look at them, you are immediately repulsed. You see those works as being outside of you, attacking you. What I was trying to do was to have something that you looked at and said, "That's normal—that's me."

Miller: You meant to have the identification come first before you started screwing around with it.

Kelley: Right, I wanted people to fall into it first, and then go, "Something's wrong." But it's too late; you're already in there.

Miller: That's exactly how the syllogisms worked in the performance pieces. The whole point was to hit you over the head with a point that would ultimately be negated.

Kelley: The great thing about the performances (this was something that I learned by going from short things to very long things) was that the negation came through time. This was something that I also discovered in early modernist literature. I was really interested in the aspect of time in the writings of Gertrude Stein because there is a constancy of tone. You're always in the present, and she did it through reiteration, saying the same things over and over again, slightly reworded. What I liked—and this is something that you see in oral poetry, things that are prewritten like *The Odyssey*—is that they're always in the constant present. Perhaps because people have a short attention span, you can get away with illogical developments if you make them unfold over a long period of time. People will assume that it is logical because they can't remember what happened before. So in my performances, say, an hour into one, I would use the same terms, but I'd say something totally in opposition to what had been said half an hour earlier, and nobody would know.

Miller: Except eventually it would catch up with them.

Kelley: Well, they knew that something was wrong but maybe not exactly. It was funny because afterwards people would sometimes come up to me and say, "I really agree with you, like with what you said about … " And I would say, "But I said five things about …" And they'd go, "Oh, I thought you said this." And it became immediately apparent that they had just projected whatever they wanted to onto the information because I gave it to them in a logical form.

That's what I really liked about these performances. People got emotionally involved in them. All this stuff started pouring out of them, and it was all about themselves. If you told them it was all about their projections, they'd get angry. That was something that I thought was really important about my artwork, that the viewer had that kind of relationship with it. The viewer is ultimately responsible for any moral point of view, and responsible for becoming conscious that they're the ones who are taking a stand in relationship to it—it's not me preaching to them.

Miller: I think that really gets at the ideological function of art, the way traditional art is set up to invite investment or belief.

Kelley: Right, like the artist is some sort of guru who is going to tell you what to think. This is really why I hate agitprop work.

Miller: Exposing how a belief structure is projected is something that runs through all your work: the performances, the paintings, and the sculpture.

Miller: Why did you stop doing performance? I know that performance anxiety made you physically sick, but were there other reasons?

Kelley: The first reason was one of ghettoization—I didn't want to be thought of as a performance artist per se.

Miller: That's true. For a long time you were categorized as a performance artist.

Kelley: I never thought of myself that way, so I realized that if I was going to find acceptance as an artist, I had to do less performance. Also, the performances became longer and longer and more complex and sometimes took a year or two to make. And then, because they were so complex and long, they took half a year just to learn. So it became this incredible process of learning these performances and doing them. Because of the rules that I set for myself, they could generally only be done once. They became so psychologically draining that I found that I could only do one every couple of years—that was a reason. Another was that they were economically impossible, especially as the performance world dried up. I'd have to travel and do them night after night after night, and I didn't want to do that. I was an artist who did them for specific reasons within the body of my work. The final reason I quit was that the last body of work that I got involved in seemed less like a random project that could be ended at will, but a project that, once started, would almost never end. I mean the *Half a Man* project.

The *Half a Man* project was so much about large, social notions of sex. The performances before were about finality: I've reached the end of this search, and so now I'm just going to make some logic system that caps it, a ritualized coming to life and then death of this logic system. How do you end something that is part of the culture at large? So I find that I keep working longer and longer and longer. If I did a performance now, it would have to be *in* time, whereas I always thought of the earlier performance as being *out* of time. But if you're doing something in time, the work becomes more like a demonstration: I'm going to tell you what I think about psychosexual problems. That's my problem, I've been thinking that I would like to do another performance, but what would it be? A live demonstration? a live sex show? or something that has the overtones not of theater but of demonstration?

Miller: Elements of that crept into your last performance with its affinities to Jim Morrison.

Kelley: It was there somewhat, but still highly theatricalized.

Miller: There were also the silly, ritualistic sections.

Kelley: Parodied ritual.

Miller: "Performance art."

Kelley: And parodied psychodrama. What I'm thinking about now is more akin to psychodrama, yet the forms of psychodrama are so bankrupt that I felt

Kelley: I always said the performances were about belief systems. I thought of them as propaganda gone wrong. It's why at the time I was so interested in, and felt such a kinship with, Matt Mullican's work. He was somebody who used these given symbols and given social structures and tried to bring them to life.

Miller: The life of a stick figure.

Kelley: Right, or early Jenny Holzer—lists of truisms. I felt very close to that work because the form said "emotion," "belief," and the more you looked at it, the more you came to realize that it was your emotions and your beliefs coloring how you understood these things. And it was up to you to examine your own internalized belief system in order to look at another belief system. I think, as I progressed, I grew apart from those artists, but at that period I felt very close to them.

Miller: They've changed substantially, too.

Kelley: I think that after doing the performances for a number of years, and always denying that I had had a belief system of my own, it started falling apart. By the time I got to the *Plato's Cave, Rothko's Chapel, Lincoln's Profile* performance, I saw that certain themes came back again and again in my work. There's an ur-group of information that I was suppressing, and I was just playing with all these rationality systems, denying that there was some core of interest in my work. I think that's why I started going into this *Half a Man* work. There were really personal associations that I talk about in a more social way without having to fall into syllogisms and logic structures and things like that. I could start to bring in these materials that, for years, I wouldn't allow myself to use.

Miller: What would you say these repeated motifs and concerns were?

Kelley: I think they're really standardized kinds of repressed things in this culture—embarrassing things, like sexual dysfunction and the scatological. I started seeing throughout my work that a lot of these traditional, low-comedy forms and subject matter were operating. I wanted to start to deal with that in a more conscious way. I think that's why people say my work is more socially directed now. It's hard for me to say; I'm too involved in it. More recently, people have politicized my work. In much of the early work, I was accused of being apolitical or even of being a terrible person or a racist because I worked with inflammatory material and denied a point of view.

Miller: The works' politics couldn't be valorized.

Kelley: The art world has come around to being able to talk about dysfunction. Three years ago, nobody would talk about that. Now every other gallery in Soho has a show about the body, or dysfunction, or some kind of thing like that.

Miller: That's almost a direct result of the Helms controversy.

Kelley: Maybe so.

I could only do a parody. To tell you the truth, I'm at a loss at this time. What are the theatrical structures that would be of interest now? In the past, I was interested in the Vienna Actionists, which is a weird collusion of art and life and politics, yet, at the same time, totally staged. Some of it was incredible, yet you couldn't do those performances now; they'd look like hackneyed sex psychodrama. They also bear some relationship to the guerrilla theater at the time. Notions of psychological psychodrama and role-playing are considered dated now. I guess maybe I'm just older. When I was younger, I was willing to throw myself into a form and just struggle with it. Now I want to know more before I do something; I want to know what the parentheses are. I would be embarrassed to go in front of people now and do a performance because I don't have the commitment to do it. I don't want other people to sit through it if I can't sit through it. That's why I stopped.

Miller: Much of your work hits upon things that haven't been acknowledged, the anonymous side of what people do. By that I mean things like the recent trend for these little gridded display shelves that have been showing up in suburban kitchens with little seeds and little bits of things stowed away in old-fashioned bottles. No one has ever written about that stuff or talked about it. But in the Midwest…

Kelley: That *is* culture.

Miller: That is culture and that's what people do. There are billions of stores that sell things like that. It's odd that it's so pervasive, but people that write don't know about it.

Kelley: There's no history of it—it's amazing. There probably will be in fifteen years. Once that particular phase of craft goes out of style, then people will write monographs about it, but now you just can't see it. I think within five or six years someone will write a monograph about macramé or something—that's a dead culture, so it can be art. Dead things are art, basically.

Miller: In a sitcom you would show someone was a hippie by having him do macramé. But no one would show people putting little seeds into little bottles; it would be confusing.

Kelley: Or it's just about a class that the viewership comes from, so they would not accept that as a joke. A television sitcom can't make fun of the viewers; they don't like it. Actually, there is a character on *Mama's Family* that makes crafts. That shows me that as a form it's dead; it has reached the level where it's no longer acceptable. Every show there's something about this old matron making a toaster cozy or something.

When I first started working with crafts, they were invisible to me also. The first piece I did with stuffed animals, for example, wasn't even about stuffed animals but was about gifts. That was because the primary discussion in the art world at that time had to do with commodification. There were these utopian ideas being bandied about, "Well, we can make an art object that can't be commodified." What's that? That's a gift. If I give you this art thing, it's going to escape the evils of capitalism. Well, of course that's ridiculous, because if you give this thing to Junior he owes you something. It might not be money, but he owes you something. The most terrible thing is that he doesn't know what he owes you because there's no price on the thing. Basically, gift giving is like indentured slavery or something. There's no price, so you don't know how much you owe.

Miller: I think you're right, but that's more like a precapitalist formation, whereas late capitalism doesn't want people bound together—all transactions should be completely aloof and fast. For example, the Indian giver: when the Indians gave the white men peace pipes, they expected something in return. The traders just thought, "Great, we got something more." You could think of the dichotomy as being Indian giver/capitalist taker, because the logic works toward accumulation.

Kelley: Actually, I'm not thinking of capitalism in the broad sense. I'm thinking of it more in terms of the mentality of the proletariat, those people that work for a living.

Miller: For rituals where gifts or some token of thoughtfulness is required, get a card or a balloon: something dispensable.

Kelley: It's only dispensable as an object. That's not what the commodity is. The commodity is the emotion. The other thing is just a ritualized object that's applied to the commodity. What's being bought and sold is emotion. I did a piece called *More Love Hours Than Can Ever Be Repaid.* I said, "If each one of these toys took six hundred hours to make, then that's six hundred hours of love. And if I gave this to you, you owe me six hundred hours of love, and that's a lot. And it adds up because if you can't pay it back right away it keeps accumulating ..."

Miller: Interest.

Kelley: If I get together five hundred of these objects, you're bowled over. That's more love than you can ever pay back. So what? You're just fucked then. I wasn't even thinking about the objects as objects. I was thinking about them as just hours-of-attention.

Miller: That's what craft forms have come to signify. That was Thorstein Veblen's critique of John Ruskin and William Morris—that the Arts and Crafts movement was simply reverting to less efficient and less economical ways of doing things.

Kelley: What? By going back to hand ...

Miller: Hand binding books and printing with woodblocks.

Kelley: He missed the point. It's more efficient in some ways because it loads the object with all this intense, ritual energy.

Miller: That was his point. In his terminology, the distinction turned on it being a more conspicuous kind of consumption.

Kelley: But of course that doesn't work in relation to the family. Okay, say you give somebody this piece-of-shit thing. You can't say it's a piece of shit—it's all totally repressed. You've got to say, "Oh, that's wonderful!" That's the connection between the luxury item and the craft. The luxury item has the façade of worth; the craft doesn't require that at all. It could be the worst piece of junk in the world, but it's not allowed for you to talk about it as a piece of junk. This is an interesting thing, because in the fine art world you can make a junk sculpture—a gear welded to an old camshaft—yet it finds a certain amount of respect by virtue of its place in the economy. It's worth a lot of money because somebody says so.

Miller: That's because junk sculpture has been legitimized and formalized.

Kelley: In terms of the present economy, you can't even see it as junk anymore.

Miller: No, it functions like a traditional art object. It's been recuperated.

Kelley: Even so, its recuperation is filtered through those that can afford it. It's a fantasy object; it relates to the dream life associated with the world of the wealthy, whereas the craft item is of the more humble family, so all these dynamics are repressed.

Miller: Don't you think that all giving contains an element of aggression anyway? That's not specific to modernity.

Kelley: Yes, that aggression is obvious. But in terms of the family it's not so obvious.

Miller: Well, in the everyday life of the family it would be too painful.

Kelley: Right, it's too painful so you hide it. Anyway, after these craft objects accumulated for a while I started to become aware of them as discrete objects—the particular morphologies of them. This is where my formal training came back.

Miller: But it was coupled with a psychological interest.

Kelley: Yes, but I wondered what the psychology was. I could study them formally, and I understood how they operated socially, but I didn't understand the interrelationship between the two. Why is this object formalized in this way? That's what I'm interested in now.

Miller: That really comes out in the objects. They're so anonymous for being handmade; it's such a generic, repeated impulse. That becomes what's disturbing about them.

Kelley: And that they're so invisible.

Miller: I remember when you first started doing the arrangements on the blankets and the afghans, and you joked that they were like Haim Steinbach's sculpture.

Kelley: That's true. I was thinking a lot about Haim Steinbach when I did them, except I was trying to put all the things into them that I felt Haim left out of his. What I saw Haim Steinbach doing was working with the ideal—art about the commodity in terms of a classical notion of perfection. To do that, you have to separate the objects from the world, put them on a stage or in a frame, like theater or a movie. They are out of this world; that's how his shelves function. Then the objects never change. They're fetishized as being perpetually brand new. They're not allowed to wear out. What I wanted was to have something that was worn yet not nostalgic. That was my problem, because in the tradition of most modern art things, "worn" becomes a cypher for "time." In almost all junk sculpture past dada, that's true. It's even true in surrealism. Worn things become a metaphor for...

Miller: They become nostalgic.

Kelley: They become nostalgic. So the problem that I set for myself is to deal with something of our time that people can't see as being of our time; they can only see it as of the past: a child's worn toy. I wanted to say, "No, this thing isn't of the past. This thing's here right now." It's not some metaphor for childhood, this is something that an adult made. It was made maybe last week. If you're seeing it of the past, it's because you're meant to see it of the past. I'm interested in how that functions.

Miller: These craft items are supposed to be nostalgic by their very design.

Kelley: They're built to be nostalgic. That's intensified in crafts because they are made with outmoded production techniques. It produces a nostalgia for a lost economy. But other things, like dolls, have to do with a certain psychology of morphology which I don't quite understand. I know why they do certain things. I know why they always make the heads bigger than the bodies—those are the proportions of a baby. So the thing automatically produces the same problematic questions a baby does. Everything else is invisible in the object, its other particularities. They are probably even invisible to the makers. The things are designed to be projected onto as generically human. This is why they're so weird: I think they are unconscious projections of the maker. These objects are invisible, yet they have a strange aura, a very creepy aura, because all the decisions that go into their production are unconscious. These toys have a really strange presence, especially when you compare them to the commercially made ones that are standardized. The makers of the standardized things have gone through and excised anything that looks vaguely personal or idiosyncratic.

Miller: Or sexual. Except, if you think of the My Pretty Pony toys, the sexualization of a pony is displaced. There's the coy posture of the thing; it's given hair, and it's candy colored.

Kelley: It's so obviously repressed that it becomes superloaded. That's something that you can only get in a commercially made thing. That effect is produced through removal. Classical objects have that feel. Repression is built into classical objects—something's missing and that's their power.

Miller: That would seem to be their arch-sublimatory function.

Kelley: I think so.

Miller: A few months ago I met an artist [Spring Hurlbut] whose work deals with what gets repressed in classical architecture. She thinks that if you go back far enough, a column represents a sacrificial victim: the capital is the head; the fluted part is the torso and legs; and the pedestal, the feet. The idea that the Parthenon, for instance, might in some way stand for human sacrifice seems antithetical to Western civilization, but that shows the self-deceptive aspect of sublimation.

Kelley: In terms of this culture and the things that I grew up with, religious illustration and historical illustration were the classical things. Bible illustrations don't bear any relationship to the humans that you know, yet you read them as being perfectly human. So they have, at the same time, something that you aspire to, yet something that frightens you intensely. Their frightening aspect is in their perfection. That's also, I think, part of the frightening aspect of advertising: everything is perfect. You like it and at the same time it's scary because you know that there's all this stuff that's left out. That stuff that's left out is you.

Miller: Yes, you're always made to feel inadequate in comparison. If there's no feeling of absence, then you don't desire it.

Kelley: That seems to me the whole lie to the notion of beauty in art. If beauty is about the ideal, it is automatically about the frightful. That kind of simple-minded notion about the function of art misses the whole point. The real appeal of beauty is the sublime experience, not some intellectual thing. It's the kick you get from that which extends beyond the thing you see—that's the aesthetic kick.

Miller: Do you think of beauty as being synonymous with the sublime?

Kelley: Unless it's strictly about mores. If it's just totally about control, then I don't think it has to do with the sublime. If something is beautiful just because it's supposed to be, then it's just about acculturation. But if it's beautiful in some way that implies loftiness, it has got to have that edge of working against its boundaries.

Miller: It's funny with beauty. It's something that the middle classes want but that art critics won't talk about.

Kelley: It's a problematic term. It doesn't mean anything except in terms of other problems. A number of years ago, there was a lot of discussion among students at Art Center about the sublime. I think many of the students used the term as a euphemism for beauty. They really all wanted to make art that they thought of as beautiful, yet they knew that the terms are problematized to such an extent that they can't make a purely beautiful object. They refused to cope with the fact that beauty is a socialized thing, that you had to examine where the terms for beauty come from. I think they were longing for some inherent standard for beauty. Sublimation as a way to mystify something.

Miller: That's awful. Why don't we talk about the banners? They've been somewhat overshadowed by the stuffed animals lately, but they were the first time that you self-consciously…

Kelley: Used a craft idiom. I first used banners in *The Sublime* project. There were references in that work to the sublimation of nature through its personification. This is where the whole thing started.

Miller: Like a Mount Rushmore idea?

Kelley: Yes. The nineteenth-century aesthetic of the sublime is all about these grand landscapes and being lost in them. You could also think about the more modern interest in blowing the small up large: the electron microscope, for example.

I had an experience when I was young, when I worked as a janitor, that became the subject for my first banner. It was a very boring job, and I worked for long hours, and I would find myself fixating on small things and going through certain kinds of mind games in order to make the experience tolerable. For example, I'd be sweeping the floor, and I'd fixate on one little piece of dirt that I would be sweeping because I would be sweeping floors all night by myself. So I'd start to play games where I said this was the best piece of dirt—that one. So this piece of dirt becomes more and more important and aestheticized. You can start to go through this whole process of deification just by picking one thing out. (Also, the banners were linked to my Catholic school upbringing—banners were something you made in religion class.) So I cut a personified piece of dirt out of felt and glued it on a banner.

Miller: What was the title of that?

Kelley: *Janitorial Transcendence.* It functioned as a mop. When I finished cleaning, it could be unrolled and it would become this banner. So this process of mopping went through this sublimatory process and became this banner proclaiming a new deity.

After that, I did the *Plato's Cave, Rothko's Chapel, Lincoln's Profile* project, which initially started off as a project about the possessive—about how ascribing a quality of possession to something would equalize everything. Like, if I said that this was an exhibition of everything from Lincoln's house, it links all this random stuff that has no link except as a possible way to psychoanalyze Lincoln. Everybody asked me why I picked those three people. I made a whole list of possessives that were in common usage, and I just picked the three that sounded best together. There was no big, intellectual rationale for it. Those were the three that sounded good together. Then I wove a set of associations between them.

Miller: That's a bit like Raymond Roussel.

Kelley: Yes, in fact, Raymond Roussel was a big influence on me. *Plato's Cave* came about because I was asked to do a site-specific installation in the anchorage of the Brooklyn Bridge. When I went to see the space, it was like a cathedral—these huge, dark, brick rooms. Nothing could compete with that architecture. So that's when I decided that I would go for a heraldic effect and use very simple things. At the time, I was getting a little tired of my own restriction to black and white—I wanted to use color. Because I was primarily based in linguistic practices, I decided I would do monochrome paintings that could only be differentiated by their separate titles.

This evolved out of the notion of the possessive. I wanted to find out who named things. The piece started out as an exploration of who named what, who titled something. I started out trying to find out who was responsible for naming all the rock formations within various caves, and who named all the colors of commercial paints. They had these flowery names, like Rock Coral and Sapsucker and Irish Setter. That exploration fell apart pretty fast, but I was left with the interest in naming.

Miller: I remember when you had all those paint chips, but at the time I didn't connect that with how naming is patriarchal—how the father's name is handed down.

Kelley: Somebody named these things, and I was interested in that process. For caves it was pretty easy because generally the person that discovered the cave or commercialized it would name the rock formation based on what it reminded them of. But a professional namer is hired to name colors. I was interested in this whole idea of possession and naming. There were three sets of four monochromes—red, yellow, brown, and white—that were identical except for their names. One set was named after the "four races," because they were the colors generically given to the four races. Then another set was named after four analogous body fluids, analogous by virtue of color. Another set was just named after the names of the color chips that they were painted from.

I then went on to other banners that made a more overt reference to the religiosity of the space. I did a banner that was a self-portrait after the shroud of Turin, which is a kind of banner, and also a banner that was an artist's conception of Rothko's bloodstain. There's a great quote from one of his friends that the bloodstain left after he killed himself was his best stain painting, the most pregnant with meaning. I couldn't find a picture of it, so I had to do an artist's conception of the bloodstain. I did do a painting of the actual stain left from Lincoln's assassination. I was also interested in the fact that Rothko's color system was the same as the Christian color iconographies for Lent. He tended to use yellow and orange as a kind of transcendent color and purple as a passionate or moody color—complementaries.

The first felt banner I did in this series was called *Lent Felt,* which was an Easter banner in Rothko colors. Then from that I did two other banners in sort of elementary-school style. I wanted to use a standard American story and present it as a modernist Christian-style allegory: an illustration of the story of Lincoln studying by candlelight. It's an image of a book with a candle on it, *Lincoln's Beacon.* Then there was another felt banner called *Youth Aspiring to Glory.* It's a simplified image of an altar boy, his head represented by a small penny, as if he is aspiring to Lincoln's image. The joke is that Lincoln's profile is on the lowest monetary unit. Our greatest president is on the lowliest coin. The banner looks like a pinhead, an altar boy with a pinhead.

Next, I did a whole show of banners in various themes. By that time I had become very interested in the use of the banner in contemporary Christianity, how modernism had been co-opted by the church. Historically, modernism was very much a break from the past and self-consciously anti-religion, and yet you see Calder and Matisse become the prototypes for contemporary Christian art.

Miller: So you make their intermarriage a kind of double blasphemy.

Kelley: Fine arts blasphemed and Christian arts blasphemed, and all in one swift blow.

Miller: Modernist churches are true kitsch and, of course, the attempt to make modernism spiritual is...

Kelley: Very sad. My artistic model for the felt banners was Sister Mary Corita, who was a Catholic nun. I understand why she did what she did when she did, and have a certain respect for it. With its sunshine aesthetic, the work implies that you're not supposed to think about negative or contradictory things. As long as you stay on the level of it's a "good time," and "fun," it's okay. That's what links it, in my mind, to what I hate most about the whole East Village movement and graffiti art, and art that's supposed to be about fun. As long as you don't think about it, or look at where it comes from, it can be good on the fun level.

Miller: "Amnesia is good."

Kelley: Sister Mary Corita, psychedelic posters, left-wing graphics, and underground comics were the first things I saw and thought of as art. I can say now that I was influenced by a lot of subcultural stuff from that period, and for years I wouldn't talk about it. I wanted to differentiate myself from it. I think now there is enough time and enough discussion of it in the art world that it is obvious how my work differs from, say, S. Clay Wilson. For years I wouldn't even talk about somebody like that because there wasn't enough knowledge of subcultural aesthetics in the art world for people to distinguish what I was doing from that. As I get older, I'm more willing to talk about the things that influenced me when I was in my teens, because I am willing to try and teach people about that material, how it functioned, and what I took from it.

Miller: Also, you're now beginning to influence other artists. Your work is being viewed as a determinant.

Kelley: It's also interesting how a lot of artists that influenced me are being rewritten back into history. For example, the pop artists Öyvind Fahlström and Peter Saul. My teachers considered Fahlström and Saul to be minor artists—Rauschenberg and Johns were their heroes. Now I think more people would agree that these artists were important artists. I always thought it was strange that they were so universally despised. Now it's a different generation of artists with different concerns, and these concerns have more to do with those kinds of people.

Miller: The whole history of pop art is being rewritten. But I'd like to talk about some of the recent pieces that were based on college flyers.

Kelley: Those were the most recent banners that I made.

Miller: When were these done?

Kelley: They were done this year. I made them and was very confused about them. I decided that I wanted to make some more banners that weren't so specifically referencing religion. I wanted them to be more contemporary but equally invisible, and to be about something that people would associate with college life. I was worried about being typecast as someone who just deals with kitsch. So I thought, "Okay, I'll just use an imaging mode that has to do with educated people but isn't considered an art form." So I decided to use college handouts, bulletin-board flyers. I'm still very confused about what they mean to me or what their final purpose is going to be. I only made four of them. I was going to make a bunch of them but then I got sidetracked and did the faculty-lounge installation *Alma Pater.*

Miller: So these turned out to be part of that.

Kelley: No, they're separate. The faculty lounge is much more understandable. It relates to something that is alien to most people now, so you could say that it represents a certain given mentality. But the newer banners don't do that.

Miller: I like how they seem completely up-to-date.

Kelley: I like them for that reason, too, and because they are kind of a collision of forms, like a felt banner that implies a certain kind of lower group activity and things that you associate with college life. College students themselves would never make anything like that.

Miller: But the handout is a low form, too.

Kelley: But it's so offhand that you don't even think about it. It doesn't take any time to do it. You magic marker a message on paper and Xerox it. It doesn't take any time, really. Yet when I started working with them, I was really interested in their particular aesthetic. Of course, that's changing now. I have a bunch of them printed that are made on home computers; they're not handwritten. They use type and that's a problem—should I use those or should I just stick to the handmade things? Should they have a gestural quality or is it okay to make ones that are purely machine derived? I think it is. I mean, what difference does it make?

Miller: It would be interesting to see if there is any difference.

Kelley: But the ones I chose for the banners are done by hand, so they have a very personal, graphic quality.

Miller: They remind me of personal ads, in a way. They try to target a very specific group.

Kelley: Some of them are very specific, like looking for a female roommate. Some of them get real specific, like: a Christian, nonsmoking, female roommate.

Miller: Or someone to play Pasolini in a student film.

Kelley: When you look at them, you don't just think about the people that made them; you think about the whole group to which these people belong, or to which you assume they belong.

Miller: In a way, they're a bit more like the birdhouses in terms of their blankness. They're not at all overt.

Kelley: That's right. They're very difficult to politicize. There's nothing nasty about them. There's nothing different about them from the originals except that they're bigger and they're made of felt.

Miller: Do they have titles?

Kelley: No.

Miller: Do you often do untitled work?

Kelley: Yes, but a lot of things have titles, too. I've always been very careful about titles. As an undergraduate student, I was drawn to the collision of title and object. A lot of the early things I did had titles that made no sense. You see that a lot in sixties art, like some of the color-field painters: Jules Olitski would give his paintings these ridiculous titles.

Miller: Those are almost like color-chip names.

Kelley: I've become very particular about the title having a certain function. So if a thing doesn't need a title, I don't give it a title. Although I really hate when an artwork is open to all interpretations. I like the interpretations to be limited so that the process is problematized. Not just any interpretation is good; there's a certain range of interpretations that are allowed. Then the interpretation becomes a problem—I like that.

Miller: I gather you try to make a certain degree of moral responsibility incumbent on the viewer, as you did in the performances.

Kelley: Yes, I always thought that was important. I never liked art to be "Oh, you're free to do whatever you want." There is a pact with the artist. You're free to do certain things within a range of freedoms that I allow—that's our pact. You are responsible for your interpretation, but you're not totally free. If you were totally free, you'd do it yourself. You can go and look at the spit stains on the wall or the patterns of leaves floating. You could let nature do the work for you; you don't need me.

Miller: That reminds me of the drawing you did of the man with the bottle of ketchup.

Kelley: Yes, the drawing was called *Freedom.* He gets so caught up with putting ketchup on his hot dog that he gets lost in association and wants to cover the whole landscape in ketchup swirls as an outgrowth of his freedom. That was a really simple-minded cartoon of that notion, of that intellect that thinks that art's about freedom.

Miller: I also think of the afghan piece you called Zen Garden.

Kelley: That really looked like a Zen garden.

Miller: But it also seemed to address interpretation. There were these lumps under the afghan and you didn't know what they were, but you assumed that they were stuffed animals.

Kelley: That's what you'd suspect. It's funny how that piece is interpreted. Because it is stuffed animals, people like to load it with psychological significance. They see the stuffed animals as hiding under the blanket; there's some psychological crisis going on. That's why I called it *Zen Garden;* I wanted to give it this peaceful, contemplative title so that anybody who started talking about the psychology of the animals hiding under the blanket would be forced to deal with a title which calls to mind a more contemplative activity.

The Arena series looks psychologically loaded, and that's why they're titled by number. Titling them by number prompts you to look at them as simply arrangements of objects on a field. Of course, it's impossible to look at them only that way. Because they're dolls, you're going to psychoanalyze them. The last afghan pieces are very decorative: they're really crude, but they are very pretty, very brightly colored, and untitled. They're like paintings lying on the floor. They're by far the most formal of the afghan pieces that I've done. I think that's why they're the end of them.

Miller: With these floor sculptures, had you thought much about floor-versus-pedestal in minimalist sculpture?

Kelley: Somewhat. I was thinking overtly of Barry Le Va's scatter pieces. When I look at his work, I think about system and antisystem. The enclosing architecture could be the system that contains the antisystem, the scatter. As in the Allan Kaprow work where he threw tires around, the Le Va pieces seem to be in a pattern that you can't understand by just looking at it. In my work, the system and antisystem aren't about architecture versus the material contained by it; they're more about social systems. There are certain things you come to and say, "That's random" or "That's not random." The placement on the floor makes you think of certain historic formal discussions. Yet the materials themselves deny that discussion, because the materials relate to hearth and home, and developmental kinds of issues. Of all my works, they are the most about categories, about confusion of category. You strive to categorize them.

Miller: I think there's a tendency to equate the afghans with rugs in these works.

Kelley: But they don't look like rugs. The materials don't have anything to do with rugs. They're blankets with totally other associations. I have done some things with rugs, but they had a different kind of association.

Miller: Like the wax-candle piece from Plato's Cave*?*

Kelley: Like the wax-candle pieces *A Hippie's Bedroom* and *Melt Down*. I've shown them both on the floor and on the wall. They function both as floor sculptures and paintings, but that doesn't matter, because those pieces aren't specifically addressing their status as paintings or sculptures. They call to mind a rug being ruined; they're about the whole fear of dirtying something. So whether or not they are paintings or sculptures, in this case, doesn't make any difference. It could be clothing—a vertical or a horizontal orientation makes no difference.

After so many years of limiting myself to black-and-white paintings, I finally allowed myself to start working with other materials. I didn't want to do it as I was schooled to do, where materials are all just interchangeable. Let's just pick three things: rubber, feathers, and wax. I see so much work that's like that. When I started using materials, I started using them for very particular reasons, so they would have the right psychological impact.

Miller: You've never fallen into that tendency to exoticize materials that comes out of arte povera.

Kelley: I've never been a fan of *arte povera* for that reason. It's like high school surrealism: I'm gonna throw a teapot in with a hankie and something exotic and weird. I don't care about that.

Miller: Do you ever think of the stuffed-animal pieces in terms of the breakdown of the nuclear family?

Kelley: Yes, I see that. Advertising still presents an idealized notion of the family, even if it doesn't exist anymore.

Miller: In a way, even the newer craft objects still have that oddly dated quality. Maybe it's just that a good number of them come from a nuclear family. Somehow we can't picture them as coming from some other kind of family formation.

Kelley: It would be interesting if we could find something that we could say is an object indicative of a single-parent situation or an extended family, but they wouldn't be considered traditional. They would be considered oddities, and crafts are traditional. They reveal a mythos, not real-life situations.

Miller: That basis in myth reminds me of something that Brecht said, that folk art is bad art.

Kelley: I agree with that. After the NEA controversies I was considering applying for a folk art grant because they so obviously exist to promote traditional values. I mean, what's the difference between this folk and that folk? They're not talking about Folk Art, they're talking about *particular* folks they want to support. If I applied for a folk art grant, how would it be determined if what I did was folk art or not? I think that's the only politically correct thing to do nowadays.

Miller: It would be a coup for you to get a folk art grant.

Kelley: It would be great. We've talked about crafts and how there's no history of crafts. There's no history of conspiracy theory either. When people start writing about that, outside of it, trying to decode it, trying to actually examine why these certain networks of information are always operative in conspiracy theory—that will be a really interesting thing. Then we'll really learn something about our society. I don't think that there's anybody in the academic world who will even go near conspiracy theory at this point. Once it starts to become obvious how it is a motivating factor in real life, then people will start to write about it as a mythology or an ideology. I'm really interested in that.

I know a few artists that are working with that, like my friend Jim Shaw, who has always been interested in that. He's one of the few artists that I know who seems to be able to deal with conspiracy theory in any enlightening manner in art. I feel it in Cady Noland, Peter Nagy, Survival Research Laboratory, Tony Oursler, and Raymond Pettibon also. I think you'll start to see a lot more artists working with that kind of stuff. It has already happened in literature with people like Robert Anton Wilson and Philip K. Dick and William Burroughs. In the past, Öyvind Fahlström worked with that somewhat. I feel connected with that. How about you?

Miller: Conspiracy theory? It makes me wonder what the dividing line is between conspiracy theory and just outright paranoia.

Kelley: Paranoia is a fear that is too ludicrous to be taken seriously, but conspiracy theory has a veneer of validity, like art. You can trace it. It's based on historical information. It can be catalogued.

Miller: But there's a paranoid component to it.

Kelley: Of course.

Miller: Over the last four or five years there seems to be an opening up in terms of your process. For example, the animals on the afghans—most people would say it's not even making anything.

Kelley: That's what people said. I was scared of that reaction at first. I thought that work would go over like a lead balloon, that I would be accused of being a lazy artist, yet I knew that's all I wanted to do—that's what they had to be. I even showed them to a lot of people and I said, "I want to talk about these things." I found that most people tended to understand them as I understood them, so I realized it wasn't just some private thing. It was really something that people could understand, so I went ahead and did it. It was by far my most successful show in New York, ever. In fact, now that's thought of as typical Mike Kelley work. Of course, everybody says that in different periods about different work, but that's what people generally think of as Kelley art. When I was younger, because I wanted to be accepted as a smart person and since I was dealing with material that generally was thought of as being stupid, I held myself back a lot more. I wanted to be seen as an intellectual, so I was unwilling to really let go. I didn't want to be typecast as a funk artist, but now I don't care. I don't want to be seen as operating within too obvious of a program.

There's a funny thing when there is a market acceptance of your work. I find myself really trying to take it all away. Like, what will people go for, will they buy a stuffed animal on a blanket? It's interesting because they do. It's not like having it in a back room someplace and people saying, "That's an interesting thing." It's part of the economy, and then it's much more charged.

Miller: There were people who thought those stuffed-animal pieces were mainly about testing the limits of what collectors would be willing to buy.

Kelley: And I got reviews that said that, and of course that wasn't my intention at all. There is a history of work that's much more ephemeral than my work. Now I do see in the marketplace a lot of work that's junky and people seem to be competing for who can make the junkiest stuff. I've always been interested in the *particularity* of the junk, how it became junk. Why is this junk and this is not junk. I don't simply go to Pic 'N' Save and get the lowest piece of shit and tape it to the wall. That seems totally about the art market. I don't care about the art market except as a part of the culture at large.

But as far as what I'm working on now, I'm sort of pulling up to the end of the stuffed-animal stuff. I'm working on what I consider will be the final work with stuffed animals.

Miller: What you have planned for the Carnegie International—to display the stuffed animals sorted out categorically on rental tables—seems like you want to push the reification of these things as far as it will go.

Kelley: It's also a denial of any psychological element. They will be presented categorically by morphology and construction technique. Then there's a photograph taken of each one with a ruler à la an archaeological artifact. Then perhaps one drawing done like an archaeological diagram of a group of the dolls. It's a simultaneous presentation of different ways of organizing the same material—presenting it without acknowledging its loaded psychological nature at all. I was thinking this might not even be necessary because of the already repressed nature of the mode of presentation, but I was thinking of having an infantilist movie screened, placed within the museum where nobody could see it. So there'd be this aspect of the adult attachment to these things, some kind of infantilist impulse, but totally denied in that you couldn't see it, hidden away someplace.

Miller: With that and Zen Garden, *I think of Duchamp's* With Hidden Noise, *the ball of twine with the unknown object. There's a hiding strain in the coffin pieces, too, the* Empathy Displacement *works.*

Kelley: Well, that's an important part of those works, that they're hidden—that's it. The empathy displacement has to do with how you empathize with a doll and the fact that the more you empathize with something, the more you don't see it for what it is because you see it as you. Blowing these images of dolls up to the human scale and having them so deadly rendered makes you more aware of the strangeness of the morphology, how it differs from you. If you saw that thing walking down the street, you wouldn't go near it. It becomes hard to project onto.

Miller: The object tends to invite the viewer to see it as human, and then you turn around and say, "Let's make it human."

Kelley: Then you don't want to see it anymore, right? I knew that wouldn't happen by just blowing them up because you'd just say that it's just a picture of the thing. You had to have something to empathize with, so I put the thing that you empathize with in a box in front of the painting. You assume the object of empathy is in the box. You assume the painting is an accurate depiction of the thing that is in the box, and you can prove that because there is a window you can look through, but you're not allowed to.

Miller: If you do look, you can only see the face through the window.

Kelley: The complete title is *Empathy Displacement: Humanoid Morphology (2nd and 3rd Remove),* which refers to the second and third removal from the platonic archetype of the human. The first removed would be your body; the second removed would be the doll; the third removed would be the image of the doll. So we're getting at some notion of the human only through a second and third remove, and even then there's all these levels of displacement. You realize that the whole function of empathy is displacement. That's what I was trying to do in these pieces.

That's the same thing that's going on in *Center* and *Peripheries,* where there is a central organizing square, but it's blank. The organizing principle that connects all the peripheries, the power base, is missing. They are paranoiac paintings in that they imply a controlling influence that's invisible. The things around the central square are a selection of images that you can choose to empathize with. One of them is a garbage bag; one of them is a stuffed-animal portrait. There are two dead people's heads and a toe.

Miller: Weren't the dead people all radicals from the sixties?

Kelley: No, one of the dead people is a murder victim, and the other is a student from Tiananmen Square. They might be alive or they might be dead, but it puts you in a position of having to empathize with someone who is more than likely dead. Most people can't empathize with a murder victim because they don't want to imagine themselves in that position—that's frightening. Yet it's very easy to empathize with a doll because dolls don't die. Also, it's very easy to empathize with a head, but it's very hard to empathize with a toe. If it's part of the same body, why is it easy to see personality residing in the head and not in the toe? It's funny.

Miller: After the Gulf War, Fox Network showed butchered bodies of animals in the Kuwait City Zoo that were, oddly, more moving than all the piles of human corpses.

Kelley: That just proves the point. You can't feel for the people who are dying because that's too close to home; but if you can go through the secondary device of the animals, then you can feel intense emotion. The plight of those people is too horrible to imagine. I know as a child I always found puppet shows very frightening, also cartoons—especially the deadest cartoons, like Hanna-Barbera cartoons. I believe they frightened me because of the intense deadness of the depictions. They were barely moving, but they were alive. They were like walking corpses.

Miller: Baudelaire preferred backdrop painting to the academic landscape painting of the day for that reason: because the artifice is seen as artifice. For him, the well-rendered landscape was completely uninteresting.

Kelley: It's too alive.

Miller: And too naturalistic.

Kelley: The most frightening media thing I can remember from my childhood was a puppet show on a children's TV program about a puppet in one of these little prosceniums who was supposed to be on an endless stairway and falls off into nothingness. You just hear the voice: "Oooooooo..." For years that has been my ideal. If I could make something that moving, that could have you frightened for the rest of your life, and all it was was a piece of clay that falls off a piece of cardboard, that so much emotion could be invested in this piece of shit—that's amazing.

✶

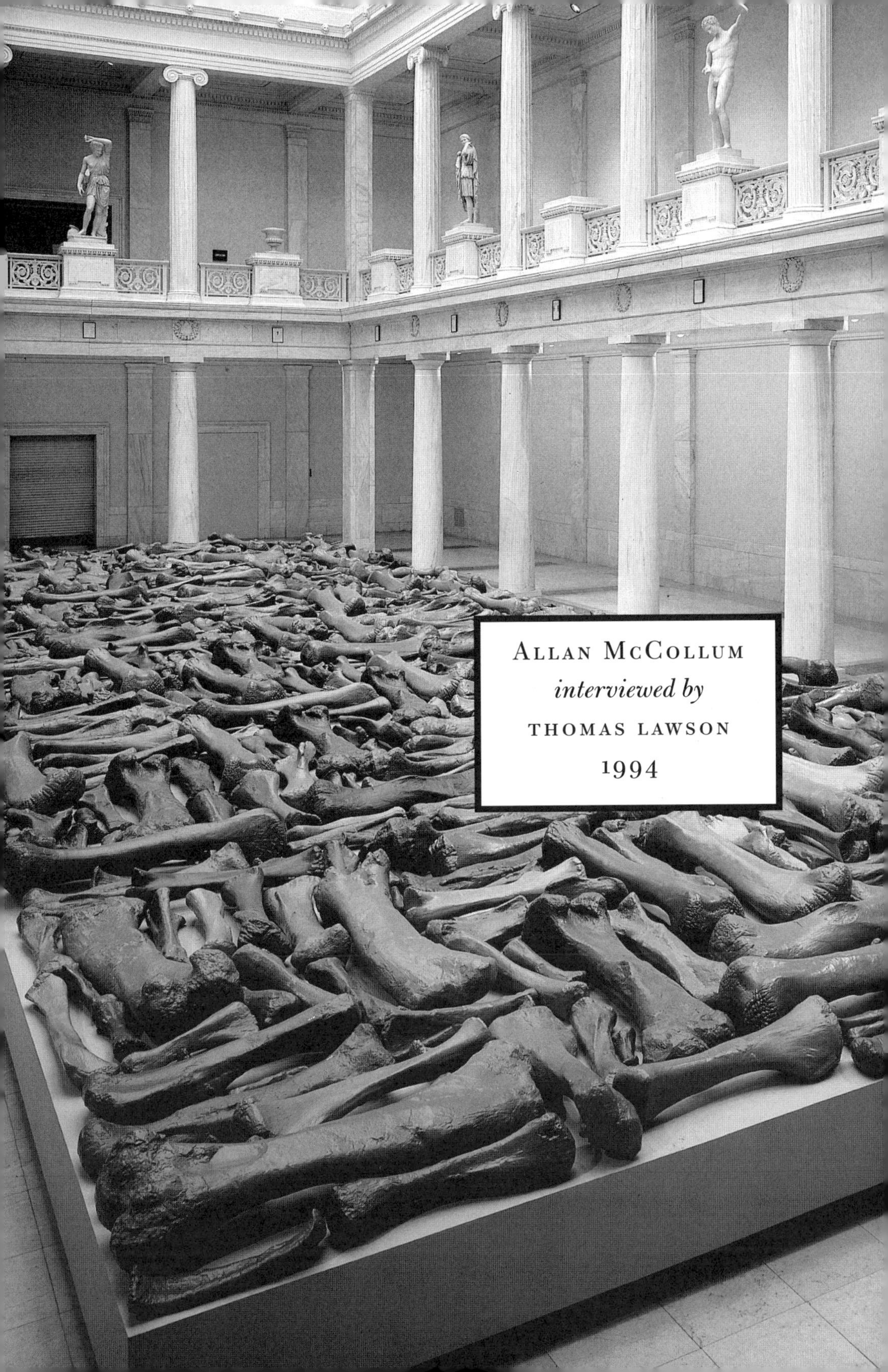

Allan McCollum
interviewed by
THOMAS LAWSON
1994

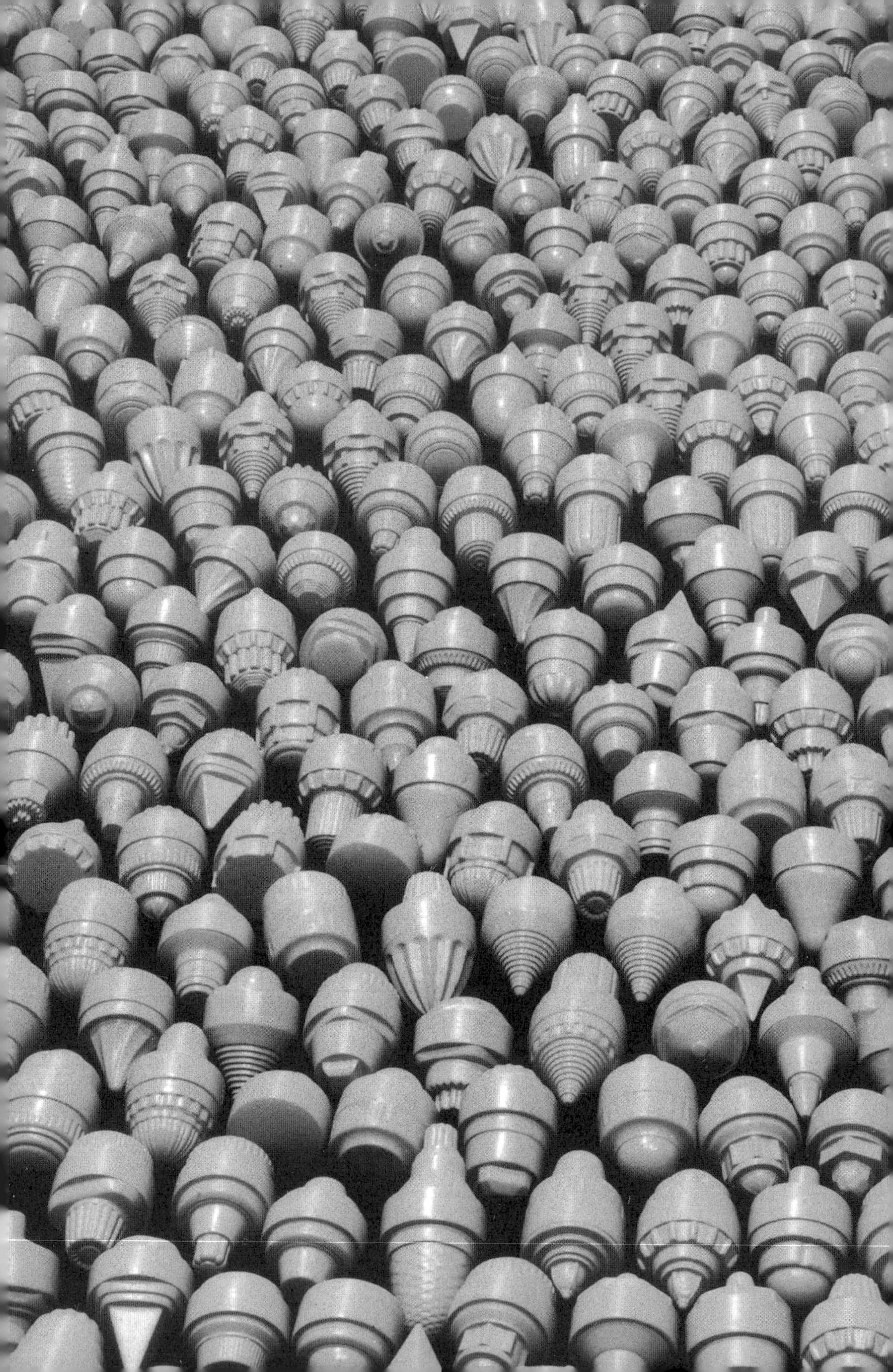

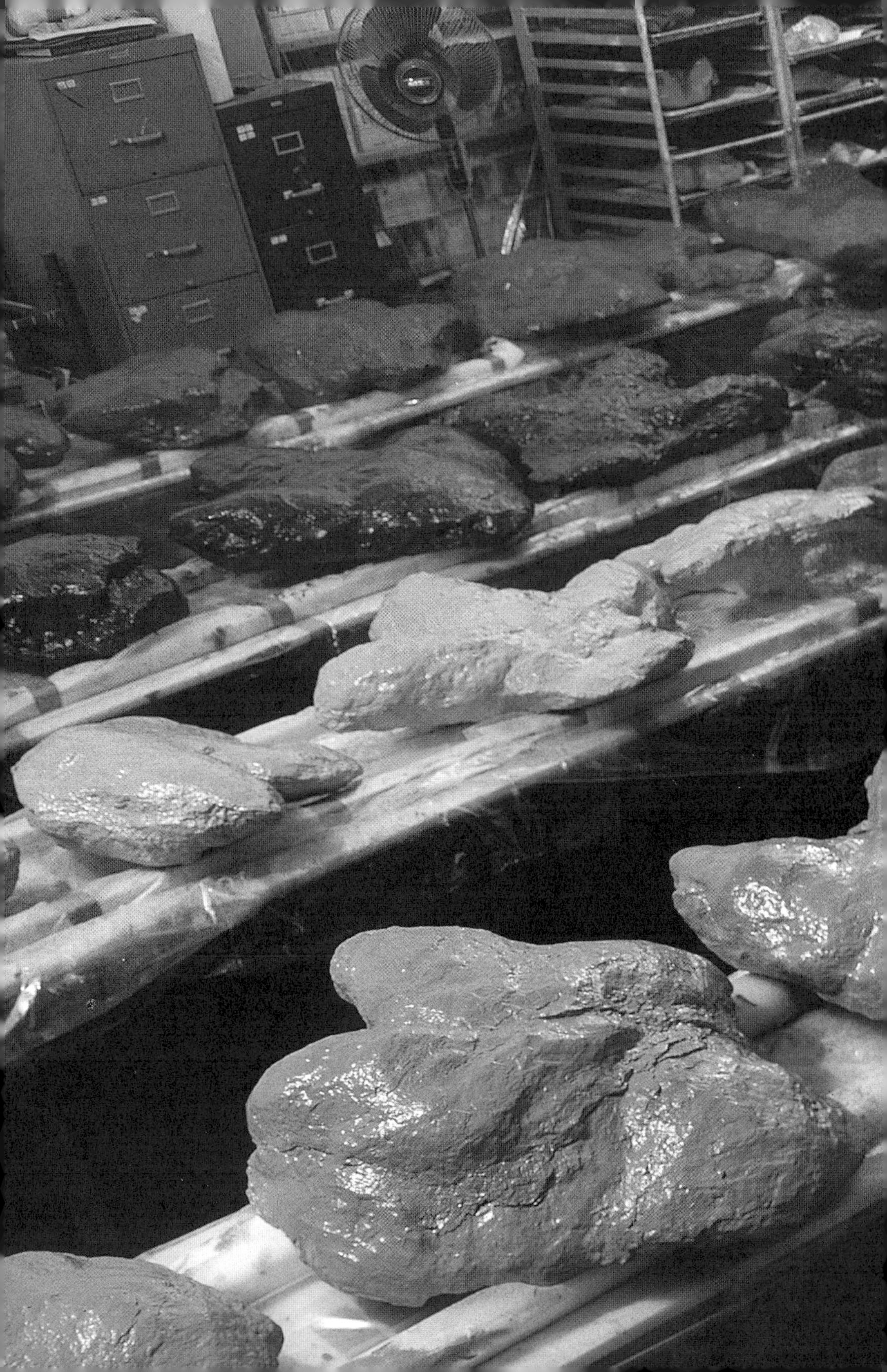

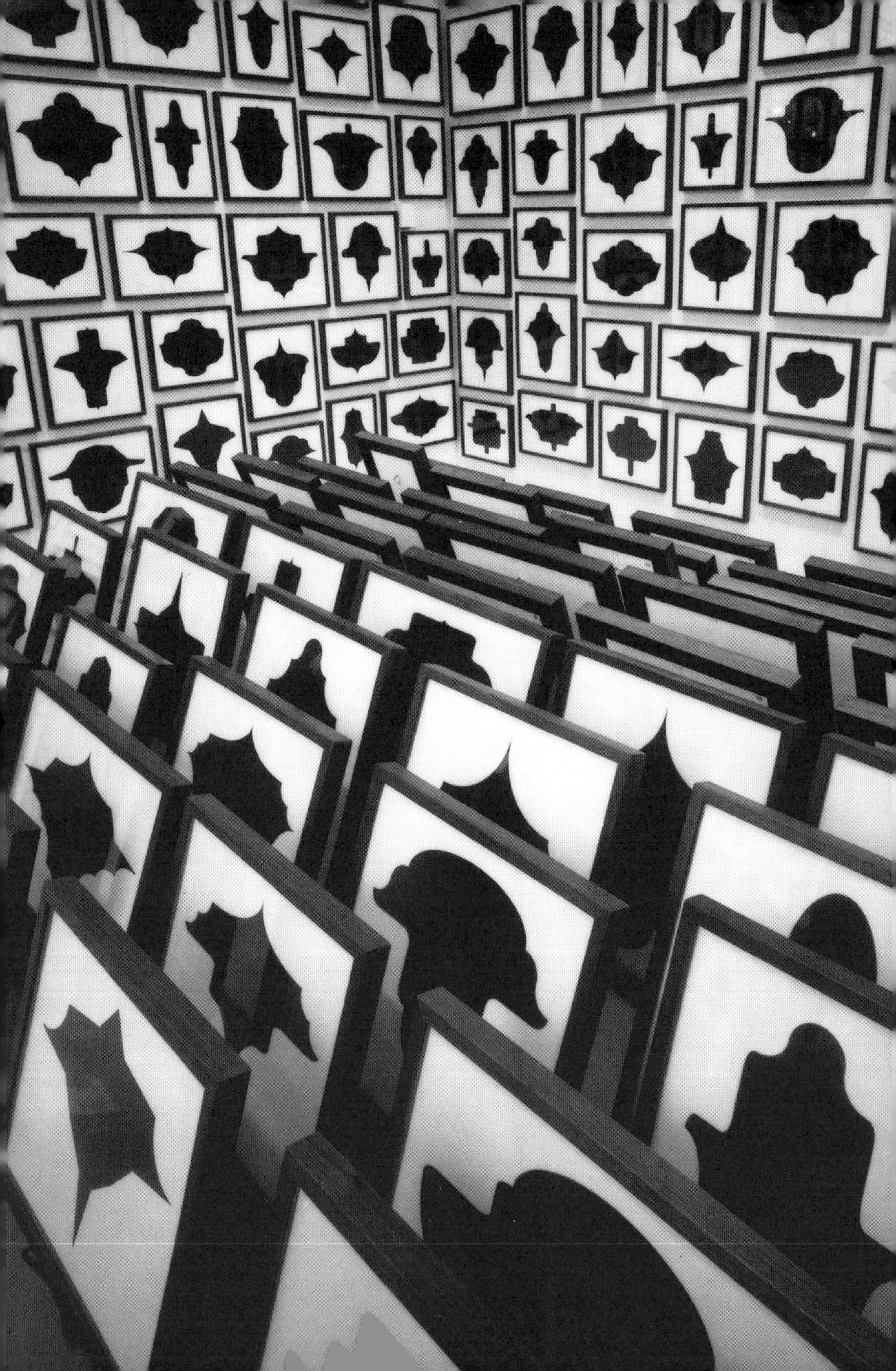

ALLAN McCOLLUM

interviewed by

THOMAS LAWSON

Thomas Lawson: In many of the interviews you've given, you sound very angry about culture, about the way the idea of the museum operates, and what your feelings are when you go into a museum. You want to know who paid for this, who cares about that. There is a real sense of alienation. It seems to me there's a lot of anger in the way you talk about your work. And until recently, I would say that you have been concerned with developing abstract methods of drumming out that anger.

Allan McCollum: I don't know that I agree with you exactly. Maybe you're right: in previous interviews I've expressed some anger at the way we always tend to define culture in terms of the interests of some privileged group. But I don't know if you can always necessarily infer that that's what my artwork is about. I think that's wrong. Maybe I'm too chatty in interviews, or maybe I dwell too much on how I feel about things in general when I should be talking more specifically about the ideas related to my work.

Lawson: So you want to keep your feelings as a person in the world separate from your thoughts as a working artist?

McCollum: No, of course not [laughs]. My work is *always* about my feelings, but I also seem to always design my projects so that they invite wider cultural analyses. I do want my work to suggest a larger picture of the way we experience culture and participate in it. I like to ask questions about how society creates objects, and what those objects mean. But when I speak of society and culture, I'm obviously speaking from a personal, biased point of view.

Back in the seventies, with the *Surrogate Paintings,* for instance, I was trying to make objects that made it easier for me to explore my own relationship with paintings in general. But I assumed that my relationship with

page 131:
Lost Objects, *installation, Carnegie International, 1991*
page 132:
Over Ten Thousand Individual Works, *1987–88, enamel on cast hydrocal*
page 133:
Natural Copies from the Coal Mines of Central Utah *(detail), 1994–95, enamel on polymer-reinforced gypsum*
page 134:
Drawings, *1988–92, artist's pencil on museum board*

paintings was similar to everybody else's. I think you could talk about each series that I've done in terms that would sound angry or fearful, but you could also use terms that would sound exuberant or playful, and so forth, or even humorous, ironic, or silly. So I want to challenge your statement a bit. At the same time, there's something about what you're saying that is true. Lately I have been trying to be more constructive than I used to be, to explore art making as something that might be *good* for something!

Lawson: Well, what we're talking about, I think, is the critical perception of your work, not necessarily what you think of your work. One of the reasons to look at what you have been doing is to understand it in the context of a progressive, thinking-through, abstract method of art making.

McCollum: There's a reduction.

Lawson: A reductionism and an antirepresentational position—for example, with the Surrogates, *you use the blank center of the issue of representation. But the real difference with the more recent works—the cast* Dog from Pompei *and the dinosaur bones—is that they bring representation right up to the surface. A lot of the discussion of your earlier work has to do with framing—framing created by the pieces or by the institution, the context of exhibition, all that kind of thing. Pompeii still provides a framework of this sort, but there is a shift in emphasis. Pompeii was this wealthy resort town of a civilization now long gone, and the odd things that are left of it are bits and pieces of everyday life, not the fabulous treasures of a power elite. So what you do with the dog is point to ordinary experience, but from this huge, extraordinary distance. You leapfrog over the historical and all that cultural baggage you dislike.*

McCollum: I think I understand. But I need to say, in the first place, I don't necessarily see the *Surrogate Paintings* as nonrepresentational.

Lawson: I know you don't. The Surrogates *could just as easily be considered representational sculpture. I think the question has to do with whether the works represent something or are about representing something. But to me the installations of the* Plaster Surrogates *always seemed to be about taking a position against representation in art—against "pictures." In contrast, the dogs and bones look like they might be pictures in three dimensions.*

McCollum: That's not exactly the way I think. The motivation behind making the *Surrogate Paintings* was to represent something, to represent the way a painting "sits" in a system of objects. If you look at installation shots, or pictures taken of art galleries—that was the picture I had in mind. I was trying to reproduce that picture of an art gallery in three dimensions, a tableau. So with the *Surrogate Paintings,* the goal was to make them function as props so that the gallery itself would become like a picture of a gallery by re-creating an art gallery as a stage set. To me, this was a clear representation of the way paintings looked in the world, irrespective of whether there's a "representation" within the painting or not.

Also there was a theatrical motivation, maybe a Brechtian motivation, in which I wanted the viewer to be self-consciously caught up in the act of wanting to see a picture. So in a sense, the emotional content of these "surrogate paintings" involved the desire to look at a picture. I was trying to trigger that desire by reproducing the entire tableau within which the viewer would be aroused to desire a picture, but at the same time, not fulfilling that desire, so that, again, the viewer would be caught in the act of experiencing this desire. There was something about what that emotion represents that I was trying to isolate. In that sense, the *Surrogate Paintings* were representational to me: they attempted to mirror the mind-set of the person looking at the painting. I don't think it's reaching to call that representational.

In order to make the *Surrogate Paintings* function as representations of paintings, I had to ultimately cast them in plaster so that the frame, the mat, and the picture were seamlessly joined by the same material. They were casts of paintings, so that they became representations of a type of object that is placed on a wall.

Lawson: They're most often talked about as "signs" of paintings, but to you, they also represent a more generalized type of cultural object.

McCollum: Exactly. But all representations are about choosing to reduce some thing to a "type," to some kind of abstraction. In 1978, when I first made notes to myself about what I thought I was doing, I remember inventing terms like "the standard, occidental, wall-mounted artifact." I know that I wasn't simply trying to represent only paintings. I remember thinking that I was just performing mimetically like most artists do. This is the way a gallery looks and feels, and I made an imitation of that. There's not so much difference between doing that and an artist deciding to paint a picture of a nude.

I was influenced by artists like Robert Ryman, Frank Stella, and Daniel Buren: people who seemed to reduce painting to an extremely simple formula —some kind of definition of painting.

Lawson: In one way, Ryman could be seen to be making a claim to finishing off the project of painting, reducing it to a simple definition with this very aggressive stance of "that's it—done with."

McCollum: Yes, but at the time, my perception was that if a painting were reduced far enough, down to its basic *identity* as a painting, the painting would become so self-referential that it would have nowhere to go except to implode and refer back to its position in a system of other kinds of objects that aren't paintings.

That was how I began to want to produce a painting that functioned like a prop. To me, this felt like the end result of self-referential painting. The painting winds up only referring to what it is not—which is the rest of the world. The distinction between figurative and nonrepresentational art did not come to mind too often, I don't think.

Lawson: To me, the referent is the key to the Surrogate Paintings *and to the* Perfect Vehicles. *The referent is just the abstract idea—the idealized idea of a painting or a sculpture. In* The Dog from Pompei *and* Lost Objects, *the referents are beings that once lived and breathed.*

McCollum: That's true. I guess you're right. But filling a rubber mold that's shaped like a painting with plaster is a very similar act to filling a rubber mold that's shaped like a dog [laughs].

Maybe I'm being obtuse here. Of course I favor idealizations and conceptualizations in my work; I guess that's obvious. And if I could have made something that was an abstract representation of time gone by, I would have. But I couldn't think of any real alternatives. So I chose things that already seemed to be representations, already utterly unmediated and anonymous—representations accidentally created by the world itself and not through *artistic* behavior.

Lawson: Yet there is a great difference between the generalized ideas embodied in your earlier works and the specific nature of the dogs and the dinosaur bones.

McCollum: There was something that appealed to me about the dogs and bones in this area of representation that you're talking about. I felt that in both cases I was working with copies produced by *nature.* I think that part of the challenge we face in living with the copies we make ourselves is that we experience them as alienating because they always seem to represent something else; they're never the thing itself. So to the degree to which we're enmeshed in relationships with our own copies in the world, we are constantly in a state of banishment from the imaginary "source" of things—from the original things that these copies seem to replicate.

This is just the modern condition, you know? This is also inherent in language and in the way we internalize things as representations. We live in a physical world that's filled with copies and representations made from molds, printing processes, templates, dies, and so forth. We live in a world filled with substitutions for things that are absent since every copy, in a certain sense, only exists because the original is gone. So copies are always about something that's absent, and in that way, they carry a sense of mourning, death, or loss. This is one way to look at our environment—maybe a particularly psychoanalytic way.

Lawson: Maybe, but there is also the mundane truth that copies are made so that more people can have them at a lower cost than the "original." I think it is too easy to get caught up in the melancholia of reproduction. Life goes on.

McCollum: I know. But there is still this very real side effect that we are surrounded not only by the presence of things that we wouldn't have otherwise but also with the absences that these copies represent. So if I have a certain mass-produced coffee cup, for instance, and I know that thousands of other people have the same cup, that's great, because I feel connected to all these thousands of other people. But at the same time, the actual reality of any *particular* coffee cup seems to exist nowhere. So, in a sense, absence is everywhere. So I sometimes experience living in the world as a kind of mourning or as a kind of longing for the things that are always absent. The presence of copies seems to amplify this feeling.

Anyway, I found that *The Dog from Pompei* and the *Lost Objects* could convey this particular way of experiencing representation because they were literally copies of objects that were long gone, never to exist again. The only way you could have a relationship with them at all would be through the duplicates created by nature. I came up with the idea of using fossils because fossils are reproductions almost by definition. Dinosaur fossils, for instance, are created over millions of years during which the bone is dissolved and replaced by silica or minerals of some kind. It's a slow process of development, and, ultimately, what you get is an exact duplicate of the original bone. So I felt that if representation is a sort of alienating mechanism, maybe these objects corrected or bridged that gap, or naturalized the relationship between the copy and what the copy represents in some uncanny, symbolic way because they are naturally made copies.

Whether or not this distinction makes any rational sense, I think emotionally it makes sense. So one of the meanings a naturally produced copy has for us is that it absolves us of the guilt for living in relation to our own copies all the time. It makes copying a natural thing.

Lawson: Are you seeking salvation for the alienation of your old work by using naturally occurring representations?

McCollum: Maybe. It's about the way we mythologize nature. I'm not offering any criticisms or solutions. I'm mostly describing what I think is a kind of fantasy or wish, and the way these naturally made copies seem to satisfy this wish in some way. I'm not trying to make some distinction between nature and culture here; I'm just saying that as a culture we make these distinctions. We might name a flower after a certain animal because it looks like that animal—we're constantly looking for these correspondences, resemblances. Why is it pleasurable to do that? I think that it's pleasurable because it makes our own copying seem like a natural process, whereas if we didn't find it in nature, we would find our own copying, our own inner representing, to be alienating or troublesomely false. In fact, a lot of "antirepresentational" artists from the recent past do view representations as alienating and delusional—encouraging illusions and fantasies and aloofness from reality. Sometimes I agree with these views.

When I first designed the *Surrogates* it was very difficult to convey to people that I considered the frame to be part of the work itself. People would generally look into the window of the mat and think that was what they were supposed to look at. So I think I was considered a monochrome painter by many people. That became a preoccupation of mine—how troublesome it was to convey the idea that the entire framed artwork was meant to be experienced as a whole object in itself.

Lawson: It is interesting that people used to think that you were a monochrome painter. In thinking that, they were thinking you were taking a position against representation.

McCollum: I think that I had thought these issues through a long, long time before I began the *Surrogate Paintings.* As I said, I had already looked at Frank Stella's paintings, Robert Ryman's and Roy Lichtenstein's paintings, and even On Kawara's paintings, as signs for paintings. And I think there are lots of ways to argue that that's exactly what they are, and perhaps intentionally so. But I don't think other people saw them exactly that way. I saw these paintings as caricatures of paintings, and therefore the work seemed to self-consciously refer to their context in the world at large in ways that other paintings don't. I'd been going through that train of thought for so many years that it took me by surprise that, even in 1978, people didn't know how to look at the frame and see it as part of the work. The *Plaster Surrogates* came out of a step-by-step logic from painting in the late sixties. It wasn't as if I one day gave up painting and simply became a sculptor.

Lawson: The Surrogates *are all in portrait form.*

McCollum: Well, yes, and I made that decision when I decided I also wanted to make a direct reference to domestic objects. A "surrogate painting" was meant to represent a painting in a museum, but, at the same time, it was meant to represent a photograph of your grandchild, or something like that. It was meant to represent a standard type of cultural object that we make, save, and value—an object in use. Anyway, I think I have to give you a little history of the decisions I made when I decided to do the dogs and bones in order to answer your earlier question.

Lawson: Do you think of them as "dogs and bones"?

McCollum: I try not to say "dogs" and "bones" together in the same sentence if I can help it [laughs]! When I thought of the idea of using the fossils (and they're both kinds of fossils, really), I was looking for a different type of object that functions as a kind of valued thing to the culture. Just as the *Plaster Surrogates* could represent the Mona Lisa or a graduation photo, I was trying to collapse two other kinds of disparate objects into one sign. I was also trying to come up with some sort of project which could represent a connection with the past, or our desire to be connected to the past.

If you look at my work from around 1975 to now, I think you can separate the work into categories of objects. And usually these categories can be defined by some attempt on my part to do a type of object which already exists in the culture, something which is collected and saved and satisfies or appeals to certain emotional needs or desires. I was thinking, "What do we have in our homes? What do we have in museums?" Well, you have certain types of objects which we value because they seem to be more than what they are.

Religious objects would fall into this category, and fine art objects, of course. So with the fossils, I was thinking of a category of object that we save to remind us that the past exists, both on a cultural level and on a personal level. It's funny, because you can make a sign for a painting and duplicate it, but you can't make a sign for an old object and duplicate that aura that comes from age. You can't synthesize or invent that; you can pretend. You can buy copies of Nefertiti or something, but you will always know it's a copy even if it's made from a mold made from the original. It doesn't give you what you would want from a really ancient object.

Lawson: I wonder. I recently got a phone call at school [California Institute of the Arts] from a woman who said she had some Egyptian artifacts that her husband had collected and loved. She wanted to get rid of them because he had died recently. I went to visit her and what she had, in fact, were a number of souvenirs her husband had bought at the King Tut exhibit when it was at the Coliseum in Los Angeles: a couple of bookends, a little cast of Nefertiti. They were objects with no value as artifacts, and they were of no value to her because she hadn't shared his interest in Egyptian souvenirs. But they did refer to some desire of her husband's.

McCollum: But they did have value to her because they had value to her husband. So much value that she wanted to do something significant with them rather than just throw them out.

Lawson: Exactly. She wanted art students to use them for drawing exercises, a step above throwing them out. There was a reluctance to toss them completely, which was her real impulse. We were talking about the satisfaction with the copy—I think her husband was completely satisfied with them.

McCollum: I don't know.

Lawson: The one original item he had in the collection was a little pyramid filled with sand that his friend made for him with sand from Egypt. This man's only encounter with Egypt was through the exhibition. But his friend managed to go to Egypt and brought him some sand and made this little, tiny pyramid.

McCollum: My grandmother's grandfather was a ventriloquist and performed around the country in the late 1800s. My grandmother lived in southeast Texas when she was a little girl, and he once brought a little present of seashells from San Francisco. She saved them, and just before she died, she divided them up, got a kit from the craft store for making little plastic paperweights, and made one for each grandchild so that each of us could have a little souvenir from her grandfather: seashells encased in polyester resin. I still have mine.

Lawson: You have so many stories from your family's history that prefigure your current interests.

McCollum: What you were describing reminds me of another story: My grandmother died in 1977, around the time I first started the *Surrogate Paintings,* and I was trying to determine the final form they would take. When she died, she left behind things that nobody knew about; they were essentially souvenirs of events that had nothing to do with anyone still around. It's an extremely strange feeling to have an object that meant something to somebody who's gone. You don't know what it meant, but because it had meant something to someone you loved, it now means something to you. It's hard to say how much the objects mean, because they only seem to *almost* mean something. But they mean enough to you that you save some of them. I remember feeling that it was this kind of imminent meaningfulness that I wanted the *Surrogate Paintings* to have. I wanted them to refer to things that we value without necessarily knowing all the reasons why.

Lawson: Like old family photographs that you find, and you don't know who any of the people are, except you know that one of them might have been your great-grandparent or something?

McCollum: Yes, exactly. And that doesn't only happen with heirlooms. I'm forty-eight now, and I have objects I've kept whose significance has been lost to me. I know they meant something to me once—related to some friend or some event, but I honestly don't remember. I'm afraid if I throw them away, I'll lose these meanings forever, but, then again, I'll probably never remember what they were anyway. But these objects have an aura of meaningfulness that's unknowable and nonspecific.

Lawson: So that's what's crucial with the Perfect Vehicles*?*

McCollum: Well, with the *Surrogates,* yes. But I guess with the *Perfect Vehicles,* the aura of imminent meaningfulness became more and more amplified and more refined.

Lawson: Because you made them look somewhat more like family heirlooms in some abstract way?

McCollum: No, not exactly. I wanted the *Surrogates* to represent both an object that the culture at large values and an object that an individual might value within his or her own lifetime. For the *Perfect Vehicles* I chose the vase as an object that seemed to have that same spread of potential meanings. If you go to the Victoria and Albert or the Metropolitan Museum, you can see vases that have similar shapes to the vases you can buy at Woolworth's. So, since I intended to make a reductive sculpture, all I thought about were the shapes. I tried to find one that could function at either end of the continuum of meaning, of value, and of enhancement.

Lawson: Why are they grouped—is it in fives?—together?

McCollum: I group them in all kinds of different ways.This is very hard to explain exactly. I think there's something very poignant about the mentality of modern man.

Lawson: Man as in mankind, or male?

McCollum: No, I mean modern human individuals. This is a very American thing: the individual's desire to seek out "needs," to define them, simplify them, and try to satisfy them. You see this especially in the production of consumer goods and in modern science as well as in the arts. I think it's a modern desire. I don't exactly know why that's the case, but it's an interesting area to explore. So sometimes when I'm functioning as an artist, I'm functioning as an individual in terms of my own feelings and wishes and so forth. At other times I try to inhabit that part of me that is a modern person who has this impulse. So there is sometimes that self-conscious conceit going on with me.

When I made the *Perfect Vehicles,* I was purposely functioning in a voice that naively (maybe) and optimistically felt that a religious object could be reduced to some kind of simple thing that one could then reproduce, that would represent all transcendent feelings at once. It's a preposterous goal, but it's the kind of thinking that people who design national symbols must go through. In order to amplify that posture, I decided that if this modern person wanted to create a highly overdetermined symbol, it would be much better to make a lot of them, speaking as this modern person who would think like this—and modern people do think like this. So I had this idea that you could create something like a power station—that was the reason to put a number of *Perfect Vehicles* together. The aura of value and significance would increase exponentially with the number of objects you put together.

But the vehicles are more than "religious" objects—they are also representations of "fine art" objects. There was something else I intended to do with the *Perfect Vehicles,* which was to depict that particular dramatic process of an object made to convey some charged meaning that is required of it by culture. As a kid growing up in Los Angeles, I remember that "perfect vehicle" was a common phrase—a film director or an actor was always searching for the perfect vehicle that would draw on his own particular, unique talent. So this idea that one could come up with a "vehicle" that was perfectly suited to expressing who you were seemed to me to be a principal "mythic quest" of the artist or poet. Everyone's looking for that "perfect" form, and the viewer is also looking for the art vehicle that somehow captures and expresses his or her own feelings. Through identification, the viewer finds his own inner truths objectified. So I was interested in the mythology and how it is mediated through objects that artists make. In a sense, it's essentially what artists do for a living, and it's also the critical basis for judging the success or failure of an artwork. Everyone's looking for this means of conveyance, and the art object occupies the center of this search. Maybe this quest had religious significance before it became artistic: an object might have symbolic significance that far outweighs its day-to-day usefulness.

Lawson: This all sounds very Walter Benjamin/Frankfurt School, which is not as interesting as your take on the Hollywood idea of the "perfect vehicle." I'd like to hear more on the film actor's search for acceptance and the mass circulation of religious objects.

McCollum: The fact that they exist in such immense quantities reinvents a whole new kind of aura—is that what you mean? I guess that's why I brought up the example of a religious object in the first place, because I wasn't talking about an object that's enshrined, that's a one-of-a-kind, piece-of-the-cross type of object. I was thinking about the plaster Madonna that—no matter how many times it's reproduced, how many homes it exists in—still has significance and meaning and aura to the person who believes.

Lawson: Doesn't the plaster Madonna represent aura, the Church, and religion, et cetera? Do the Vehicles *represent the "aura of art"?*

McCollum: To me they do. Maybe that sounds too simple. I was trying to come up with an object that represented all of those mechanisms of looking at a thing and being caught up in some transcendent feeling that wasn't in the thing itself, but the thing itself acted as a catalyst for these other feelings and, in that sense, functioned like a vehicle. And I think I was trying to represent this kind of object as part of my work. But like you said, by doing them in quantity, I was also contradicting the idea of the unique, singular...

Lawson: Is it the quantity that creates the idea of absurdity?

McCollum: Or intensity.

Lawson: There's a funny intensity.

McCollum: Faced with large quantities of the same object, maybe you come to realize that what you're feeling couldn't be real because it's absurd to think that the "Holy Spirit" is more present in ten thousand plaster Madonnas than in one. But in fact, if you saw ten thousand Madonnas and you believed, you probably would feel that. There's that discrepancy about what makes sense and what doesn't make sense, especially in the context of religious feeling. So even a deeply religious person in the presence of ten thousand Madonnas might consider it to be slightly absurd. But at the same time, they might realize that the power of belief exists within themselves and not in the bits of plaster. I'm not sure.

Lawson: But laughter is one response to your work.

McCollum: I understand what you're saying. There have been times when you go into somebody's home—a mother of a friend or something—and see the objects that they find so valuable, like this pyramid you were talking about, or the pencil that says "I like Pussy"—was that your story?

Lawson: That was Richard Baim's story [laughs]. They didn't know the American slang. He saw this pencil at an Italian friend's parents' home in Tuscany. They had many pet cats and cat knickknacks, including this pencil their son had innocently (or not so innocently) brought back from America.

McCollum: You go into somebody's home and you see something funny in the objects that they value, and it makes you uneasy. Let me say that I don't think the *Perfect Vehicles* are as funny as other people do. I do understand that they're funny, but I don't think they're as funny or ironic as other people seem to think they are. And while I don't necessarily look at them and have what you'd call a religious experience, I do look at them and think that I might, maybe, if you know what I mean. I don't make them with the kind of irony that people seem to project onto them because I'm actually very suggestible. If I see an object that someone else values to the extreme, I'm moved by that. As I said before, I would have a hard time throwing something away that someone else valued, even though I didn't understand why it was valued. So I suppose the *Perfect Vehicles* can appear as comedic to some, and I recognize that they do. But this always hurts me a little bit. To an outsider, the overvalued object seems silly and is made even sillier by the owner's emotional investment in it. But I want my work to amplify the poignancy of the estrangement from belief that we suffer in the face of the unfamiliar values of others.

Lawson: No, I think that's where the poignancy is: they're absurd and funny, but you know that they also refer to an idea of value.

McCollum: Maybe what you think of as "funny" I think of as "poignant." I must feel that the poignancy increases as the sense of the comedic increases.

Lawson: I can't bear to watch situation comedies because you can see the jokes coming. At a certain point, I can't take it any longer. Is that poignant?

McCollum: Well, look at the tragedy of being an alcoholic and the number of jokes ridiculing alcoholics. It's funny and it's not funny because it's tragic, and maybe there's a difference between the way you and I look at things, too—you favor the comedic over the poignant. There's something tragic and poignant, it seems to me, about looking to an object to have meaning when obviously the object is just functioning as a symbol. There's something sad about that because it means that what you want, you don't have; all you have is the substitute, and that can be seen as basically sad.

I once read a book by a famous clairvoyant who claimed that he could see people walking around who had died but couldn't leave the "earth-plane." And the reason they couldn't was that they were addicted to something. He said he once saw the spirit of an alcoholic curled up in a barrel of wine. And he claimed that people addicted to nicotine have a hard time leaving this earth-plane because they're constantly looking for cigarettes, and re-creating what he called "dream cigars." So that would be horrible if it were true, but it's also funny.

Lawson: That's ridiculous.

McCollum: Well, if a man puts flowers on his wife's grave, would that strike you as funny?

Lawson: No. Grieving for a lost love or honoring a memory—these are genuine human acts. But claiming you can see lost souls in empty wine glasses and dirty ashtrays is just nonsense.

McCollum: These are all similar kinds of concepts to me. I think that each series that I do tends to explore a different kind of valuation or kind of meaning or significance that we look for, that we value in an object. We tend to separate our valuations into categories, but they all blend into one another. The *Perfect Vehicles* are similar in many ways to the *Plaster Surrogates*—sort of a three-dimensional version of them. On the other hand, the *Perfect Vehicles* have that reference to transcendence that is much more obvious, as you pointed out. That aspect overlaps into my other projects. They all form a project as a whole, I suppose, which in the end might form a certain picture of my emotional life. I suffer estrangement from tradition, and that sometimes makes me really unhappy. I hope I'm depicting some kind of more universal condition, especially with regard to the objects we value. I tried to make the *Perfect Vehicles* look like they were made with a great deal of care, which they were. They take a long time to make in the studio.

Lawson: Why is that?

McCollum: Well, you think that it's easy to make something look perfect, but it isn't [laughs]. We use rubber molds and make the objects out of plaster, and it takes hours and hours of sanding and shaping. Even though the mold is as perfect as we can make it, every mold warps. And then there are coats and coats of paint.

Lawson: Are they usually one color?

McCollum: They usually are.

Lawson: Sometimes they have stripes, don't they? That must make them more difficult—to get the stripes perfect?

McCollum: You're not being sarcastic, are you [laughs]?

Lawson: Me [laughs]? Do you still call them Perfect Vehicles *when they're large?*

McCollum: Yes, they're just the same; only bigger!

Lawson: But they're not just the same; they are bigger. I remember being at your opening when you first showed them and standing around talking. As I moved my head in conversation, I glimpsed one out of the corner of my eye and, for that moment, thought there was someone standing beside me. It was a little startling.

McCollum: Of course they're going to have a different kind of presence. In designing the *Perfect Vehicles,* I was trying to make some objects that were highly overdetermined and that were maybe even inexhaustible in their potential as symbols. I chose a particular kind of vase to copy that had a lot of masculine characteristics as well as feminine, and that had certain references to machines as well as to the organic. I tried to elaborate upon the typical kinds of things people say about vases representing femaleness: wombs, breasts, and at the same time giving them an almost military, phallic presence. Anyway, I was aware that they also had an ambiguous anthropomorphic presence which just didn't work as dramatically on a small scale.

Lawson: So the big ones are more perfect?

McCollum: Yes! And also because they don't reference the mass-produced object so readily. At the moment when I started showing the *Perfect Vehicles*—because of what some popular, younger artists were doing at the time—I didn't quite anticipate that that reference to mass consumption was going to be favored so strongly in people's perceptions of the work, especially by younger art critics. They were being perceived in a way that I thought was out of balance. The large ones sort of solved that dilemma, I think. The larger ones are necessarily more singular. And also a lot heavier.

Lawson: They're different materials?

McCollum: They are, but that's a technical thing.

Lawson: You think? The big ones are concrete, aren't they? Doesn't concrete have a different connotation from plaster? You don't have a material content? One of the funny things about them is, either way, they're closed off. But critics have tended to make an issue of the fact that the small ones are solid and the big ones are hollow. Which is obviously…

McCollum: Of course they also have material content. Concrete has a different connotation from plaster. I chose plaster for the smaller ones because it runs the cultural gamut from its common use in simple children's crafts to its sophisticated use in commercial reproductions and artists' studios. Gypsum has been in use for thousands of years, so to me it has a feeling of being a very primary material.

If I felt I could have made the larger *Perfect Vehicles* solid, I would have. It's just that you'd need a crane every time you moved them. That was an important point, that they be solid; I was looking for an object that would grow in meaning and value through projection. That meaning would be projected onto it, or into it. I felt that if they were hollow, that hollowness would be confused with whatever meaning we might feel was inherent in the vehicle itself. In other words, if you can't physically put anything in it, then you're only going to put meaning into it—you can't put flowers in it, or ashes. Even though the large ones are hollow, the lids are part of the form as a whole, and they don't come off!

Lawson: I had a teacher in primary school who would tell off noisy kids with the phrase "Empty vessels make the most noise" [laughs].

McCollum: I've heard that expression. But "empty vessels" is different from *Perfect Vehicles* [laughs]. This reminds me of an article I read in a magazine about a wealthy nineteenth-century American who was constantly going back and forth by ship between England and Boston, and he owned these two oriental vases, each about six feet tall. He loved them so much that when he traveled back and forth he took the vases with him. This image of somebody carting around these cumbersome exteriorizations of some quality of great inner significance is an image that reoccurs in my thinking about most of the objects I make. I always picture people carrying my objects around before I make them, especially the bones. To carry around a dinosaur bone would be particularly poignant and cumbersome.

To me, the dinosaur bones, being so huge, seemed like the perfect metaphor for the way that a copy embodies an absence because dinosaur bones only come to us as copies in the first place. They represent this enormous, monumentally sad absence of a whole world we'll never retrieve again. To me, making copies from a mold feels like constantly trying to bring something back that used to be there but isn't anymore. You take a cavity that's made of rubber and you fill it with plaster and you pop it out and it looks just like the original, but it isn't quite. So you do it again and again and again.

With the fossils, I was trying to further extend this picture of the dramatic role objects play in emotional life. What I felt was missing from the picture was a kind of connectedness to history—to time, to the past. So, as I've said before, I was looking for an object that would really do that and not simply be a copy of something else that did that, or an arbitrary sign of something that did that. But there are very few kinds of objects that I could possibly imagine that might give you that sense, while at the same time being infinitely reproducible. Instead of focusing on historical relics or heirlooms or certain types of things that we could easily find, I found myself having to choose something that was quite atypical. My feeling was, since the fossil was already a duplicate, there wouldn't be any loss of authenticity by reduplicating it; I would simply be extending a series which was already begun, in a way.

Even more to the point, the Pompeii relic was a *cavity,* not a solid thing. The dog was killed in A.D. 79; it was smothered and then it deteriorated within its own cavity. But the cavity itself wasn't discovered until 1874, and it was only at that point that it was filled with plaster. The Vesuvius Museum made the mold for me in 1991. It's an object that's difficult to date. I was tempted to date it A.D. 79 because that's when the original cavity was made. So it's a problematic object in that it's a copy—a copy of an object that only existed as a copy to begin with, without having had a "real" existence during any prior point in history.

Lawson: Or existed as this empty space that once was a dog—it's a representation of a moment in time.

McCollum: In the title of the piece, *The Dog from Pompei,* I chose to give Pompei the present-day spelling, because that's where I obtained the cast dog, in present-day Pompei. But it was Pompeii—double *i*—at that moment in time when the dog died. Copy editors are always changing my title back to the ancient spelling because they think that it's more correct. So everyone seems to be confused about how to date it.

I determined that I wanted to make an object that offered a connectedness to the deep past. I also determined that it had to be something that wasn't connected to any specific culture. Usually, if we go to a history museum, we don't see things like the Pompeiian dog; for example, we see things that belonged to a particular king or era or battle, and you know they're artifacts or relics that have to do with some individual or culture. Obviously the dog did come from Pompeii and refers to a specific geological event. In the end, it's only a dog: it's not made of gold, it's not carved, it doesn't reflect any style or any culture. At least that's the way it seemed to me. I was originally looking for the famous loaves of bread when I went to Pompeii. It turned out that those loaves of bread are real.

Lawson: The bread is preserved?

McCollum: Yes, and I was so disappointed because I remembered, as a child, reading that the Pompeiian loaves of bread were cast in plaster—but I remembered wrong. So that narrowed down the choices.

There was a chest with doors and hinges which they had cast. They had found a three-dimensional rectangular cavity, and they plastered the sides with concrete and excavated it and it turned out to be a chest with molding and everything. They wouldn't let me do it. It looked very much more like an art object of a more abstract type. It would have had a whole different slew of references.

Lawson: What kind of issues did the curators and conservators at Pompei raise?

McCollum: I was very lucky because they didn't get all that involved in the end, but early on there were issues. There were certain things that had been very well documented and other things that had not been documented. The chests were discovered more recently, and that seemed to be a big issue.

Lawson: It was infringing on their potential commerce, in a way.

McCollum: My dealer in Naples and I wound up getting the dog from a museum that was a little to the side of the site called the Vesuvius Museum. And what they had was a secondary cast of the dog, as there had only been two or three copies made. And the reason that they were able to get their copy had to do with somebody who was related to somebody the museum people knew who had worked on the site and was allowed to make a copy for them. It wasn't the actual first cast dog that came out of the ground. I kind of wish it had been, but ultimately it doesn't really matter because since then I've made three additional molds. It doesn't matter because they all have the same relationship to the original cavity. A young man who was working on the site at Herculaneum, who was an archaeology student and friends with the site's restorer, knew the director of the Vesuvius Museum and they let us do it. So I didn't have to go through Rome; I only had to go through Pompei. That made it much easier. We applied to Rome for permission to use the other objects, and they refused us.

I ultimately chose the dog. At first I was afraid of the drama of the thing, it seemed so incredibly overdramatic, dramatic beyond any necessity. But in the end I think I chose it because it is so poignant, so evocative. I mean, people have actually cried when they've seen it—when they see my copy of it. When I had the show in Madrid, somebody cried. It has nothing to do with what a wonderful artist I am.

Lawson: Oh, I don't know. You shouldn't downplay your role. It is the way that you draw attention to the object that makes it seem so moving.

McCollum: Whenever I see it, my initial feeling is to feel sorry for the dog—to feel empathy for the dog. But how empathetic can you really feel for a dog that died nineteen hundred years ago? It's almost a preposterous emotion. I think, in a really interesting way, it introduces a feeling about time that is very familiar and intimate. How can I say this? It seems to me if we didn't have artifacts to remind us about the past, everything would disappear. We would be living in the continual present all the time. The only way we have any sense of the past is through artifacts, or memories—if memories can be called artifacts. We either have inner representations or outer representations, but we don't have any actual experience of the past. We can have wonderful representations of the past, voluptuous and emotionally charged representations of the past, but they're always going to be just representations and stories. I came to feel that the dog seemed to exemplify this drama and was a dramatic object that embodied that feeling of estrangement from the past even as it invoked the past.

Lawson: Does the dog encourage a narrative? Or does the repetition of the dog prevent that from happening? Last time we talked, you said something about the dinosaurs—that the fact of their existence is so strangely threatening because they represent an environment that would have been hostile to humans. And in a way, the dog does the same thing because it is a record of a moment when the earth was hostile to humanity.

McCollum: When I originally wanted to use the loaf of bread, I wanted to use an object that had utterly no significance, that was mundane, that was domestic and ephemeral, that was only accidentally preserved, and that was unsettling exactly because it was so common. Because to look at the ghost of a common, everyday object that's nineteen hundred years old is unsettling or is provocative, not because it belonged to anyone in particular, but simply because it's still here, and we recognize it.

Here's an example: When I was a truck driver in the sixties, I worked for an art-handling company in Los Angeles, and I once delivered something to a collector in San Francisco. He tipped me: he put a trilobite fossil in my hand, and I said, "What is this?" And he said, "It's a trilobite. This is 300 million years old." I looked at it and thought, "My God, holy cow!" But on the way out the door, I thought, "Yes, but any rock I pick up might be 300 million years old!" So I don't know how to explain it very well, but I wonder why is it that we don't perceive every rock that way? It isn't uncommon to find a 300-million-year-old rock—they're probably in your garden—and why doesn't that amaze us as much as an imprint of the trilobite amazes us? It amazes us because there's more of a story there, more of a drama.

Lawson: There's the evidence of life.

McCollum: And death—that's a story. To a geologist, any stone is a story, but not to most of us. So I'm interested in how that is suppressed, how we walk around not only not thinking about death but not thinking about time, not thinking about how much time has passed on this planet. To me, this daily amnesia is a good symbol of unconscious repression in general. It's something that is so obvious to all of us and we all know it, especially if the object is a bone, because it's obviously an allegorical thing, too, a reminder of death. The planet's been here—I don't know how long it's been, billions of years—and life has been around nearly that long, and we don't dwell on the significance of this on a daily basis. The awareness of time falls into that category of other things that we push out of our consciousnesses, like sexuality, violence, death, and so forth. And we save objects which seem to me to allow us to dwell on this only when we feel like it. Or we create archives that we visit to look at these things on special occasions. I'm personally surprised that everybody doesn't collect fossils. Why wouldn't everyone want three or four fossils? They have a significance that goes beyond any artwork. Yet people are generally more apt to have artworks than fossils.

Lawson: I know I keep trying to beat this dead horse, but I'm just trying to get something clear. You have this great interest and respect for fossils, for example, because they work as souvenirs of long ago—it makes you think of the fragility of life. It seems to me that before you started working on the fossils, your work was generated out of your disappointment with cultural artifacts. They represented a cultural memory that was an alien one to you—it was the memory of a power elite rather than the memory of the ordinary person. So by leapfrogging over history, so to speak, you have found a way of getting at the issue of time and memory that avoids the issue of culture.

McCollum: Yes, you're right. I see what you mean better now. It was a conscious choice, similar to the way that I avoided making "pictures" when I did the *Plaster Surrogates*. When I decided to do the *Surrogates,* I had two ways to go: I could have done either every image or no image. I opted for no image. I guess in the same sense I wanted to produce an object that carries with it that deeper scope of time—the scope of time which obliterates or relativizes history. It would have seemed overly limiting to choose a particular historical period. Pompeii, of course, existed during a certain period. So you can't say that the plaster dog works perfectly on that level, but you can say that it's very problematic to date the thing. But the dinosaur fossils do leapfrog over the problem, like you say, and I was surprised to find how satisfied I was to produce the *Lost Objects.* They satisfied a lot of my visual needs in terms of their forms, as well as my intellectual interests in what they were capable of signifying. And they're so monumentally sad.

Sometimes I almost self-consciously functioned as an American when I was plotting out the dinosaur project. I went out to Utah to see Dinosaur National Monument, where a lot of those fossils were found that I borrowed from the Carnegie Museum of Natural History to make my molds. I enjoyed the discovery that people in Utah, especially the people that I talked to who work in museums there, claim dinosaur bones as their heritage. It might seem peculiar to you as a European, but responding to that as an American, I totally understood what they meant. I think that from a European perspective one might think, "It's not your heritage; if anything, it's the earth's heritage." So I think what you're perceiving is true, that there is an element in my work of wanting to neutralize all of the complicated factors when it comes to cumulative culture. There are so many other ways that beautiful objects can come into existence! I think this is very American of me.

In a sense, culture is too much to have to think about. It's too much to have to know. This is probably not only an American impulse; it's probably more generally a modern impulse to want to reduce things into some simpler form. I'm not trying to tell you that I think this is just an observation of yours, because I do think it's there in the work, but I just want to contextualize it. I didn't think that you could get at that feeling of "timeness" without leapfrogging over cultural artifacts. What was I going to choose—something Sumerian? or Mayan? It would always be something from somewhere. Then it would be, why choose that and not the other? So I narrowed it down to a very rare, almost curiosity type of object, more than a historical type of object. And really, now I can't think of any other object that satisfies those criteria that I have just described and that comes to us as a copy but still has that direct, indexical relationship to the past—can you? Fossils are the ideal thing since they are by definition traces or imprints.

Lawson: I didn't see the Carnegie installation. I just saw a photograph, which was shot from the balcony looking down. In thinking about the piece, had you been thinking about the exhibition's context and how your work would look with European art? It's quite striking. You could start to make all sorts of associations about these limbless, classical sculptures looking down on broken bones.

McCollum: I think I liked the room mainly because it was big and very grand, and maybe it would lend a little drama to the piece. I don't know. More significantly, if you walked through the door in back, you walked right into the Natural History Museum. It was the only gallery that connected to it. I didn't mind the classical sculpture surrounding the room, but I didn't mean to make too big of a drama between nature and culture. It was as much happenstance as anything else.

One of the things that I think is unique about my work, and it's a big problem that I have, is that it doesn't have any site, really. I mean, the *Plaster Surrogates* and the *Perpetual Photos* have to go on a wall—that's about it. I design the objects before I really know what I'm going to do with them—that's the case with the bones. I'd been wanting to do cast dinosaur fossils for years, but I had no access to any. I happened to be invited to be in the show at the Carnegie Institute, so I was finally able to get access to fossilized bones. As I said before, I pictured people carrying them around, but I didn't really know what I was going to do with them. It was the same with the *Individual Works*: I didn't know what I was going to do with them, and I still have a problem with not knowing what to do with them.

Lawson: That's connected to the whole idea of identifying a need, fulfilling it, simplifying it, and culling it, because it is all done in a vacuum.

McCollum: Yes, I guess so. It's appropriate that I find myself in this dilemma, and it's appropriate that I find myself with so many objects that I don't know what to do with.

Lawson: Storage is so predominant in your studio. Your studio is itself becoming a kind of museum archive. With your method of production, you're always in production, aren't you?

McCollum: I tend to keep producing. I usually keep going on with a project until it completely bores me to death. I'm interested in the quality an object has when you know there will likely be more of them. But any one of my artworks may be made up of hundreds of smaller artworks. I produce works in collections, so if I'm doing an exhibition, I may have a single collection on exhibit, but there may be hundreds of objects in that single collection to look at. So I have to produce them one at a time.

Lawson: "Collections" sounds like a marketing device of some sort—the fashion industry presents new collections.

McCollum: Doesn't it also sound like the Museum of Modern Art, or any museum or patron? It's not my fault that the fashion industry imitates the language of the cultural elite [laughs].

Lawson: What's behind the idea of a collection?

McCollum: People collect objects. Having just one of them doesn't convey that fact, so that's why I like to make lots of objects. It's contradictory in a business sense because it makes my life really complicated, and my art dealers don't like it.

I just did a drawing show at a gallery in London last year, and since they had all the framing done over there, I naturally expected them to attach labels to the backs of all 2,070 drawings the way galleries generally do. Well, they labeled a hundred or so, but then they got bored and frustrated and stopped doing them. I was kind of irritated by that, but they were thinking that I've got to be nuts, expecting them to label 2,070 drawings. So I had my assistant sent to London to help them. It's paradoxical that I produce objects that have to be individually registered and individually signed and considered, but the artwork itself, as a whole, becomes a collection of maybe 400 or so of these individually considered objects.

Lawson: Even in a hypothetically limitless market, you will have a storage problem.

McCollum: I'm that kind of person. I tend to want to fill a space when I see it. If I have an extra corner in my studio, I say to myself, "I can store such and such there," so I make some more. Working in extremely large quantities is inherent to my thinking because in trying to construct this picture of art objects and emotions in interaction, I want to take into account not only the relationships that the art objects have to one another but also the relationships they have to all the other kinds of objects in the world that are not art objects. It seems to me that one of the determining features of an art object is that it's a unique object almost by definition. I don't think that the meaning of the uniqueness can really be understood without recognizing it in relation to objects that are not unique, that are largely mass-produced objects. When I began to think most about this particular issue—about uniqueness as a quality which is only defined by its opposite—I guess I got involved in mass production in a minor way.

Lawson: With the Surrogates?

McCollum: With the *Surrogates,* yes. I originally began using mass production in the late sixties as a kind of dramatic device. But then I began to realize that this was an interesting dilemma in the way that I just described it. I don't know how to say it. It's our conception of what artworks are, and should be, and how we expect them to function. We expect them to be rare, and we expect them to be emotional, passionate, and we expect them to be spiritual (maybe) and spontaneous. We expect art objects to symbolize what it means to be human—to have qualities that a machine cannot reproduce.

I began to recognize that the issue isn't simply how we define what an art object is, but how we define what it means to be human. And for whatever reason, when we say something is human, we are usually referring to all the qualities that are not mechanical. So how are we to understand what it means to be human if we don't also understand what we consider to be nonhuman and mechanical? In a similar way, art objects are expected to be about passion, spirituality, expressivity, spontaneity, and the recording of special, magic moments, and so forth—the kinds of things we find in a typical expressionist painting. How can we understand what that means if we don't realize that the artists who produce these artworks exist in a culture that is saturated with copies and mass-produced objects that are often all essentially the same? In a world where everything is "unique," the concept of "uniqueness" would have no significance.

To me, this contrast became more interesting than either the works of art themselves or the mass-produced objects. This is what I became interested in at the end of the seventies. I grew interested in how that dichotomy itself describes a picture of who we are at this historical moment. Then I began to consider that there was a kind of group denial of what mass production was expressing. If it was a general expression of who we were, then it must be expressive of something. We think we know what we're expressing with works of art—and you've written about this particular aspect of expressionism—how interesting it is that all this expressionism looks alike, and so on. It's peculiar that we burden the artist with all this expectation of being expressive and relieve industry of this same expectation. I feel that if you look for human values only in artworks and pretend that human values are not relevant in industry, then you're creating a situation where people feel no moral responsibility for what's being mass produced.

And so I felt compelled to think about these things and explore these issues to try to produce an artwork that also depicted what I felt industry expresses, and produce a kind of object that was at the same time a mass-produced thing as well as an art object. To make something that was a reconciliation at a higher level—that was my conceit. Not some artwork that was referring to mass production, or vice versa, but something that reconciled both forms of expression into a single form. And I began to think about how many ways industrial production seeks to imitate nature, for instance, in its repetition, in its fecundity, and in its quantity.

There is something so sensual and almost mind-boggling about the *Individual Works.* They are designed to appeal directly to a sense of touch with all of those little shapes that are so eroticized. There seems to be so much reference to the body. When I looked at the table filled with over ten thousand works, I felt like there was an extension or a projection of the human body, in a sense, my own body—not only because I'd touched each one and made each one, but because the little shapes often resembled little penises or little nipples or other little bodily passages. I borrowed from industrial design all those little tricks that make you want to touch something, that appeal to your sensuality and your desire. I chose to make shapes that, in a similar way to the *Perfect Vehicles,* could appear both biomorphic and mechanical.

When I made those salmon-colored *Individual Works,* I expected that they might have the effect of synthetic intestines. I was looking for a color that would resemble synthetic flesh, so the table would almost look like an operating table, a mechanized depiction of a dissection table that had gotten out of control. In the same sense, I chose green for the other ones so they'd refer to vegetation and growth.

Lawson: Like scenarios in a horror film?

McCollum: Well, I suppose.

Lawson: That they might hatch or something?

McCollum: Well, that could be. To me that's the way the world looks; that's the way industrial production seems—kind of maniacally proliferate. At the same time, it seems almost to want to reach for the sublime, to represent our wishes for abundance: to heal the sick and feed the hungry and to produce a more egalitarian society. All these feelings go hand in hand with our horror of technology and weaponry. Industrial production certainly isn't without its emotive qualities. It is clearly a reflection of our dreams being made real in some way, and our nightmares.

Lawson: There's the argument that art is useless whereas the industrial object is useful. You work with industrial techniques—from a kind of mechanical drawing to assembly-line production—to make objects that are designed to have no use.

McCollum: Well, I think that's a particular way of looking at use. There is, of course, already such a thing as the mass production of art objects. If that's someone's definition of industrial mass production, then it shouldn't seem possible to produce art objects industrially. But people do this all the time. They produce souvenirs and tchotchkes and religious symbols and so forth. It's very common that we produce objects that are for symbolic and aesthetic use. I make a special point with the *Individual Works* to make sure that they are not useful. They don't even have bottoms, so they can't be used as paperweights. That's something that I had to figure out, and it was much harder making them without bottoms because they needed a two-part mold, and they'd roll off the table during production. In many ways, I really like this work because these objects are an attempt to come up with your "basic treasured object." I had this continuum in my mind: I had the feces of the toddler at one end of the spectrum (which might be the first valued object) and the Fabergé egg at the other end. And in making all these design choices there was that intestinal quality.

Lawson: From the chicken's point of view?

McCollum: A Fabergé egg is essentially an object of pure value, maybe even to the chicken [laughs]. The process of producing the *Individual Works* in quantity becomes part of the drama of experiencing the work, I think. It certainly does for me. And I produced those *Individual Works,* of course, without ever seeing them on display because I don't have room to display them. So they're made on a table and then put into boxes.

Lawson: In your studio, where they're made on trays like cookies, that gives you one sense of what they might be, yet the end result is different.

McCollum: To this day, I honestly don't know what to do with them. Two different museums bought groups of over ten thousand. I've made over thirty thousand so far. Ten thousand seems to be the low end of what they call a short run in industry.

Lawson: In a funny way it seems like an excess, but it's really not at all.

McCollum: That's true. Once I had a job for somebody else, and I had to come up with twelve hundred wooden pegs of an odd size. I didn't want to make them myself so I looked in the Yellow Pages for people who did wood turning and found a company whose claim was that there was no job too small. They said they did short runs. So I went all the way over there and told them I wanted twelve hundred pegs made, and they said, "We won't do twelve hundred objects." And I said, "You said, 'No quantity too small.'" They said, "Yeah, but twelve hundred?" I asked, "What's a short run?" And they said, "It would have to be at least ten thousand."

But the effect of the *Individual Works* is peculiar because they create something like a moral problem. I created a system that produced them all to be unique, which is all very intellectual, arithmetic. Once they're all out on the table, then they're an experience that I find unsettling. Sometimes I find it exalting and sometimes I find it nauseating, especially when, for instance, I've started to look to see if I can find the one that I'm looking for. There's just so many discriminations that have to be made that I start feeling nausea.

Lawson: Can you remember each one?

McCollum: I remember the molds. I've made only about three hundred molds. Each mold creates half an object—they go together in over forty-five thousand ways. When and if I produce more molds, the yield will rise exponentially. I certainly could say to myself that I would like to find the one that has such and such a top and such and such a bottom—I could do that. A lot of the objects, the little shapes and parts that I use, have personal significance to me. They come from very specific moments, like the object you have—one of the shapes came from a friend's childhood toy and another shape came from my flashlight. I've used the shapes of objects found on friends' front yards, or in friends' houses, on trips abroad, vacations, hardware stores in Europe, so that when I look at that vast array of unique objects—*Individual Works*—I'm also experiencing a flood of memories as well.

I find that the work replicates a kind of day-to-day drama. It's a moral drama. It's making decisions about what's important and what isn't: what people are important, what people aren't important; what things are important, what things you throw away, what things you keep; what person you want to talk to and who you don't; who your friends are. These constant choices we make in a field of billions of people are probably essentially experienced on some level as a kind of moral pain, like the pain suffered by a military officer when he decides to send soldiers into battle knowing that a certain percentage of them are going to be killed.

And I think that, in a sense, this moral pain is what *Individual Works* are a "picture" of. I also think it's the same moral pain represented by the whole continuum of objects, from the mass produced to the unique, from the common to the rare, and so forth, because I think this continuum obviously (maybe not obviously) represents the way we construct a class society. The way this society is organized, the way we organize objects, reflects the way we are organized by society.

I have to say, there's an effect that I try to achieve with my work... Have you read *Jealousy* by Robbe-Grillet? I don't believe the word *jealousy* is ever used in the book, in spite of the title. All you experience as a reader is the narrator's description of what he is looking at. He's looking at the trees and he's looking at the veranda and he's looking at the letter in his wife's handwriting that he sees in his friend's pocket. He thinks, "Maybe..." And there's this obsession with looking that's described over and over again as his eyes go back to certain things and to his memories of seeing certain things. He's jealous, he's frightened, he's angry. You intuit those emotions; you're not told he feels this way. The feeling grows in you as you're reading, as the character increasingly "looks" at things in a way that's conditioned by his feelings. I was hugely influenced by Robbe-Grillet in the sixties. And I think it's that way of developing emotional self-consciousness that I try to accomplish—that it isn't located in the objects; it's a kind of halo effect that emerges in the experience of the objects. It's a recognition of something unconscious that slowly emerges, so that the pain of social inequity is replicated in the way we organize objects. One of the things I'm doing with the *Individual Works* is trying to re-create that drama. This is the kind of effect that I try to achieve with my work: how I described looking at ten thousand objects as nausea or moral pain.

Lawson: Do the Drawings *refer to moral pain as well?*

McCollum: The *Drawings* and the *Individual Works* were born out of each other; they were similar projects. The *Individual Works* came first. I wanted to speak about the impulse to do these projects in the terms you brought up earlier, about representation versus antirepresentation. The *Perfect Vehicles,* in a sense, represented a very specific type of symbol, which you could define as a single object that might represent "eternal truths." That's a common type of symbol—a single thing that represents a lot.

I think I wanted to question or explore this particular structure: one thing representing everything. We look at the American flag and it represents all Americans or the "Spirit of America," or whatever. What if instead we had 300 million individual symbols that somehow represented the multiplicity of the country? I wondered if there wasn't some kind of hierarchical thinking or aristocratic model that we follow in the way we make objects and organize them when we create symbols. It almost seems to be our primary definition of a symbol—that it represents something larger than itself. Otherwise you wouldn't need the symbol; you'd just have the thing itself.

So I was thinking about how difficult it is for us to conceive of the quantity of people on the planet and how, before we knew how to conduct demographic studies, no one knew how many people were on the planet, and this was a mysterious concept. But with communications as they are now, it's a serious emotional problem, dealing with the knowledge of how many people are on the planet and what it means when we hear that twenty thousand people died in an earthquake. It's difficult; it's a moral problem.

I began to wonder if maybe part of that problem is that it's exacerbated by the structure of our symbols, where one object represents many things. Maybe an alternative or additional kind of symbol making could exist where thousands of things were represented by thousands of things. I wondered what that would look like. I was thinking about people when I designed the *Individual Works*: what people must mean when they talk about the human soul, individual souls, and how you would depict that. With the *Drawings,* I chose this kind of heraldic image that might even suggest a clan or family symbol but carried that idea through into a slightly more complex system that could produce millions and billions of separate images—potentially one for every human soul on the planet. In a sense, I was creating a heraldic system for individuals rather than for families or nations. With both of these projects I'm dealing with huge quantities. I mean, the *Individual Works* are being shown in lots of over ten thousand, and the *Drawings* are shown with as many as twenty-five hundred in one exhibit. I hoped to create a picture of what it might look like if we thought differently about making symbols in the first place.

Lawson: How did you go about making the Drawings*?*

McCollum: I designed five curves and a system of formats or little matrixes. I inscribe these curves into the matrixes and use an arithmetic system to make sure that I don't repeat myself. Then I draw these five curves in every combination on paper. So far, I haven't made a drawing with more than four curves.

Lawson: Do the curves have personal references for you the way the forms making up the Individual Works *do?*

McCollum: No, they're just geometric. I had plastic templates made at a factory where they make architectural templates out of that green plastic. But, no, they don't have any of that kind of significance for me.

Lawson: The piece is more diagrammatic, in a sense. The Individual Works *seem to spin off from all these other associations, but the* Drawings *focus in on the idea in a more abstract way.*

McCollum: There was so much hyperextended sensuality in all those multiple references in the *Individual Works*. I think that with the *Drawings* I was looking for something that was balanced and stable, so I chose symmetrical shapes and a traditional art medium. It was the only series I've ever done using a traditional art form: graphite on paper. That's why they're simply called *Drawings*. In a sense, it was about the desire to look for social stability through identification, hence the reference to heraldry—about making a stable symbolic system to accommodate the chaos of huge numbers.

Lawson: The Drawings *are much more austere in appearance than the colored plaster works.*

McCollum: When I walk into exhibits of my drawings, I feel like I'm walking into an ancient archive. There's a kind of spiritual stability in them for me, whereas the *Individual Works* are transgressive in all different kinds of ways.

Lawson: The Drawings *are harder to gain access to; they're just there. With the objects it's obvious that you have a real desire to tell stories, to insert a narrative content in the work. And while looking at these objects, people have these realizations about different kinds of moral situations, or realizations about the passage of time. I think making narrative, representational paintings is no longer feasible, or reliable, or doable. It seems that now we need to make movies, or get into some kind of elaborate installation type of work, or some kind of time-based work if we want to tell a story. But you've been able to do it in this perverse way by holding on to "traditional" cultural objects like the vase. You've been able to get this poignant effect from a group of things that, on the face of it, shouldn't produce that effect.*

McCollum: Before I was an artist, in the early sixties, I thought that maybe I wanted to go into theater and had gotten a bit interested in writing plays. There was one play I never saw produced, but I read it—*The Kitchen* (1959) by Arnold Wesker. Do you remember it? It was a one-act play structured on the rising tension and stress that takes place in a restaurant kitchen as the rising demand for producing food and getting it out there during a rush takes place. I'd worked in a lot of restaurants and knew this structure, so I was intrigued by this play. It depicted the increasing tension between the employees: increasing anger, increasing arguments. In the end, it calms down, back to normal, and you get the sense that this happens every four hours. That was the play, sort of "found theater." It was an allegory for the way working people are caught up in the drama of economic demand and endless production. All the characters were cooks and waitresses—it was a wonderful play.

This particular drama had such an influence on me. Reading John Cage, I noticed how he would substitute other sequences of events for traditional musical structure. I was attracted to that as well. After learning about the wide variety of Fluxus performances based on the substitution of non-narrative "events" for traditional storytelling, I quickly fell into imitating the task-oriented performance in my studio. So the objects that I produce are always the result of multiple sets of applications of simple tasks.

One performance that has stayed in my mind was the one by Yvonne Rainer where she and a group of dancers carried furniture and carpeting from the lobby of the theater to the stage, and that was it. She did many other performances that challenged preconceived ideas about narrative. Carrying furniture from one place to another is only a narrative if you really want to think of it as a narrative. In fact, there may be no other way for us to perceive any sequence of events, really.

I think the question for me was, "Where does that narrative structure exist?" Does it exist in the event? in the script? in your head? In the sixties this was a very crucial question. Many people were interested in the nature of what we universalized as in-the-world, as opposed to invented, cultural structures. Is the narrative scenario something that is universal, or is this in the event itself, or is this something that we bring to events? These were the kinds of questions that a lot of people were asking. I was also especially influenced by a group of radical performance artists in San Francisco who called themselves The Diggers. I never met these people; I just remember anecdotes. But they invented the Free Store. Do you remember that?

Lawson: No, that is too much a part of American history for me.

McCollum: These actors were interested in artistic social intervention. I believe they were actors who had studied Brechtian strategies. They were interested in economics, and they were interested in how we perceive one another in the economic world that we live in and how we function there. They came up with this series of quasi-theatrical interventions that invited or forced you to consider economic exchange as a possible site of creative awareness and change. That was one of their strategies—just to use the word "free" and attach it to things. Especially things such as "free love" that were already free, so there was an obvious and paradoxical irony. Or the Free Store: it was a real store that opened in a storefront and everything was free. They spent a lot of time going around to bakeries and meat markets in the middle of the night and finding things that people didn't want, soliciting donations from all over the city.

Lawson: Real things were free?

McCollum: Real things. You'd go in there and get food or clothes or whatever they were able to come up with. I guess the idea of a store where you get something for free is only appreciable in terms of knowing about the enormous amount of trouble it was to keep the store functioning. And that's what I mean by a story. It's that sense of a drama that only becomes radically moving if you know what it took to make it happen. Getting up at three in the morning every day and going out to all the bakeries...

Lawson: So this is different from Oldenburg's store?

McCollum: It was very different, although it could have been influenced by that. It seemed to be an attempt to question what certain forms of economic exchange signify. Our traditional economic concepts limit our ideas about what's possible. The Free Store suggested a more creative way to look at what a store might be and to generate all kinds of implications as to other kinds of "valuation." I was struck by this experiment.

Lawson: Did you know about Oldenburg's store at that time? I ask since he made plaster objects. Did you know about that wedding-cake piece he did in L.A. in 1966—plaster cake-slice souvenirs for a curator's wedding party?

McCollum: I didn't know the whole story until I read it in your essay! [in *Claes Oldenburg: Multiples in Retrospect 1964–1990* (New York: Rizzoli International Publications, Inc., 1991)].

Lawson: That was one of Oldenburg's best multiples. I especially like that the guests at the wedding party took away their slices as party favors.

McCollum: Me, too. In my own work, the way art circulates among people is really primary in my thinking. Artworks sometimes seem to be just like tokens, or coins, circulating from person to person, or from gallery to museum to auction house. They accrue meaning and value at every step. Circulating like coins but much more slowly, of course, and on an entirely different historical scale. But they're always *moving.* They always have a kind of trajectory, and this trajectory develops the meaning of the work and one's experience of it.

Also in the sixties, around 1967 or '68, I remember reading about an event staged by the BMPT group in Paris. Each of the four members of the group had their own particular abstract painting that was reproduced over and over again as a group. The paintings themselves were indefinitely reproducible, depending on the circumstances they were shown in. In this particular event, they displayed one each of their four paintings—each the same size—on a theater stage, and invited an audience to view them. The curtain went up for one hour, and then it came down. That was it. They isolated the event of looking at a painting as a single dramatic moment.

Reading about this event had an early effect on my thinking. I was interested in ways to isolate the act of looking at a painting from the actual painting itself. This thinking really culminated when I began doing the *Surrogate Paintings:* the painting as a token, a sign of itself, or a prop, around which meanings and desires play out some kind of drama.

Lawson: But it has always seemed to me that the positions staked out by Buren and Mosset and the others are always just that—positions taken, poses struck. I have always found it difficult to accept the political content in the work of radical-chic intellectuals with an eye to career improvement. You, at least, have the desire to reach out to the common person, the uninitiated person who's not an art lover. The very particular decisions that you've made all along have been much broader in their implications.

McCollum: Well, these artists have always been really important to me. I'm sure my mentality and my background are different, and maybe I do imagine a different kind of audience when I'm working. I don't really know. But their work means a lot to me. I'm glad you think that, though. In other words, you don't think that a person needs to have followed art closely to feel like there are issues they can relate to in what I'm doing?

Lawson: I think that the Surrogates *still operate in that space where they look a little like abstract paintings. Big installations of them, where you had five hundred or so on the wall, probably transcended that. It is such an obsessive and absurd experience that there is a good chance that even someone who doesn't know the particular crevices of the argument might get a sense of what is going on. I think with the* Perfect Vehicles *it becomes clearer because they're not art objects per se; they refer to these vast cultural and emotional constructs that more people are likely to have a memory of, or a knowledge of, than of painting or art history. In the* Individual Works *the objects are recognizable in a way, but you don't know what they are, or you can't pin them down as art. They're not recognizably art. They're recognizably something else.*

McCollum: I agree.

Lawson: Because the Individual Works *don't have bases, they're not sculptures. They don't have hooks on the backs, so they're not paintings. They're homeless. The more recent pieces,* The Dog from Pompei *and the* Lost Objects, *are very direct.*

McCollum: It's back to what you said at the very beginning. The works seem to want to leapfrog over art history in their effect. Is that what you said?

Lawson: I think they do manage to get past the complexity that modernist avant-garde activity has created—the reliance on a complex barrier to understanding as part of its method of working. Starting from a very valid premise—questioning an issue of culture—such work has created a situation that's possibly worse than what it sought to fix. Oddly, there lies the place for reinscribing recognizable objects into the discourse, a strategy which obviously plays into the difficulties of being retrograde. So the question is, are you advancing or retreating when you start making work that can be described as figurative?

McCollum: I don't think that's the issue! Especially at this point in time. I don't know that it makes sense anymore to say that the main barrier separating modernist avant-garde artwork from the majority of people is that these works lack imagery, or that they're nonrecognizable, or anything like that. I think that the key to this separation lies more in the quantity, or the lack of quantity, of these artworks. I mean, artists seem to have just accepted, without question, that it's their calling to produce *rare* objects. This seems to me to be the reason that avant-garde activity is isolated from the people at large.

These days it's possible to learn about the philosophical complexity of all these "issues" on your own from reading and visiting museums and so forth. People aren't stupid. But what really is a barrier, I think, is this focus on making rare artworks that preclude participation by the majority of people through any real ownership and (worst of all) by censoring objects created in larger quantities before they're even made. We always seem to reinvent a class system of objects to accommodate the already existing class system, and I think this artificially limits what we're able to express as artists.

It's so funny the way people think. What might be considered beautiful in a small quantity of one or two is supposed to become less beautiful in larger quantities. And in mass quantities, things can even begin to seem hideous to some people, especially to connoisseurs, and "common" clearly becomes a negative, not a positive, quality. So when artists try to be progressive and at the same time produce rare objects, I think they are often working against their own stated intentions whether they mean to or not. I think they operate out of a blind spot.

Lawson: I tend to agree. Susan [Morgan] and I have a friend who trades in craft items from Central and South America—beautiful things and silly things, well made and improvised. She is fond of saying that while she admires quality, she loves quantity. I think that this—Claudia's dictum—expresses a kind of joyfulness, an acceptance of difference that has to be at the heart of any progressive idea of art making.

McCollum: It's a shame the way artists are always letting themselves be maneuvered into making these objects, objects which are meant to function in this kind of role. It doesn't even necessarily make sense, this idea that beautiful things should only be made available in small numbers. Yet in the art world we seem to accept this limitation without much question.

In the everyday world, we all know that a large quantity of anything can be beautiful. Everyone loves to watch the clouds, for instance, which are always unique and constantly plentiful. And we all seem to agree that trees are beautiful, and flowers and grains of sand and all the other millions of unique biological and geological formations around us. So in everyday experience there just doesn't necessarily seem to be any conflict between what's common and plentiful and what's unique and irreplaceable when it comes to recognizing beauty.

I think that we all lose out when we ask our artists to eliminate their feelings about large quantities from their vocabulary of expression just to please a certain exclusive group. And for this reason I think it's really important that, as artists, we should feel free to take a stand on this point by making as many artworks as we want.

✶

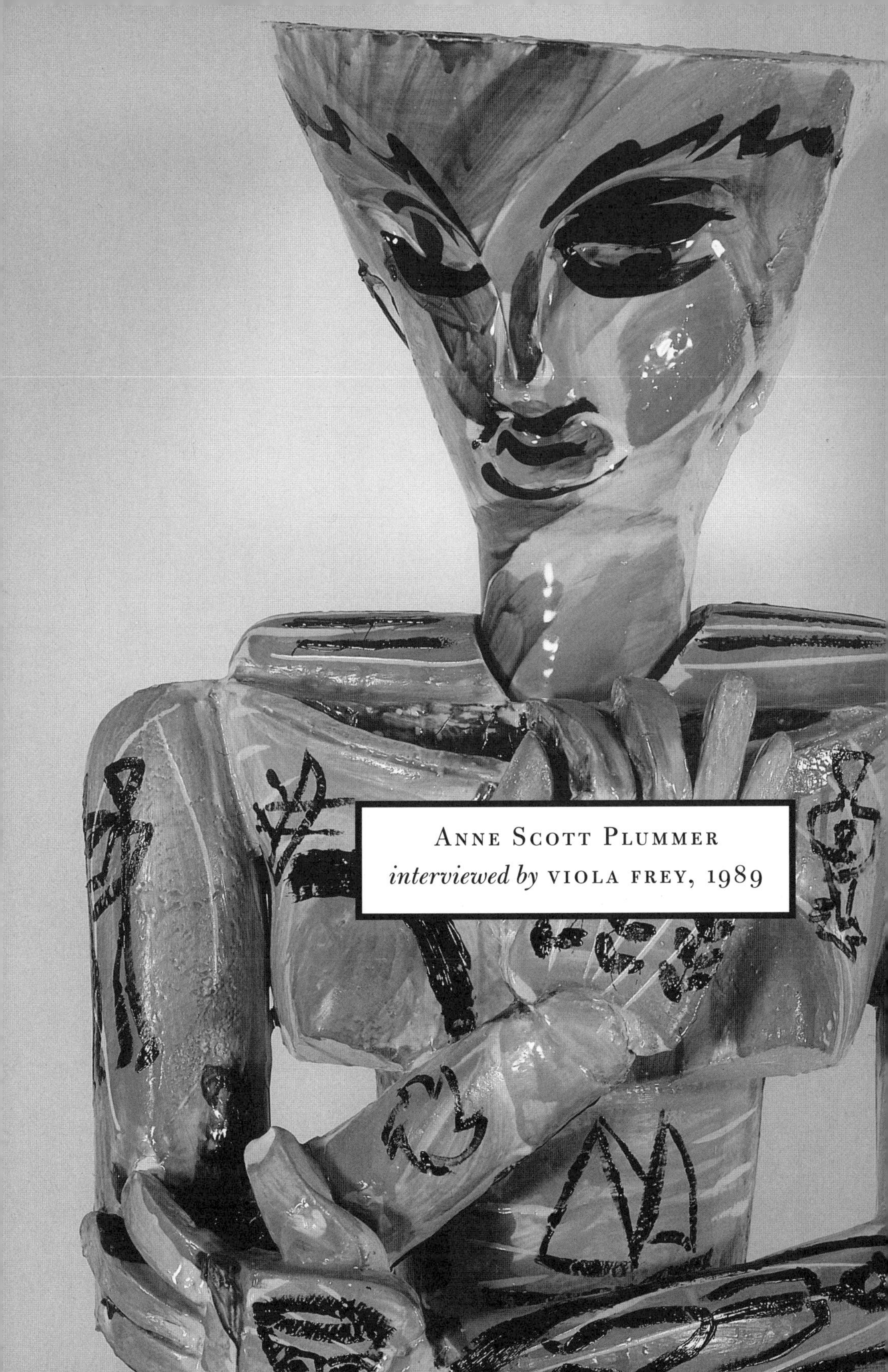

Anne Scott Plummer

interviewed by VIOLA FREY, 1989

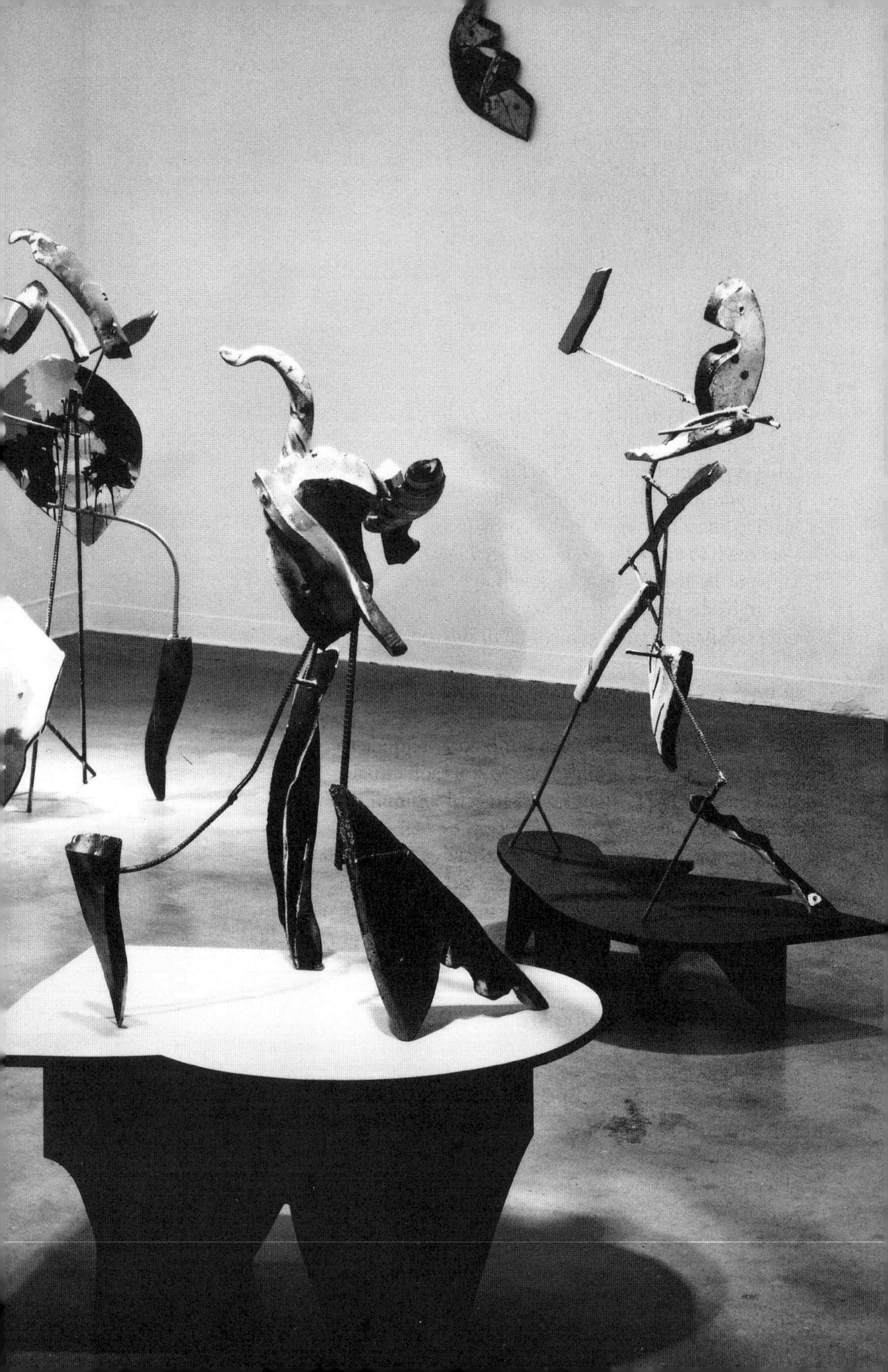

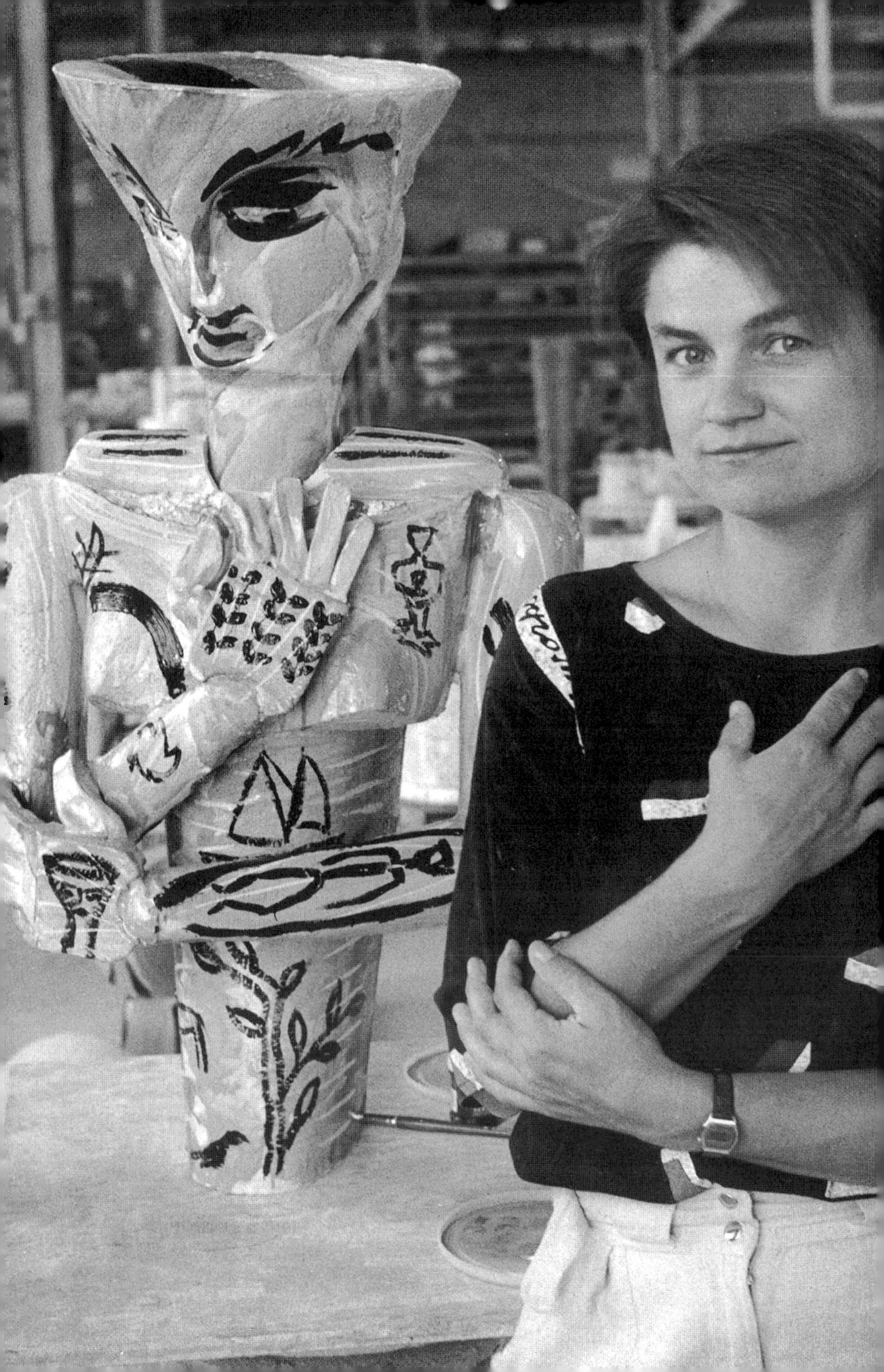

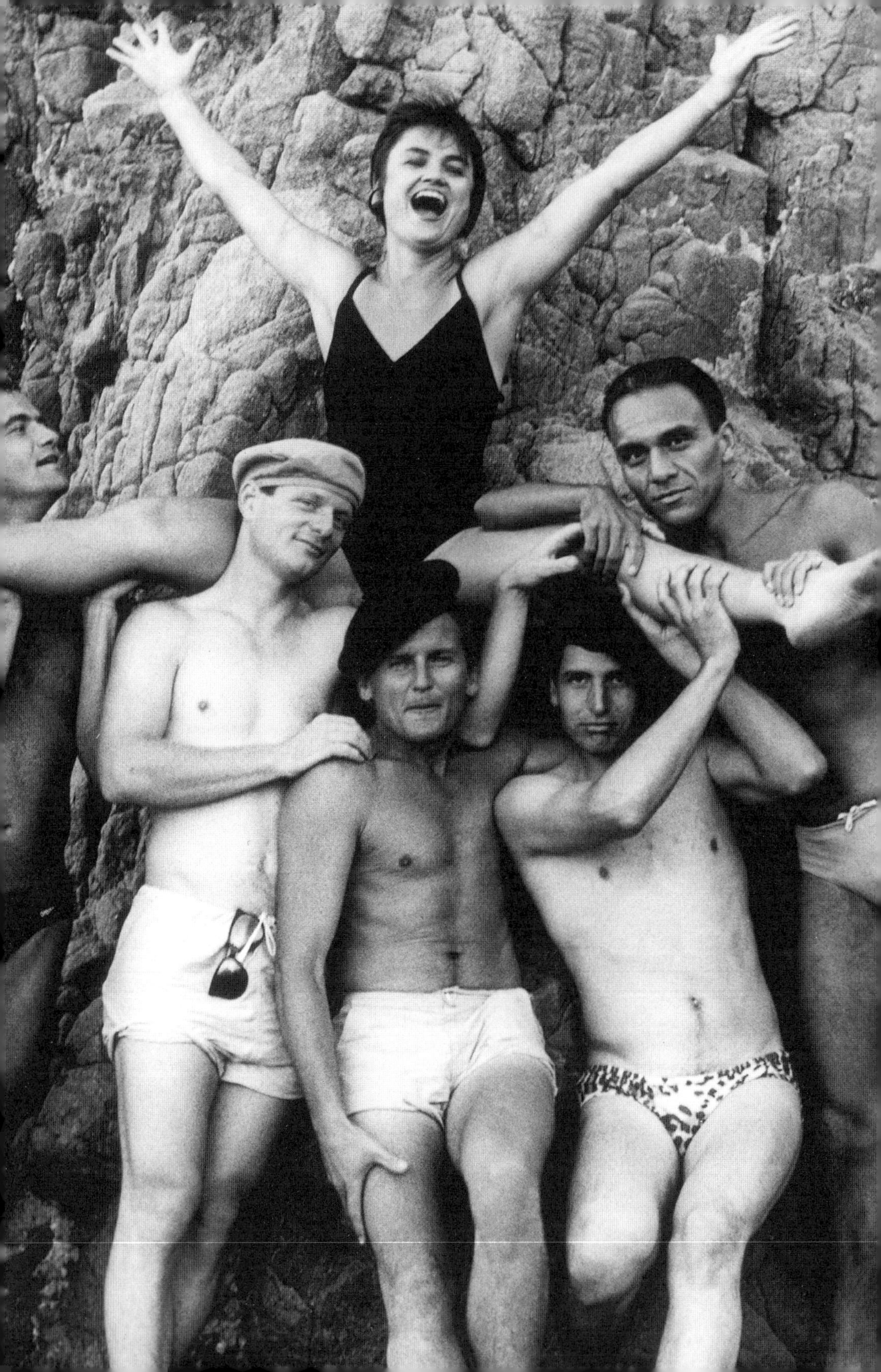

ANNE SCOTT PLUMMER

interviewed by

VIOLA FREY

Viola Frey: Have you always worked in clay?

Anne Scott Plummer: From the time I was a little kid, I was always interested in painting. Both my parents went to the Rhode Island School of Design—my mother was working on an art education degree and my father was studying textiles there. That was when Rhode Island was a big textile manufacturing state. The story my parents tell of how they met is that my mother hung up some of her watercolors and they dripped on my father's dyed yarns. So when I was a kid, my mother, who never completed her degree, always encouraged me to do art projects. She remained a Sunday painter. I would paint using the leftovers on her palette. I was also fascinated by the figure drawings which she had done when she was in school.

I won first prize in a local art show when I was twelve or thirteen, and my mother won second prize for her painting. When they told me I had won first prize, I assumed it was in the youth category, but I was astounded, then gratified, to find out that I was considered an adult. Since then I've considered myself an artist.

Frey: How did you *get started working with clay?*

Plummer: In high school I made my first painted sculpture. It was a formed canvas, three-dimensional. Something about that really struck me: this painted sculpture. I had never really thought of it before, having something three-dimensional, sculptural, and being able to paint it as well. That's one of the things still fascinating to me about ceramics. That combination of painting and sculpture is so natural, so integrated. Clay looks right when it is glazed. It doesn't look as if you've applied paint on something three-dimensional; it looks as if it's all one material.

page 167:
Industry, *1986, low-fired vitreous china with glazes, 37 x 18 x 14 inches*
page 168:
Fired Punk Rock, *1981, installation at the Libra Gallery, Claremont, California, ceramic with glazes and acrylic, steel, wood with plastic laminate and acrylic, 72 inches high, each*
page 169:
Anne Scott Plummer with Industry, *1986, low-fired vitreous china with glazes, 37 x 18 x 14 inches*
page 170:
Anne Scott Plummer at Matador Beach, California, 1985, promotional photo for the Ecole des Beaux-Arts, Paris

Nevertheless, my father didn't think it was such a good idea to go to art school. It was in the late sixties, and the people at Rhode Island School of Design were walking around barefoot with torn jeans and all, and that didn't make a big impression on him. So I just chucked the whole thing. I'd go to art school later.

Frey: What did you do then?

Plummer: I took a brief side trip as an air traffic controller in the air force. I was rebelling. It was a way to be independent from my family, to get away from their control.

Frey: Being an artist wasn't enough of a rebellion?

Plummer: I guess not. After the service and before I went to Rhode Island School of Design, I lived in Provincetown on Cape Cod for four years. I had a painting studio there and started to make pots to earn my living. I worked as a carpenter in the wintertime. In the summer I got together with a potter and learned how to make pots. I thought it was a great way to earn a living, and that was really my first introduction to ceramics. I didn't think of it as fine art. I sort of painted on the surface of these pots.

I also socialized with artists, and I modeled for artists, so I saw people working. These were artists who worked at the Provincetown workshop. It gave me an opportunity to watch serious young artists working: painting, sketching, and hanging their exhibitions. I had always thought I was a natural-born artist and didn't need to go to school. But after a while I realized that there were things I could learn in school.

My first year at Rhode Island School of Design was a real breakthrough for me. In that first year, the freshman foundation year, we explored a lot of different materials, and the whole idea of combining materials seemed natural after these experiences. I loved it, and I stayed up all night doing lots of projects because it was such a welcome challenge.

John Gill was one of the people who worked with clay in a real sensitive way that had an effect on me. Up until then I had been working with people who had this aggressive, the-bigger-the-better attitude toward working with clay. John Gill was a big man, but he had a very subtle, sensitive approach to the material. Jackie Rice was the head of the department the last two years I was there. She was very inspiring to me because she exposed me to the work of many contemporary ceramic artists and to their ideas. She really elevated my perception of working with clay as a fine art material.

Frey: Now you're a California artist—how did you make the transition from there to here?

Plummer: Well, I came here to go to graduate school. I came out to Claremont without having been to Southern California. I packed up all my things into a drive-away car and took off across the country. Just that experience alone was great. I love to travel, and there is something wonderful about driving cross-country. You really know what ground you've covered.

I worked with Paul Soldner at Claremont. That was who I came out to study with. I had read an article about him in *Ceramics Monthly* that made me realize he was an important artist and someone that I wanted to be involved with. Soldner really teaches by example. He emphasizes an intuitive approach; he does things because they feel right. Roland Reiss is another artist I worked with in Claremont. He is intellectual and conceptual in his approach to art, and this balanced with Soldner's more personal, value-oriented approach. The other great thing about Claremont is that there are fifty grad students, so there are lots of people to talk to. My work really started to develop in graduate school.

Frey: Other than these professors, what else has inspired you in your work?

Plummer: The other thing that inspired me was my uncle, Galway Kinnell, who is a well-known poet. When I was a child there was a certain disapproval expressed by the family because he wasn't well known. He was struggling. He was very involved in the civil rights movement, and his poetry reflected that. He just got by financially. The little information I got about the things he thought about made a big impression on me. He gave us things like a book of the stars, the constellations, and he talked about the stories behind them, the myths that they illustrate. He brought me a penknife that he said was the kind of knife that art students in Paris used to sharpen their drawing pencils, and that was one of my prized possessions for a long time. Of course, my mother didn't think I was old enough to have a knife. I was a little kid then. I thought his lifestyle was fascinating and exotic. He traveled a lot and thought about different things than I was exposed to. He was involved with the world at large, not just the small community that I called home.

Frey: I see. You did a series of pieces about Sun Valley. What was that all about?

Plummer: I first went to Sun Valley in the summer of 1980 as a graduate student. One of the other students was associated with Sun Valley Center of Arts and Humanities. It sounded great to me, so I went there. It's a ski resort in the winter, and it's really beautiful in the summer: there's still snow on the peaks, and it's cool and green.

I went up there as a student that one summer, and I went back two other times as an artist-in-residence. The first time I went back in 1983, I did the kiln pieces. They had recently built a big wood-fired kiln and were doing a few firings in it. It's a big communal project, firing a wood kiln up. All the wood has to be chopped into small pieces, and the whole thing gets loaded with the work of maybe fifteen people. Then there's the firing, which involves constant stoking and monitoring of the smoke coming out, constant adjustments, and the continuous chopping of wood. This is an all-day, all-night project. I got involved in it, and I fired a few pieces in that kiln. It got me thinking about how closely ceramic artists are associated with the technology of kilns—what a symbiotic relationship there is between the ceramic artist and this kind of magical process of firing. So I did five or six pieces that explored the relationship between the artist and the technology of firing. The largest one was *Spirit of the Wood Kiln*. It was an image of that big kiln with bright red, drippy, fiery glaze. On the outside, I drew images of the whole work process, all the manual labor involved in loading up and firing the kiln. It had a head coming out of the top that represented the spirit of the kiln because kilns seem to have their own personalities, their own souls, especially those bigger kilns. This is acknowledged by the practice of making a kiln god or goddess to help ensure a successful firing. This relationship is magical, and it's also unpredictable. There's a feeling of a greater force, a greater creative force contributing to the artwork. That's how I feel about it.

While artist-in-residence at Sun Valley Center in 1984, I met Jean Biagini, an artist from Aix-en-Provence, France. His work that summer involved some real interesting site work out in the Craters of the Moon national monument, one of the largest lava fields on earth. Before he returned to France, he invited me to work at the Ecole des Beaux-Arts in Aix-en-Provence for the following year. I was really excited. In the meantime, however, Biagini was appointed the head of an international artist exchange program in Paris. I guess he misunderstood and didn't realize that I was coming to Aix. I misunderstood and didn't realize that he wasn't going to be there. When I got to Aix, he wasn't there. I met him later at an opening in Marseilles, which is just south of Aix. He told me that I should get in touch with his friend Georges Jeanclous in Paris, and that I probably would prefer to work in Paris anyway.

He was right; Aix was a charming place, but Paris is an international art center. I called Jeanclous, went up to Paris, and showed him my portfolio. To the amusement of his students, I tried to speak in French. He played along and nobody spoke English to me after that. He let me work in the studio there at the atelier with the students, and he suggested that I do some figure drawing. This resulted in a series of figurative work.

It was a very romantic situation for me, just the idea of working in Paris right across from the Louvre at the Ecole des Beaux-Arts, this old venerable art institution surrounded by the beauty of Paris. I was in heaven the whole time.

I was very impressed with the outdoor figurative sculpture in the Tuileries. I wanted to get some of that monumentality and universal impact in my smaller pieces. One of the pieces I did was *David and Goliath*.

Frey: I'm surprised that you got anything fired at the Ecole.

Plummer: I fired the work myself when the students weren't using the kilns. My work had to fit into the small kiln that was available.

The other interesting thing that happened was that I started thinking about Los Angeles, the uniquely L.A. things and the American things about my life and art. And those things came into my work. For instance, I did my first modern centaur piece, the half-woman/half-car. She was on a freeway, listening to a saxophone-playing muse. I guess by being in Paris I suddenly became aware of things unique to our culture, like jazz, which is so admired there. I even missed the mobility of intracity freeway travel. I began to see the potential of those elements as images for my work.

It was a real nightmare bringing that work back to the United States. I packed it all up in boxes, which were difficult to get to begin with, and loaded everything on a train bound for Frankfurt, where a cousin of mine lives. Because I had ten boxes and you're only allowed three, including luggage, I put everything on the train very early before any conductors were around. I was advised, "Get it on the train before they know you have too much." I had to take two trips in a taxi to get it to the station, and when I arrived, there were no porters around, but I still got all the boxes on. As the train started off, one of the first things that they said was that the train would be separating. The front half of the train was going to Frankfurt, and the other half was going somewhere else. I enlisted the help of a couple of young women who spoke a little bit of English. I asked them if they would claim the pieces as their own when we went across the border because I had too much.

They said sure, they'd do that. Then I asked them if they would mind helping me carry the boxes up to the front half of the train. So, one at a time, we carried these big boxes through the narrow little aisles. Between each car there were about four doors—vacuum-shut doors. It was a big deal to open them, squeeze through the door, and get on to the next, and then, of course, we bumped into every single person along the aisle to the right part of the train. Then we had to find places to store all these boxes, and of course everyone had put their luggage up on the luggage racks. Well, we had about two and a half hours. When we got to the biggest box, it wouldn't go through the doors. There was a stop just before the train was to separate. It was a sixty-second stop. I said, "Look, we're gonna have to run outside the train with this box. We've got sixty seconds to run the length of the train, and then we'll jump back on the other end." The conductors were warning us to remain seated unless it was our destination. In spite of the warning we jumped off the train with the box—two of us because it was oversized and heavy—and ran down to the other end and jumped back on just before the train started up again, with us kind of hanging off. Then the train split up.

The next ordeal was the German customs officials: "What's all this? What are you going to do with it?" I don't speak any German, and they didn't speak any English. Fortunately, one of the girls who had helped me spoke German and interpreted.

"What's the work?"

"It's art."

"How valuable is it?"

"Oh, not valuable at all."

"Then why are you bringing it here?"

"Well, I'm just bringing it to my cousin."

"What are you going to do with it? Are you going to sell it?"

"Oh, no. I wouldn't think of selling it. In fact, it's not even finished yet. Look. Look at it."

And it's true—it wasn't finished. It wasn't even glazed. They didn't have glazes at the Ecole des Beaux-Arts. Jeanclous didn't use glazes, so he figured that nobody else needed to either. Anyway, with the help of this girl I didn't have to pay any duties, but they had to rip open all the boxes to look at the contents and see that they were actually worthless pieces of art.

I finally got my work to my cousin's. She had a small apartment and didn't have room to store all the boxes. In fact, she didn't even have room in her car to get them home. By the time she sent them to me, every single one of them was broken. I glued them together and painted them. They're still some of my favorite pieces.

Frey: You were chosen to work at the Kohler Arts Center. What was the program there like?

Plummer: It's an ongoing program called Arts/Industry at the Kohler Company and the John Michael Kohler Arts Center. Actually, the Kohler Company and the Kohler Arts Center are two separate organizations. The company is family owned; they say it's the biggest family-owned company left in the United States. A brother and sister still own it. The city of Sheboygan organized the Kohler Arts Center and bought the former Kohler family house for it; the Arts Center has an independent board of directors. They initiated and cosponsor this Arts/Industry program at the Kohler Company that is pretty unusual. There aren't too many companies in the U.S. where artists come in and actually work using the technology of the company.

Frey: What was it like, working in the factory?

Plummer: Working at Kohler was an incredible experience. There was a huge, open studio. It went back so far you couldn't really see the end of the room, and it was full of what looked like huge naked men. It turned out that they were seen slides of my installation work at the LACE exhibit and asked me if I ted to do a proposal for an installation in their main gallery for the follow- month. In just a few days I put a cardboard model together. Then the job to blow it up in ten days to forty by sixty feet for the gallery space.

For my subject matter I used my experience of living at Kohler, of being in country. I have always dreamed of living in the country, having a garden, ng out by the woods in nature. I contrasted my impressions of city and ntry living in this installation. At Kohler I was in the country, but it wasn't at I expected at all. The people just talked about their motorcycles, beer, bratwursts. It was not the pastoral life that I fantasized about when I ught of country living.

I was happy with the *Fastlane Tractor* installation, and kids loved running und in it. Overall, you really got a sense of moving through time and space, nging environments, different things happening. It kept your attention.

Frey: It looks like it was a very successful installation piece.

mmer: It resulted in a lot of breakthroughs for me: the use of different mate- s, the large scale required, and the integration of kinetic and audio elements h the visual nature of my work. The installation was built to compel view- to experience the space in different sensory ways as they moved through different environments. I used projected images, music, and sound effects enhance all the environments. There was a silo mounted on a world that wly turned, a flat world platform. It was the kind of thing that kids ran and nped on. There was a hay loft with real hay that you climbed stairs to get to. ere was even a section with a swing that kids would swing on.

There was a limited budget for materials, but the resources of the com- nity were really fun. Because it was a small community, we could call up so- l-so, who would say, "Oh yeah, there are some old plows up there; you ıld use one of those." Those kinds of things were available.

Frey: Have you done any other installations since that experience at Kohler?

mmer: Yes, *La Donna Mobile,* in the spring of 1987. It was outside in Los geles. It was constructed out of wood and about twenty-two feet high.

Frey: Earthquake proof?

mmer: It was pretty solid. Someone could have run into it with a car. We d eight or ten people on it when we were installing it. I brought it over in a truck in sections. It was inch-and-a-half plywood, and it was overbuilt. It ighed a ton.

It was at an intersection and was really appropriate for the site. I love the age of a modern centaur: half-woman and half-car rather than half-horse. ople were always backed up in traffic right there, and so there was this idea flying off out of the traffic. Something that I really feel in Los Angeles more just naked from the waist up. The molds on their work be pants, creating the illusion of nudity. Every time I walked as if I was going into a men's locker room. It was a bi However, it was a great experience to be there because of able to me. I spent a lot of time up in the mold-making d was assigned to help the artists with their molds. He r about the techniques of mold making. It got me thinkin technology in a different way.

The kilns are a hundred yards long, a football field kiln. You load your stuff on these little cars, and it goes moving belt; it's really a little train. A day and a half later it other end, and your things would be fired.

The slip for slip casting comes out of hoses from this l It's like the hose you use to fill your car with gasoline. lever, you have gallons and gallons of slip to use in you there is on a big scale. The cart you use to move your worl hundred pounds. Everything is far away. They have all th but it would literally take me about fifteen minutes to walk to the wood shop.

I was there for about three months and did a lot less w inally planned to do. I made molds bigger than I had ever r ger than I had made. I used some of their glazes and some was able to use my own palette. I think that the forms tha more rigid than I had in mind. As it turned out, I wasn't ab clay because it was so nonplastic. Since then I have use mold making I gained, and it has had a profound effect that time I wouldn't consider making, say, twenty molds in body of work. It seemed like too much work. Since the ex have been able to do that.

The biggest of the pieces I made there is *Industry,* so the kinds of work involved in making it. It wasn't a summ felt like a summer of hard labor, but at the same time it wa This piece represents that. There is a sink pedestal that is the piece. The factory workers made that element. I made elements by modeling original forms, making molds, casti and finally assembling all these cast pieces—including th make the sculptural form. Later I glazed it.

At the end of my residency, they had some schedulin Arts Center. An artist who was supposed to do an installat than anyplace else that I've lived is being part of my car or my car being part of me, of being intimately involved with the vehicle, much more than I should be.

Frey: That's one of the reasons I moved from San Francisco to Oakland: it took me two hours a day to commute by public transportation. I figured that was months out of every year.

Plummer: I proposed doing a similar piece at the San Francisco Airport: half-woman/half-airplane taking off.

Frey: What do you feel your subject matter is?

Plummer: Well, subject matter...people make differentiations between theme and subject matter. Or do they? Are you making that differentiation?

Frey: I think every artist has his or her subject matter; then there are many themes within that. And for an artist it's always a search; for instance, someone might describe my subject matter as going from abstraction to realism, or from realism to abstraction. I just feel that all artists are moving. They have to move. "Move" is the operative word—such as moving from a personal to a public sense. All that together and more is my subject matter.

Plummer: That makes sense to me. I utilize my personal experience, but I definitely am also exploring some basic human dilemmas. I want to communicate with the viewer first on a gut level: a psychological, emotional, spiritual, visceral level rather than in an intellectual way. That's how I respond to art. That's the kind of art that I like—the kind that immediately affects me. I think that the power of art lies in that kind of direct communication with something other than your mind, with a deeper part of yourself, a more basic part.

Primarily I address some of the dilemmas of human existence through the use of the figure. For instance, *David and Goliath,* which I did in Paris, addresses an important psychological reality that we encounter today. To me, that story is about facing an insurmountable challenge, of being presented with something that you cannot overcome, something that is much larger than you, something that poses a challenge at which you should fail. In the face of certain failure, you attempt to overcome the obstacle anyway. When you succeed, you experience that sense of bewilderment, relief, and awe. The moment after beheading Goliath, David can hardly believe that he has succeeded and becomes aware of the help of God. He feels an inner strength of which he was previously unaware. That's the moment that I want to convey to the viewer. By using the figure, I try to create that experience for a viewer with my work.

The process of making art is important for me. In fact, the creative process itself is the most important aspect of art making to me. The end product is gratifying, but it's no longer living art in my mind. Living art is the act of creation. I do not have a precise image of my finished piece before it is completed. I do have a basic concept, and I work towards that. Shortly after I begin, the piece generally takes on a life of its own. It starts to have its own spirit, its own character, and its own input. Then there's a sense of collaboration because the work is speaking back to me. I see new things through it. *Siren Song* is a good example. Before the bisque firing, the image was of a seated woman blowing a conch shell as a trumpet. She was using nature to amplify her message. The bisque firing distorted the piece in such a way that she is now listening to the message from the conch shell. That is the "happy accident" that Paul Soldner talks about; he utilizes it a lot with firing. Soldner espouses leaving your technique open enough for there to be accidental results. Sometimes those accidents simply result in discarded pieces, but other times, as in *Siren Song,* a "happy accident" results in a piece superior to the one you may have originally conceived. I still puzzle over what it all means after I finish it. I don't have all the answers, and that's what keeps me excited about doing this work.

Frey: In some of your early pieces, you used molds of familiar objects such as roosters.

Plummer: I'm doing a couple of different things with them. In one way I use them as abstracted forms. Actually, a lot of people who aren't familiar with the ceramic process never see the rooster or the fish or the duck unless you point it out. They don't catch on. It's for form and texture. Sometimes, in a figurative sculpture, I'll use a mold as a kind of headdress, like an explosion coming out of the head, more than as a literal reference to the rooster or fish. This is also a play on the fact that these cast objects are very low art with distant origins in higher art. I'm returning them to the realm of high art in a backhanded way.

Frey: This country, Japan, and Canada are the only countries in the world where you can get these kinds of ready-made things.

Plummer: That's good news. That means that I can go to Japan and work.

Frey: It's interesting that molds are used worldwide and cross time and cultures. They go back hundreds of years and they go across all cultures.

Plummer: Like all the Buddhas and traditional Chinese vases.

Frey: And Greek vases and Walt Disney.

Plummer: Things that are from the eighteenth and nineteenth century.

Frey: They're all there. I think I read once that in order for them to continue production of those figurines, they have to sell at a rate of about a hundred thousand a year for the image to become popular enough to continue. Why are people still buying eighteenth-century Meissen figurine groups, or even worse?

Plummer: Because they're familiar, and people want art; they want decoration. They can understand them, and little ceramic things are so intimate. You can pick them up and they're nice to touch. They're more comforting in a way than something you put up on the wall. Not everyone wants to be challenged by their home environment; they feel challenged enough by the environment outside. They want to be comforted at home, so they surround themselves with these little familiar things that make them feel good.

Frey: That certainly is part of it. If you think of the eighteenth- and nineteenth-century figurine groups, the farmers were depicted as being happy, even with patches on their clothes. That was to make poverty and hunger less of a threat, to take the tigers and panthers and make them also into less of a threat. Comfort is one of the reasons people look at art or even want art.

Plummer: I think artists and people seriously involved want art that is challenging, but the vast majority of people want comfort, reaffirmation. They want art to make them feel good about themselves and don't want art to be difficult, challenging, or to show the dark side.

Frey: Well, what are you working on now?

Plummer: On pieces that relate to the ideas I was exploring in Paris. Those pieces were very small and unglazed. The new work is larger, more complex, and involves a wider range of images. The pieces incorporate my own forms as well as found forms from molds. Also, I was just commissioned to make a sculptural fountain for a courtyard in a restored fifties apartment building in the Hollywood redevelopment area. It's a lot of work, but I am excited about having an outdoor piece that utilizes the dynamics of moving water. I also want to enlarge my figures to monumental scale and include more narrative elements, such as the environment and multiple characters.

Just when I think I know what I am going to do next, a new project presents itself and my work changes direction.

✶

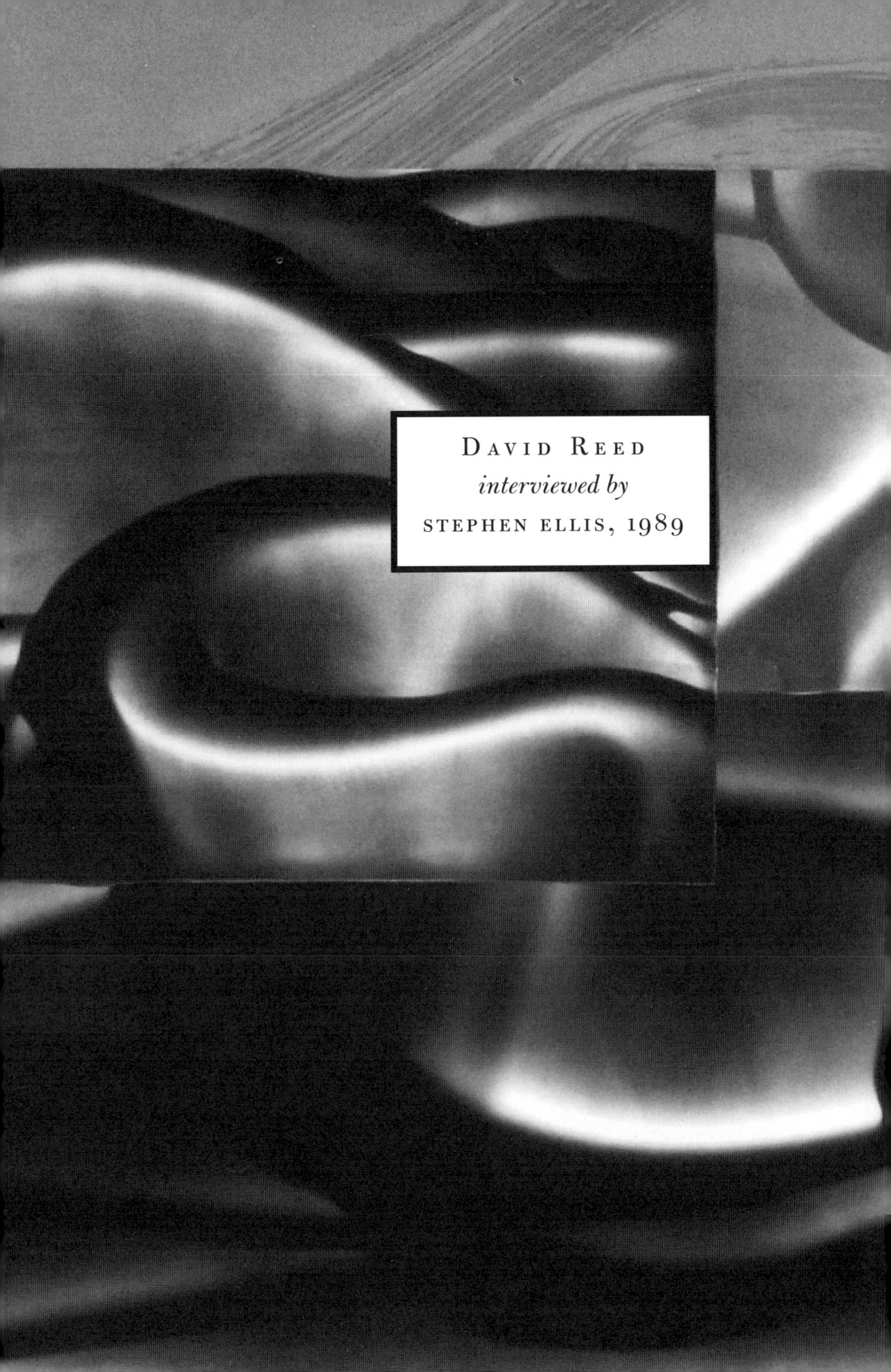

David Reed
interviewed by
STEPHEN ELLIS, 1989

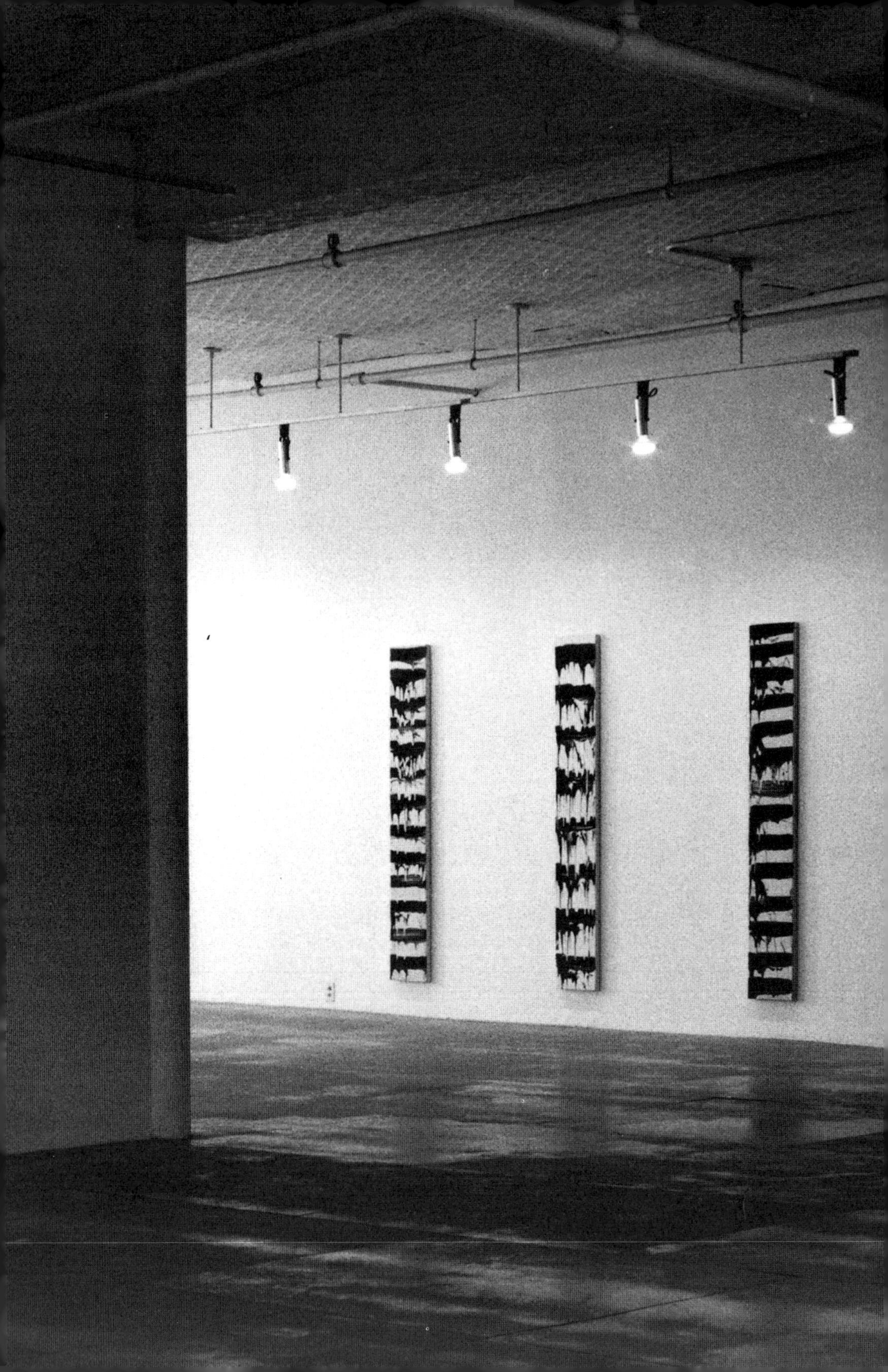

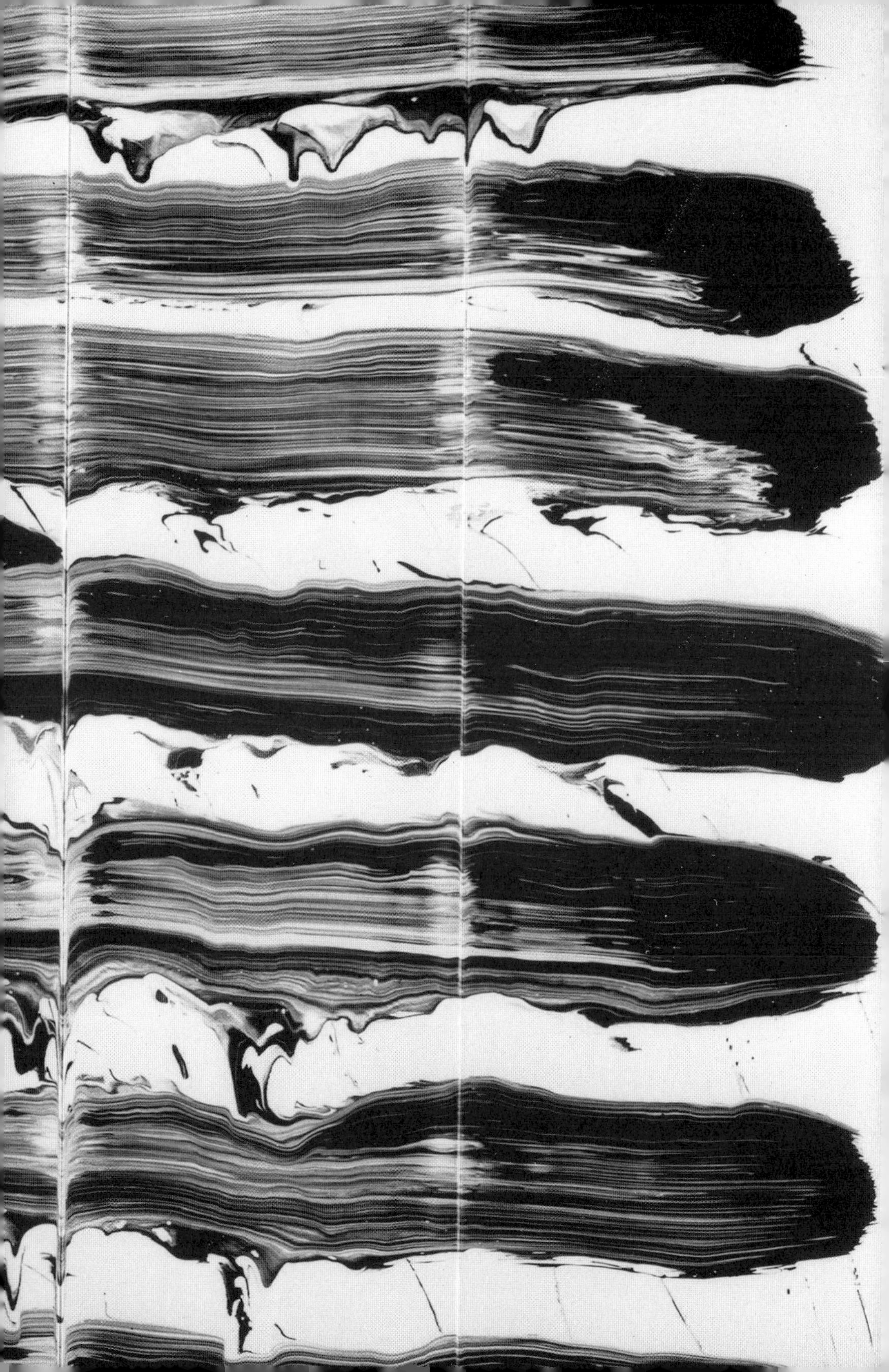

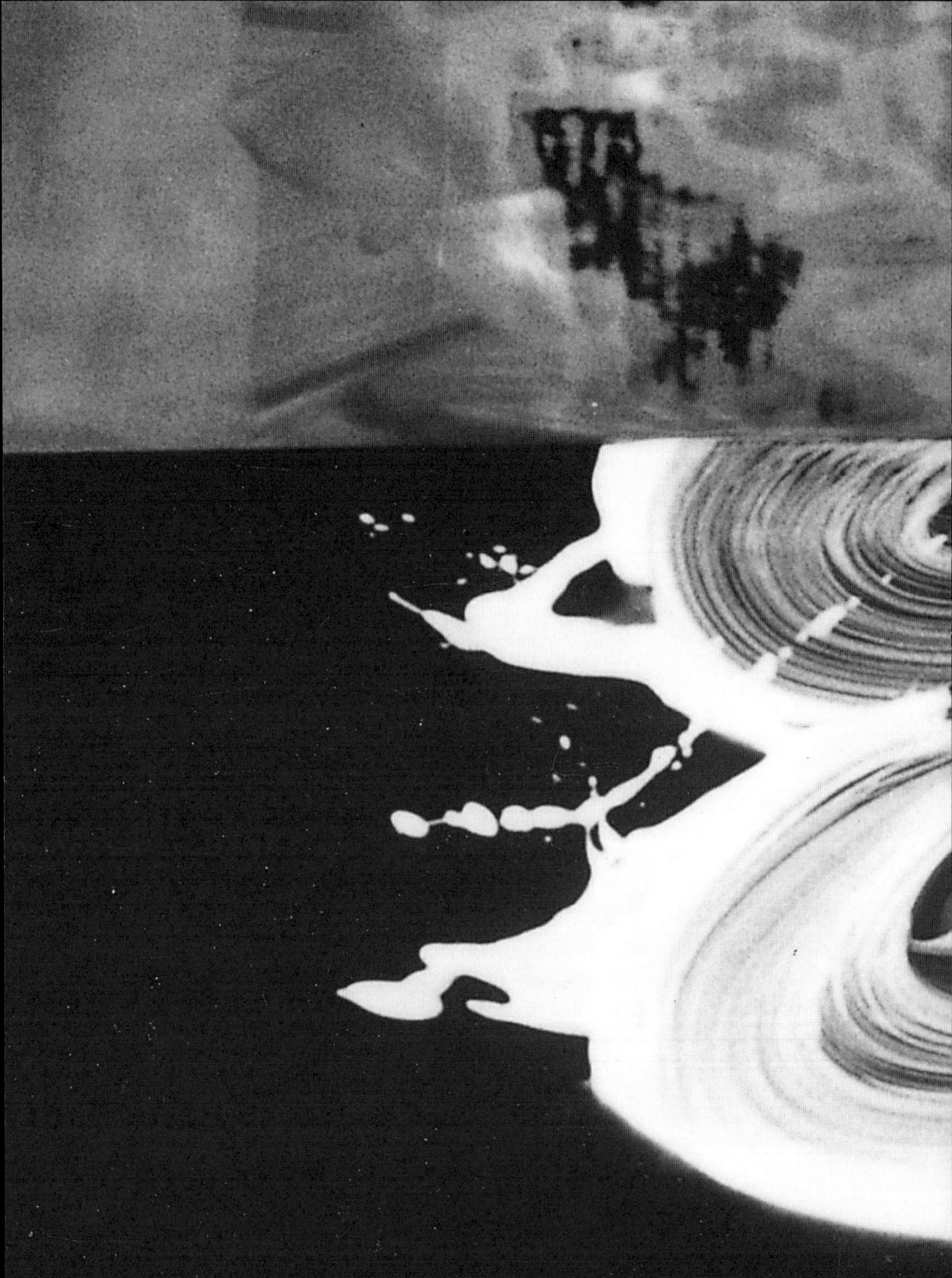

David Reed

interviewed by

STEPHEN ELLIS

David Reed: When I was supposed to paint a still-life setup while ignoring everything else in the room, I couldn't do it. I hated it—I wanted to paint the space between me and the still life and everything behind it. It was the first time I'd lived in New York, and I felt confined. I missed the spaces of the West. In the middle of a snowstorm, I got in the car and drove south to the Grand Canyon, "the home of American painting," to paint landscapes. I had read that Jackson Pollock was a road surveyor at the Grand Canyon, and I was convinced that the experience of a space too huge to comprehend would lead to what interested me in painting. I ended up near Monument Valley. Sitting beside my shack and looking out, I felt like I was on the moon or in the center of a huge void. I pretended that I could see ideas floating in from the East or West Coast. They came out into this desert void and expanded like balloons until they burst.

Stephen Ellis: It sounds as if you're describing a painting. Although one tends to read painting in terms of an iconography of objects, of nouns, something also happens that's like a verb. Painting communicates kinesthetically, like dance. It doesn't matter whether it's representational or abstract: when you look at the Creation of the Planets *on the Sistine Chapel ceiling, where God is flying through space like Superman, you inhabit his body in your imagination. The drama comes from a physical identification with the mass and velocity of his body. Gestural abstraction is like that, except that you feel the movement of the painter's body making the mark. I've often thought about this, looking at your paintings. They're not theatrical in the sense of an exaggerated dramatic effect; they're theatrical because you transfer yourself into the action of the painting.*

page 183:
Number 261 *(detail), 1987–88, 25 x 102 inches*
page 184:
Installation view of first one-person show, Susan Caldwell Gallery, New York, 1975
page 185:
Number 72 *(detail), 1975, oil and alkyd on linen, 76 x 57 inches*
page 186:
Number 187-3 (Hollywood) *(detail), 1982–84, oil and alkyd on linen, 24 x 96 inches*

Reed: I think that's true. There's a real equivalence between identification with the gesture of the figure in baroque painting, for example, and with the gesture in abstraction. Both figurative and abstract painting can cause identification, can act as a mirror for the body looking at the painting. Sometimes people say that the marking in my painting looks like drapery. But I've come to think of the marking as more like the billowing cloaks that cover the figures in baroque painting. In my paintings the strokes are draped very loosely. They've either just flown off the viewer's body into the painting, or they're about to fly off the painting onto the viewer. The movement is what is important. It reveals the gesture of the body.

Ellis: It's also a trace of the body. Viewing the gestures in your paintings, one imagines the actions that made them and reads the meaning of the painting through that physical identification.

Reed: The Carracci had a theory about how to express the emotions, the *affetti,* in pictorial terms. They had books illustrating certain hand gestures that had specific meanings for them. Their goal was to make the viewer feel particular emotions through the language of the bodies in their paintings. I hope to find some equivalent for that effect in abstract painting, which deals with forces and relationships rather than objects. The specificity of the gesture identifies an emotion.

Ellis: In Norman Bryson's book Vision and Painting, *he uses the word* deictic *to talk about this "verb effect." It's something that has always been a fundamental part of oriental painting, where, in contrast to most pre-Romantic Western painting, the trace of the movement of the artist's hand was always valued. In contemporary painting, the idea of the expression of forces or ideas through the gestures of the body has unfortunately become bound up with a narrow, melodramatic reading of Action painting.*

Reed: Yes, not only has that narrow vision limited how painting is seen, but its future possibilities as well. There are new combinations of surface and gesture to be tried.

Painters discover in the process of working that painting itself is a kind of nonverbal thinking. This kind of thinking is difficult to describe—often it can't be expressed in language for a generation or two. What can't be verbalized is unnerving. When I first started working abstractly, part of me would identify with the painting, as if I were inside it working through the forms. Another part of me would stay outside and watch what was happening. I felt split in two. I was afraid that I couldn't come back together again. In some of my first stroke paintings, the idea was to work so quickly that I knew I could get the two parts back together. Finally, I decided that this experience of being split apart was necessary to make a painting. I learned just to grit my teeth and take it. Then in Tom Wolfe's book *The Right Stuff,* I read about a similar experience. When the test pilots for the X-2 got up to the edge of space, they reached a point they called the "break off." The pilot was no longer in his body but saw himself from above and behind at the same time. He felt at one with the plane. He belonged in space, not on earth, and could do anything he wanted—then he crashed. I still have to go through that break-off point with each painting, but now I know it's part of the process.

Ellis: Here in New York you see a drama of experiences shattered into fragments: the rhythm of movement in the streets, the scale of people in relation to buildings, the quality of light. These shattered perceptions, reassembled in paintings, can create an image of this *time and place without actually describing specific objects.*

Reed: Painting can reflect our current environment. It has to be radically reinvented to be relevant to the present. I want my paintings not to be nostalgic or sentimental—that means they have to be about this moment. A corollary of that is that they should be an integral part of life, not separated in museums or galleries. Paintings belong where they can be a part of normal life, seen in private moments of reverie.

Ellis: But at the same time you feel this responsibility to the present, you're also obsessed with Italian baroque painting. How did that begin?

Reed: I'm glad you bring up the baroque in the context of the present. I love some baroque paintings, and I've been inspired by them (especially the color), but I can't use their compositions and figurative or representational devices. What they did has to be done again in a different way.

I first found out about the baroque through studying with Bill Midgette at Reed College. There was a rainy day and we couldn't draw. The light wasn't good enough, so he took us upstairs to show slides. He put up Rubens (I guess he's an honorary Italian). I thought, "Oh God, this is going to be so boring. How am I going to keep from going to sleep?" But his enthusiasm was so infectious that the paintings came to life for me. Fifteen years later, when I was walking through the Metropolitan Museum looking at those big, dark paintings you don't look at much, I noticed Guercino's *Capture of Samson* and stopped. The excitement that I got from Bill Midgette all those years ago helped me see the painting. Strangely enough, my entry into the painting was the way Samson's foot is crammed into the bottom right edge. It reminded me of a painting by Elizabeth Murray in which an abstract form is jammed against the same edge. Also, I missed Midgette, who had died a couple of years before, and seeing that painting established a direct communication with him again. I became obsessed not only with that painting but with others of the period, with trying to understand them.

This contact I've reestablished with Midgette is very important to me. It's helped me understand that painting is the discovery of something new. More recently I've lost another painter friend, Nicholas Wilder. One of the last things he did was to take a trip to the Prado in Madrid. When he returned, he described each room to me and drew a diagram and located the paintings he thought I could learn from, especially Northern paintings, which I still haven't learned to see.

I don't want to be the first painter, and I don't want to be the last. I want to be part of a continuum. The image I have in my mind is of a conversation with the artists of the past. We agree or disagree but carry on a dialogue.

Ellis: But before your formal education as a painter, what were the things you looked at, the things you saw when you were growing up?

Reed: My first memory is of looking at the peach-colored stucco wall of my parents' house. I remember looking at the light moving across it while playing with some bright red, yellow, and blue beads. Much later, visiting my parents in San Diego, I noticed the drip pattern on their bathroom floor: a Jackson Pollock floor. It's all black and white and it's terrific. I sat down and suddenly I felt right at home. I realized I'd memorized those abstract patterns. After that, I started noticing the California environment—especially the stark contrasts of black and white that the intense light produces. If you think of the Spanish Missions, you imagine them in the starkest light. A light that strong is dangerous, so it's disguised with bright pastel-colored houses and signs.

The good California painters, like John McLaughlin, deal with a counterpoint of color and black and white. I'd love to have a collection of California art that was all black and white. I connect Californian and Neapolitan painting because Naples has the same light—and the same threatening undertones. I thought maybe I was exaggerating this until I saw Hitchcock's *Vertigo,* which is set in northern California. When the hero is deceived by the girl he's following, the scenes are all in flat, pastel colors. When he's pulled into the reality of the situation, the screen is crossed with black and white diagonals.

Ellis: The movies have become such a rich reservoir of visual ideas for every sort of painting. Painters don't have to deal with literal narrative anymore because the movies do it so perfectly. Why bother to compete? You can isolate the essence of the visual ideas and use them for your own purposes.

Reed: When I was painting landscapes near Monument Valley after college, I worked out a lot of the visual ideas I still use. I always thought the ideas came straight from nature. Then last summer I saw a series of westerns in CinemaScope and realized how much those films had influenced my work: my preference for long horizontal canvases, extended forms, and lateral compositional movements. The directors using CinemaScope thought it suited the way the eye actually sees, more than the square format of earlier films. I think they were right.

We're used to seeing images in a different way now. Our eyes scan information in a different way than they did in the past. We're used to seeing images move on a flat screen. We expect them to move and look for ways to get them going. We're used to watching images change over time, and movement suggests this change—that's why I'm interested in the brush mark and the gesture.

Ellis: What about kinetic art?

Reed: No, I mean implied movement. Attempts to make a painting move mechanically are too simplistic. When you look at an isolated part of any of my long horizontal paintings, the other parts, which you see out of the corner of your eye, seem to move, because peripheral vision is especially sensitive to movement. But when you look directly at the movement, it stops, and peripheral movement starts somewhere else. I can reinforce this effect with paint—some areas are blurred like out-of-focus photographs, and others are rendered sharply. I'm very interested in the sense that one event in the painting leads to another in a process that happens in time, as it does in a film. I want to put time back into abstract painting so that you have to go through a decoding process in order to understand what the painting is about.

Mondrian and the other pioneers of abstraction wanted to make abstract painting timeless. When you look at a classic Mondrian, you perceive it all at once. Even when you look at a single part, you are still so aware of the whole that you don't get any sense of looking at the painting in time, at one part after the other. But now this desire for timelessness seems nostalgic. I'm surprised there hasn't been more recent abstract painting interested in time. It's not that I want to eliminate this awareness of the whole. I want to test it, stress it, to see how far it can stretch.

Ellis: That reminds me of one of the most interesting devices in fourteenth- and fifteenth-century Italian painting, the simultaneous narrative. By representing scenes occurring in different moments of a story all together in the same pictorial space, the artists injected a sense of time into painting that it doesn't otherwise have.

Reed: There were several examples of that in the recent show of Sienese painting at the Metropolitan Museum. The one that especially struck me was *Saint Anthony at Mass* by the Master of the Osservanza. The artist wanted to portray a religious awakening, but how do you represent something as nebulous as a moment of sudden insight? Saint Anthony is shown once as a boy kneeling before an altar, then as an adolescent listening to a priest read the Gospel, and possibly a third time as an older monk praying in the background. When similar shifts of time are implied in an abstract painting—through the changes of focus I was talking about, through overlapping sequences of gestures—they can create several temporal orders. Also, color has its own tempo. It moves at different speeds depending on whether it's interrupted or flows smoothly throughout the picture. The combined effect of these color movements produces pictorial light.

Ellis: The light that makes a container for the abstract events in the painting.

Reed: Exactly. During the Renaissance and the baroque periods they had a wonderful religious light that always came from above. Now we have a technological light, the light of a TV or movie screen, which is directionless—homogeneous across the screen—and increases the intensity of every color. Since we see this light on or through machines, it seems beyond the human, even immortal. To that extent it's similar to the divine light in the older paintings. Technological light can be suggested in an abstract painting, but made more sensual and material than it is on a screen or in a photograph.

I insist that my paintings have a wide range of light and dark, as well as a wide spectrum of color. Greenbergian formalist painting suppressed value contrast in order to stress the flatness of the picture, and by doing so it eliminated a lot of the expressive possibilities of abstraction.

Ellis: Using contrasts of value and hue contrapuntally creates a much richer expressive range than either one taken in isolation, almost an orchestral range. Together they pull you physically into a deeper, more ambiguous space.

Reed: It's always been a challenge for painters to integrate strong contrasts of value and hue. The artists who followed Leonardo wanted to combine his subtle way of veiling forms in shadow with stronger local colors, but it turned out to be a surprisingly difficult problem. The darker tones of the shadows obscured the bright local colors of the drapery, for instance. Having to describe objects limited the ways they could use value gradation and color intensity together to create space and light. Abstract painters don't have that limitation: we can solve the problem they couldn't.

Ellis: Ultimately, what you respond to in painting—more than the formal invention or the intellectual argument—is the moral quality of the decisions involved. I mean moral in terms of the risks the artist takes, not in terms of conventionally good or bad behavior. In fact, the formal and conceptual aspects of a painting are really only traces of those decisions. You sense their character immediately; they give some paintings, which otherwise are trivial, their power. Confronted with Les Demoiselles d'Avignon, *you're overwhelmed with Picasso's courage in the face of a total loss of meaning. That quality of risk is the most important thing. With it, painting is meaningful; without it, it's nothing.*

Reed: You'd think the moral universe of painting would be simpler, that it wouldn't have all the complications you have in life. In fact, it's filled with *all* the ambiguities and moral complications one experiences in life. It isn't different. It isn't separate.

Ellis: Part of the reason people become artists is a fascination with that risk. The studio becomes a kind of moral laboratory, though it's an artificial one compared with real life because the stakes are lower—after all, a painting is only a piece of cloth. But once paintings go out of the studio, they become symbols of a specific moral vision, of what's meaningful and what isn't—at least, that's the way I understand Gerhard Richter's dictum "Painting is a moral act."

Reed: Painting is high risk because you can't get back to an earlier state as you can in some of the reproducible media. In writing, film, and photography, for example, you can return to an earlier version if you screw up. With painting, you can't; you're lost if you want to go back. I was reminded of this recently when looking at a landscape by Annibale Carracci with another painter, Guy Goodwin. Several men and women are in a boat in a kind of swamp. There's a city in the distance. The sun is setting; it's about to get cold. One man is pointing the way and talking to the oarsman. They want to get home, but without realizing it, they're going in the wrong direction, away from the city. We had the melancholy feeling that they were never going to get home. The most striking formal device in the painting is a tree in dark silhouette going across the whole foreground. The oarsman is pushing his tiny oar against this huge tree. Nature is going to overwhelm them, just as a painter can be overwhelmed by painting. You can get lost and never get out again.

Ellis: It's true, the impossibility of returning to a previous state in a painting is an unalterable condition. You have to become the person who can make the paintings you want to make. You may admire something—like these marvelous Italian paintings—and think you'd like to make something similar. But you can't just make a work that superficially looks like the thing you admire; you have to become a person who acts with the same consequence or breadth as the artist you want to emulate. You have to hold the stage of your own theater with the same authority. To do that, you intuitively design your persona as an artist over a period of years, and that construct is your ultimate creation—the art just renders it concrete. The idea of Cézanne isn't tables tilted up toward the surface of the picture or asymmetrical jars, any more than the idea of Picasso is gluing newspaper to canvas, or the idea of Beuys is stuffing forlorn objects in vitrines. The idea of Cézanne is an unbelievable rigor of perception, and of Picasso of courage in the face of the chaos of modern life, and of Beuys of the redemption of nature and history from the abuses of power. If there's any ideal in being an artist, that's it.

Reed: Perversely, it's possible for an artist to realize the idea in his work when it's nowhere in his life. Caravaggio was a horrible person—he killed a man over a bet on a tennis match. In life, he couldn't control his violence, but in art, where he could view violence dispassionately, he investigated it with more conviction than any of his contemporaries. He wasn't repelled by parts of life that would disgust other artists. He painted to explore the forbidden.

Ellis: That certainly yanks him out of the museum.

Reed: Yes. As one of my favorite art historians said about another seventeenth-century artist/murderer, "He was neurotic, even bizarre, but undeniably distinguished" (laughter).

Ellis: Finding something useful to contemporary painting in the baroque Italians is a real act of recovery.

Reed: People think of Annibale Carracci as some kind of academic hack, when really the work is wonderfully relevant today. It can be brought to life again. I'd love to be part of that.

You know, I just understood something about Annibale Carracci. He had a patron, Cardinal Farnese, who had an important collection of Greek and Roman sculpture. He hired Annibale to invent new "Greek" frescoes to go with his sculpture because all the ancient paintings were lost. At the time, scholars were saying that art history was over—painters could only imitate the antique and Michelangelo. But Annibale's vision was so compelling; it not only recovered the past, it opened up a future for painting.

The point of the story is that we're not controlled by the past any more than Annibale was. We're not in a helpless position. We define the past for ourselves, just as we do the future—which, anyway, always opens up in the least expected place.

✶

Laurie Simmons
interviewed by
SARAH CHARLESWORTH, 1992

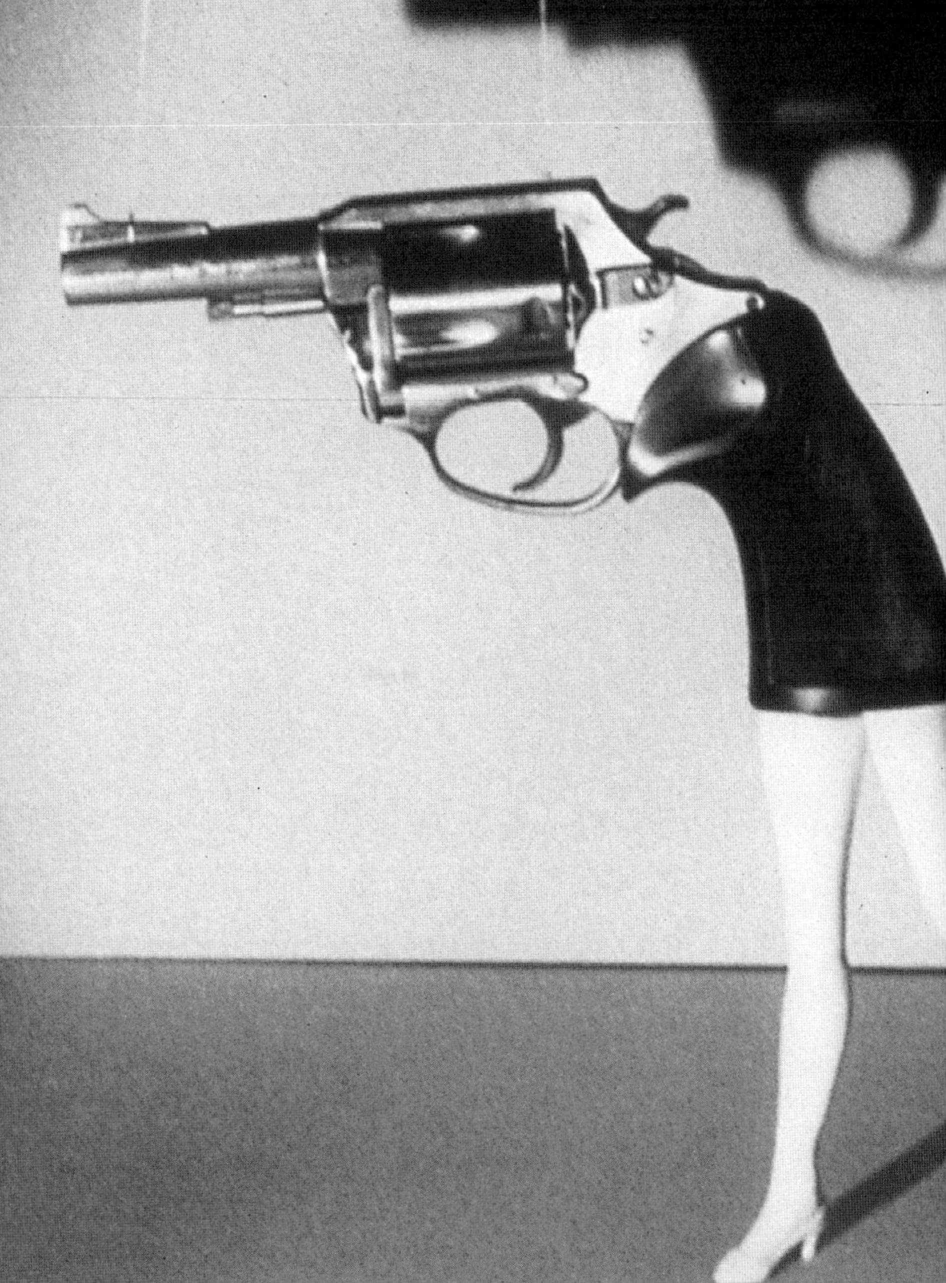

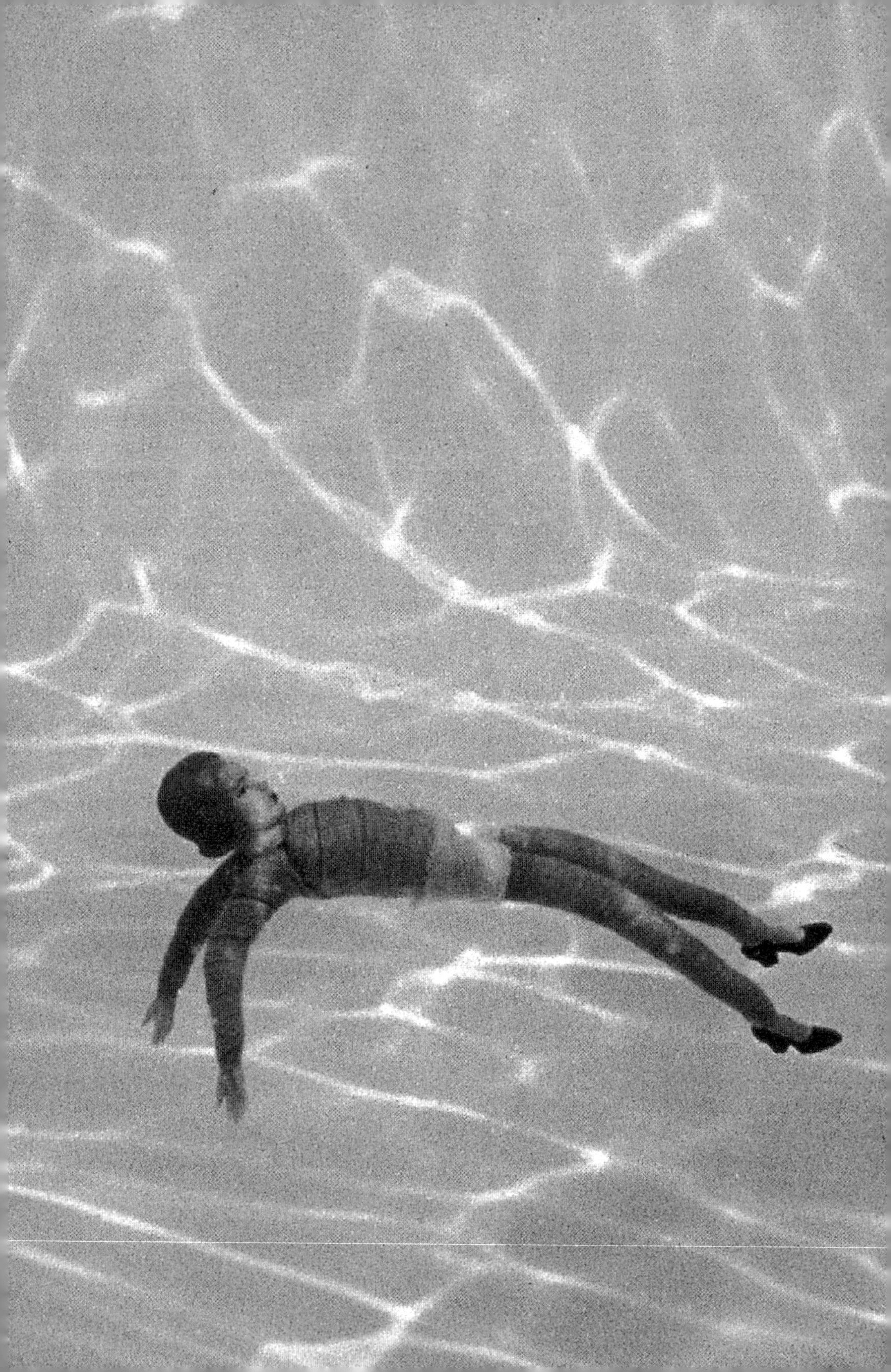

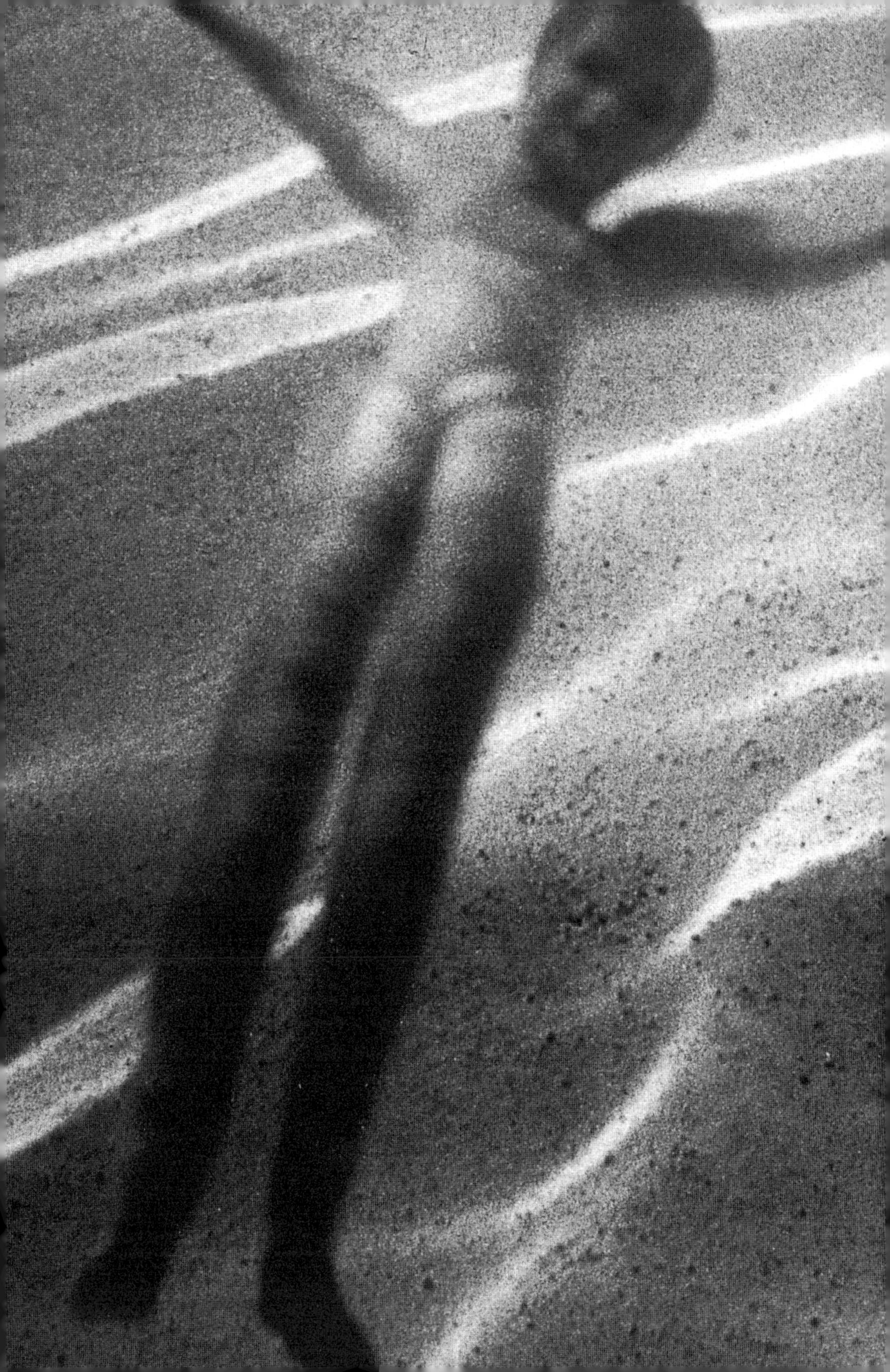

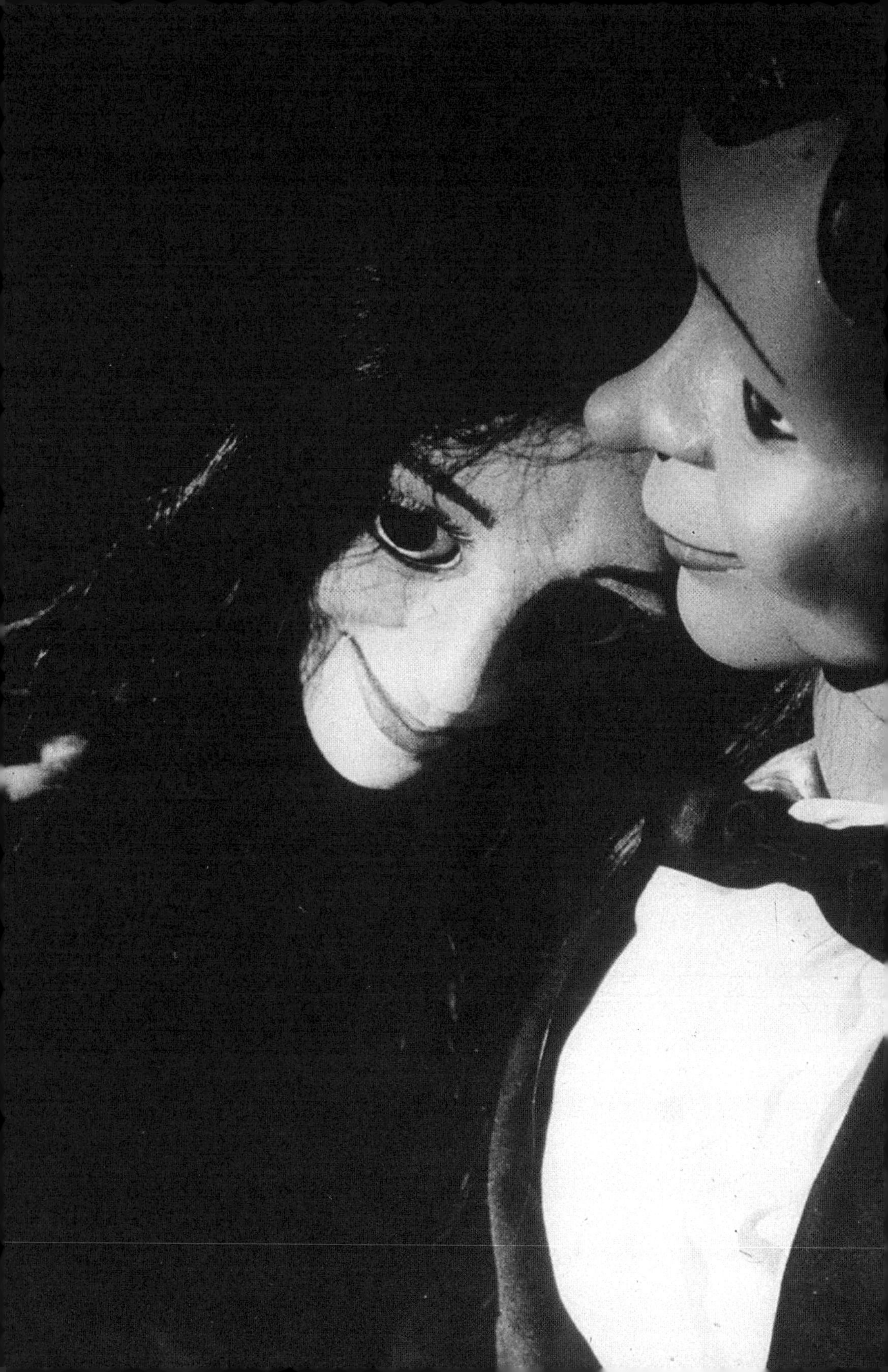

Laurie Simmons
interviewed by
SARAH CHARLESWORTH

Sarah Charlesworth: The very first thing I wanted to ask you is why photography? How did you choose this as your main medium? Did you have a background in photography? How did it evolve?

Laurie Simmons: No, I had no background in photography. As far as I know, you didn't either.

Charlesworth: Well, I did and I didn't. It was a funny thing.

Simmons: You probably had a camera and took snapshots from the time you were a little kid, like I did. In college, I enrolled in a photography course, thinking I might like to learn. I walked in and said,"This isn't art. I won't waste my time on this." Later, I realized that in order to find a voice for myself as a woman artist, I had to reject painting and sculpture, so photography became interesting in a new way.

Charlesworth: How would you describe the lay of the land in New York when you arrived in 1973?

Simmons: During the early seventies, several years had elapsed since art school, and I had done what I was supposed to do in terms of my generation: I'd lived on a commune; I had driven around Europe for seven months and slept in my car; I was heading for Afghanistan and made it as far as Turkey.

Then I came to New York. I came here to be an artist, but I didn't just start out making art. I moved into a loft on the Bowery and started going to every show that I possibly could, every performance, good and bad—and in the early seventies there were any number of horrible performances we could go see any night. I saw every film I could at every museum. I looked at a lot of fashion photography, particularly Deborah Turbeville's pictures. Conceptual art just exploded for me. My biggest question was, how did they manage to keep this a secret from me in art school in Philadelphia? You had to make a decision about what you wanted to do, what position you wanted to take before you made any work. As someone new in town, fresh out of art school, I felt absolutely paralyzed.

page 195:
Walking Gun *(detail), 1990, black-and-white photograph*
page 196:
Female Doll Underwater *(detail), 1981, black-and-white photograph*
page 197:
Male Doll Underwater *(detail), 1981, black-and-white photograph*
page 198:
The Music of Regret II *(detail), 1994, black-and-white photograph*

Charlesworth: So what medium you were going to use was not really a prime question. The question was more about finding an idea that you wanted to pursue, and then pursuing it in a form that was suitable. I went through a stage where I said that my writing and my conversation were my artwork. I remember declaring, "I'm working in groups and publishing a journal. That's my work as an artist for now." This was my practice before I started to make something concrete.

Simmons: There was a kind of freedom and also a kind of self-consciousness at the same time. The boundaries of what was art were broken so wide open that going to the bathroom and brushing your teeth potentially became issues for one's work. I feel like that's starting to happen again.

Charlesworth: I would say it was more than self-conscious. It was a kind of rigor: you really had to be able to explain why you were doing something, even if it was a strange, far-out thing to do. It wasn't like you could just fumble around.

Simmons: I was drawn to process art, where the things that usually held the art together, hidden and out of sight, would come out and become the work itself, like tape, or cardboard, or whatever. I liked seeing things used that were not precious and not particularly beautiful. It opened everything up. Autobiographical information—conversation, interactions—could be documented in a way to become part of somebody's art. Mel Bochner laid down stones; Barry Le Va moved himself around a gallery space; Smithson pushed dirt; Hanne Darboven counted. Things needed to be documented in some way, and the snapshot seemed to be the method of choice. I looked at a lot of story art at the John Gibson Gallery and discovered John Baldessari and Jan Groover at Sonnabend Gallery. Photography was being used in a much more casual way than it had been by the people who were carrying large-format cameras and tripods around at my art school.

Charlesworth: I think it was more than casual. It deliberately contradicted that fine art photography aesthetic. I remember a piece Doug Huebler did following bird calls in Central Park. I thought it was brilliant because it undermined all sorts of aesthetic assumptions about quality.

Simmons: When it all came together for me was at a Jan Dibbets show at Sonnabend that I saw in 1973. I talked to someone from the gallery who told me that he had taken these little photos to the corner drugstore to be developed. That seemed so radical to me, because that meant I could just pick up a camera without having prior knowledge of how to work in a darkroom. It meant that I could take a picture for the sake of taking a picture. To me, that was the moment of freedom; I could pick this contraption up, this camera, and not be tied down by the history of photography if I didn't want to be. Even though this history was only a hundred years or so, it still felt very weighty to me.

Charlesworth: Well, it was an oppressive tradition. It was fetishized and very conservative in many ways. Another thing in the air at the time was feminism. It was very much part of the experience of our generation, and whether or not you decided to call yourself a feminist was not the point. There were questions, issues of gender politics, in the air. How did feminism influence you in this period?

Simmons: I felt a kind of relief when I moved to New York City, because I had been living in a commune-like situation in upstate New York, where there were many people still living the "tune in, turn on, drop out" life. I was a hippie. And a number of women that I knew at that time were part of a radical lesbian group. So the first late-sixties brand of feminism that I was exposed to was a very rigid, hard-core, fierce feminism that involved a lot of negativity towards men. When I came to New York, I was relieved to be able to shave my legs and wear lipstick without anyone breathing down my neck. My first encounter with feminism was frightening, but very exhilarating, too.

Charlesworth: It sounds funny, but I understand perfectly. I was intimidated by the life issues, choices, and challenges that were emerging. But you were saying...

Simmons: So the attitudes that I was encountering in New York, and the women I met, were much more relaxed and, in a sense, more open, more fun.

Charlesworth: Were you part of a women's group?

Simmons: Not formally, but you could say that there were informal women's groups happening everywhere, every single day, just in terms of being together, going to dinner. We ran around in packs, and the conversation was intense soul searching—exhausting, when I think about it in retrospect. For me, the last thing on my mind, because I felt so young and unformed, was the idea of marriage and children. I felt like I had rejected the notion of family when I was in my teens. My friends were so much more interesting and more important to me than family. In the late sixties, there was a total revolution going on, and we were all so eager to become part of it. I always find the question "Do you consider yourself a feminist?" to be such an odd question, because what else could one be? What would it mean not to be a feminist?

Charlesworth: How did these experiences enter into your artwork?

Simmons: Again, it was a question of finding a place to work that could be my own. I figured out in that first period in New York that it wasn't going to work to be a second-generation anything, and that's what I saw going on around me. I was so naive and so unformed, but I was smart enough to know to wait until I could figure out what was going to be my artwork.

Charlesworth: I don't think you had a choice. You would have been slaughtered otherwise. At that time there was no such thing as a second-generation conceptual artist, and besides, what do you do after somebody does a show of dictionary definitions of nothing?

Simmons: It's a very tempting place to work, to pick up where somebody has left off and start from there.

Charlesworth: I don't think it was possible. The ideas at that time were so singular and so radical. We were forced into the unknown, and it was incumbent upon our generation to find its own terms. As young women influenced by conceptual art, we were in the position to be on the cutting edge, and yet there were no givens, no formulas whatsoever to follow. I noticed in your notes that you had already started collecting objects to make photographs long before you came to New York.

Simmons: Yes.

Charlesworth: You must have had some idea in the back of your mind.

Simmons: When I was living in the country, I was collecting all this stuff, and I didn't know what I was going to do with it. I found a toy store that was going out of business in a town in the Catskills called Liberty. I went up to an attic, and they were selling everything they had. It was like a strange dream. There were toys all over. They were boxed and unopened: toys that I'd had as a child, toys I'd gotten for Christmas—the same dollhouse, the same dolls, board games, tea sets. Not just similar—the very same brands and boxes that I had played with. So I started buying this stuff. It was really cheap and they let me have as much of it as I wanted. Then I found an old general store, and in the back of the store I found wallpaper, rolls and rolls of wallpaper. Like the stuff you'd seen, maybe not at your house, but at your aunt's house or at a friend's house. I started buying this stuff compulsively, not knowing what I was going to do with it. The feeling was not that of a collector, but a sense that a time would come when there would be a use for this. I didn't know that I would ever use it in my art, but nevertheless I knew it inspired me, and I carted it with me wherever I went, thinking I would put it to use sometime.

Charlesworth: Obviously, this material was stimulating something in you about your own memory and growing up in the fifties.

Simmons: Yes, and that stimulation ultimately turned into a desire to start making things. I had the advantage of never believing that I would amount to anything as an artist. The pressures coming to bear on a young artist arriving in New York in the early seventies were very different from those in the early eighties. I had no belief that I would become successful or would be able to make a living from my work. Simply to be able to make work and live like an artist was the payoff. These were the goals: to believe that you were an artist and to make work. That's what we were all there for. It was an activity that one could do very privately. You know, you'd be out at a club at midnight and someone would say, "I've got to go home and do some work." There was nobody banging down the door to your studio. You might look at what a friend was doing, but basically, you got a job, you went out to parties with friends at night, and sometimes you went home early to do your work. So I had a camera and I got some film. I started working with these setups. I have some pictures from this time that I love to look at that are completely silly, where I drove toy women around in plastic toy trucks. This was around 1974. Everything was black and white.

Charlesworth: You must have been responding to something in your own memory when you saw those old toys and furniture, but is there an aspect of the work from that period that was consciously critical, from a feminist point of view? Were you attempting to make a statement about how you saw women's lives?

Simmons: I would very much like to say yes, but really, in retrospect, I was simply trying to re-create a feeling, a mood, from the time that I was growing up: a sense of the fifties that I knew was both beautiful and lethal at the same time.

Charlesworth: These pictures are so nostalgic. I say that because nostalgia is something with which one has a love/hate relationship. It's not clear-cut. We were raised, in a way, to be housewives, and in your early pictures there are women bending over an oven. It's been interpreted historically as a feminist critique. Yet, when you really look at the pictures, it's not clear whether you're criticizing women's roles or fantasizing about them. It's almost as if both things are going on at once. They're dear and they're dead; they're nostalgic and they're scary.

Simmons: They're not about us. Maybe they're about our mothers, grandmothers, and aunts. At the time, I had not spent many hours bending over a stove or cleaning a bathtub. I was something of a tomboy for the times, and I didn't have as deep an involvement with dolls and dollhouses as these pictures would suggest. I think a kind of playacting was going on, setting up these things, that was less about the act of playing and more about the re-creation of a sense of visual memory or history.

Charlesworth: Yes, but isn't this something that goes on throughout your work? Even now, the style of your dummies is originally from the fifties, isn't it?

Simmons: Yes, they're like the first Jerry Mahoney dummies that I saw. I wouldn't make dummies like the ones I see now. They look terrible to me—polyester leisure suits, terrible human-hair wigs. My dummies have plaster hairdos and beautiful tweed coats.

Charlesworth: Would you say your work is a way of exploring your own memory?

Simmons: That's one level of it, but really just a part. I mean, exploring my own memory is so personal, so individual, that it feels like there wouldn't be room for anyone else. It's a generalized memory, it's of a particular generation, and a particular way of growing up in a homogenized environment. It didn't necessarily have to be suburban. Certainly the TV shows at the time that idealized the American family were about the suburban family. They weren't *Roseanne* and *All in the Family*. It was *Ozzie and Harriet, Father Knows Best,* or *The Donna Reed Show*. All those women wore dresses and heels while they vacuumed, and seemed thrilled with their position in the home. The suburban experience was a common experience, even if you were living in a city or in the country. That's what was idealized on TV.

Charlesworth: What is it about miniatures? You always seem to be drawn to things that project into very small scale.

Simmons: That's simply about control.

Charlesworth: On a psychological level or a technical level?

Simmons: Both. It's about being able to make a large world manageable. The end result of a photograph is ambiguous, and even though these things are small, I try to convince the viewer that they're very large and very real.

Charlesworth: You frequently play with tricks of scale. You can photograph Jimmy the Camera with real legs right next to a small object on toy legs. You like that ambiguity of the final product where you don't know exactly what's what. It doesn't matter how you got there.

Simmons: I love it. I love the confusion in the studio. I feel like I'm making a movie of colossal scale—an epic. I have to move in for close-ups and rig up what seems to me complex special effects. Of course, in the end, it's all just between me and myself. Setting up a photo feels like composing the first few notes of a song on a piano—seeing the final enlarged photo feels like the realization of a full-scale musical. I think a lot about the work of Ray Harryhausen who did the most wonderful, but flat-footed, special effects in films like *The Seventh Voyage of Sinbad.* There were flying carpets, clumsy cyclopes, and a woman you could hold in the palm of your hand. He's one of my heroes.

Charlesworth: You've said about your work that you felt like you just got on board, as though you were getting on a train. You "got on your work"; you "got a process." How has your work evolved for you?

Simmons: The big question for me is, why did my work start where it started? That's the question I find really difficult to answer. Once it started, once I got onto it, the direction became very obvious. It would reveal itself to me. The question that will probably take a lifetime for me to answer is why I started where I did, and why at that point in time did I realize I'm making my work? But to try to answer your question, I always work on a series: I start it, I work on it for a while, and then it's over. Then there's a kind of grieving period, a period of assessment. But often, when I've been working on a series, there's the germ of an idea for the next pictures.

Charlesworth: To what extent do you feel that your work is in a discourse or a dialogue with other work around you?

Simmons: I don't exactly think in those terms, but I've always felt that it is important to be thoroughly aware, read magazines, catalogues, see shows, know art, and generally maintain an informed position. As I mentioned before, I feel that my thought process was opened by the use of photos in the work of some conceptual artists. During the early eighties I started to recognize interests that were similar to my own in the work of other artists, and I feel that my work shares ongoing concerns with other artists I respect. I just don't like to use the word *history*. I certainly feel part of an art community whose work is public by nature.

Charlesworth: At one point, you described a false start, a body of work that didn't have it. Is this one time that your intuition led you astray? Does that frequently happen?

Simmons: It happened in a very grand way that time. For months I staged dance recitals where real people, nondancers, danced a ballet. They were dressed in tutus and ballet slippers, made up, and put on a stage, where they were asked to dance and feel like ballerinas. I wish I had videotaped it. I got very involved before I called it quits. This followed an underwater series that didn't seem to have a lot of connection to the type of pictures I had done before.

Charlesworth: Were you dissatisfied with the underwater pictures?

Simmons: When I made them, I was uncomfortable with the pictures that came before, the dollhouse pictures. Embarrassment has been a key feeling for me through all my years of working. I've come to realize that I often feel embarrassed when I stumble upon something new, something out of my own unconscious, which later feels right to me.

Charlesworth: Imagination?

Simmons: Yes, and if I feel embarrassed, as if I didn't want anybody to see the pictures because they might laugh at me, it often means that I've done something that has a certain power. This would happen frequently early on: the things that embarrassed me the most would often get the greatest response from other people. But when I did the underwater pictures, I think they were a reaction to the fact that I was playing with dolls and photographing dollhouse furniture, doing something that could be construed as dumb or childish. It was around 1980, and a woman I was very close to died. It was my first real encounter with death—someone my own age, someone whom I really loved—and I think that I wanted a change partly to escape that experience. Somebody gave me an underwater camera, which I had been using to photograph little frogmen inside a fish tank, which was very much in keeping with the work that I had been doing. Then I had the idea to take the camera underwater myself and take the props with me. Once I got underwater with this camera and felt the sensation of weightlessness, I thought, "I could live here." I felt utterly at home. I saw how people looked underwater through the camera, so elegantly distorted and beautiful. It was a very powerful visual experience.

Charlesworth: Did you feel that this underwater work was some false track in and of itself? It was quite unique. It stood out from things that had preceded it and many things that have followed it.

Simmons: It still does, and I still feel that I'm trying to explain its existence in terms of the rest of my work. I guess I move farther and farther away from trying to explain it. It exists.

Charlesworth: In dealing with the miniatures, the dolls and dollhouses, what about the whole issue of role playing and substituting of one thing for another—the way all the models became metaphors? Then in the underwater pictures you were suddenly in real life; there wasn't so direct a metaphor there. What about the dialectic between authenticity and inauthenticity in the work?

Simmons: You mean, over a period of time? Well, I thought that I had dealt with artifice, with dolls, with issues of playing, with surrogates. Again, a kind of embarrassment set in, and I thought, "I don't want to play anymore." I wanted to work with real people because that seemed more grown-up, more important.

Charlesworth: More authentic?

Simmons: Yes, exactly. There's a play back and forth.

Charlesworth: So what was the dissatisfaction there? Does it come too close to traditional fine art photography when something is just beautiful and you take a picture of it? Had you lost your critical relationship with the body of work, or were you beginning to?

Simmons: The pictures of people swimming underwater seemed like an antidote to dealing with the dolls and the artifice. But I felt I had lost a certain critical edge, that I'd gone too far into the area of what you're calling authenticity. So what I did next was a natural step: I took a bunch of dolls and threw them into the water and photographed them as they were falling. I tried to recoup some of the edge or feelings I felt I'd lost by photographing real people. There was this play, back and forth, back and forth. I've tried to deal with real people in photographs in other ways, using Jimmy DeSana's legs with the camera, and then using plastic legs for the rest of the series.

It's interesting that the work I'm least comfortable with, except for *Jimmy the Camera,* are the photographs where I used real people. Every time I've photographed a human and tried to get the same off-balance feelings that I get using the dolls, I feel that I've failed a little.

Charlesworth: Will you talk about your experience of finding a social context, a theoretical context for your work?

Simmons: It became clear at the end of the seventies that I had been working on my own secret, quiet project using photography at the same time that a number of other people my age had been working on their own secret, quiet photographic projects. It's confusing as an artist—you don't know whether to be overjoyed or feel scooped. My first show was at Artists Space in 1979, and that's when I met Helene Winer, who was then director and later became one of my dealers. That's also when I met Cindy Sherman, who was working at Artists Space, and she showed me a body of black-and-white photographs that she had been working on. I discovered there were a number of people around who were making work that I could relate to—Barbara Kruger, Louise Lawler, Sherrie Levine, you, and Cindy Sherman—work I still relate to today.

Charlesworth: But it also helps to connect your ideas with a larger sense of the importance of your practice as well. I think one of the things that was interesting at the time was that photography itself was being used in a different way. Before, you described taking a photography course and thinking this was not an interesting medium, and then, suddenly, there was a way in which the medium could be a vehicle for making art. Photography itself was being redefined. And it was from within the context of an art practice; it had nothing whatsoever to do with the very alien and precious tradition of fine art photography.

Simmons: It seemed like a brave new world, with no rules.

Charlesworth: What about perversity? There's something that frequently strikes me as perverse about your work. In the fake fashion photos, the use of cheap or ugly clothing seems slightly perverse, or in the tourism pictures, the dolls are garish colors, or there's garish lighting. Is there some streak that you recognize as perverse that goes through the work?

Simmons: Quite honestly, I'm attracted to these colors and materials, issues of conventional taste aside. I'm certainly not trying to appear naive or perverse. I'm interested in a direct approach, stripped of all intentions to shock.

Charlesworth: I think your work approaches a lot of things that are almost taboo, even the use of dolls. A lot of the subject matter that I've seen in the Ventriloquism series is mildly distasteful, or makes me uncomfortable.

Simmons: I was going to use the word *discomfort*.

Charlesworth: I can never put my finger on exactly what it is. You said before that embarrassment is one of the motives that you recognize in your work, and that you consider it almost a healthy thing. Perhaps it's when you're dealing with subject matter that is charged for people, in a way. The minute something's taboo, and you know you're not supposed to go in there, then you know there's some energy there.

Simmons: Obviously, we can't all go around pulling our pants down in public, but maybe there's a way that we can re-create some of those "I dare you—I'm a jerk" feelings in our work. Maybe this gets back to the perversity you were talking about. In my work I can approach subjects that make me feel as uncomfortable, as revealed or stripped bare, as pulling my pants down in public.

Charlesworth: Do you feel you're being the most honest in your work when you're willing to be embarrassed?

Simmons: Yes, but embarrassment is not something I always feel when making the work. I've described this way of working to you before, and I know that it drives you crazy, but I have a whistle-while-you-work mentality. I really have a good time. I like working alone, and there's an aspect of ease that I know irritates certain artists who struggle. So the embarrassment usually comes afterwards. Maybe it's about being really uninhibited and stepping back and thinking, "Oh my god." Maybe it's like having wild sex. Maybe it's like really being an asshole at a party and waking up the next day and thinking, "Oh god, I put the lamp shade on my head."

Charlesworth: It's more about private space and public space. The way you work is very private, and the act of making a show and making work public is very revealing. There's a dialectic in your work between the private and the public, and in making something public.

Simmons: I think that's true, because talking about it is making me uncomfortable.

Charlesworth: I'd like you to talk in broader terms about what has gone on in your work and in the work you identify with. In the eighties, work has often been described as "critical" or "postmodernist." Do you relate to either of those terms? Had they meant something to you?

Simmons: Critical, yes. Postmodernist—my first experience with the term *postmodern* was in terms of architecture and quotation.

Charlesworth: It was a word you've always hated.

Simmons: I have an ambivalent relationship to it.

Charlesworth: What about critical*? How do you feel about that? That's the handle that everybody would use, particularly to describe feminist work.*

Simmons: Well, it describes most work I'm interested in. I think of good work as having a critical edge. That could be abstract painting; that could be sculpture—work that in some way separates itself from historical aspects of beauty and the sublime, work that engages the viewer on a political or psychological level. For me, it's got to ask some pretty tough questions or make me squirm or make me jealous.

Charlesworth: I see it as a historical phenomenon. During the eighties much of the art that I thought was interesting was involved in trying to examine mechanisms or cultural devices for making meaning. There was a lot of discussion about the way visual language was functioning in the culture itself, the way advertising formed stereotypes, advanced values, and presented itself as a role model. Some people were directly engaged in conscious critical practice, like Barbara Kruger. She clearly politically positioned herself in that regard. But wouldn't you say that your work also took on the same kind of examination of inherited role models?

Simmons: Maybe it relates to the history of our generation, the feeling of standing on the outside of mainstream culture and questioning it. Maybe it's a habit we got into.

Charlesworth: I don't think it's a habit. I think it has to do with certain art historical problems that we inherit. I mean, modernism was very isolated from culture at large. Remember "high art" and "popular culture"? It was only at the beginning of pop art that mundane and "quotidian" culture, as it was fashionably called, became subject matter for art. Our generation began to explore some of that, and it's in your work.

Simmons: In this case, I'll say that being a woman forces you to examine your role as an artist because of the number of obstacles jammed in your path. A man might be comfortable inside the tradition of modernism, but if a woman attempts to plug herself into it, the resistance is staggering. Then she/you are simply forced to question your position in society.

Charlesworth: Yes, but I think for both men and women artists it was being brought up from a number of different perspectives—in the seventies, with the influences of semiotics, deconstructivist theory, all that. It was very much an ongoing cultural question-asking. I think it's too easy to say, "I work alone in my studio and what happens, happens," because I don't think you would be as important an artist as you are if it were that simple. The reason why there's a context for your work is because it's a historical phenomenon. A whole generation is asking questions of its time. What about the Tourism series? How would you define the issues of that body of work?

Simmons: Tourism was one of the most satisfying groups of pictures I've ever taken, starting with the fact that there were all these places that I wanted to go but couldn't. I thought if I could move this surrogate figure (a stand-in for myself) through an interior space, like a house, which is a metaphor for psychological space, I could certainly move her out into the world. "I have places to go, people to see" was my attitude and the attitude of the pictures. Let me backtrack a little to tell you how the Tourism series started. I was in Greece in 1983. I was standing on the Acropolis, in front of the Parthenon. I was with a couple of friends, and it was really hot and crowded and polluted.

Charlesworth: And you had a camera?

Simmons: I had a camera, but it was not something that I really felt like using. There were guides everywhere speaking in different languages. There were people hawking souvenirs. It was an unpleasant experience, and I said to my friends, "You know, you get a better sense of this place in books. You can see it better in pictures." The people I was with were irritated by what I had said, and they were teasing me about it. I started thinking about how experience has been mediated for us through textbooks and tourist guides. The images have been shown to us over and over again, so many times that by the time you come to the real thing—what a letdown. It's so much more beautiful in a travelogue. My grandfather, who was quite a character, used to sit on a beach chair on Long Island in front of the ocean and say, "This view is worth a million bucks." He traveled a lot by ship; he could go anyplace he wanted, but he would prefer to sit on a beach on Long Island and think it was the most beautiful thing he's ever seen. He had no interest in looking at the ocean from any other vantage point. He felt he'd seen everything from his one perspective. How many ways can you see the ocean? How many ways can you see the Parthenon? There's something about looking at an image of a place in a book and having it idealized for you in a certain way, and then when you actually get there and you see what humans and pollution have done to the place, it's disappointing.

So I went over to one of the tourist shops and bought a page of slides of a number of Greek archaeological sites. They were all faded, kind of blue, like a cerulean blue. I brought them back to the studio, and I set up some dolls in front of these pictures. That was the first picture in the series. After that I became an armchair traveler. I started gathering background images compulsively before I ever shot again. I have notebooks full of tourist attractions, wonders of the world, grand hotels, beaches, castles, and so on. Then I started shooting the Tourism series. I tried to find monuments that were easily identifiable, and, as it turns out, they were all extremely phallic-looking: the Taj Mahal, the Eiffel Tower, the Pyramids, St. Basil's.

Charlesworth: Were you consciously talking about the dominance of male culture in the work?

Simmons: It became clear to me that the great sites of the world were built by men for the enjoyment of men, and I liked the idea that these small plastic women that I work with could walk through it all in a casual, carefree way. I had the feeling that I could go anywhere, be anywhere, do anything. I had a good time doing it.

Charlesworth: In the Tourism series, and in other bodies of work where there's a play between the authentic and the inauthentic, there is a questioning about what is reality. Which is real—is the monument real? No, it's a picture. Is the doll real? No, it's only a doll. Were the pictures real to you? Were the dolls real to you?

Simmons: I think that the pictures are the most real thing: the purity of these monuments with nothing around them, standing still with a perfect sunset or a perfect sunrise. The Pyramids, the Great Wall of China with nobody walking along it—this is the way they're meant to be seen. This is the way I first encountered them in textbooks as a child. Perfect pictures. Then, when you get there, they're much too big and chaotic to be understood in human terms.

Charlesworth: It's something that's happened to us, living in a world of pictures. We've inherited a visual icon, and it is something very real and yet very different from what the real Parthenon is. It's the idea of the Parthenon, the idea of the housewife.

Simmons: Why would you want to sit in the back row and see live theater when you can see people kissing close up on the movie screen? The way that things have been brought to us in all their greatness, up close and personal, makes the real thing feel so small, so human. We've been spoiled, overindulged, spoon-fed bigness.

Charlesworth: In the earlier works, with the housewife doll leaning over the bathtub, etc., there's a love/hate dynamic—the model which failed you, but to which you're still nostalgically attached.

Simmons: Some of the great moments of my own life were during my childhood, acting or singing in a play. I knew what I wanted to be—I wanted to act. I wanted to perform. It became clear I could never do it, but those moments are some of the key moments of my life, when I felt absolutely the biggest, the best, the fullest, the most wonderful. It's curious to me—if those early experiences were so stimulating, so life enhancing, why didn't I move in that direction? Well, I didn't. But I make my work to re-create a kind of stage where I can feel powerful. Certainly the way I was describing moving the women through the landscape underlines a sense of strength and control. So there is a nostalgic attachment to that period of time and those feelings.

Charlesworth: Are the dolls surrogate "you's"?

Simmons: I think they're more surrogate "me's" than anybody else. Call them a generalized memory, but they've got to be a version of me.

Charlesworth: In the walking pictures, and even before that, in the talking pictures, you were beginning to take things that are inanimate objects and bring them to life, which is a little different than when you're just using dolls. You're actually animating them. You're giving them a personality, or reading a personality into something that is actually inanimate.

Simmons: Precisely. I love that.

Charlesworth: It goes right through the most recent body of work, like the Magnum Opus, *where you bring all these little characters which you've already created in other pictures—like a camera on legs, or a microscope on legs, or a perfume bottle on legs. You've created little personae, and then, in the* Magnum Opus, *you bring them all out to parade and wave goodbye, because you go on to the next body of work. I'm trying to get you to dwell on that aspect. What is that thing that you love?*

Simmons: I'm trying to figure it out. The desire to animate everything may refer to an early time in my life when I experienced a certain amount of loneliness, dread, and thought how wonderful it would be if all the things around me could become my friends. I know that childhood desire wasn't exclusive to me. I see my own children doing similar things, figuring out if their toys can speak, or finding a face in some object and making it talk. It's about softening the condition of loneliness and making friends out of thin air. The idea that objects can befriend you, and fill a lonely void in life, is a child's idea that certainly translates into an adult's desire to consume. But as you become older and more mature, you distance yourself from it; the idea becomes more diffused and, let's say, more amusing. How funny that my purse can dance with money clinking in it. How odd if my camera could walk away. I have an emotional distance from it, but it's still based on these very intense childhood feelings.

Charlesworth: You have children, and here in your studio you have dummies that you're dressing up in little clothes. From here, you go upstairs and dress your daughters. There's a very close parallel.

Simmons: I guess there is, but it doesn't often cross my mind. My pictures feel more connected to my own childhood.

Charlesworth: Do you think you're playing out other possibilities—choices you didn't make?

Simmons: It's like I'm allowing myself to be a birthday cake on a pair of legs, a piece of cheesecake, literally and figuratively. Using a sexy pair of Japanese metal legs and attaching a toilet to it—maybe that's a way to be down and dirty. There's a real resonance there for me. There's got to be a way for me to be these things when I make these things.

Charlesworth: I always found in my own work that whenever I thought I had some theoretical reason for doing something, years later I could read a clear psychological reason into it. I think now that one's conscious and unconscious reasons for creating a body of work go hand in hand. Sometimes you see more of one [kind of reason] in somebody's work, but I think even with the most rigorous conceptual artists, you can tell.

Simmons: I agree, and I think it's uncomfortable for any of us to talk about our unconscious motives, even if they've come to light.

Charlesworth: People feel comfortable with clear handles. You have a funny way of working that you call intuitive, and you trust yourself, which is a big thing. It's like taking a leap off the side of a building to say, "Yes, I'm going to make it. Just because I have an interest in it and I feel like making it, I'm going to make it." Then you dive off. That, to me, is very scary—when you decide to trust something without being able to give an explanation or anchor it theoretically.

Simmons: Isn't that why we're visual artists? Isn't that what it's about to be an artist? You can talk about what you do and you can try to precontextualize it before it's done, but ultimately there's something about the way it looks that makes it wrong or right. At least, that's my final level of judgment—the way it looks. If it's got the look that you want to know better, then you just keep going deeper and deeper into it.

Charlesworth: When something's finished, do you like it?

Simmons: I love it. There are still a couple of images that I feel uncomfortable with. But I know my own work; I know what I think. I'm not really interested when people say this is a strong picture, or this is a weak picture. I know what's weak and strong.

Charlesworth: I always feel, when I finish a body of work, slightly dissatisfied. I always feel like I've got to go back and try it over again. The way that you trust your instincts—you don't cross-examine it so much. It's quite unique. Some people have a big game plan, and some people have their passions, but you think, "Oh, this would be interesting." You just go with it. I think it's trusting yourself that permits you to go into zones that might be uncomfortable. Even when you explore things that are embarrassing, as you yourself describe them, you recognize it as a strength. If I'm embarrassed about something in my work, I want to hide it. To me, when I'm uncomfortable about something, it indicates a fear. If I make work and I feel really uncomfortable, nobody sees it.

Simmons: There's another aspect of my work that I rarely mention, and that is sadness. People like to talk about the humor in my work. I don't respond to that; I don't see it. I try to be good-natured about it. But I think there's an element of sadness in the very first picture that still exists in the most recent pictures. That's an aspect of myself that's very hard to describe. I don't fully understand why it's there.

Charlesworth: Do you suppose it could have something to do with the fact that your work touches on things that could be considered idealizations, dreams of the way the world is supposed to be? You said at one point, "This is how the Parthenon is supposed to look, but it doesn't." Is it about the loss of innocence?

Simmons: Yes, but it feels like I was born with the loss, that it came to this planet with me. This brought to mind one of my earliest heroes, a person whose face I used to draw over and over as a child, and that was Emmett Kelly, the sad clown.

Charlesworth: That's interesting.

Simmons: I learned how to draw Emmett Kelly when I was very young, and I drew him over and over. He was such an important figure in my life, along with Margot Fonteyn and Danny Kaye. They were my heroes. To think about Emmett Kelly, he's a walking contradiction—the sad clown. Clowns aren't supposed to be sad, and I wonder how I saw him as a child. What kind of image was that? What did it mean? I can't remember if he ever did funny things. Lots of people find the dummies sad and poignant, and other people simply write them off as weird and eerie. When I say I don't respond to the humor in my work, I also don't respond to the strangeness of it. I don't find it eerie or weird or funny. It just gets back to being sad.

Charlesworth: It seems from a number of things that you've said throughout our conversation that your art has become a vehicle for you to overcome a certain sense of isolation. You've mentioned it in terms of your experience as a child in looking at objects around you and wishing that they could come alive, and you've talked about your experience as a young woman artist working alone. It seems, as for most artists, that you really work through a feeling, and in this case maybe the feeling is of isolation and loneliness.

Simmons: The peculiar thing is I've set up a life that contradicts these feelings in my work. I've surrounded myself with friends. I've got sisters, a husband, kids. I'm always on the phone. My life is not a lonely life; it isn't a sad life. Yet, that is a lot of what I often feel my work is about. When you work, even if there are six people running around the studio, I believe you have to work alone. You must find a private space. If you're not making work in that private space, you're not making good work. I believe that. And I think that going into that private space is the point in my life when I do have to confront being alone.

Charlesworth: We've touched on the issue of inauthenticity in the work, but it seems that what we're circling around is an honesty and directness masked within inauthenticity. There's a real emotion, whether it's love or sorrow. I know that in your own life you have had some very close experiences with death. You have had several close friends who have died. Is the presence of death in your life something that your work talks to?

Simmons: It's all very mysterious to me. Experiencing the deaths of friends felt like a confirmation of many things that I had already known and felt. These feelings have never been alien to me. I may touch upon death and AIDS somewhat in my work, but it's going to take some years for me to get enough distance to make it my subject.

Charlesworth: I'm trying to negotiate between certain parameters. There's Laurie the private person with her own psychology and emotions, her own drives, and there's Laurie the public person who is also a part of the culture and a time period and a city. I think your work is to be interpreted between those twin, conjoined contexts. I would like to come further into the present. It's a very peculiar time right now, in terms of history and art history. A lot of the political and social forces that have acted upon us and influenced our work are breaking down now. We can't trust the same secure sense of history. The economy is breaking down; Russia is falling apart; the Cold War is over. The art world itself is in a very unstable situation. There is death all around us. Even in terms of an art historical project, it appears to me that there isn't any clear trajectory right now in the public arena. How do you read this moment as a platform for going into the future, going into the next body of work, going into the next decade?

Simmons: Well, I feel that if I'm honest about sadness being a mood that permeates everything I do, then I'm much more comfortable now than I was ten years ago when things weren't quite so dark. This is the right time for a sad person to work.

Charlesworth: Now I feel a need in my own work, or in the work I'm beginning to look for in the world, to create something that is perhaps healing or regenerative, affirmative. I'm almost embarrassed to say it. I feel that it's time to begin affirming, to instruct. It's not just a time to react but a time to construct ways, models, laws, artwork that is positive, that is not just negative or reactionary. How do you feel about that?

Simmons: There has always been an aspect of that in my work. I don't feel that my role as an artist has always been to point out the negative—to point out that a woman was trapped in her home in high heels. My work in the past and the present has been about underlining a certain condition and leaving the final judgment, the possibility to interpret, to the viewer.

Charlesworth: I feel that same way. That's why I tend to use the word explore *rather than* teach. *I don't feel that either your work or my work is didactic. And I don't think that was the intention. I think that it was in the process of exploring that…*

Simmons: The work is there, pointing at the truth of a certain condition. Many people look at my work and simply laugh in amusement and walk away; some people find a certain pathos in it and then draw conclusions. And in the drawing of conclusions perhaps there is something to be learned, and it's not blatant. I've never made the kind of work that hits you over the head and says, "This is the way it is and you better listen up, motherfucker." I've never been able to make work that is aggressive in that way. And I feel that my work is autobiographical, historical, and current, and that I can only point up the conditions of the period of time that *I've* lived through and do it from the perspective of a woman. That's my subject. A lot of those subjects are out there, but I can't project myself into the minds of others.

Charlesworth: There's a great deal of ambivalence in your work about the traditional women's roles that you talk about. You talk about growing up in the fifties, and styles from the fifties, but that's getting to be almost fifty years ago and now it's gone. The time we grew up in is over, and we are raising children and we're making a world for them. The work that's most interesting to me is the work that's dynamic and that shifts in time as a person matures and evolves. As the culture changes, the issues change.

Simmons: If the issues are there and they're contemporary issues and I have to dress them up in the clothes of the fifties to be comfortable with them, well, as long as the potent subjects are present, I don't think it matters how they dress.

Charlesworth: Let's talk about the dummies a bit. You're making sculptural work that looks just like your photographic work—I find this really interesting. How do you feel about the dummies in conjunction with the rest of your work? Is it a new venue, or is it a one-shot thing?

Simmons: I don't really know the answer. I made four trips to Vent Haven, the ventriloquist museum in Kentucky. When I was there, I photographed a lot of dummies. There were six hundred dummies in the museum, and I handled them a lot. They were all sitting in chairs set up in rows, like a big school auditorium. I had to pick out the ones I wanted to photograph, so my relationship to shooting them was a lot like making friends when you were a kid. The curator of the museum was very nice and let me carry the dummies to a makeshift studio I had set up. I would come back from each trip to the museum with ten to twenty images of the dummies and edit what I wanted to show in the ventriloquist-dummy portrait series. I realized a few years later that I missed the objects, holding them and carrying them. In the case of the dummies, I felt a range of feelings was lost in the photographs that I thought would be appreciated if I showed the actual dummies—the poignancy of the faces of these guys, and their hands, the tactile quality of their clothing, how "cunning," as mothers and aunts used to say, their shoes were. There was something that I really liked, and I was intrigued by their clothes. So I decided to have one made, have six made, have a hundred made, and see what it was like, to sit them in little chairs and…

Charlesworth: Trust your intuition.

Simmons: And deal with them more as objects, though I hate calling them objects. They're like people. In terms of authenticity and inauthenticity, going back and forth between real people and dolls, for me there's also a going back and forth between men and women. I feel if I remained exclusively in the domain of women, I would be excluding men as viewers, that they would not be interested in my work. The idea of men not being interested in my work makes me uneasy. I want everyone to be interested in my work, which isn't the way all artists feel. A number of artists want at least some people to hate their work.

Charlesworth: Oh, they just say that.

Simmons: That's true. Working with the dummies seemed to be a way to work with the idea of dolls, and men. Because a man might respond to a doll in his own image. Also, it seemed like...

Charlesworth: Getting them under control.

Simmons: Yes.

Charlesworth: Although they are obviously men—I didn't even think of that—they're dummies.

Simmons: They're very much men. Like all my series, it has a title: Clothes Make the Man. It's one image, one face. It took a year working with the dummy maker to get the face just right. We worked for months on the hairdo alone. Now this dummy is just being re-created as many times as I want. The only thing that differentiates one from the next is his suit of clothes.

Charlesworth: What about the chairs they sit in? Are they like the chairs at Vent Haven?

Simmons: It's just a chair that I like. One chair. I only want them to be differentiated by their clothes.

Charlesworth: It's funny that you say that. All their suits are almost identical.

Simmons: But they're not.

Charlesworth: A little blue jacket, a gray jacket, a plaid jacket...

Simmons: But they're not.

Charlesworth: Yes, but they're not wearing leather jackets.

Simmons: They're all suits, but that's the point. Do you remember the movie *The Man in the Gray Flannel Suit*? There were real issues of conformity when I was growing up: how important it was to be like other people, how important it was for our parents to conform to a certain social group and have their children conform to a certain mode of behavior.

Charlesworth: I remember people saying, "Boy, she's a real nonconformist!"

Simmons: Right. Or if my mother was uneasy with a person she met, her way of describing this person to me without being too negative was, "You'd like her, Laurie, she's very different." That became a veiled way of saying that somebody was somewhat off, marginally accepted.

Charlesworth: So what about the clothes? Are they talking about conformity?

Simmons: The differences in these suits are dramatic in terms of where you'd wear them, how you wear them, what type of tie you wear. A bow tie and a straight tie have very different meanings. A bow tie means you're a more extroverted kind of guy.

Charlesworth: A nonconformist.

Simmons: Something of a nonconformist. These modest little differences in clothing represent a world of meaning.

Charlesworth: So is "Clothes make the man" our tactic?

Simmons: Well, do you think that clothes make the man? Do you?

Charlesworth: No. What do you mean? The thing that I relate to most in what you're talking about is Detroit turning out yet another new car, and you're making dummies that are identical, like a car factory. Within a context that is all about unique imaginative expression, you're making these models almost on an assembly line. Then the differences that they have are minute differences.

Simmons: But you'll be able to tell them apart easily. You'll say "the guy in the brown tweed jacket," or "the guy in the gray plaid jacket." It's not going to be that hard to tell them apart.

Charlesworth: I suppose it's like a mother with sextuplets saying, "But I can tell them apart." Are they children?

Simmons: No, they're men.

Charlesworth: Throughout the work you toy with the idea of human—almost human, not quite human, a little too human. You like to get close to this human/inhuman idea, to confuse the difference between the two.

Simmons: That confusion or gray area is a place I like to dwell. That's where my subjects come from. Decisions about scale and color come from this place, too. I can always spot something in my work that's familiar, though somewhat torqued. You can see something like this happening with kids. It's about scale. They can spot an animal or another child or a toy from miles away. They recognize their own kind; they're always attracted to things that remind them of themselves. This can be true of adults, too.

Charlesworth: I do remember my son always responding to pictures of children. We may be touching on unfamiliar territory to all of us, but much of making art or looking at art is about the mirror stage of looking back at one's self. Does this do anything for you, the mirror-stage-like fascination with the almost-human, as a way of looking at the self?

Simmons: Definitely.

Charlesworth: You've never said that before. I've never heard anybody say that about your work.

Simmons: Going back to the time I spent at Vent Haven, it was interesting to me because, as I said before, I ordinarily find that making my work is a pleasurable activity. I did not like being in Vent Haven. Maybe I finally started to find the subject matter a bit eerie. I didn't like the smell of the museum; I didn't like setting up my work outside the studio; I didn't like having to select the dummies out of a group. It seemed less like fun and more like work, and what kept me going was knowing that when I got back home I could process the film, edit the images, and I would have something very separate from that place. There was something far too real about that place. It took itself too seriously in terms of the history of ventriloquism and all the documented stuff, the books, the tapes. It had none of the qualities of seeing a ventriloquist and dummy perform. I felt far away and a little bit homesick. Also, I'm an artist, and there, I felt like a journalist. There are truths I simply don't need to know.

Charlesworth: I've always felt uncomfortable with dummies.

Simmons: Why?

Charlesworth: To me, they're bizarre, strange, weird—there's something about the psychology of it that's weird. Ventriloquists are kind of weird. You know, those movies about split personalities.

Simmons: I can say, with the exception of one, that all the ventriloquists that I've met have been very unusual people.

Charlesworth: Split personalities?

Simmons: No, let's just say very unusual people. They're not like other actors or performers that I've met.

Charlesworth: How do you feel about the dummy sculptures? Do they make you uncomfortable?

Simmons: No.

Charlesworth: Do you feel nurturing towards them?

Simmons: No. Well, protective. They're breakable.

Charlesworth: I always feel that when you talk about any of the work with the dummies, you actually recognize them almost as if they had personalities. A lot of the portraits that you've done are exactly as though you were doing portraits of real people in which you read a personality into the dummy.

Simmons: Absolutely, but none of this happened until the picture was my very own, until it was back in the studio, edited, and taken out of the context of Vent Haven. When I was there, I merely went through the selection process, set up the background.

Charlesworth: But that's denying the issue of making the choice: "Don't look at me—I just went there."

Simmons: I just went there and picked the one with the blond hair.

Charlesworth: You just went to a ventriloquism museum?

Simmons: I have a very strong identification with the portraits. They seem like archetypes to me, like your teacher or your friend or an aging cabaret singer you heard many years ago.

Charlesworth: You almost like them and they're almost real, but they're not. There's something that draws one's emotions and denies them at the same time. It brings up a very iffy emotion.

Simmons: What's confusing about dummies is that they have the potential to speak, to have a voice. But they need to have a ventriloquist.

Charlesworth: You? Do you think that the dummies are the beginning of a new body of work? And what are the issues taking shape?

Simmons: During the later part of the eighties, I was dealing with the superficiality, with the exterior mode we inhabit, with the confusion between ourselves and our possessions: a self-image based on what we do and where we live and how we function and certain kinds of cold disappointments in terms of truth and lies. One of the things I'm working on in my new work is imagining the daydreams and the night dreams and the fantasies of the characters that I've created. Now I'm concerned about what's going on inside, and that's where I feel I'm going. Now I think it's important for me to address their inner lives. What is making them put one foot in front of the other?

Charlesworth: You will continue to do photographs.

Simmons: Of course.

Charlesworth: For me, this sculptural work says something different than the photographs. You were saying before that images are more real to you than objects sometimes, and that the process that things undergo in being photographed enhances them, to you, more often than not. I frequently feel that, too, and I think it's an unusual idea because the convention says there's the real thing, and a photograph is just an "image" of a real thing. Do you feel photography has some special, unique power to make something that's never been made before?

Simmons: Yes, I definitely do. I feel photography, the way you and I use it, has the ability to translate something that is small and terribly mundane into something very grand and dramatic. To me, it's almost like the creation of a play or a movie: the inherent ambiguity of the photograph is what gives it its power. It means that a world is opened up to you, and it can happen in a four-by-five-inch picture you see in a book. I feel, again, that it all started when we were children.

Charlesworth: So that photographs do not refer to anything specific. For example, a dollhouse.

Simmons: No.

Charlesworth: They are something in and of themselves.

Simmons: Yes. Can you remember a time before you could read, sitting on somebody's lap, looking at a book, and being read to?

Charlesworth: Sure.

Simmons: And how large those pictures loomed, how big the pages were to you as a child, especially when you had no relationship to written language? I can remember the sensation of almost standing inside the image on the page. My boundaries became somewhat blurred, and for an instant, I existed within the story. I'd like to go there again.

✦

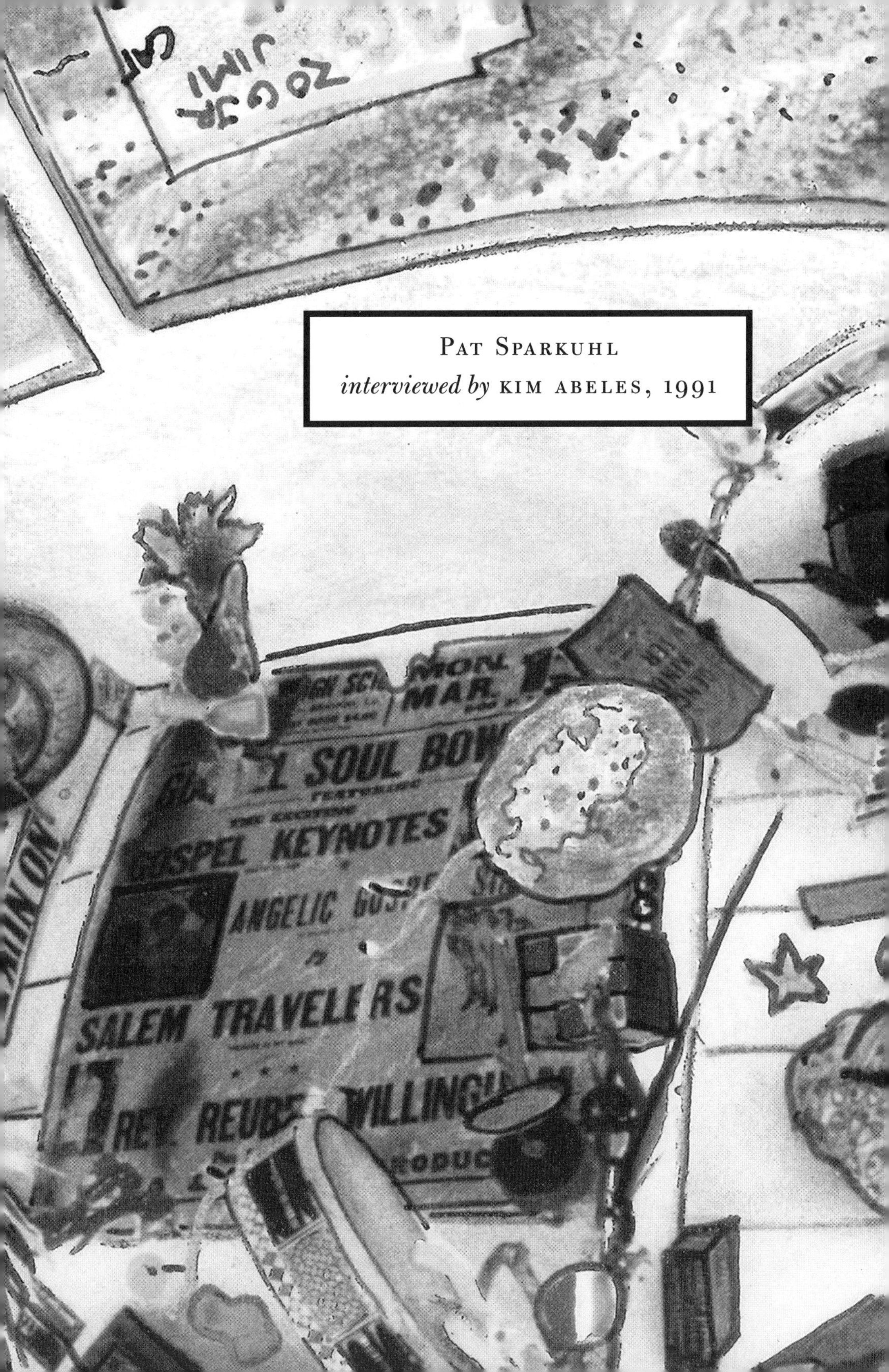

Pat Sparkuhl

interviewed by KIM ABELES, 1991

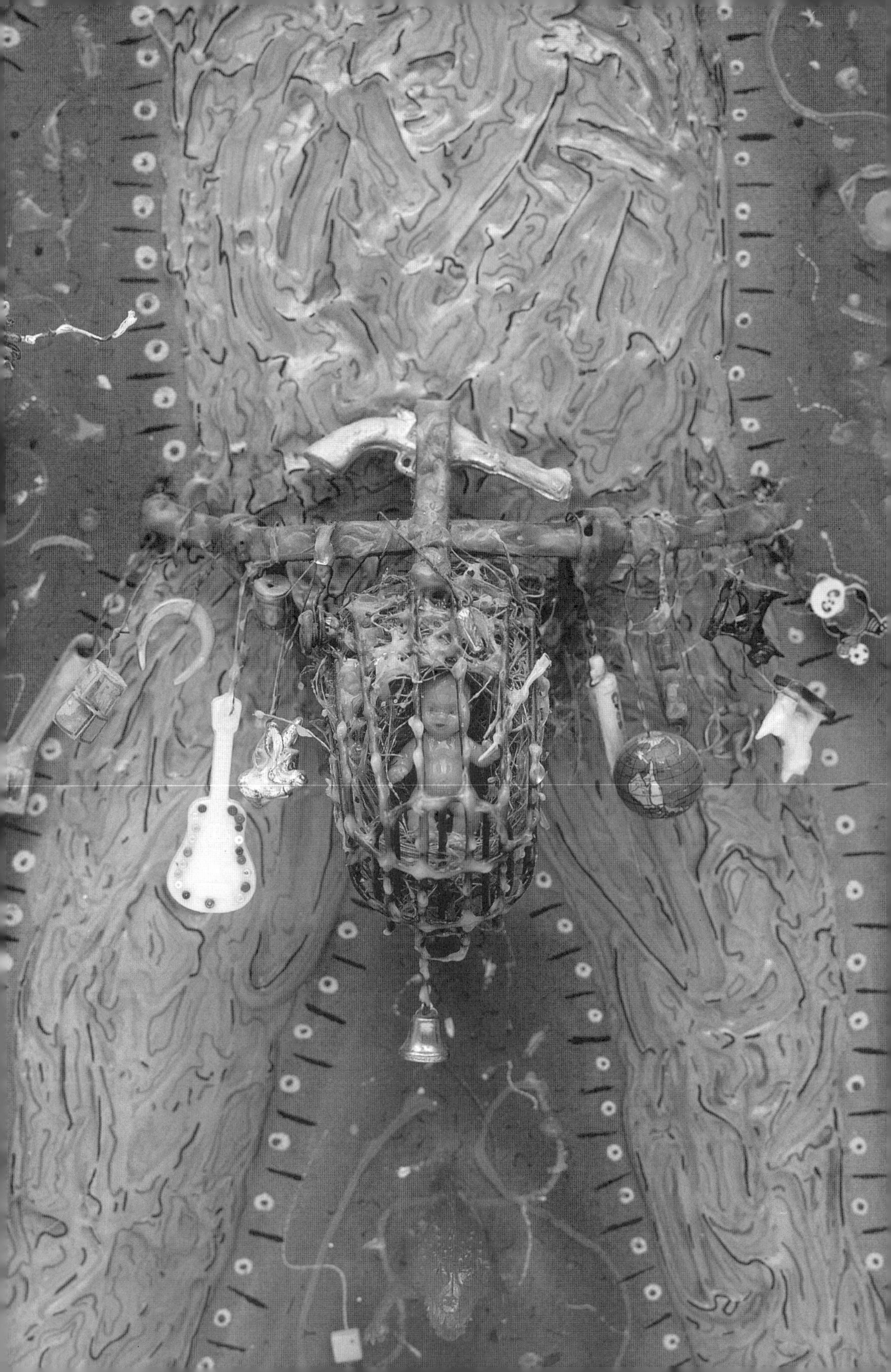

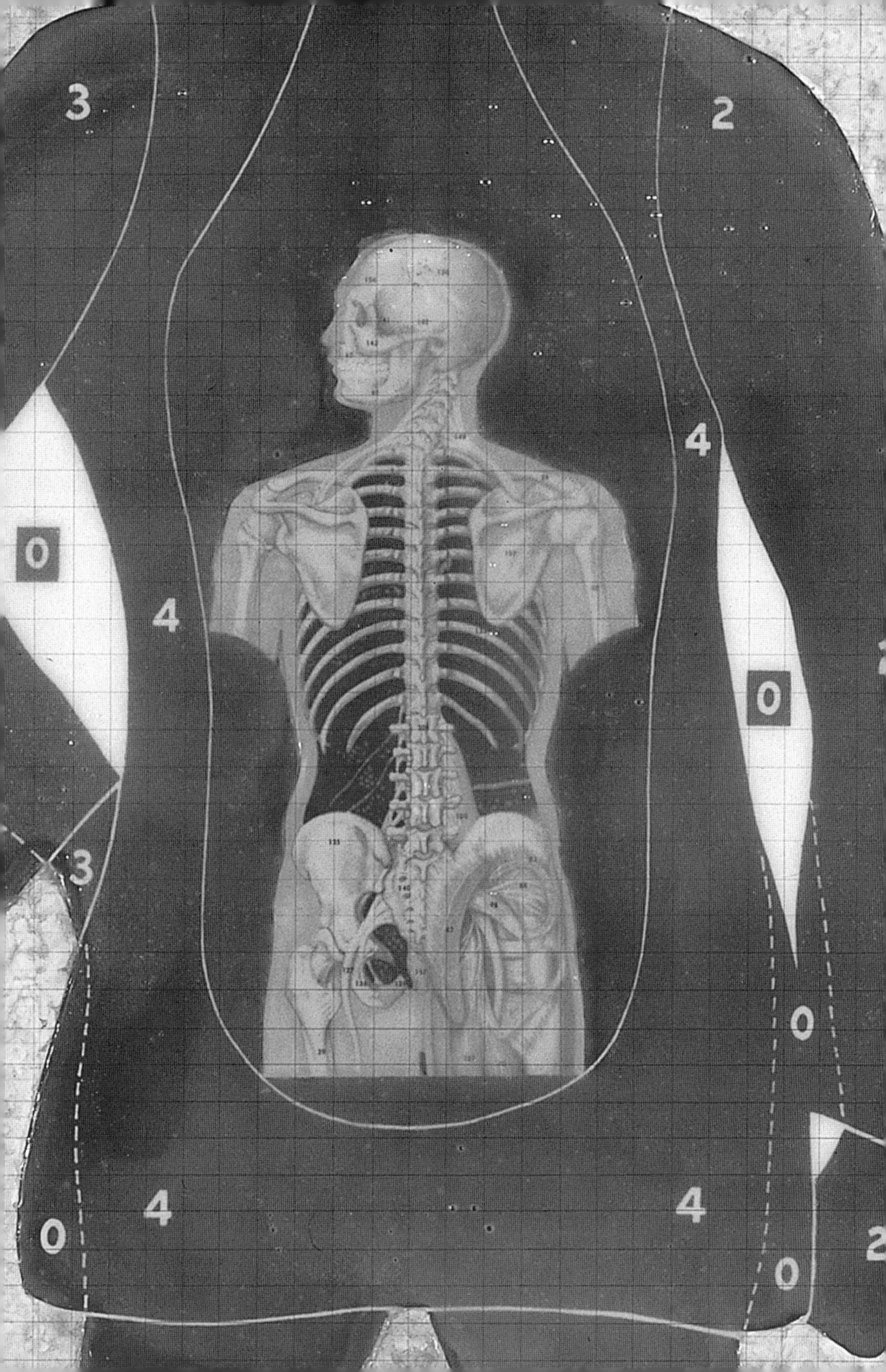
3
2
4
0
4
0
3
0
4
4
0
0
2

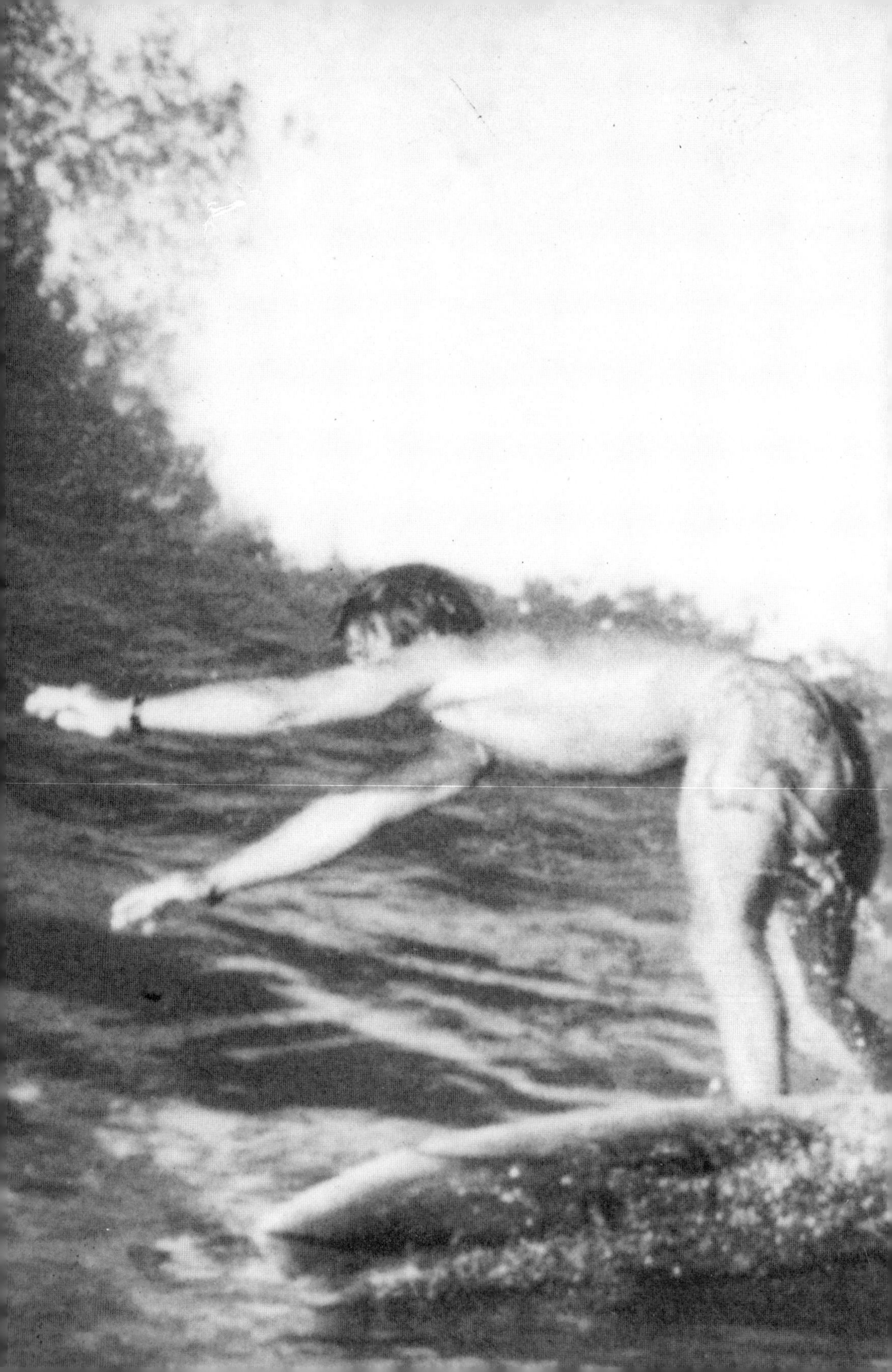

Pat Sparkuhl
interviewed by
KIM ABELES

Kim Abeles: It has been said that artists reflect society even if it's unconscious on their part. You, however, are an artist who deals directly with social issues. In a culture where so many people are apathetic and in an art world that is dominated by the last outrageous auction price, how did you get involved with this kind of work?

Pat Sparkuhl: My involvement has to do with my personal history, my own frame of reference as a basis for developing this body of work, and my perceptions of the particular issues with which I deal.

Abeles: How is this attitude reflected in a work like the Marilyn Chambers piece?

Sparkuhl: *Marilyn's Chamber* was based on a former model for Ivory Snow. In 1971 I surveyed fifty-five Ma and Pa grocery stores for a photo essay at the Bowers Museum in Orange County. At the time there was an article about Marilyn Chambers's controversial involvement in porno movies. I wanted some Ivory Snow boxes with her picture on the front for a future piece. The Ma and Pa stores would be my only source since media attention had resulted in the boxes being rapidly removed from major supermarkets. I went to a small store in Orange County. Sure enough, there were six boxes left. The final piece focused on my frustration with real estate development, machismo, and the cliché of the "ten" as brought out by Bo Derek in the movie *Ten.* Where I live, real estate people have speculated heavily for fifteen years, making huge profits at the expense of our town. I wanted to show how real estate people score and evaluate things and apply it to this kind of macho "ten."

Abeles: So the original project of documenting those Ma and Pa stores is reflected in the Chambers piece?

Sparkuhl: Yes. Without an understanding of the cultural lag between the megamarkets and the Ma and Pa stores, the piece could never have come about.

Abeles: How many children do you have, Pat?

Sparkuhl: Two.

page 221:
Fisheye View of Dining Room Ceiling *(detail), 1990, hand-colored photograph, 16 x 20 inches*
page 222:
Kid in Me (for Cory) *(detail), 1988–89, mixed-media construction, 29½ x 66½ x 6 inches*
page 223:
45-22-38 *(detail), 1982, mixed-media construction, 41 x 46 x 3 inches*
page 224:
Pat Sparkuhl surfing at Rockpile, Laguna Beach

Abeles: You often use dolls in connection with ideas about the destruction of the world, potential destruction with bombs and so on. I wondered if the arrival of those children altered the amount of political input in your work, or if that's always been there.

Sparkuhl: The political aspect has always been there. Ever since I saw Ed Kienholz's work in that infamous show in March 1966 at the Los Angeles County Museum of Art, I have realized that there is a political dimension that I can work towards. At that time I was not so focused on art per se but on the possibility of how I could view a social context in artwork.

Abeles: Do you think artists have a responsibility to do social and political work?

Sparkuhl: It goes back and forth, as in the old cliché "art imitates life and life imitates art." I think it's like respiration—the yin/yang. There's a balance that occurs, but the responsibility is a personal one.

Abeles: Yes, but many artists ignore this. You're obviously a symbolist, yet there's a certain literalness about the way you use the objects as symbols. Two pieces that come to my mind are Search'n *and* Young Kids Getting Pushed Around, *in which they're literally being pushed around in the sculpture. How specific do you want the reading of these pieces to be when a viewer approaches them?*

Sparkuhl: I am currently focusing attention on this aspect of my work. In *Young Kids Getting Pushed Around,* the symbol of a lemon pie represents the idea of a lemon as rejection and the idea of manipulation that parents impose on children. I tried to deal with it directly so one can see the manipulation of different nationalities in the lemon pie. You literally rotate, or push, the sculpture in a circular manner. I tried to get a more abstract rather than a direct reading so that the narrative is less literal.

I find that a clear narrative polarizes viewers. Those who agree keep looking and thinking; those who don't, walk away. Since I want to get people off the fence and get them to deal consciously or unconsciously with my work, I try to get enough of an abstract quality into it.

Abeles: So it's more like presenting a forum, a form of discussion. Some of the symbols are repeated in different works. Dice are used a lot, teeth are used, and wishbones. Are you developing a language that is meant to stretch from piece to piece?

Sparkuhl: To a degree, yes. Many of the issues that I like to deal with pose a moral gamble. I like to use wishbones and dice a lot. Different colored wishbones represent luck, good and bad. In some pieces, I'll use black wishbones, and in other pieces white or yellow, and so on. In *Young Kids Getting Pushed Around,* I have rose branch wishbones that are thorny. I try to have some kind of a line connecting the work to the symbols, a kind of psychological dynamic in terms of how one would approach the moral level of the work.

Abeles: The wishbone with the thorns that you mention points to another method you use, the combination of something horrifying with an object that is nostalgic or romantic. Is that to create tension?

Sparkuhl: That kind of tension and contrast is ever present in our society. I manipulate the possibilities of embellishing an object, or the form itself, to give a bit of repulsion. You want to come closer, but you are repulsed at the same time.

Abeles: Eastern philosophies have that yin/yang, but we in the West approach it differently because we evaluate things as bad or good.

Sparkuhl: We have definite perspectives on the value of things.

Abeles: Which is advantageous for your work, assuming it's a Western viewer. The viewer comes to it with those ways of morally judging everything. You play off that assumption.

Another contradiction is that edge of humor you have in the titles of your work. Is the humor a kind of comic relief to all these very heavy subjects, or is it a kind of cynicism, or is it the yin/yang you mentioned?

Sparkuhl: It is really all of those. I attempt to lighten up the issue and create more access to it for those people who choose to deal with the titles. I also like double-entendre. This idea of releasing a little bit of tension is something personal. I want to make a statement that the viewer can have some connection with. I guess I'm approaching the issue from a few different angles at once. I deal with play in most of my work. I incorporate some level of play, whether it's in the painting of the object, the manipulation of the object, or in the title itself. I want there to be an element of openness.

Abeles: Sometimes I look at your pieces and they're so deadly serious. Then I look at the titles and they become full of whimsy.

Sparkuhl: It's like that Andres Serrano photograph and the recent furor about the NEA. Had there been no title on it, that piece could be in every church in the United States. The title changed its whole demeanor and how it's perceived. It's so attractive and so ethereal, yet you see *Piss Christ* associated with it, and it takes on another meaning. It's just like the cost of a work. As soon as you look at the price, it affects your perspective on what you're seeing; it changes the attitude you have about the work.

Abeles: Every politician seemed to want to say that Serrano title. Even if they were furious about it, they seemed to relish using it.

Sparkuhl: What an opportunity! When could a politician say "piss Christ"? They could say it publicly, and people were supportive.

Abeles: Your pieces also poke fun specifically at the middle class, as in The Blind Taste Test *piece. It seems grounded in the middle class.*

Sparkuhl: My father was in medicine. An interesting aspect of my family was that my mother, a nurse, was a Democrat, and my father was a Republican. They were both very intellectual in their approaches to life, yet one was very concerned with feelings, and one was very caught up in the work ethic. So I grew up in an environment where possessions were a given, but because of my mother's influence I wanted to connect with middle-class values.

I am the youngest of four boys who grew up assuming we all would pursue careers in medicine. But along with medicine, there is a class consciousness because of the pedestal that society has created for doctors. I had difficulty coming to terms with this, so I sought out friends who helped me resolve the contradictions that I found in my own family. It was an unconscious rejection of upper-class values that led me to seek out a particular group of friends who happened to have middle-class values. I'm sure that comes through in my work.

Abeles: Since the fifties the middle class has been presented as a warm area in advertising.

Sparkuhl: Well, all the advertising was aimed at the middle class, or middle-class values. That was the basis of our society.

Abeles: To be middle class was a goal, but that's not the goal anymore. Does that change the nature of your pieces, or the way the earlier ones look now? Aren't they going to be relics of a disappeared culture?

Sparkuhl: Maybe—only time will tell. We'll see. I know what is changing things for me: having a family, having children. Having children has caused me to loosen up considerably in terms of how I deal with objects. Objects are very important to me. I feel objects are the basis of our society, and I want to present them in a way that I feel reflects our society and how I feel about specific issues.

Abeles: Are your narratives influenced by the objects, or are the objects influenced by the narrative?

Sparkuhl: It depends on the issue. If the issue calls for certain objects to be incorporated into the piece, I seek them out. If I'm working on a piece and allowing time to go by for its development and a particular object happens to play into it as a form or an influence, then I allow that to happen.

Abeles: What about Chatterbox*? Did it arise from your being interested in the way teeth looked? Is that how that piece came about?*

Sparkuhl: I had been painting teeth for quite a while, using them in different things. I saw an opportunity to paint a variation of teeth. The basic idea is that of a dog trying to get through a cage. Whenever we pick out a dog, we go to a shelter. There are always a few dogs growling and snarling at the cage. What I wanted to do was simulate that feeling in terms of people talking and placed into a confined area, so that the concentration and variation of all these mouths chattering would come through.

Abeles: In that same piece, and also with some of the iron pieces, the viewer shares a feeling of participation or potential movement. Is that something that you want in these? There's a psychological involvement because of the potential movement.

Sparkuhl: Well, it must be unconscious.

Abeles: Much of your earlier work is aligned with the pop art movement. Some of the pieces use flags, for instance, Untitled Flag for Women. *Is there a historical reference to Jasper Johns in addition to the obvious social and political elements you address in these pieces?*

Sparkuhl: Actually, with *Untitled Flag for Women* I was not consciously thinking of Jasper Johns. I wanted to deal with the plight of women and how women have been exploited for centuries in our society. And deal with war, the exploitation of war, and how it is ever present in the world these days. I wanted to apply the universal concept of war to women of the United States. I eliminated the flag's stars to change the scale and substituted a camouflage field for the blue ground. The relationship of war to the stripes would be much more significant than the standard three-by-four-foot flag with the stars and stripes. Any reference to Jasper Johns was purely unintentional, but the association is fine. I don't mind that.

Abeles: What is your connection with the pop art movement?

Sparkuhl: I did my master's thesis on advertising and subliminal conditioning. As a graduate student I was very interested in how advertising influences the public. This perspective was automatically incorporated into my work.

Abeles: This calls to mind the piece with the pornographic playing cards.

Sparkuhl: I did a couple, one called *Stacked Deck* and the other called *Eye Poppers.*

Abeles: Do you see those as being pornographic simply by your presentation of those images, or do you see those as moving away from pornography into moralism?

Sparkuhl: They're both based on generalized male perspectives. In the fifties, if a woman had big breasts, she was called "stacked." I got some fifties cards in Las Vegas. What I did was to play on the attitude of stacking the deck, which is literally manipulation of the deck. One manipulates the deck for one's own benefit. I manipulated the deck for mine. I was essentially showing a stacked deck of stacked women.

The piece called *Eye Poppers* is a more contemporary deck of cards, which I laid out like a photographic contact sheet. I made a contour cut around each woman and pulled her out of the environment. That's based on a stereotypical male perspective. When guys see a nudie, they don't see the rest of the environment; they just see the naked figure. That's what they're doing most of the time consciously, and if not consciously, they're unconsciously projecting her out from the environment so that she becomes the only thing they see.

Abeles: So you bring men's fantasies into reality, which may startle them into seeing what they're doing. Have people responded at all negatively to pieces like that?

Sparkuhl: You know, it's interesting. I have never gone by the name Patrick; I've always gone by Pat. People say, "God, she must be quite a gal to deal with this kind of issue." So if they don't know, they see Pat as cross-gender, and it doesn't matter. In that respect it's been okay. But whenever I've been around the piece or they know that a man did it, there've been responses like, "You're a sexist fool," "What audacity you have," "What a put-down on women." Absolutely not. It's never been intended as a put-down. I see that perspective in our society and try to be objective about it; it's a perspective based on gender, and I try to bring it out in my work.

Abeles: What do you think it means when people respond so differently? Once I took students to see a piece by Alison Saar, and a couple of black students were very alarmed by images of black men upside down and sus-pended. As soon as I told them the artist was a black woman, they said, "Oh, I see, it's a critique of society." What does that imply? It seems so limiting to the way we view art, that we always will stereotype even if we're critiquing.

Sparkuhl: Which is okay. I think that's the way it is in a society where we are so overwhelmed with information. The media tends to polarize people. News is designed to create reaction, yet sometimes results in apathy. By the time children are five years old, they've witnessed countless thousands of deaths on TV. They have become so callous to the idea of death that when they see a dead person or a photograph of a dead person, they don't respond to it very much. It's the same with social issues: male/female, black/white, green/purple —it doesn't matter. When an issue is so polarized, people want to align with something. They want to connect: fusion by delusion. They think the connection is sincere, but they're really deceiving themselves because they're not looking at the real picture.

Abeles: We're all simple-minded people, I guess.

Sparkuhl: The news media are a more contemporary, mass-psychological way of organizing certain perspectives in our society. The way they channel or present information to an audience determines how the audience will respond.

Abeles: I've heard it said that Ted Koppel is just as influential as the president. Was your move from more graphic work to assemblage a natural development or a conscious decision? You always added objects to those graphic pieces, but the work became much more three-dimensional.

Sparkuhl: I've always enjoyed the idea of containment. From the mid-seventies to about 1982 I dealt with containment in a box. The idea was to create a shrine. Maybe there was a relation to Cornell's boxes, not a conscious effort to reproduce like activity but rather to deal with my own kind of containment in this shrine. I've always enjoyed the religious overtones that I tried to incorporate in these boxes by enshrining something. Like making an icon.

Abeles: Because advertising is our new religion?

Sparkuhl: I did a few pieces on smoking. I wanted to fuse elements of religion and the politics of smoking.

Abeles: You're not a smoker, right?

Sparkuhl: No.

Abeles: I wondered about your personal involvement in pieces, if these are issues you read about or see in society, or if they're issues that involve your family or close friends.

Sparkuhl: In the last seven or eight years I've dealt a lot with child issues. Does that mean I am using my children as inspiration or motivation to deal with an issue? I am definitely influenced by what goes on around me and encourage those influences. I also read about issues, many of which seem absurd. Many times something bad is happening and nothing is being done. That's where the politics come in, along with the idea of mixing religion, God, and country. Religion and smoking are naturals for me because they are major idols in society.

Abeles: Do you think that art can have an influence on society? I just read an article on AIDS and art. There are critics who think there's no possibility of change due to art and that it's inconsequential whether artists do political work or not.

Sparkuhl: Look at the art market. Money influences people's thinking. In the last ten years art has made quantum leaps in the marketplace. So if for no other reason than cost, people are going to look closely at artwork.

Abeles: How about your use of Christian iconography? Why did you select that?

Sparkuhl: I was brought up Catholic but was not too interested in going to church. I think the only time I was motivated to go was during grammar school. I had a girlfriend who went to Sunday school and I wanted to see her, so I went to Sunday school.

My real focus on religion is based on morality. Religion has formed the basis for moral perspectives in society. My use of religious symbols automatically makes a connection with the moral aspect of what I'm dealing with. Many times this charges the way people see the relationship of their own symbols to other issues.

Abeles: I am curious about how the steam iron with the crucifix came about. It's a very powerful image that implies tattooing or branding. The crucifix is imprinted so that if you actually used the iron, you would get a scorched imprint of the crucifix. To me, it implies I would put that iron to my flesh.

Sparkuhl: Perfect—that's what it's about. The piece evolved at a time when I was overwhelmed by all the born-again Christian activity going on around me. It was more than a trend; it was a crusade that peaked in the mid-eighties.

I love looking at things in Goodwill stores. One day as I was rummaging through a store, I saw a Gothic arch on a shelf. I thought, "God, there's a religious image right there." It was a simple, hand-held iron, and I envisioned it as something used to iron out problems. There was something that was very provocative about it. I brought it home, and I kept looking and looking at it. I thought a lot about the born-again activity and how crazy it seemed to me—again, fusion by delusion. So I thought, "Here is something that irons out problems, the wrinkles in your life."

Abeles: And also is a labor-intensive activity.

Sparkuhl: What really struck me was that shape. Historically the Gothic arch is a religious symbol. Rather than ironing out problems, I wanted to create a branding iron because I saw people figuratively branding each other as born-again Christians. Another religious symbol is the wire rosary-viper element. Here again is a kind of push and pull—a viper with fangs, and yet at the same time, it's a rosary. I fused the two issues. To allow the user a greater connection with God, I put a "GOD" label on the heater control knob.

Abeles: Another piece that interests me is Crutch Fetish, *partly because of the powerful scale and the way the connections are made.*

Sparkuhl: The image focuses attention on the upper crutch. I wanted to make it more of a form than an implement or tool. I also wanted to deal with an architectural aspect that suggests rhythm. The intent was to have a tenuous balance of crutches teetering on just one crutch in the middle. The entire group of crutches depends on one little pin.

Abeles: So that piece is more formal?

Sparkuhl: Definitely more formal, and more playful.

Abeles: How about the 100 Hot Spots*?*

Sparkuhl: Sputnik was really the inspiration for that piece. I approached land as a human element and ocean as a void. We concentrate more on land because that's where we live. What I did first was to paint all of the land area on the globe as if it were textured flesh. Abstractlike, swirly wires extend from the globe.

Abeles: Those swirling wires appear often in your work. They are like energy.

Sparkuhl: Energy symbols. I wanted abstract shapes with swirling wires circling the globe. Two global issues interested me: war zones and strategic areas. I put map pins to identify strategic areas around the world where war has occurred or is on the brink of occurring.

I think of it as a shrine image. It is a mobile shrine. It's on casters because war happens in so many parts of the world. You can simply move it from location to location. The modular pedestal combines an architectural form with an altar.

Abeles: Earlier, you mentioned moving the new work more into abstraction in order to generalize the themes. Is that correct?

Sparkuhl: I sometimes feel schizophrenic. I find myself dealing with very literal matters at one time and then swinging over to intensely abstract ones at other times.

Abeles: When you speak of abstracting the work, do you mean expanding it?

Sparkuhl: I'm talking about incorporating forms in a way that the work becomes more abstract. For instance, I dealt with rhythm and architecture in a piece that I call *Record Tower.* It is about the passing of the vinyl record, about the heroic stance that records used to have in our society. I heated about a hundred records, and when they were warm, deformed them in varying degrees to create three groups of deformity. Then I stacked them to create a tower that symbolizes, to me, the social issue of change in our perspective of what the vinyl is. Now it is just useless. I was able to deal with the idea of rhythm itself or a concept of rhythm, repetition, and form.

Abeles: So you're making strength from simplicity. The steam-iron piece is a simpler piece.

Sparkuhl: Less is more. One aspect of my work has always been allowing things to take their own time. If it takes a year, a year and a half, or two years, it doesn't matter. I try to deal with things as they happen. By allowing things to go on and on for so long, I have to focus my attention on sculptural sketches. In this work I limit the amount of materials that I incorporate and see what I come up with.

Abeles: Your works on paper are so different from the sculptural work.

Sparkuhl: In 1981 I started working on paper, drawing with Prismacolor, and making different types of graphic work. It was an investigation of very clinical and modular symbols. For the last five years I've dealt with another side of myself. It is about color and free form, yet still expresses an attitude about the social condition. I love color. In my earlier work, I didn't focus on it much. I used mostly somber tones, which were effective for those pieces. Recently I have looked at color and fragmentation. How to deal with the idea of fragments really excites me because we are in such a fragmented society. I have been working on pieces dealing with the idea of repetition of spots of paint on the wall in a rhythmic manner. I love repetition. There's something that has always intrigued me about repeating an image to make it more anonymous. It gets back to the middle class. In our culture the middle class is anonymous. By focusing on repetition, the individual image becomes more and more anonymous, more like a member of a group.

Abeles: How do you select your themes and determine which subject you'll develop as opposed to another when the world is full of so many ideas, events, tragedies, and social issues?

Sparkuhl: I try to deal with my life and my own history. Impersonal history puts me on the outside—I deal with issues at a subjective level. They are very important to me, based on my frame of reference and activities, leading me to have certain feelings about issues.

Shoeshrine Box is an example. I have very strong feelings for Mexico and its culture. I started college in Mexico City. As a child I used to go around our neighborhood trying to shine people's shoes for ten cents, just for fun. In Mexico little shoeshine boys were everywhere. The idea of the kids scurrying around with their shoeshine box trying to make a couple of pennies, pesos, or centavos really touched me. They were always so happy, greeting you with a smile. They were also very religious. I tried to fuse the elements of the shoe, a shoeshine, the religion, the color typical of Mexico, and mobility.

Abeles: How did Jesus Heels *develop?*

Sparkuhl: As a student on an overseas trip, years ago, I did a project collecting pop tops at various ports of call. My plan was to do a pop-top survey of the world. I also wanted to do something that directly related to my walking from place to place. I enjoyed walking rather than taking taxis or buses, as it let me connect with many people. The more I looked around, the more I was intrigued with all the heels that I found. They had a direct connection to what I was doing—all the walking. So I started collecting heels from every port and ended up with over a hundred of them by the time of my return home. Each of the heels was bagged and labeled with the port of origin. Many times I lay these heels out, thinking, "What the hell am I going to do with these things, anyway?" They're so unique—unique to the individual who walked. They connected to what I had done, walking everywhere in my travels. It struck me that when upended, the heels resembled headstones. There was a sense of repetitiveness and yet each was unique. Maybe these heels could have been from people who walked for Jesus. The phrase "Jesus heals" just struck me: "Jesus heels" as a kind of play on words.

Abeles: This is the second time you've mentioned a shape, such as that of the steam iron or of the heels, referring to something else. Is this part of your idea about using abstraction in the new work? Is that what led you to this?

Sparkuhl: In part it did because I wanted to focus on forms more than content. I wanted to emphasize the forms in relation to the sense of fragmentation that I see in society. By avoiding the literal content of the object, it is easier to "read" its form. I started drawing forms that related to one another. For instance, a treble clef was important because of the idea of music and rhythm. Then there are certain basic forms—squares and rectangles, wedges and circles—as well as forms that are close to me, such as bones. We have a couple of dogs—the idea of dogs chewing bones. I like the idea of incorporating a bone or two in a piece. I looked at some of the shapes my kids make as inspiration also.

Abeles: So they become language symbols.

Sparkuhl: More recently this work has been a response to the changes in the landscape that are going on where I live. I did a piece called *In Roads.* It concerns the idea of a line, which represents the freeway system interacting with the changing landscape. In Laguna Beach people can afford virtually anything. Every imaginable exotic car is available, and they're all going fast. What I attempted to do is create an atmosphere of bright coloration and texture to develop a sense of something very much in transition. I used color on color. The line with blurs of color represents the cars on a freeway leading nowhere. The landscape forms a colorful transition. Everything is focused on trendy colors.

Abeles: How has living in such close proximity to the ocean affected your work?

Sparkuhl: We moved to Laguna when I was ten. I remember my father brought home a surfboard, and I thought we were going to the snow. I had no idea of what a surfboard was. Going to the beach soon became an integral part of my life. I loved the water. The ocean offered a perspective that I had never experienced—the ocean and the movement of the waves. Surfing became my entire focus. I mean one hundred twenty percent. What was so wonderful about it was that it was an individual endeavor. It was something that I could work with by myself. There was a connection with nature. No one else would bug me about it. It was something that was separate from my family. I wasn't just "the youngest child." The issue of being the youngest wasn't really negative, but I was always associated with it. I wanted to be my own person. Of course, at the time it wasn't conscious when thinking about surfing, but the involvement I was developing with the ocean was very significant to me.

Abeles: Surfing and the ocean have a lot to do with rhythm and repetition, and finding a place within the rhythm.

Sparkuhl: All those elements became intuitive, not anything that I had to work out.

Abeles: Do you still surf?

Sparkuhl: Yes, it's still important to me.

Abeles: I've been told, once a surfer always a surfer.

Sparkuhl: I lived on Maui for a while in 1968–69, before the incredible influx of people from the mainland. Five of us would surf the best surf on the island where now there are three hundred people. It was like a sexual experience: the idea of fusing with something that is very important to you. When you're in the ocean for years and years like that, it becomes a companion. I often chuckle when I'm down at the ocean and I see people who aren't familiar with it. They think they can walk straight into a wave as though they are invincible. They think they can overpower the ocean. Invariably they're tossed to the shore, eating sand, a humbling experience. The relationship that I developed with the ocean endowed me with a humble perspective on what natural elements can do.

Abeles: Those contradictions again.

Sparkuhl: The older I get, the more surfing becomes a kind of therapy when trying to get away from the craziness that goes on around us. It's a great way to develop an intuitive feel for possible rhythms, which I want to deal with.

Abeles: You might wind up like Duchamp, but surfing instead of playing chess the last years of your life.

Sparkuhl: Well, I've been surfing for thirty years and I've known guys in their seventies who still surfed. I hope that when I'm seventy not only will I still be surfing but, like Duchamp, I will still reflect our place on the planet.

✶

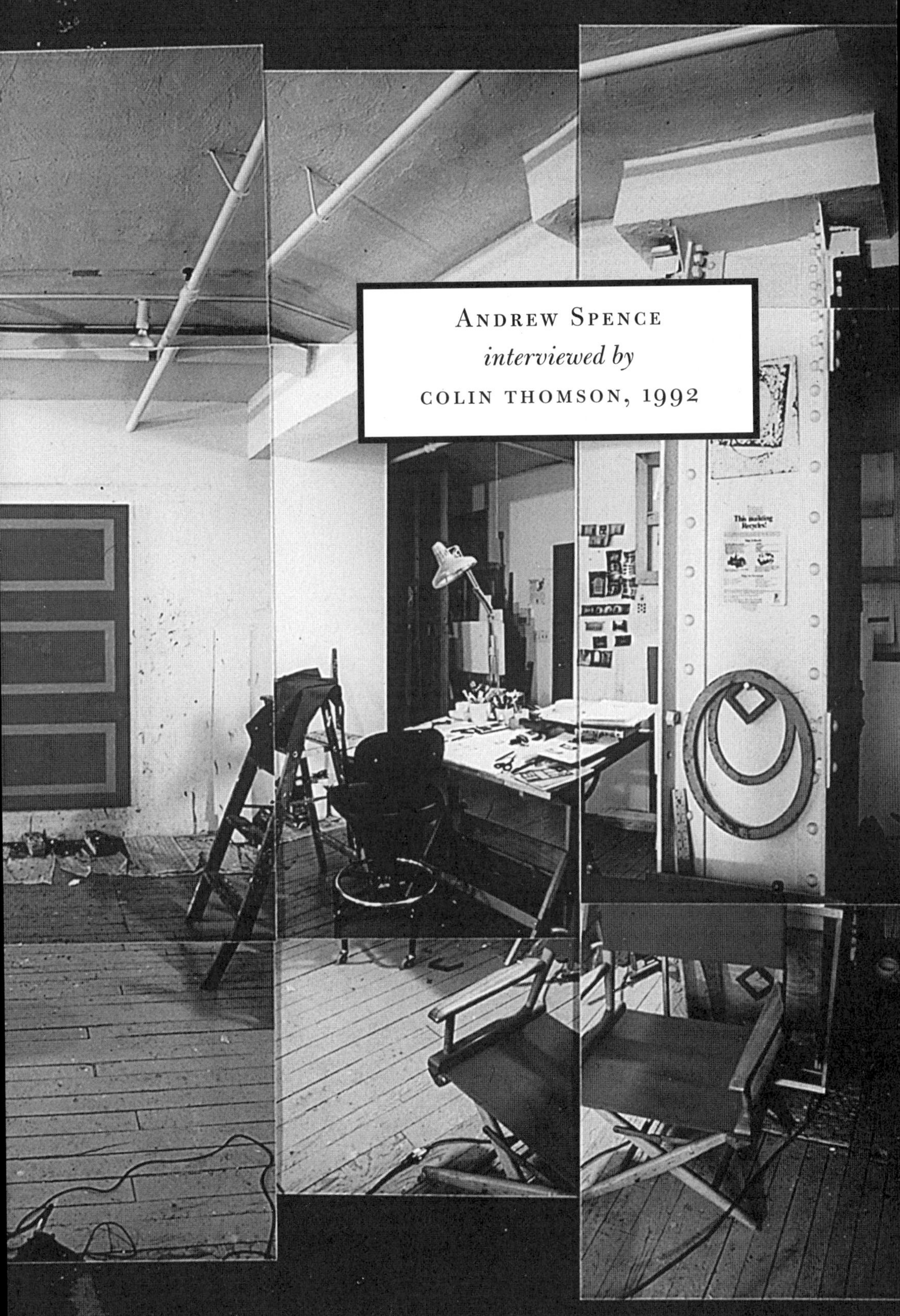

Andrew Spence *interviewed by* Colin Thomson, 1992

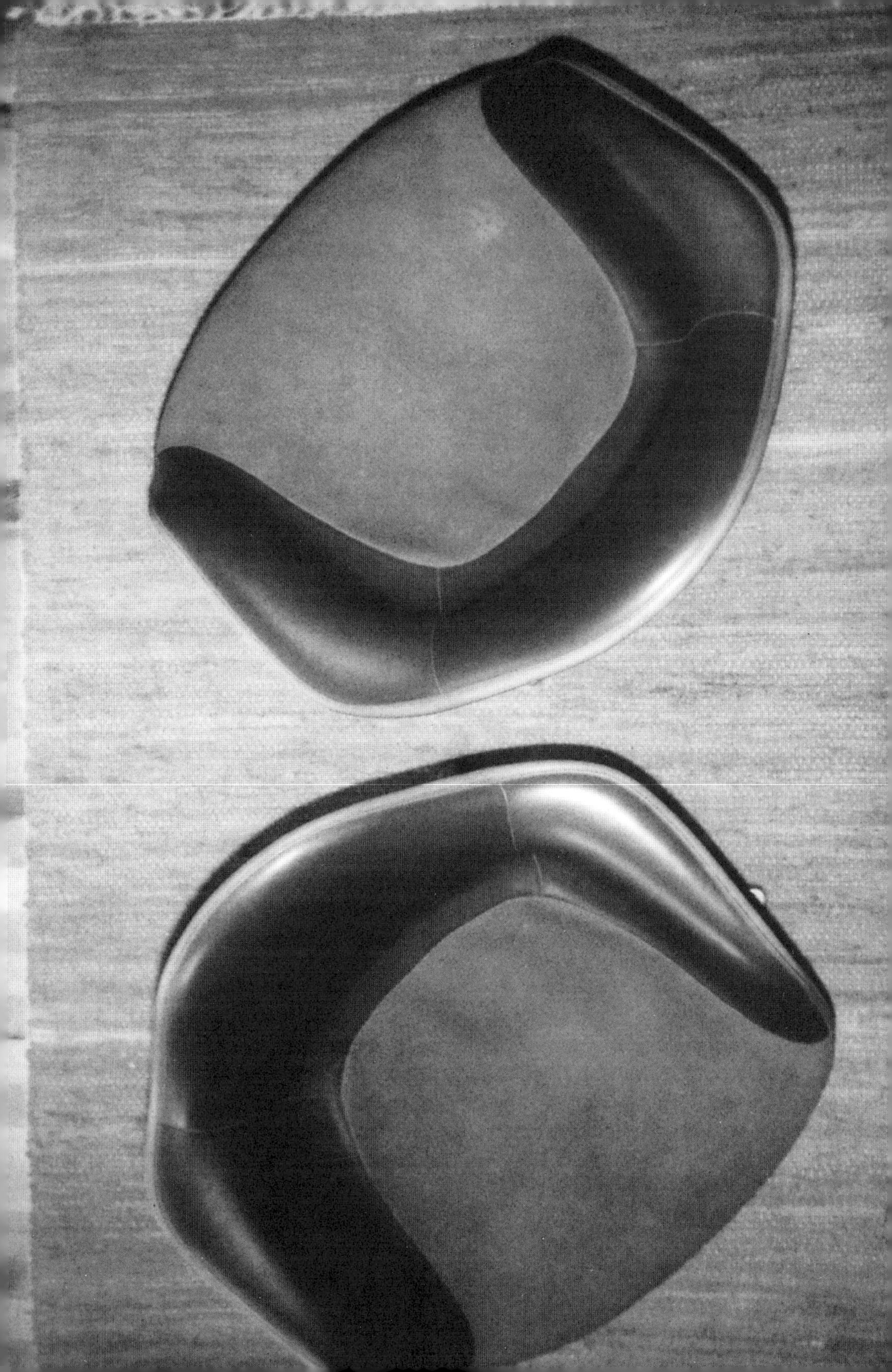

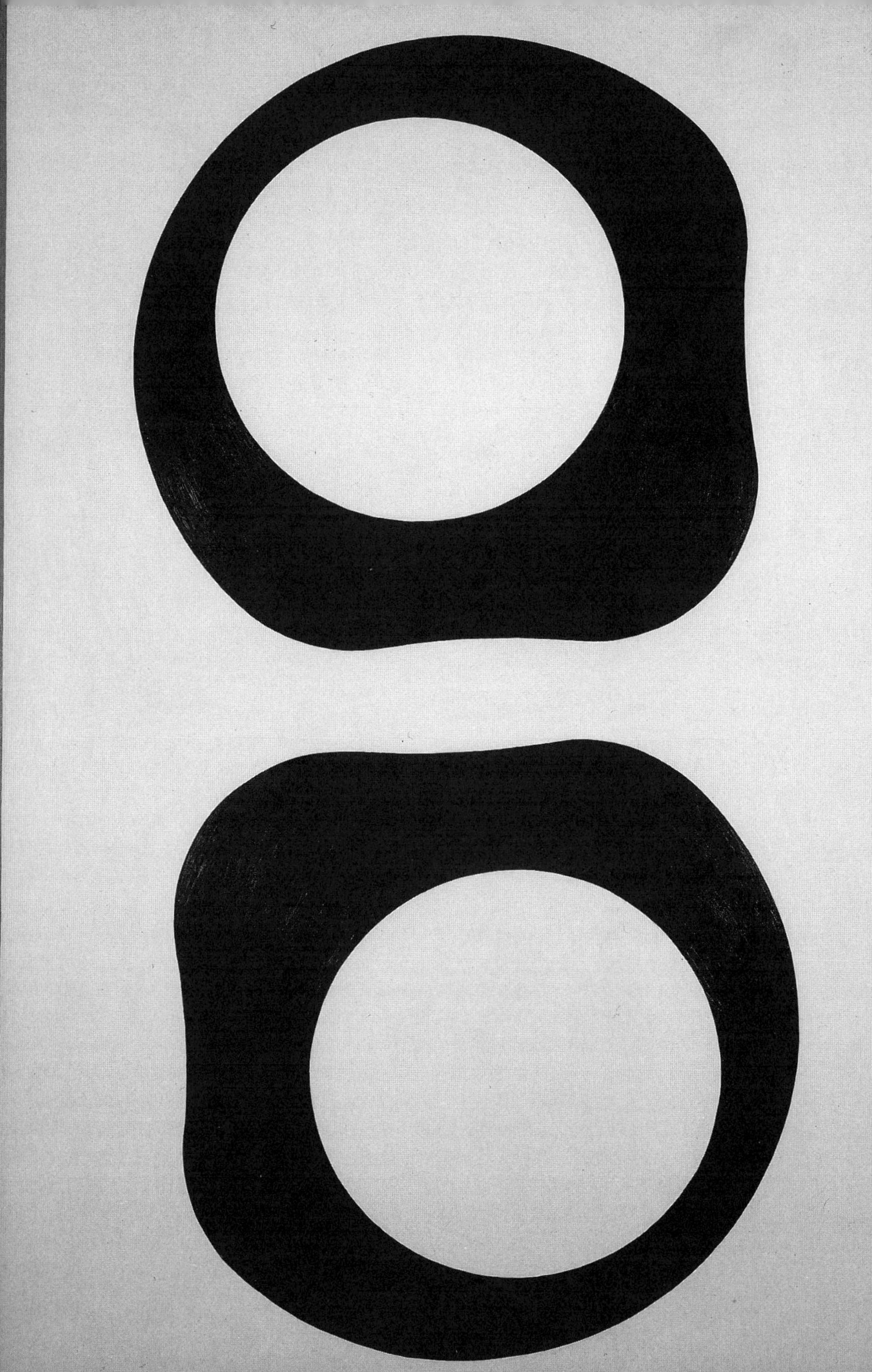

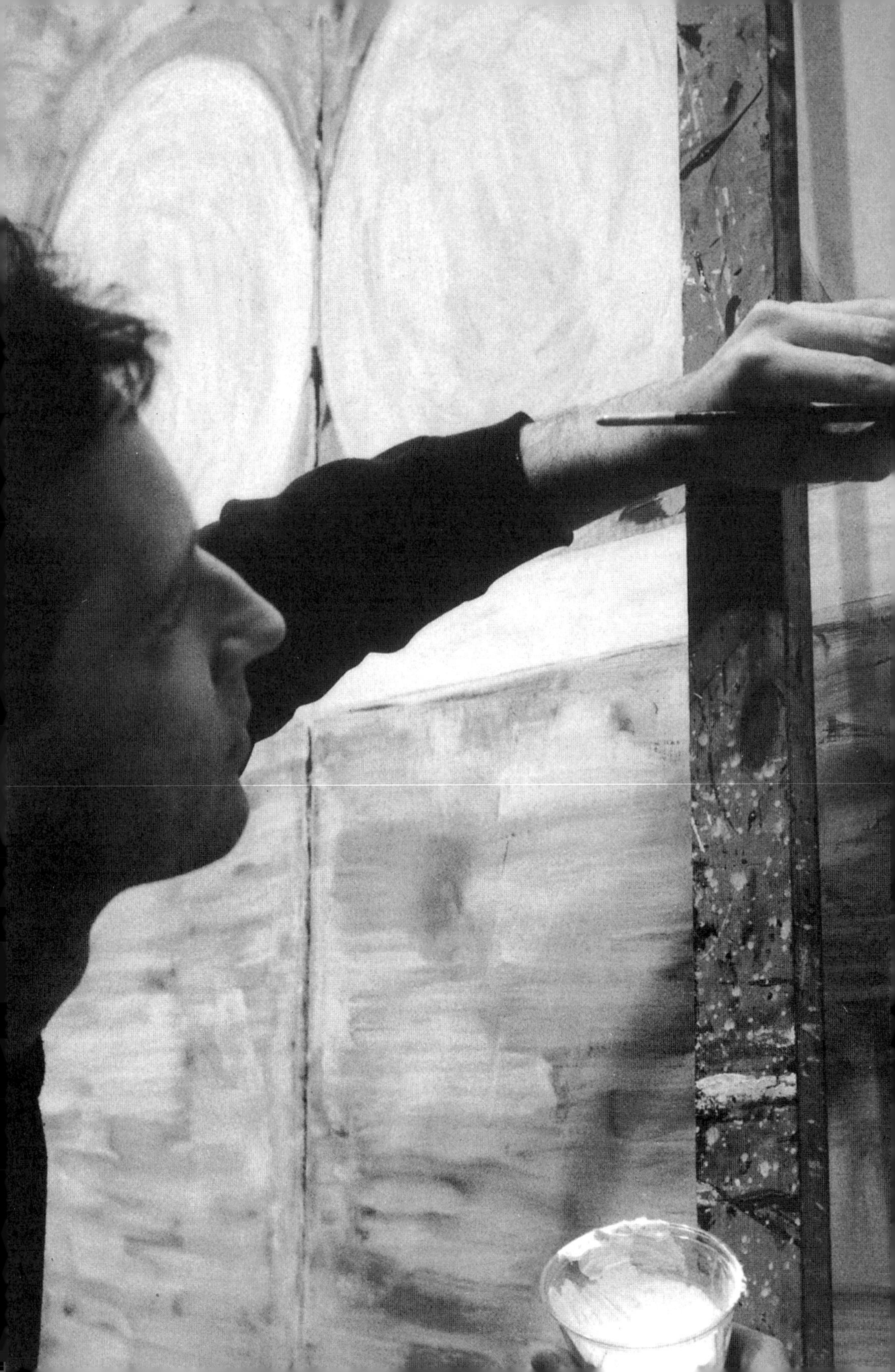

ANDREW SPENCE

interviewed by

COLIN THOMSON

Colin Thomson: I've known your work for about twelve years, since we first met in Los Angeles. I think it's interesting that the work you were doing then and the new work have a lot of parallels. The intentions in that earlier work are also in what's happening now. Would you speak about what you were doing when you first became an abstract painter—what you thought was going on in your paintings?

Andrew Spence: By the time you and I met in 1977, I was constructing molded modular paintings based on loosely formed ideas about prefabrication and Southern California architecture. Prefabrication was significant to me for being such a major part of the Southern California landscape—meaning tract homes and industrial parks. This is a theme that goes back to 1969 when I first met Esther McCoy, an architectural historian with whom I studied and later befriended in Los Angeles. So that's how I became aware of architecture and wanted to somehow involve it in my work.

Thomson: Didn't she do a big show on Rudolf Schindler and a book about California architects?

Spence: I don't know about a show on Schindler, but she did work in his office back in the thirties. She worked on a design show at the Whitney and a show about the Case Study House program at the Museum of Contemporary Art in Los Angeles. She has also written several books on Southern California architects and was one of the authorities on the subject before she died.

Thomson: Did you have any idea at the time that you might be interested in being an architect?

Spence: Not at that point. But earlier on, when I was first starting out in college, I thought I might become an architect or designer. Eventually those aspirations faded away as my interest in painting got stronger.

Thomson: During that period, which California painters were you familiar with? Who were you looking at?

Spence: In 1971 I took a job at an art warehouse and met some painters who were still getting established and

page 237:
Andrew Spence's studio, New York, 1992
page 238:
Detail of advertisement for Eames chairs, Harper's Bazaar, *1957*
page 239:
Swivel Chairs *(detail), 1986, oil on linen mounted on wood, 84 x 60 inches*
page 240:
Andrew Spence at work in his studio, New York, 1992

were also working there. Eventually we took an interest in each other's work. We would go to artists' studios to pick up or deliver artwork and had a chance to see not only what they were working on but *how* they were working as well. You'd peer in and see what people were doing. It was interesting that no one was really making images. They were making process art and conceptual art. A lot of people were doing sculpture that hung on the wall. The most established painters were making very decorative paintings—lots of patterns and bright colors. Everybody, including myself, seemed to find a way not to make a painting using an image. By 1974 I knew most of the Southern California artists through that job and Nick Wilder, who was an art dealer at the time.

Nick's storage at the warehouse was one of the most interesting to me and contained several of John McLaughlin's paintings. These paintings caught my attention while I was working on an inventory. They were so different from what was generally around—very minimal, geometric, and calm. The tension from the calm was weird. It took me a long time to figure out what in particular attracted me to McLaughlin's work. I finally did come to an understanding about this attraction, and it's been a measure for me ever since.

Charles Eames's designs had the same effect on me as John McLaughlin's paintings. I saw a show of his work at the art gallery of the University of California, Los Angeles. Actually, I had to pick them up and deliver them to his office.

Thomson: You didn't actually know these people, so you were developing in Los Angeles as a painter in a rather cloistered environment. Is that incorrect to say?

Spence: I didn't live in a neighborhood full of artists. Most artists lived near the beach in Venice. Not being from California and not having gone to a Los Angeles art school, I always felt that I was peripheral to the local scene. When I wanted to see more work than I saw at my job, I would go to galleries. I didn't socialize with artists other than the ones that I worked with. I never worked the art circuit as some did.

Thomson: Then you became involved with Nick Wilder.

Spence: Yes, Nick would visit his storage in the warehouse quite often. We became friends, and every few months he would stop by my studio for a visit. In 1974 he invited me to show with him. I made a body of work that consisted of about ten paintings of acrylic Rhoplex on canvas. Every painting was just like the next painting except that they were of different colors and sizes. One half of the canvas was one color and the other was another color, but very close in value. I was trying to create an interesting looking surface—like a detail of a section of a building. The surface was supposed to be the image. It took a while to realize that the paintings in this show looked great as an installation, but on their own there wasn't enough to see and they didn't hold up.

One time, someone who was unfamiliar with contemporary art but knew I was an artist stopped by for a visit at my studio. He commented on being interested in seeing my work sometime as he stood right in front of one of my paintings. While looking at the painting, he asked what it was for. Embarrassed, I replied that I used them for sound baffling. From that moment I wanted my work to be more communicative to people. I started looking around my environment for less abstract references than the surface of a wall and became interested in the colors used for automobiles, recreational vehicles, and other industrial purposes. I liked the way recreational vehicles were painted: a white ground with top and bottom accent-color stripes. The surfaces were usually made of aluminum stamped to look like wood grain, which amused me. My wife, Sique, and I would go through trailer parks taking snapshots. We even went to a mobile-home factory and saw how they were made.

Thomson: You really made a conscious decision that you would find a more interesting subject matter, and that you would find it not in your studio but by going out.

Spence: Yes, I wanted my work to be reflective of my environment and my place in time. Pop art was important for that—at least it was for me—as was all painting before photography was invented. Before photography, painting was the only visual recording of history. I wanted an abstract format to function in the same way and to communicate my point of view about my surroundings to people.

People started responding to the work better. They weren't so much aware of it looking like the side of a trailer, but there was some kind of association being made. That was an interesting observation: there was the beginning of some kind of response.

Thomson: So after these earlier paintings you started constructing a surface on the painting that would actually lump out along ridges.

Spence: Just before I left for New York in 1977, these earlier paintings led to molding bas-relief surfaces made out of acrylic Rhoplex mounted like a painting on either plywood or canvas. I would paint on these surfaces as if they were sectional pieces of a larger whole, such as a building façade or the side of a trailer. The effect was similar to an imprint.

Thomson: But this two-step system of working would also serve as a distancing effect between what the painting would look like and how you were working on the painting. So it wasn't suddenly all in your hands.

Spence: I was still experimenting on how and what to paint on these new surfaces and tended to keep the painting very simple. The paint jobs on trucks, trailers, recreational vehicles, and cars were used as references for the painting part of this process.

Thomson: When you came to New York and these references seemed less relevant to you, where did you go for your subject matter?

Spence: That's when I started drawing images using geometric shapes as opposed to the façades and bas-reliefs that I was doing in L.A. I realized very quickly that West Coast references didn't make sense in New York because everything in New York is a hundred years old and made out of brick. Prefabrication wasn't as relevant here. I began to have difficulty focusing on new source material. In a way, maybe there was too much information. I had to just start over. I went back to the drawing board.

I don't know why I wanted to do the geometry, but I think that, again, it comes out of architecture. Also, it's better organized, and I need to be organized. It seems to have something to do with that. I was drawing a lot of rectangles and squares and circles and other geometric shapes. I selected the lasting ones for painting ideas. This way of working was very random and had its problems. Every time I got something that I liked, I had to go run through my reference books just to see if I'd seen it someplace, or whether someone had already done this, or ask myself, "Why do I like this?" or "Why does this look so familiar?" This approach to painting was very unsettling.

So I started looking at things that I admired for their design qualities and abstracting them into images for paintings. This helped me narrow down the range of possibilities to forms that had personal significance. The paintings that resulted from this approach were immensely satisfying. I realized that if I wanted to get to an original form I had to dig deeper inside of myself.

I also began realizing that the more eccentric my work became, the less it looked like other people's work. That was a refreshing thought, so I would try to find eccentricity within myself. For one painting, I interpreted the experience of seeing a raft floating on a lake through some trees as a geometric, abstract image. This approach took the emphasis off the random search for subject matter and allowed me to concentrate on the painting process.

Thomson: Almost as if working from a narrative.

Spence: Sometimes, yes.

Thomson: At least a soliloquy to yourself.

Spence: Yes, but it wasn't easy, and it took a long time to get that going.

Thomson: When people are looking at your paintings, how do you feel about them tying into your original thought? For instance, the painting Swivel Chairs *has as its subject Eames chairs. Do you feel that recognizing the Eames chairs might co-opt people from seeing beyond the image of chairs?*

Spence: I do wonder what people actually see. When I'm painting, I'm also the viewer. I see the abstraction—that is what's important to me. I hope other people see that too. Recently, I made a painting using a gate as a source. It worked well as an abstraction, but the gate was still recognizable to some, while others saw it as a ping-pong table. I think that people who *want* to see beyond recognition of the subject matter will do so. As for the titles, they are just names so we know which painting is being referred to when we talk about it.

Thomson: Do you feel that some of the paintings are paintings and others are objects?

Spence: My early paintings from California are about looking like objects, both in the sense of their shapes and in the way they are painted. Do you remember when all cars seemed to be two-tone? And now they are all one color. It's interesting to think about this—was it just the fashion, or did it have something to do with the economy, cutting costs by eliminating a color? Or is it a change in taste, in ideas about what looks modern? I was interested in these design decisions and the way they affected people.

The New York paintings are much more pictorial. The images are abstracted from everyday objects that are interesting to me because they have an intended purpose for existing, which is connected to the way they look. It's the shape that's invented. You can look at that Sony cassette recorder you're using for this interview and wonder why the buttons are where they are, or whether there is a better arrangement, or whether it's a good idea to have the microphone positioned on the corner. Everything has a purpose that helps to define its shape: form follows function.

Thomson: Everything is a sculpture.

Spence: Why is a chair so many inches off the floor? Why is a steering wheel placed where it is in a car? There is a reason for everything in design and architecture. The Museum of Modern Art's design collection includes a leg splint that Eames made for the army or navy during World War II. I used to have one hanging on my wall—it was a beautiful object and really comfortable, too.

I've been collecting old fishing lures that also have to do with my art. They are the epitome of things man-made. These lures are supposedly designed to catch fish, but they are really designed for people to buy; the fish aren't buying them. They are very seductive and extremely elegant. The shapes and colors are quite extraordinary.

I discovered, by reading and doing this kind of work, that certain colors are more attractive to people than others. Attraction to a particular color doesn't seem to happen on a universal level but seems to be determined by geography—it varies from city to city.

Thomson: Are there any colors that you are not attracted to?

Spence: No.

Thomson: Do the paintings usually start from an idea such as "Here is what the image will be," or do you just have a feeling that you need to do, for instance, a black painting now?

Spence: I'll use either approach to make a painting. If the image comes first, then the color will come later, or if a color comes first, then the image comes later. I'm flexible about possible changes, but I have to have something in order to get started.

Thomson: Is there ever a situation where there is no idea, no new painting coming out?

Spence: Yes, it's very frustrating and seems to happen at some point every year. I still go to my studio to draw and work on other projects. I keep sketches and notes going back over the years that pertain to completed paintings and paintings that were never made. Sometimes I can find something there. I think ideas are everywhere, but you have to be in the right frame of mind to see them.

Thomson: How many variations are there from the original idea before you make the actual painting?

Spence: I do as many variations of an idea as is necessary to determine whether or not I want to proceed to the painting stage. This could take anywhere from a day to a few weeks. These variations on an idea are worked out in small drawings on a sketch pad that function as visual notes—drawings that try to clarify ideas by developing colors and shapes. Trying to invent a shape is a hard thing for me to do, and it often takes a long time to decide whether or not I like something. I try to sketch out as many possibilities on a shape as I can think of to know which one is most right. I also try to limit my options to certain criteria which use visual rather than verbal language. I can't really explain the criteria because they're too elusive.

If you were to look through one of my sketch pads, you would see several pages filled with variations of the same drawing. You would also see an idea or image among many other ideas that crept in and began to develop on a page. Then, on the next page, there may be two or three more variations of the first image, and some other ideas. There are times when I exhaust all the possibilities before realizing that it is not going to work out as a painting. At that point, I move on to something else.

Thomson: So by the time you start working on a painting, you're fairly clear about what you're doing?

Spence: Yes, but that changes as the painting develops. Hopefully, at a certain point, a painting will begin to tell me what to do as it takes on a life of its own. The original idea may become less important, and the changes that take place might even obliterate it. One of my paintings started out as an image of the picture window in my studio. The drawings were way too literal even though they were only grid patterns. I kept increasing the thickness of the lines, making the grid appear fatter until it became more of a shape and less gridlike. The image got better and became resolved after superimposing some rectangular shapes for balance. By this time, the idea had nothing to do with the picture window and looked more like a section of a building façade. I used green paint for vegetation and named the painting *Ivy Windows.*

The progression from one painting to the next is very important to me. I have to make the first painting in order to figure out what the next painting is going to be. There actually is a relationship between paintings. Perhaps it may not be about the object, but on a visual level there is this progression. I like to establish a rhythm that leads to future paintings.

Thomson: Could this rhythm be a color progression?

Spence: Not exactly. I think it's an intuitive progression in which color is a factor in the same way that scale or subject matter might be a factor in determining the movement from painting to painting. I try to work on three or four paintings at a time in different stages of development. If the rhythm established by this way of working is interrupted by one of the paintings not going as planned, then I would prefer to stop working on everything and concentrate on the problem at hand.

Thomson: It's funny—you work on a flat surface and deal with associative images, but you're also dealing with the history of abstract painting. A lot of humor happens in the juxtaposition of all those different elements. You're playing with more than a full deck of cards in some ways, because as you're working on the paintings, sometimes ideas will become apparent that you didn't even know were there.

Spence: I like using formal elements in my work. I'm not sure, however, if this formalism comes out of art history or is just something that already exists in the nature of the man-made objects that are my subject matter. The tongue-in-cheek aspects that may occur in my work are amusing but are not intended to be the main focus—just one of the elements involved. That painting over there in the corner is called *Hanging Table.* It's about a folding table that hangs on the wall when not being used, like a painting or a Shaker chair. That may be amusing, but as an abstract painting *Hanging Table* is dealing with serious formal issues that are important to me.

Thomson: Looking back at your résumé, how did you get from Bryn Mawr to Norman, Oklahoma?

Spence: I applied and was accepted at the University of Oklahoma in Norman. After high school I decided to radically change my environment and experience another part of the country. I had some friends that were already there and liked it. I studied art there, and the art department was good. There was also an interesting architecture department that was located at one end of the interior of the football stadium. You would have thought that it would have been located in some kind of modern building, but it was one of the more architecturally interesting buildings on campus. Another part of the campus still consisted of some old, wooden, one-story army-type buildings left over from World War II when Oklahoma University was a military base.

Thomson: So would you be in your studio on Sunday and hear forty thousand fans going bananas above you?

Spence: The art studio was located in another building. I don't remember hearing crowds; I was too busy trying to control the art materials that I was using.

Thomson: Were you influenced by pop art at that time? Did you see yourself as a future pop artist?

Spence: I was just learning about pop art. I never really thought about being a pop artist.

Thomson: Eventually you made it out to California.

Spence: After two years at Oklahoma University I decided it was time for a change of scenery if I wanted to pursue painting seriously. I applied to Tyler School of Art in Philadelphia and spent my junior year attending their program overseas in Rome. After my senior year I graduated from Tyler and headed out to the University of California, Santa Barbara, for graduate school. I was a teaching assistant in the art department there, and they gave me a forty-foot trailer as a studio.

Initially, California was like paradise. The climate was mild and sunny all the time. Fresh fruit, vegetables, and flowers grew all year round. The freeways had ocean views and were wide and smooth. Even the air was clean and clear in those days. At dusk people would parade out to the bluffs overlooking the ocean to watch the sunset. To me, this was amazing—I had never seen anybody do this before. The sunsets really were spectacular.

After the University of California, Santa Barbara, I moved to Los Angeles, got a job, and ended up staying for several years. Los Angeles is where I entered the art world.

Thomson: One funny thing about your paintings is that your ideas started to come to you in Los Angeles. I do feel that your work is very personal. There are not ten other people working in your style.

Spence: Everything in Los Angeles seemed like it was new. There wasn't any sense of history. For me, it was a good place to try out new ideas and to experiment. Most of the people that I knew came from other places like Nebraska, Arizona, or Mexico. Other than Sique and Nick Wilder, I don't remember meeting anyone else from the East Coast. I think that growing up in the East affected my outlook on California.

Thomson: There was a time when Nick Wilder started painting seriously after he quit art dealing. His paintings were geometric abstractions. How did you feel about this, since you had this special relationship with him that basically covered your entire life as an artist?

Spence: Early on I realized that we were each pursuing totally different ideas in painting. The fact that we both chose a geometric format was coincidental. It was my understanding that Nick actually painted in a geometric style before he was an art dealer. I think that our friendship intensified because of our common interest in geometric abstraction. We were secure enough in our own work to avoid feeling threatened by one another. We could share things like ideas or technical problems openly. To have had a rapport like that with another artist was very special to me and one that I will always remember.

✶

Artists' and *Interviewers'* Biographies

Kim Abeles
Kim Abeles received an M.F.A. in studio art from the University of California, Irvine. She has been the recipient of many grants and fellowships, from the California Arts Council and the J. Paul Getty Trust Fund for the Visual Arts, among others. She has had solo exhibitions at the Laurence Miller Gallery, New York City; Phyllis Kind Gallery, Chicago; and Santa Monica Museum of Art, California. Her work has been featured on radio and television broadcasts on CBS (by Dan Rather), CNN, and CBC. A major exhibition of her work, *Kim Abeles: Encyclopedia Persona, A Fifteen-Year Survey,* sponsored by the United States Information Agency, will tour Latin America during 1996–97, following its domestic tour. A bilingual second edition of the award-winning exhibition catalogue/bookwork is forthcoming. Abeles is represented in the collections of the Museum of Contemporary Art and the California Afro-American Museum, Los Angeles. She has received commissions for the Santa Monica Bay Restoration Project and the California Bureau of Automotive Repair for her environmental artwork. She has also received commissions for the Panorama City Public Library, the State Archives in Sacramento, and the Metropolitan Transportation Authority's Art for Rail Transit in Los Angeles.

Vija Celmins
Vija Celmins was born in Riga, Latvia, and came to the United States with her family at the age of nine. She grew up in Indiana and received an M.F.A. from the University of California, Los Angeles, in 1965. Her solo exhibitions include a 1973 show at the Whitney Museum of American Art, New York City; a traveling midcareer survey, *Vija Celmins: A Survey Exhibition,* organized by the Newport Harbor Art Museum, California, in 1980; shows at McKee Gallery, New York City, in 1983, 1988, and 1992; *Vija Celmins,* organized by the Institute of Contemporary Art, Philadephia, which traveled from 1992 to 1994 to the Walker Art Center, Minneapolis, the Whitney Museum of American Art, and the Museum of Contemporary Art, Los Angeles; and most recently, a show at the Cartier Foundation in Paris, September 1995. She has received fellowships from the National Endowment for the Arts in 1971 and 1976, a Guggenheim fellowship in 1980, and an award in art from the American Academy of Arts and Letters in 1995. She lives and works in New York City.

Sarah Charlesworth
Sarah Charlesworth was born in New Jersey. She holds a B.A. in art history from Barnard College, New York City. Charlesworth has had recent individual exhibitions at the S. L. Simpson Gallery, Toronto, and Jay Gorney Modern Art, New York City. Her work has been shown at Galerie Rizzo, Paris, and included in the group exhibitions Photoplay, *independently curated;* Commodity Image, *International Center of Photography, New York City;* Image World, *Whitney Museum of American Art, New York City;* Art and Its Double, *Fundación Caixa de Pensións, Madrid; and* A Forest of Signs, *Museum of Contemporary Art, Los Angeles. She is represented in public collections such as the Museum of Contemporary Art; Whitney Museum of American Art; National Museum of American Art, Washington, D.C.; Museum of Fine Arts, Boston; Victoria and Albert Museum, London; and Stedelijk Museum, Eindhoven, Holland. Charlesworth lives in New York City.*

Chuck Close
Chuck Close was born in Monroe, Washington. He earned a B.A. from the University of Washington, Seattle, and a B.F.A. and an M.F.A. from Yale University School of Art and Architecture. He received an honorary doctorate of humane letters at Skidmore College, Saratoga, New York, in 1993, and honorary doctorates of fine arts from Colby College, Waterville, Maine, in 1994, and the University of Massachusetts, Amherst, in 1995. He won the Academy-Institute Award in Art from the American Academy and Institute of Arts and Letters, New York City, in 1991. A major retrospective of his art was exhibited by the Walker Art Center, Minneapolis, in 1980. The traveling exhibition ended its tour at the Whitney Museum of Art, New York City, in 1981. More recently, the Staatliche Kunsthalle in Baden-Baden, Germany, held a retrospective of his work, which traveled to the Städtische Galerie, Lenbachhaus, Munich. Close's work has also been featured in solo exhibitions at the Museum of Modern Art, New York City; Los Angeles County Museum of Art; Chicago Art Institute; and Stedelijk Museum, Amsterdam. His work has been featured in the group exhibitions Documenta 5, *1972, and* Documenta 6, *1977, in Kassel, Germany, and the Whitney Museum of American Art biennial exhibitions of 1969, 1977, 1979, and 1991. In 1992 Close was elected a member of the American Academy and Institute of Arts and Letters. Forthcoming exhibitions are the Carnegie International, Pittsburgh, fall 1995, and a major retrospective at the Metropolitan Museum of Art, New York, fall 1997.*

Jimmy DeSana
Jimmy DeSana's first solo exhibition was in 1979 at Stefanotti, New York City. He also had exhibitions at the Galleria Trisorio, Naples, Italy; Oae Gallery, Minneapolis; and Oggi Domani and the Pat Hearn Gallery, New York City. His work was most recently shown in a solo exhibition at Galerie Jablonka, Cologne, and in the group exhibition *Hollywood, Hollywood, Hollywood* at the Art Center College of Art and Design, Los Angeles. Other group shows include *Photomodern: Issues in Photography,* Atlanta, and *Kenneth Anger Retrospective* at the Whitney Museum of Art, New York City. Jimmy DeSana died in 1990.

John Divola
John Divola received an M.F.A. from the University of California, Los Angeles. He is a four-time recipient of the National Endowment for the Arts photography fellowship and has also received a Guggenheim fellowship. His work has been featured in numerous one-person and group exhibitions in the United States, Canada, Europe, Australia, and Japan. Significant exhibitions include the Whitney biennial exhibition and several group exhibitions at the Museum of Modern Art, New York. He is currently chair of the Department of Art at the University of California, Riverside.

Stephen Ellis
Stephen Ellis was born in High Point, North Carolina. He received a B.F.A. from Cornell University, Ithaca, New York, and attended the New York Studio School, New York City. His solo exhibitions include those at the André Emmerich Gallery, Elizabeth Koury Gallery, and Koury Wingate Gallery in New York City; Galerie Ascan Crone, Hamburg; Galerie Thomas von Lintel, Munich; and Galerie Nathalie Obadia, Paris. His work has appeared internationally in numerous group exhibitions, most recently Transatlantica *at the Museo Alejandro Otero, Caracas, Venezuela. Ellis has received grants for painting from the National Endowment for the Arts and the New York State Foundation for the Arts. He has been a staff writer and an associate and contributing editor for* Art in America. *His articles have also appeared in periodicals such as* Bomb, Parkett, *and* Tema Celeste.

Judy Fiskin
Judy Fiskin was born in Chicago. She holds a B.A. in art history from Pomona College, Claremont, California, and an M.A. from the University of California, Los Angeles. She has had recent solo exhibitions at Curt Marcus Gallery, New York City; Patricia Faure Gallery, Santa Monica, California; and the Museum of Contemporary Art, Los Angeles. She has been featured in numerous group exhibitions, including *Typologies: Nine Contemporary Photographers and Special Collections: Photographic Order from Pop to Now,* originating at the International Center of Photography in New York City. She has served as associate dean of the School of Art at the California Institute of the Arts, Valencia, and has received two grants in photography from the National Endowment for the Arts. She lives in Los Angeles.

Viola Frey
A native Californian, Viola Frey received a B.F.A. from the California College of Arts and Crafts, Oakland, and an M.F.A. from Tulane University, New Orleans. Her work has been featured in solo exhibitions at the Asher/Faure Gallery, Los Angeles; Nancy Hoffman Gallery, New York City; and Rena Bransten Gallery, San Francisco. Group exhibitions in which her work has been shown include Pygmalion: The Female Form in Sculpture, *National Museum of Ceramic Art, Baltimore;* American Pop Culture Today III, *La Foret Museum, Tokyo; and* Quatre Americains à la Manufacture de Sèvres, *American Center, Paris. Frey's work can be viewed at public installations at the Los Angeles County Museum of Art and in New York City at the Metropolitan Museum of Art and the Whitney Museum of American Art.*

Felix Gonzalez-Torres
Felix Gonzalez-Torres lived and worked in New York City. He received a B.F.A. from the Pratt Institute, Brooklyn, and an M.F.A. from the International Center of Photography at New York University. He had many significant solo exhibitions at museums including the Solomon R. Guggenheim Museum, New York City; Hirshhorn Museum and Sculpture Garden, Washington, D.C.; Renaissance Society, Chicago; Museum of Contemporary Art, Los Angeles; and Museum of Modern Art, New York City, and galleries such as Andrea Rosen Gallery, New York City; Jennifer Flay, Paris; Ghislaine Hussenot, Paris; and Galerie Peter Pakesch, Vienna. He taught at New York University and the California Institute of the Arts, Valencia. Gonzalez-Torres received grants and awards from the National Endowment for the Arts and Gordon Matta-Clark Foundation, among others. Felix Gonzalez-Torres died in January 1996.

Mike Kelley
Mike Kelley was born in Detroit and resides in Los Angeles. He earned a B.F.A. from the University of Michigan, Ann Arbor, and an M.F.A. from the California Institute of the Arts, Valencia. He has exhibited at the Hirshhorn Museum and Sculpture Garden, Washington, D.C.; Rosamund Felson Gallery, Los Angeles; Juana de'Aizpuru, Madrid; Galerie Peter Pakesch, Vienna; Galerie Jablonka, Cologne; and Metro Pictures, New York City. He has participated in group exhibitions including *Helter Skelter: L.A. Art in the 1990s.* In 1994 the Whitney Museum of American Art, New York City, organized a retrospective of his work, which traveled to the Los Angeles County Museum of Art and Munich. Kelley is also a writer, performance artist, and musician. His *Three Blowhards and a Little Lady* was performed at Beyond Baroque, Venice, California, and *My Life and Media,* at Broadway Cinema, Cologne. Kelley has taught at the California Institute of the Arts, Valencia; University of California, Los Angeles; and Art Center College of Design, Pasadena, California. He has received a National Endowment for the Arts grant and an Artists Space Interarts grant.

Thomas Lawson
Thomas Lawson was educated at the universities of St. Andrews and Edinburgh in Scotland, and City University of New York. He has shown regularly at Metro Pictures, New York City; Anthony Reynolds Gallery, London; and Richard Kuhlenschmidt, Los Angeles. Lawson's work has also been exhibited at numerous galleries and museums around the world, including the Brooklyn Museum; La Jolla Museum of Contemporary Art, California; Museum of Contemporary Art, Los Angeles; Third Eye Centre, Glasgow; and National Gallery of Art, Sydney, Australia. His essays and reviews have been published in Flash Art, Art in America, *and* Artforum. *He has been awarded fellowships from the National Endowment for the Arts. Lawson is dean of the School of Art at the California Institute of the Arts, Valencia.*

Allan McCollum
Born in Los Angeles, Allan McCollum lives and works in New York City. His work has been exhibited in museums internationally since 1969, including solo exhibitions at the Stedelijk van Abbemuseum, Eindhoven, Holland; IVAM Centre del Carme, Valencia, Spain; Musée d'Art Contemporain, Nîmes, France; the Centre d'Art Contemporain, Geneva; Museum Haus Esters, Krefeld, Germany; and Sprengel Museum, Hanover, Germany. McCollum's work has been featured in such publications as *Allegories of Modernism: Contemporary Drawing* (Museum of Modern Art, New York), *A Forest of Signs* (MIT Press), and *Beyond Recognition: Representation, Power and Culture* by Craig Owens (University of California Press). His work is in the collections of the Museum of Modern Art, New York City; the Museum of Fine Arts, Boston; and many others.

Michael McMillen
Michael McMillen was born in Los Angeles. He graduated from San Fernando Valley State College, California, and earned an M.A. and an M.F.A. from the University of California, Los Angeles. His solo exhibitions have been presented at many venues, including L.A. Louver; the Patricia Hamilton Gallery, New York City; Dart Gallery, Chicago; and San Francisco International Airport. McMillen's recent group exhibitions include an installation at L.A. Louver and Beyond Appearance, *at Armory Center for the Arts, Pasadena, California. Cited by* Esquire *magazine in an article on the "men and women under forty who are changing America," he has been awarded grants from the National Endowment for the Arts and the Louis Comfort Tiffany Foundation. His installations have been exhibited at the Los Angeles County Museum of Art; Kukje Gallery, Seoul; and Sun-Moon Lake, Taiwan. McMillen lives in Santa Monica, California.*

John Miller

John Miller lives in New York City. He received a B.F.A. from the Rhode Island School of Design, Providence, and an M.F.A. from the California Institute of the Arts, Valencia. His work has been shown recently in the solo exhibition The Middle of the Day, *Metro Pictures, New York City; at Galerie Barbara Weiss, Berlin; at Hotel Krone, Gais, Switzerland; and in* Wind from the East, *Richard Telles Fine Art, Los Angeles. He has participated in numerous group shows, such as* Altered States: American Art in the '90s, *St. Louis Museum of Art, and Pièces-Meublées, Galerie Jousse Sequin, France. A prolific writer, Miller has published pieces in* Suture: Phantasm der Volkommenheit *(Salzburg Kunstverein) and in* Artforum. *His work is in the collection of the Whitney Museum of American Art, New York City.*

Anne Scott Plummer

Anne Scott Plummer was born in Providence, Rhode Island. She holds a B.F.A. from the Rhode Island School of Design and an M.F.A. from Claremont Graduate School, California. She recently won a major public art commission to produce an eighty-foot cast-concrete relief mural for the city of Rochester, Minnesota. Solo exhibitions include the installation *Mural/Manchild in the Making,* at the Rochester Art Center, and a show of recent sculpture at the Conkoing Gallery, Mankato State University, Minnesota. Plummer has participated in many group exhibitions, including *Revolution in Clay: The Marer Collection of Contemporary Ceramics,* which traveled to nine venues throughout the United States. Her work is in the collections of the Vallauris International Museum of Ceramic Art, France; the Downey Art Museum, California; and the John Michael Kohler Art Center, Sheboygan, Wisconsin. Plummer is an assistant professor of art at Winona State University, Minnesota.

David Reed

Born in San Diego, David Reed lives and works in New York City. He received a B.A. from Reed College, Portland, Oregon, and attended the New York Studio School and the Skowhegan School of Painting and Sculpture, Maine. He has been awarded fellowships from the National Endowment for the Arts and from the Guggenheim and Rockefeller foundations. A recent exhibition of his work was at Kölnischer Kunstverein in Cologne. He also shows at Galerie Rolf Ricke, Cologne; Max Protetch Gallery, New York City; and Patricia Faure Gallery, Los Angeles.

Tim Rollins

Tim Rollins was born in Pittsfield, Maine. He holds an A.S. from the University of Maine, Augusta, and a B.F.A. from the School of Visual Arts, New York City. He also studied art education at New York University. Rollins cofounded Group Material, New York City, and founded K.O.S. (Kids of Survival) and the Art and Knowledge Workshop, Inc., South Bronx. In recent years, he has had solo exhibitions at the Fundación para el Arte Contemporáneo, Mexico City; Hirshhorn Museum and Sculpture Garden, Washington, D.C.; and Mary Boone Gallery, New York City. Most recently, he has participated in group shows including Malcolm X: Man, Ideal, Icon, *Anacostia Museum, Washington, D.C.;* Black Male: Representation of Masculinity in Contemporary American Art, *Whitney Museum of American Art, New York City; and* Signs Taken for Wonders, *Kunsthaus Zurich, Switzerland.*

Laurie Simmons

Laurie Simmons is a native New Yorker. She received a B.F.A. from the Tyler School of Art in Philadelphia. Her work has been exhibited at Metro Pictures, New York City; Galerie Philippe Rizzo, Paris; S. L. Simpson Gallery, Toronto; Daniel Weinberg Gallery, Los Angeles; and Galerie Jablonka, Cologne. Simmons's work was also included in the 1985 and 1991 biennial exhibitions at the Whitney Museum of American Art, New York City, and the biennial exhibition of Sydney, Australia. Her photographs are in the collections of many museums, including the International Center of Photography, New York City; Musée d'Art Contemporain, Montreal; Museum of Contemporary Art, Los Angeles; Stedelijk Museum, Amsterdam; Museum of Modern Art, New York City; and Philadelphia Museum of Art. A retrospective of her work organized by the Baltimore Museum of Art will open in fall 1996.

Pat Sparkuhl

Pat Sparkuhl received a B.A. from Chapman University, Orange, California, and an M.A. from California State University, Fullerton. His work has been exhibited at the Museum of Science and Industry, Los Angeles; Laguna Beach Art Museum; and Angeles Gate Cultural Center. Recent exhibitions have included *Fabric of Life,* Riverside Art Museum; *Outside the Mainstream,* Irvine Fine Arts Center; *Reflections on AIDS,* Orange Coast College; *Seriously Sexual,* BC Space Gallery, Laguna Beach; and *Artists' Pin Auction,* Muckenthaler Cultural Center, Fullerton. He recently sat on the panel "State of the Art in Orange County," Griffin Fine Arts, Costa Mesa, California. Sparkuhl lives in Laguna Beach.

Andrew Spence

Andrew Spence lives and works in New York City. He received a B.F.A. from the Tyler School of Art in Philadelphia and an M.F.A. from the University of California, Santa Barbara. One-person exhibitions of his work have been held in Chicago; New York City; Miami; Boston; Worcester, Massachusetts; and Los Angeles and La Jolla, California. Spence has been featured in a biennial exhibition and the group show *1980s: Selections from the Permanent Collection* at the Whitney Museum of American Art, New York City. He was awarded a grant from the National Endowment for the Arts in 1987 and a John Simon Guggenheim Memorial Foundation fellowship. His work has been reviewed in periodicals such as *Arts Magazine, Art in America, Artnews, Artforum, Vogue,* and *Elle,* and is represented in public and corporate collections including the Baltimore Museum of Art; Museum of Modern Art, New York City; Hirshhorn Museum and Sculpture Garden, Washington, D.C.; Metropolitan Museum of Art, New York City; and Cleveland Museum of Art.

Colin Thomson

Colin Thomson was born in London. He received an M.F.A. from Yale University and has studied at the Skowhegan School of Painting and Sculpture, Maine. He received a National Endowment for the Arts fellowship in 1991. His most recent exhibition was Works for a Funhouse *in New York City. Other exhibitions were* Directions in American Abstraction: A New Decade, *Southern Alleghenies Museum of Art, Loretto, Pennsylvania, and a group show at the International Sculpture Center, Washington, D.C. Thomson lives in New York City.*